REQUIEM FOR MODERN POLITICS

REQUIEM FOR MODERN POLITICS

The Tragedy of the Enlightenment and the Challenge of the New Millennium

WILLIAM OPHULS

WestviewPress

A Division of HarperCollinsPublishers

Published in 1997 in the United States of America by Westview Press, 5500 Central Avenue, Boulder, Colorado, 80301-2877, and in the United Kingdom by Westview Press, 12 Hid's Copse Road, Cumnor Hill, Oxford OX2 9JJ

Library of Congress Cataloging-in-Publication Data
Ophuls, William. 1934–
  Requiem for modern politics : the tragedy of the enlightenment and the challenge of the new millennium / William Ophuls.
    p. cm.
  Includes bibliographical references and index.
  ISBN 0-8133-3142-0.
  1. Liberalism.   2. Liberalism—Moral and ethical aspects.
3. Environmental policy.   I. Title.
JC574.064   1997
320.5´1—dc20   96-34216
                                                                                          CIP

Interior design by Tom Beckwith

The paper used in this publication meets the requirements of the American National Standard for Permanence of Paper for Printed Library Materials Z39.48-1984.

10   9   8   7   6   5   4   3   2   1

CONTENTS

*There are a thousand striking at the branches of evil
to one who is striking at the root.*

—Henry David Thoreau

PREFACE

THE ARGUMENT OF THIS WORK IS THAT MODERN POLITICS has reached the end of its tether. The modern political paradigm—that is, the body of political concepts and beliefs bequeathed to us by the philosophical movement known as the Enlightenment—is no longer intellectually tenable or practically viable. We are therefore in deep political crisis and confront the necessity for an abrupt and decisive change to a radically different type of politics. But we cannot hope to attain the latter without understanding the former, so what follows is about the crisis: it is a critique of the old order, rather than a vision of the new. Thus the reader must not expect a formal presentation of the new paradigm of politics or of the philosophy that will justify it. I leave that to the future.

However, my vision—a politics of consciousness rooted in a new conception of natural law, a politics appropriate to the dawning age of ecology—is inevitably implicit within the critique, so I invite the reader to attend to the subtext of the argument as well as to the text. Moreover, the vision is clearly, if briefly, sketched in the Prologue, Conclusions, and Epilogue. This is to show that my critique is offered in a positive spirit: if I write about the death of the old order, my aim is not to spread doom and gloom but, rather, to prepare the ground for the new.

Because we confront a paradigm crisis in which the governing ideas of the modern polity are at stake, my analysis is primarily concerned with the deep structures of politics—the dominant cultural premises, values, and self-images. These ideational structures largely determine the institutional and ideological structures that in turn form the matrix for events, most especially those events that we label "problems." Although sociological explanation and institutional reform are useful during normal times, when a fundamentally successful system merely needs reforming or fine-tuning, they become largely irrelevant in time of crisis, when the basic ideas of the system itself need changing. Worse, once a political system is in crisis, superficial analyses are likely to mistake symptoms for causes, and conventional reforms based on these analyses will therefore fail—in fact, they may well make matters worse, as we shall see repeatedly in what follows. In short, I follow Thoreau in focusing on roots rather than on branches.

This book continues the exploration of our paradigm crisis begun in *Ecology and the Politics of Scarcity*. As in that work, I aim to raise critical and disturbing questions about the fundamental direction of modern industrial civilization, for this is the indispensable first step in finding genuine solutions to its problems. In other words, I seek not to provide answers, much less easy or pat answers, but instead to reveal the tragedy of a way of life being destroyed by its most basic principles—indeed, by its very virtues.

To this end, I reexamine the familiar and the obvious from a point of view that challenges deeply held beliefs—beliefs about our peculiar form of politics, about the modern civilization in which it is embedded, and, ultimately, about the very enterprise of civilization itself—so that we can see issues afresh and understand clearly why the stale old answers will no longer serve. I have therefore made a conscious effort to stand mostly outside, if not in opposition to, the usual framework of political discourse in our time, especially the narrow spectrum of political thought endemic to the United States (where so-called liberals and conservatives only quarrel about spoils—"who gets what, when, how"—not fundamentals). I have also made ecology a key element of the analysis because I believe it reveals aspects of social reality otherwise hidden from view.

The measure of my success will not be whether the reader agrees with me in all respects—I anticipate rather the opposite reaction—but instead whether he or she comes to understand that the old ways of thinking and acting are moribund and that we must begin to talk about what will take their place. What follows is therefore an invitation to the debate, not the last word on the subject. As Virginia Woolf wisely says in *A Room of One's Own*, "In a question like this truth is only to be had by laying together many varieties of error."

One possible source of error in what follows is the work's very ambition. Ranging over most of human history and many different fields of knowledge is not without risk, as pointed out by the cultural historian Johan Huizinga: "In treating of the general problems of culture, one is constantly obliged to undertake predatory incursions into provinces not sufficiently explored by the raider himself." And the unfortunate corollary is that time expended on predatory excursions is necessarily time subtracted from exploring one's own province. Thus I have undoubtedly overlooked important findings or slighted the work of others. But to wait for mastery of an enormous "literature" in many disciplines, much less complete and certain knowledge, would mean never to write. At the same time, I have had to take certain thorny issues largely for granted— for example, power and human nature—because discussing them in any depth would take me too far afield and turn an essay into an encyclopedia. By its very nature, therefore, my work is condemned to be one of Woolf's "varieties of error."

Another possible source of error, or at least confusion, is language. Much of our inherited conceptual baggage and current vocabulary is ill-suited for discussing the defects of the current order. For example, as Neil Evernden brilliantly shows, the very word *environment* evinces and perpetuates the mind-matter and man-nature dualism that is intrinsic to modern thought and that many regard as the root cause of our ecological debacle. To put it more bluntly, the language of modern life is fundamentally anti-ecological. Even politics is dominated by the ethos of economics: we talk about "values" rather than "principles" or about "output" instead of "excellence," and words like "truth" or "beauty" are utterly proscribed. In this and in the many other ways noted in the text, our materialistic and rationalistic culture protects itself by effectively ruling other worldviews and forms of reasoning out of bounds. Thus a radical critic of that culture has to struggle to avoid being misunderstood or even dismissed out of hand. However, for the most part, I have not tried to invent a new language or new worldview here—that is the task of a future work devoted to the epistemological revolution of the twentieth century and its political implications—but have instead taken our language as given, using it to expose the contradictory and self-destructive nature of the political reality it reflects. In other words, I have simply done my best with the obsolescent conceptual and linguistic tools available. I nevertheless urge the reader to peer between the lines for the new political reality being born in our time, but whose proper language has yet to be invented.

The discussion focuses on the United States. This is appropriate given that America was explicitly founded on and exemplifies so clearly the characteristic features of the modern political paradigm. It is thus the perfect case for examining its contradictions. But America is special, not unique: modern principles, practices, and institutions now pervade the globe. My findings therefore apply more generally (as I have tried to make clear in brief asides). In other words, my argument transcends the case used to make it.

To put much of the above in a nutshell, this is a dialectical and visionary essay. It is dialectical because it attempts a critical inquiry into received values and assumptions with the aim of correcting or rejecting them. It is visionary because it suggests, at least implicitly, that we need a polity based on radically different values and assumptions. It is an essay because it is literally a first trial of new ideas, not a finished theory.

It follows that I am not a scholar writing for the academy but, instead, what the Germans call "a thinker for the world." Although I hope scholars in many disciplines will find my argument both interesting and well founded, I address all concerned about our political future. Yet this is not meant to be a popular work in the usual sense: rather than aiming for topicality or "relevance" (although the analysis certainly illuminates current affairs), I have tried to place our current situation in a long-term historical and philosophical perspective.

In this light, although I have striven throughout to convey essential truths that are not in conflict with the best scholarship, the reader must avoid judging this work by the standards appropriate to an academic treatise or scholarly monograph. The Introduction, for example, is painted with a broad brush and therefore contains statements that will raise polemical hackles in some quarters. But this is, to reiterate, an essay whose importance (if any) lies in its general thesis. Thus my request to the reader is not to boggle at particulars but, instead, to allow room for the latter to unfold. Although I have done my best to make each step of the argument convincing, I suspect that it will persuade either as a whole or not at all.

I must also crave indulgence for not being able to do full justice to the philosophers whose ideas I have borrowed to elucidate our predicament, for this is a political argument, not an intellectual history. For example, I present Hobbes minus most of his subtlety and brilliance—which leaves only his force. But vulgarization is the fate of every political theorist, not of Marx alone; and since my subject is liberalism as a political and economic reality, not as a subtle and complex philosophical position, I shall quite naturally and appropriately focus on what can be called vulgar liberalism. Moreover, as befits a critique, I shall be presenting primarily the negative side of liberalism, not its humane, liberating, uplifting aspects, which are well known and extolled in countless other works. Nor must the reader look for philosophical consistency or try to identify me with a particular theorist: my use of Aristotle or Rousseau at key points in the argument does not mean that I am bound by them. At the same time, I have done my utmost to be true to the essential spirit of all the theorists cited.

All of the above means that I have minimized the work's scholarly apparatus, because scrupulous documentation of each fact and quotation would have obscured rather than advanced the argument. Instead, I have tried to honor Montaigne's request for "books that offer the results of learning, not those that set it out." For better or for worse, what follows is the result of my learning since the publication of *Ecology and the Politics of Scarcity*, not of the tortuous path leading to it. However, major influences and borrowings of ideas are clearly indicated in the text, and the Bibliographic Note and annotated List of Sources show to whom and to what extent I am indebted (and where support for my statements and positions can be found). They also suggest avenues for further exploration if the reader is so inclined.

In addition, I have tried to make the reader's life as easy as possible by prefacing each chapter with epigraphs that tell its story in a nutshell and by concluding each chapter (except for the Introduction and Conclusions) with a summary section. In this way, those oppressed by the frenetic tempo of modern life can quickly gain an overview of the work and decide for themselves what to pursue in depth.

Finally, my debts, both personal and intellectual, are so numerous and large that I must acknowledge most of them in summary fashion by thanking all who have been generous with their time and ideas as I planned and wrote this book over a span of fifteen years. A few debts, however, are too great for such general recognition. First, the work was conceived (in a very different form) during my two years as a visiting professor at Northwestern University. That my experiment with academe was not successful in no way reflects on my unfailingly supportive colleagues or their institution. At the risk of slighting others, I extend special thanks to John McKnight for his genial companionship and many contributions to my thinking (much of which he will probably disagree with); and also to Robert Lineberry, to whom I owe "hyperpluralism." Second, I benefited greatly from the discussions at Esalen Institute's invited conferences on "Appropriate Governance." I thank Esalen itself for its nine years of support as well as my fellow participants, who furthered the development and clarification of my own ideas by generously and convivially sharing their own. I owe a particular debt to Don Michael, both for his leading role in founding and maintaining the group and for his friendship and encouragement over the years. Third, I thank the Gleeson Library of the University of San Francisco for borrowing privileges. Fourth, I thank Dick Lamb for sharing his knowledge of books and publishing. Fifth, I thank Jack Kornfield, Dick Lamb, and Don Michael for reading an early draft and making helpful suggestions for revision (which does not imply that they endorse the ideas herein). Lastly, my deepest thanks to those who have been good and helpful friends during my own peculiar journey of discovery, especially Ed, Shiva, Dhira, Jack, Michael, Dora, Eduardo, and Hardy. Despite help from all of the above, as well as many others, plus the best efforts of my own muses and daimons, this work undoubtedly contains many residual errors and shortcomings for which I alone am responsible.

William Ophuls

PROLOGUE

The major advances in civilization are processes which all but wreck the societies in which they occur.

—*Alfred North Whitehead*

I HAVE A VISION. ALTHOUGH ITS ROOTS ARE ANCIENT, it owes as much to the totality of current scientific understanding as to perennial wisdom. Its essence is simple: I envision a politics of consciousness deeply rooted in a renewed erotic connection to nature and to the mysterious and sacred realm out of which both man and nature arise. But destruction is the precondition of creation. We must therefore begin by examining modernity on its funeral pyre, for it is from the ashes of the old order that the phoenix of the new will rise.

INTRODUCTION

The origins of evil lie far back in time and it is one of the functions of history to trace them out.

—G. M. Trevelyan

MODERN CIVILIZATION, IN ALL OF ITS ASPECTS and everywhere on the planet, is plunging ever deeper into a multiplicity of crises that call into question its governing principles, practices, and institutions. In this "crisis of crises," there is one that has yet to receive the attention it deserves: the impending failure of liberal polity, the modern system of politics founded on the tenets of classical liberalism and the rationalistic philosophy of the Enlightenment. Liberal polity is based on intrinsically self-destructive and potentially dangerous principles. It has already failed in its collectivist form and, contrary to the view of many, is now moribund in its individualist form as well. Moreover, the exploitative economy intimately associated with liberal polity is fraudulent in its premises and is now approaching bankruptcy—again, in both its market and nonmarket forms. In addition, the merely purposive rationality that helped to create and sustain a liberal polity and an exploitative economy expresses modern man's will to power and wreaks increasing havoc both on nature and on man himself. Thus the three main components of modern civilization—liberal polity, exploitative economy, and purposive rationality—are riddled with inner contradictions. That civilization is therefore collapsing. As a result, the latent totalitarianism of modern politics is likely to manifest itself with increasing force in the years to come. In short, without a major advance in civilization, we confront a political debacle.

This harsh and sweeping assessment of our predicament, which will be elaborated and supported in the main body of the book, is intended to promote not despair but simply a realistic understanding of the political challenge confronting humanity on the threshold of the twenty-first century. Indeed, it is only by exposing the intrinsically self-destructive nature of modern politics that we can reveal the only real solution to our multitude of problems—*which is to change the way of thinking that caused them.*

Unfortunately, when most people call for solutions, a different way of thinking is usually the last thing they have in mind. What they want instead is something that will not challenge their assumptions, shock their sensibilities, or violate the conventional wisdom. Much of what follows is therefore designed to make it absolutely clear that no such solution exists—that trying to solve our problems in terms of the basic principles of liberal polity is a lost cause, because it is these principles that have created the problems in the first place. In this way, the necessity for a new vision of politics that directly addresses the egotism and destructiveness of the modern way of life will follow as a matter of course. In that sense, not just the Conclusions, wherein I briefly sketch the essential spirit of the new vision, but the work as a whole is the "solution" to the problems it describes: it tries to exemplify a different way of thinking.

Although modern civilization is the primary focus of analysis, a critique of civilization itself is necessarily implied. As we shall see, our version of civilization differs not in kind, but only in degree, from all past civilizations. That is, it intensifies and amplifies the basic tendencies that have characterized the entire process of civilization, especially in the West. Moreover, as the etymology of the word *politics* indicates—it is from the Greek word *polis* meaning "city," which in its Latin form, *civitas,* is also the root of *civilization*—politics and civilization cannot be discussed in isolation, for any system of politics necessarily contains some notion of civilization as well. In addition, it is not easy in practice to distinguish between the problems created by human nature in general and those created by the particular nature of modern men and women, whose way of thinking and behaving has been shaped by the peculiarly selfish values of modern politics. Thus although my principal aim is to show that the Enlightenment, in seeking a cure for civilization's ills, only succeeded in making them worse, causing us to become embroiled in increasingly intractable and dangerous contradictions, we must first place modern civilization in context by examining its ecological basis and historical evolution.

Why ecology? Because from the biological point of view civilization is the story of man's struggle to transcend nature, so it is critical to understand just what we are struggling against. More important, it has now become apparent that victory is by no means assured. Unfortunately, despite rising environmental concern, few understand basic ecological principles or their radical social, economic, and political implications. In other words, few comprehend the degree to which ecology contradicts the modern way of life, root and branch. It is therefore essential to begin by laying a firm foundation of ecological understanding. Moreover, ecology is not for environmentalists alone: its principles and methods of analysis can be applied more generally. In fact, as we shall see, many of the proudest features of modern civilization—our agricultural productivity, our economic abundance, our medical marvels—appear in a more humbling light once they are examined from an ecological perspective. In short, ecology is a basic ground of my critique (and of the vision that grows out of it). Accordingly, the first half of this Introduction is a short course in human ecology.

Similarly, the rationalistic thought and liberal politics of the Enlightenment cannot be fully understood apart from the historical forces that produced them. The second half of the Introduction is therefore a short course in human history designed to reveal how our peculiar form of civilization and its characteristic politics evolved. We will then be in a position to analyze the modern order to show why it is moribund and why a new vision and philosophy of politics is essential.

To sum up, modern government is failing almost everywhere in the world, but especially in the United States. Most informed persons are aware of this, but few understand why. The reason is straightforward, albeit unpalatable: the fundamental premises of modern polity are false and unsustainable. It is our most basic and cherished principles—individualism, liberty, materialism, rationalism, or, in short, the whole set of liberal-democratic values that we inherited from the Enlightenment—that are the direct and proximate cause of the failure. But its ultimate roots lie more deeply buried, so we must begin by tracing out their origins in human ecology and human history.

The Challenge of Ecological Scarcity

The viability of an industrial civilization that lives by exploiting nature is now threatened by the emergence of ecological scarcity. Simply put, ecological scarcity refers to the impact on human society of the so-called environmental problematique—that is, the whole complex of interrelated environmental problems, ranging from atmospheric pollution to zoological extinction. These problems, together with the laws of ecology that underlie them, generate a closing circle of scarcity that is making it ever more difficult and expensive for us to continue to "develop" economically as we have in the past.

Unfortunately, ecological scarcity goes largely unperceived. Although concern for the environment is greater now than twenty or thirty years ago, it is still quite shallow. Most attention is given to particular symptoms, especially if they seem dramatic or threatening, rather than to underlying causes. But basing the environmental case on particulars is bad ecology and poor strategy. For example, although the evidence for global warming continues to accumulate, it is not yet certain that its consequences will be as catastrophic as some have claimed: hidden feedback loops of which we are currently unaware may mostly nullify the impact of the so-called greenhouse gases, resulting in no discernible climate change despite greatly increased emissions. It is also conceivable that the same feedback loops could, by increasing cloud formation, induce significant global *cooling* in the next century (and various acts of God, like extensive vulcanism, or of man, like nuclear war, would also result in cooling). But if global warming is not a sure bet, does that mean we can relax? Obviously not, because by chemically assaulting the biosphere, humankind is, in effect, running an unplanned experiment with the atmosphere that entails grave and unpredictable risks—if not of major climate change, then of storms, droughts, or other instabilities that may be equally unpleasant.

Nevertheless, even if global warming eventually proves to be a false alarm, it is still significant, for lurking behind it we can see all the basic forces creating ecological scarcity: more and more people desiring to live higher and higher on the ecological hog, and possessing ever more powerful technological means to do so, have begun to overstress the natural environment (which provides life support for human and nonhuman populations alike) and hence to deplete the resource base upon which economic activity depends. In other words, ecological scarcity is created not by any particular factor, for human ingenuity can usually find a way around specific obstacles, but instead by the mutual interaction of all the many different factors that make up the environmental problematique.

Ecological scarcity is therefore an overall social challenge rather than a series of discrete problems for specialists in ecology, economics, and engineering. Take, for example, population growth: almost 100 million people are added to the Earth's population each year. Such an increase in human demand for resources has not only major ecological and economic implications but equally large social and political consequences—not just for the nations concerned but for the entire community of nations. Indeed, the past decade has made it clear that many problems not customarily perceived as ecological in nature, such as explosive urbanization in the Third World and illegal immigration in the First, are in fact deeply rooted in overpopulation and deteriorating environmental conditions—that is, in the closing circle of ecological scarcity. And the worst is yet to come, predicts Robert Kaplan, a journalist who specializes in Third World problems:

It is time to understand "the environment" for what it is: *the* national-security issue of the early twenty-first century. The political and strategic impact of surging populations, spreading disease, deforestation and soil erosion, water depletion, air pollution, and, possibly, rising sea levels in critical, overcrowded regions like the Nile Delta and Bangladesh—developments that will prompt mass migrations and, in turn, incite group conflicts—will be the core foreign-policy challenge from which most others will ultimately emanate, arousing the public and uniting assorted interests left over from the Cold War.

As this quote illustrates, the forces producing ecological scarcity, like population growth, never act alone: they mutually exacerbate each other, so that the eventual environmental impacts are multiplied. And they also act across the board, ultimately affecting everyone everywhere to some degree, for the planet is an ecological unity. Thus even if modern civilization could find the means to solve any one of these problems in isolation, it cannot expect to overcome all of them simultaneously: like Gulliver trussed up by the Lilliputians, industrial civilization will find itself more and more tightly bound by the web of interacting forces that make up ecological scarcity.

Another way of viewing ecological scarcity is to use an economic metaphor: like spendthrift heirs to a great fortune, we are living off ecological capital instead of income. That is, instead of depending on natural flows such as solar energy, we consume stocks that have been built up over millennia, such as fossil fuels and even fossil water. This can hardly go on for much longer. Indeed, by exceeding the planet's ability to provide matter and energy over the long term, we are progressively eroding or destroying the physical basis for maintaining future consumption at anything approaching current levels. What is worse, if we continue to spend biological capital to support current consumption, we risk not having sufficient stocks of depletable resources left to make possible the very difficult and costly transition to a new energy regime based on sustainable resources such as solar energy. Our economic prodigality is therefore setting us up for a precipitous ecological fall.

Consider the fate of the forests. Everywhere on the planet, they are being destroyed by the greed and shortsightedness of governments, corporations, loggers, and ranchers; devastated by a multitude of poor peasants who ravage them for fuel, food, and, above all, a plot of land, however unsuitable for long-term cultivation; choked and poisoned by acid rain, ozone, and a host of other noxious "side effects" of development. The Amazon and other tropical rain forests are particularly endangered: unless current trends are speedily reversed, in a few decades only relict islands of their former vastness and magnificence will remain—none of them, in all likelihood, large enough to be ecologically viable over the long term. In short, the great forests of the planet are becoming extinct.

But the forests are not islands separate from the main. With the trees will die all those species of plants and animals associated with them, including many of possible benefit to man. (About half the world's variety of plants, insects, and animals is found in the tropical rain forests alone.) Already populations are declining and rates of extinction accelerating as the ecological fabric that supports biodiversity unravels in what is tantamount to a biological chain reaction. In a generation or two, we will look back on a biological catastrophe comparable to the mammoth extinctions of the Cretaceous—but caused by human action. More important, however, along with the trees we will lose all the critical functions that forests perform in the biosphere—some of the most salient of which are flood and erosion control, promotion of rainfall, moderation of local climate, regulation of global climate, and even, conceivably, the balance of oxygen and carbon dioxide in the atmosphere. So the death of the great forests tolls the bell for us as well. When they are gone, we will inhabit a radically impoverished world, perhaps an unlivable one.

As this example shows, one need not be a nature mystic to embrace ecology. The suitability of the planet for human occupation is degraded when we mistreat nature. And it is indeed *our* well-being and survival that are at stake. The planet itself will easily survive anything mere human beings can throw at it, even total nuclear war. After all, the Earth has in the past experienced lengthy ice ages, collisions with large meteors, and other major geophysical events, some of which have caused cataclysmic extinctions; yet it has continued to abide. However, if nature is well-nigh indestructible, its particular manifestations (among them man) are anything but. Despite his puniness in the cosmic scheme of things, man is entirely capable of rendering the biosphere uninhabitable for himself, as he already has for a multitude of other species.

In sum, although the particular aspects of the environmental problematique, like population pressure or rain-forest destruction, are bad in and of themselves, ecological scarcity is something much more pernicious: it is the multiplicative interaction of all of these factors to form a powerful ecological dynamic that directly challenges the industrial basis of modern civilization. And this ecological dynamic ultimately rests on the operation of basic physical laws. This is why much of the debate over specific environmental problems is beside the point. Facts and opinions, even "scientific" facts and opinions, about particular issues may change, but underlying ecological laws and principles do not—and it is these that tell us that we are exceeding the carrying capacity of the planet and that all of our attempts to evade ecological limits are bound to be self-defeating in the long run. Understanding the environmental problematique in terms of its underlying dynamic would also help to eliminate one of the least edifying features of current debate: the tendency to blame others. (Thus, for example, Americans castigate Brazilians for destroying the Amazon, even though we have already chopped down most of our own primeval forest and continue to log what little remains.) To understand the dynamic is to see that we are all implicated, albeit in varying ways and to different degrees, and this is the beginning of ecological wisdom. Let us therefore examine some of these basic laws and principles and their implications in more depth.

The Laws of Thermodynamics

Human beings have profoundly affected natural environments ever since the discovery of fire, with consequences that have deeply influenced the course of both biological evolution and human history. But the Industrial Revolution and the new technologies associated with it have made possible a more intensive exploitation of our biological capital than ever before. Unfortunately, although technology enhances our ability to extract useful matter and energy from one part of the ecological commons, it inevitably imposes losses elsewhere that are greater than the gains—and the more powerful the technology, the greater these losses.

That technology, especially intensive modern technology, is ultimately a destructive force is due to the First and Second Laws of Thermodynamics, among the most basic known to science. They state that matter and energy can neither be created nor destroyed, only transformed; and that all such transformations consume or degrade usable matter and energy. This loss of usable energy is called entropy. For example, when we burn coal to generate electric power, only about 35 percent of the energy released becomes electricity; the rest is wasted, dispersing as low-grade heat into the environs. In addition, the original matter not converted into electricity or heat turns into numerous unusable, unrecoverable, or even dangerous waste products, like the sulfuric acid that causes acid rain or the carbon dioxide that contributes to global warming. And even the electricity itself decays into useless low-grade heat once it has done its work. The high-grade energy or potential for work contained in the coal has thus been exhausted—in other words, lost to entropy. To keep electric power flowing, we have to extract and burn coal continuously, resulting in a continual increase of entropy. Our increasing reliance on technology has therefore set in motion a thermodynamic vicious circle in which the ultimate product of all our economic activity is entropy—an increase in disorder, decay, depletion, and degradation within the biosphere as a whole, due to our escalating demands. Ecological breakdown and backlash are simply nature's way of presenting us with these unpaid thermodynamic bills.

The entropy law is not, of course, the complete story, or the biosphere would not exist. But the creative force of nature operates only over the long term, whereas the acceleration of entropy via technology occurs in the short term, so human destruction has begun to overwhelm natural creation. Moreover, the rich beauty of the biosphere results in large part from nature's skillful accommodation to the Second Law: from the thermodynamic perspective, life is but a marvelous device for trapping incoming solar energy and using it to maximum effect before the energy is degraded and reradiated into space. In other words, paradoxically, the seemingly negative entropy law is itself a major part of the positive creative force!

It seems that our economies are based on a thermodynamic delusion. Indeed, the word *production* as a description of human economic activity is a misnomer. This is especially true with regard to "crude oil production": we produce nothing, but simply siphon up what nature produced eons ago. In other words, although we attribute the gains from economic activity to human effort and cleverness, what we actually do is use technology to extract or expropriate these benefits from nature, while at the same time inflicting costs on nature that greatly exceed them. The benefits are therefore a by-product, for what we mostly "produce" is entropy. For example, our apparently very productive agriculture is anything but: growing one calorie's worth of corn using intensive methods requires the expenditure of about ten calories of energy in the form of fuel, fertilizer, and other artificial inputs. What is worse, high-energy farming causes soil loss, pollution, and other harmful "side effects"—so the higher our agricultural "production," the higher the thermodynamic costs. But as we enjoy the benefits and have hitherto succeeded in displacing or ignoring the costs, intensive agriculture seems "productive" to us. It is this parochial view that ecology exposes as deluded.

In essence, as we shall see again when we explore economic development and its consequences in Chapters 3 to 5, our so-called affluence has been acquired by dishonest means: we do not account for what we steal from nature or sweep under the ecological carpet; or for what posterity will have to pay for our pleasures. Thus the more we develop, the deeper we go into thermodynamic debt and the more we ultimately impoverish ourselves.

Since the accelerated production of entropy resulting from economic development is the consequence of basic physical laws, no amount of money, energy, or technological wizardry can eliminate it. True, we can make our technologies more efficient in thermodynamic terms—a process called "etherealization." For example, using optical fibers made from sand instead of copper wires refined from ore reduces the thermodynamic costs of telecommunications. However, this process cannot continue indefinitely, for neither matter nor energy can be manufactured out of thin air. And even optical fibers and solar energy or other "soft" technologies exact a thermodynamic price that is not trivial (given large populations and heavy demand).

Moreover, what we can do in theory and what we can do in practice are two different things. Indeed, our ability to innovate has begun to be outrun by the pace of events and the size of the problems. A joint report of the U.S. Academy of Sciences and the Royal Society of London issued in 1992 stated: "If current predictions of population growth prove accurate and patterns of human activity on the planet remain unchanged, science and technology may not be able to prevent either irreversible degradation of the environment or continued poverty for much of the world." In other words, the days of easy and automatic technological advance is over; "progress" against ecological and thermodynamic limits will come much harder in the future. In fact, given some aspects of the ecological backlash—such as the rapid increase in insect resistance to pesticides and in microbial resistance to antibiotics—we shall have to run very much faster just to stay in the same place. In the end, the idea that we can flout the Second Law in perpetuity or build an artificial human technosphere exempt from ecological limits is a delusion.*

Hence we humans cannot for very much longer evade the basic ecological requirement imposed by nature on all living things: to stay within the limits of the carrying capacity of the ecological commons. These lim-

---

*Contrary to the pronouncements of diehard technological optimists, space colonization is not an answer. The entropic costs of lifting mass into orbit will restrict space exploration and eventual colonization to a tiny vanguard. Extensive trade in matter and energy is also ruled out, except in some remote science-fictional future in which we have mastered the force of gravity. Nor can we "decouple" ourselves from nature here on Earth, at least to the extent envisioned by those who would have us live in artificial ecologies based on such emergent technologies as biotechnology, nanotechnology, and fusion power. Even if these unproven technologies are eventually found to be both economically practical and ecologically harmless, replacing nature as the maker of all the basic requisites of life for large numbers of people will take infinitely more capital, knowledge, and managerial skill than we now possess or are ever likely to acquire.

its may be manipulated technologically for human gain—indeed, they must be if we are to live as anything but simple hunter-gatherers—but not in ways that consistently violate natural laws and cycles or to an extent that overstresses the resilience and health of the biosphere and its subsidiary ecosystems. All the various manifestations of ecological scarcity that we read about in our newspapers are signals to us that we have already transgressed the limits and have begun to destroy our life-support system.

Technological intervention in nature does indeed foster entropy, but does this mean that our situation is hopeless or that we need to give up all the perceived gains of scientific advance and economic development? As the previous paragraphs show, the answer is clearly no, *provided we learn to understand and respect nature instead of merely exploiting it*. Although all human interaction with the environment necessarily involves some disruption of natural cycles, and therefore has entropic costs, different types of technology and different ways of life have radically different ecological consequences. Consider, for example, the horticultural agriculture of Bali, where farmers have maintained the fertility and health of the soil for millennia using only the natural flow of solar energy, as contrasted with the mechanical agriculture of Iowa, where farmers mine the soil for short-term profit and require vast inputs of polluting fossil-fuel energy to produce a crop. In other words, technologies can be more or less thermodynamically efficient and ways of life can be more or less ecologically harmonious. Many earlier forms of technology, such as the wind and water mills of medieval Europe, were relatively less entropic. Possible future forms of technology—more "ethereal" and based on sustainable flow resources such as solar energy—promise to provide a sufficiency of material well-being at reasonable ecological cost. But more efficient technologies must be *matched* by more harmonious ways of living. At the very least, since continual growth in human numbers and in human demand must eventually overwhelm even the most efficient technology, the goal of economic life must be redefined as plenitude for a reasonable number of people rather than as affluence for an ever-growing population. Thus a technological future in reasonable harmony with the laws of ecology and thermodynamics is attainable, *but it depends on a political decision to live a different kind of life*.

Such a decision cannot be long deferred, because our current economic and technological mode of existence is so ecologically destructive that it threatens to wipe out important parts of our global life-support system and deplete critical resources within little more than a generation—and too much ecological destruction and depletion would foreclose the possibility of a relatively benign economic future. To revert to the metaphor of the spendthrift heir, instead of husbanding our estate to provide a comfortable living in perpetuity, we are squandering it to sustain a high level of current consumption. We are therefore devouring our patrimony, and a day of reckoning must come when the reality of ecological poverty dispels the illusion of economic wealth.

An Abnormal Era of Rapid Economic Growth

If the process we call economic development is as ecologically noxious as claimed, what accounts for its apparent success? In essence, extraordinary and unrepeatable conditions. First, Europeans, who had previously been tightly constrained both economically and socially, "discovered" the great frontier of the New World—a cornucopia of rich resources available for the price of killing, enslaving, or colonizing the native inhabitants. Second, spurred initially by resource shortages and then by the process of conquest itself, Europeans also invented technologies that gave them both the power to kill, enslave, and colonize on a global scale *and* the ability to exploit the resources more "intensively" than the allegedly benighted natives could do. Third, because these resources, not only in the New World but everywhere on the globe, had not been exploited intensively before, they were available in their most pristine and concentrated form. As a consequence, the ecological costs of the early stages of economic development were relatively modest. Moreover, due to lags in natural systems, the costs of development have tended to manifest themselves well after the benefits were received. To the casual eye, therefore, development has seemed unquestionably beneficial.

Once the cream is skimmed off, however, the ratio between economic benefits and thermodynamic costs deteriorates. First, the latent price attached to past development becomes manifest. (A prime example is the nuclear industry in the United States: we must now spend billions cleaning up contaminated facilities and disposing of toxic wastes, a price that was not part of our original calculations.) Next, economic development is subject to diminishing returns. Exploiting resources of lower quality normally requires a greater technological effort and the expenditure of more matter and energy. Thus we must now drill for oil at great depths and in remote and hostile environments, so it takes much more energy to obtain energy. In brief, as delayed reactions and diminishing returns force up ecological costs, the price attached to development rises inexorably over time.

Unfortunately, because almost all of these costs are "external" to the market, they are not ordinarily reflected in the price mechanism. To return to the example of electric power generation, the harm caused by acid rain to lakes and forests or human health is not included in the price of electricity. Nor are the true costs of producing corn reflected in its cash price: ecological losses like soil erosion and pesticide pollution or social losses like the decline of family farming are ignored by the market. In other words, the cash side of the ledger may show a substantial profit even though the thermodynamic accounts are drowning in red ink. Indeed, this is the story of the Industrial Revolution in a nutshell: technological cleverness has allowed us to lower market prices by driving up ecological costs. In the end, therefore, economic development is intrinsically predatory and destructive.

This conclusion, which will be supported in greater depth in later chapters, is bound to be vigorously resisted by an industrial civilization dominated by the economic ethos. But the challenge of ecology can no longer be avoided. Mounting thermodynamic costs signal the end of an abnormal era of ecological abundance in which extraordinary factors and forces permitted rapid economic growth with little regard for the damage done to the natural environment. Like it or not, we shall soon be obliged to create an economic system capable of transmuting illusory, short-term quantitative growth into genuine, long-term qualitative development that harmonizes the interests of man and nature.

From Pioneer to Climax Civilization

The challenge is not confined to the economic sector, because all our principles, practices, and institutions are products of this abnormal era—one in which we could simply appropriate the found wealth of the New World, Africa, and Asia and then develop these virgin resources without having to count the ecological cost. The rights of man, individualism, egalitarianism, mass education, social mobility, liberal democracy as well as socialism in various forms, and many other characteristic features of modern industrial civilization are outgrowths of the abnormal ecological circumstances that created and sustained this era of rapid growth. Now that these circumstances have changed, human institutions will have to adapt. Both the necessity of change and its required direction can best be understood by reference to the model of ecological succession, which illustrates how natural systems deal with the problem of thermodynamic costs.

Ecological systems vary in their degree of organizational integration or "maturity," from "pioneer" ecosystems at one extreme to "climax" ecosystems at the other. As these names suggest, the former are relatively crude or undeveloped, whereas the latter have attained the highest level of biological maturity that climate and other factors allow. The best exemplar of a pioneer ecosystem is a field of weeds; of a climax ecosystem, a coral reef or a tropical rain forest. Pioneer ecosystems use the available matter and energy with low efficiency to foster rapid growth, so they are made up of very large numbers of just a few species competing fiercely with each other as they grow very rapidly during relatively short and simple life cycles. By contrast, climax ecosystems use the available matter and energy with much greater efficiency to support a more complex biological structure made up of relatively small numbers of many different species, who tend to live in cooperative symbiosis with each other during long and complex life cycles. To use the language of finance, pioneer ecosystems produce a high yield, climax ecosystems a rich capital stock. The pioneer stage is therefore characterized by *quantity*, the climax stage by *quality*. If biological evolution is a movement toward greater organic complexity and richness on the planet, then climax ecosystems are the best exemplars of this tendency.

But what causes ecosystems to become qualitatively better and to move toward the climax? Simply put, immature ecosystems are forced to evolve toward greater maturity by the emergence of thermodynamic costs. Quantitative growth brings larger numbers, more wastes, and numerous other perturbations and problems that challenge the system (just as more people now challenge industrial societies). The result is a developmental crisis. To avoid collapse, the system must respond by achieving a "higher" level of organization that allows it to damp the perturbations and turn the costs into benefits—for example, by evolving feedback loops that limit populations, recycle wastes, and increase symbiosis. A political analogy may help: just as a large city can no longer be governed by a town meeting, which is an institution suitable only for small villages, so larger and more complex ecosystems need a more intricate and highly developed form of "governance" than do simpler ones. Pioneer ecosystems thus outgrow the relatively straightforward mechanisms by which they are governed and evolve toward greater organic complexity; and a process of ecological succession through a series of "developmental stages" of progressively greater maturity occurs, bringing into being ecosystems that can handle matter and energy more efficiently through better organization. Over time, this process produces a climax, the most mature ecosystem possible given local conditions.

It is therefore in the nature of things for relatively immature ecosystems to work themselves out of a job. Their very success, by generating all the problems that accompany increased size and complexity, renders them obsolete. Or, to use another political analogy, pioneer ecosystems exemplify the qualities or virtues needed to conquer and colonize new territory, whereas climax ecosystems exemplify those needed to consolidate the gains and create the highest quality of life thereafter.

This ecological model captures the predicament of late-industrial civilization precisely. The past five hundred years of conquest and colonization have been characterized by (1) extensive settlement of new territories; (2) explosive growth in the population of one species—humanity—to the detriment of others; (3) exponential increases in the exploitation of matter and energy, most of which is wasted; (4) deliberate destruction of older, more complex natural systems in favor of simplified, artificial systems and monocultures; (5) intense, and at times bellicose, competition; and (6) chronic instability in the form of cycles of economic boom and bust. These outcomes collectively exemplify a pioneer stage of human ecology. Our pioneering industrial civilization has pursued and accomplished its evolutionary task of colonization and rapid growth. It has thereby created the conditions that make it both possible and, barring total breakdown, inevitable for a more ecologically mature civilization to take its place. The qualities and virtues of the pioneer stage, which were necessary and appropriate to that stage (practically and perhaps morally as well), will serve the human race no longer. Now the qualities and virtues of a climax civilization have become imperative.

However, it is important not to make the climax into a fetish. Nature is more turbulent, dynamic, and changeable, even in the relatively near term, than ecologists originally believed. (In the longer term, of course, anything goes: after all, much of the Sahara was arable five thousand years ago; and the face of the Earth was largely icebound a mere twenty thousand years ago.) In other words, the climax is not a fixed or static goal to be achieved at all costs. Indeed, although the most mature ecosystems, such as tropical rain forests, are the most stable under normal circumstances, they are also the most ossified—and hence liable to collapse if overstressed. Rather than take the tropical rain forest as a model, then, we would be wiser to strive for a social order marrying the maturity and stability of the climax to the greater openness or progressiveness of the pioneer stage. And a model for such a way of life exists in nature: ecosystems that are repeatedly stressed develop a dynamic climax, like the "fire climax" of environments subjected to periodic fires. In short, the resiliency and scope for future development of the less mature ecosystem are desirable qualities that we may not wish to abandon altogether, even as we find ourselves obliged to move toward greater maturity.

At first glance, the message of ecology seems to be almost entirely negative: we are being forced by natural limits to abandon a way of life and a political paradigm which have been extraordinarily successful and to which we are strongly attached. But the model of ecological succession actually contains a positive message. If rambunctious biological growth creates conditions for higher-order complexity and richness in ecosystems, whereby quality replaces mere quantity, could not the same be true of social systems? Perhaps, therefore, the succession we are about to undergo should not be seen as a hateful necessity but, rather, as a desirable virtue to be actively cultivated: an ecologically mature civilization might also be a better civilization—a civilization that allowed our culture, through a renewed connection with the life process, to recover a sense of organic wholeness and meaning noticeably absent from modern life.

The Historical Origins of Liberal Politics

But rather than anticipate the Conclusions, let us now turn to the story of man's struggle against nature, to the history of civilization and the process of social evolution that produced the liberal paradigm of politics and the Industrial Revolution. We will then be in a better position to appreciate the nature and depth of the political crisis of our times.

What follows is an epitome, not a complete or balanced account: my sole aim is to trace the ancestry of modern politics to show why political evolution took the course that it did. I begin in prehistory with primal society and then move swiftly through successive historical stages, ending with the seventeenth-century revolution in political thought that gave birth to modern institutions.

Why begin in prehistory? Because the origins of current evils do indeed lie far back in time, as Trevelyan asserts. But surely not as far back as the Stone Age? In fact, yes. As the very word *prehistory* reveals, we tend to believe that real human life began only a few thousand years ago with the rise of civilization, so our standard account of who we are ignores everything that precedes it, even though this earlier period spans the larger part of humankind's time on Earth. But the child is father to the man, and civilization arose according to a certain dynamic that has had fateful consequences—for politics above all. If we wish to understand fully the forces that gave rise to liberal politics or that are now tending to destroy it, we must trace the story back to its origins, to the primal matrix that gave birth to civilization.

The Stone Age

In primal bands of hunter-gatherers, rule is widely shared in that decisions tend to be made by consensus. The chief is only the first among equals: he can persuade, but he cannot enforce. And the liberty of the individual is guaranteed by the ease with which he can vote with his feet. Primal society is therefore founded on charisma and consent, not hierarchy or coercion. Similarly, although social roles are sharply differentiated according to age and sex, there is nevertheless a basic mutuality, if not always a strict equality, within the group. That is, food and other critical resources are almost always equitably shared, and differences in wealth are slight. Moreover, none stand apart as isolated individuals: within the band all men are brothers, all women sisters. Even consciousness is largely shared: a common mystical participation in the living power of the cosmos, as well as a communal set of rites and rituals by which this power is invoked and appeased, is the most characteristic feature of primal society. Since animism, by its very nature, involves a direct relationship to the cosmos, access to the spiritual realm is available to all. Thus the shaman does not monopolize spiritual power: he is, like the chief, only the first among equals. Indeed, both the chief and the shaman, however charismatic, are regarded as servants of the group and judged accordingly—by the benefits they bestow on their fellows. In short, in virtually all important respects, the primal band is the original home of liberty, equality, and fraternity.

This is not to romanticize primal peoples. Despite their efforts to live in harmony with nature and with the great spirit that animates it, they could be quite destructive ecologically, and many extinct species owed their demise to overhunting or habitat destruction by our remote ancestors. In addition, the awesomeness of the invisible world and the perceived insecurity of life sometimes combined to overwhelm the group psyche—with baneful results, for minds dominated by fear, especially fear of the spirits, could easily go astray. Depending upon the group, therefore, certain aspects of primal life could be both harsh and primitive, and some customs and practices were indeed savage in the pejorative sense.

Nevertheless, paleolithic life was by no means essentially depraved or deprived, as we are wont to believe, and the image of bestial savages eking out a pitiful hand-to-mouth existence is utterly untrue. On the contrary, anthropologist Marshall Sahlins calls the Stone Age the "original affluent society," because our ancestors in fact enjoyed a kind of paradoxical abundance in which all their basic human needs were reliably met without undue effort except under unusual circumstances or in exceptionally harsh environments. "Even the poorest recorded huntergatherer group," says another anthropologist, Mark Cohen, "enjoys a caloric intake superior to that of impoverished contemporary populations." True, life was hard in certain respects. For example, even though adult populations were quite healthy, and many lived to reach elderhood, the average life expectancy at birth was low, because infant mortality was high. Yet the preponderance of the anthropological and archeological evidence suggests that, for all its rigors, this way of life was deeply satisfying—in large part because of primal man's communion with his fellows, with his surroundings, and, ultimately, with the cosmos. Hence material poverty was compensated by social and spiritual riches.

Some readers may find it hard to accept that primal peoples actually lived a decent life. We too easily forget that all the key inventions and innovations upon whose foundation civilization was ultimately erected were made by these supposed savages. In other words, our ancestors were not brutes but scientists, philosophers, and artists who created human culture. The astonishing cave paintings of Altamira, Chauvet, and Lascaux attest to the high cultural level attained by paleolithic man. That we do not perceive this is due to the ravages of time and to an arrogance that is only slowly being dispelled as archeologists, anthropologists, and prehistorians document the achievements of our forebears. In addition, we tend to forget that popular understanding of the lives of hunting and gathering peoples and primitive agriculturalists is largely based on the prejudicial views of their conquerors—that is, on the propaganda of soldiers, missionaries, and colonizers who had a vested interest in making the natives appear savage. Indeed, as most anthropologists concede, even their own profession has not been entirely free from prejudice. Moreover, by the time anthropologists got around to studying true hunter-gatherers, most had already been driven into remote and inhospitable environments by farmers and herders or corrupted by contact with civilization. In any event, most of ethnography deals not with paleolithic hunter-gatherers but, rather, with primitive agriculturalists—and, as we shall see in the next section, much of the savagery and deprivation that we attribute to the former in fact belongs to the latter. In sum, our primal ancestors were not the taboo-ridden, benighted, impoverished creatures of popular imagination but men and women as fully human as ourselves, whose way of life was both successful and satisfying.

The Neolithic Transition

Why then did primal peoples abandon this way of life for one that involved less freedom and more toil? This is a critically important question, the answer to which is pertinent to much that follows. It will help to explain, for example, the underlying dynamic of the Industrial Revolution and also to illuminate the fundamental choice now confronting humanity. The answer is, in essence, that they were obliged by ecological scarcity to invent agriculture.

As a mode of production, hunting and gathering require a relatively large amount of territory per person. Moreover, the characteristic social organization of the primal band is a function of its relatively small size. Overpopulation is therefore a menace both to its livelihood and to its social character. The typical response of a group with too many people is to split up, rather like a cell undergoing mitosis. Once all territories are fully occupied, however, the excess population has nowhere else to go. An enlarged population must now struggle to subsist within the old territory; but this process begins to deplete the resource base, aggravating the imbalance between people and resources. In other words, overpopulation initiates a vicious circle that draws the noose of ecological scarcity ever tighter around the group. Primal peoples in this predicament responded by inventing a new way of life: because game was scarce and tubers were hard to find, they began to herd animals and plant crops instead. In short, peoples who could not or would not control their population eventually had no choice but to revolutionize their means of production by practicing agriculture.

But this gradual change in the ecological basis of subsistence had profound sociopolitical consequences. First, agriculture necessarily raises the issue of ownership, and from property inevitably follows polity. It is as Jean-Jacques Rousseau said in his *Discourse on the Origin and Foundations of Inequality*: "The first person who, having fenced off a plot of ground, took it into his head to say *this is mine* and found people simple enough to believe him, was the true founder of civil society." Second, agricultural systems have to be managed in ways that a natural resource base or even pastoral flocks do not. Agriculture depends on withstanding environmental fluctuations (such as variations in rainfall) and the consequences of ecological simplification (such as insect pests). It is also vulnerable to the effects of bad practices (such as erosion). Thus the higher the level of agricultural development, the greater the need for managers standing over and above the cultivator. Third, and most important, larger numbers cannot be governed and more output cannot be obtained without a corresponding increase in social organization—and, in the final analysis, the latter requires political coercion.

The so-called Neolithic Transition from hunting and gathering to primitive agriculture is therefore a transition from a natural economy to a *political* economy in which production is socially organized to increase output by artificial means. In the process, the band grows into a tribe, and the chief becomes a "big man"—that is, a real ruler who possesses the means of coercion. And so the seed of tyranny is planted. The tribal ethic in which the earth belongs to no one and the fruits to all (at least within the tribe) no longer holds: for all practical purposes, the earth now belongs to these "high chiefs" or proto-kings, who distribute the fruits as they see fit. Naturally, the family, friends, and henchmen of the chief are favored, so proto-classes begin to form. But when some within the tribe are "more equal than others," men and women are no longer brothers and sisters as they once were; so reciprocity is no longer the invariable practice, and the decline of liberty and equality is soon followed by that of fraternity. Rousseau's description of the political consequences of the agricultural revolution is right on the mark: it "destroyed natural freedom for all time, established forever the law of property and inequality, changed a clever usurpation into an irrevocable act, and for the profit of a few ambitious men henceforth subjected the whole human race to work, servitude, and misery."

As if this were not bad enough, even man's spiritual life is now controlled by "a few ambitious men." Partly because political rule needs ideological backing and partly because life has become more insecure and less satisfying, the shaman turns into a proto-priest responsible for supplicating and appeasing the capricious gods upon whom agricultural success seemingly depends. There is also a tendency for the society to become riddled with strict taboos and savage customs designed to ward off hostile forces and attract divine blessings.

Neolithic proto-civilization therefore constituted a tragic fall from primal grace. The loss of aboriginal liberty, equality, and fraternity was particularly grievous: all the characteristic evils we associate with politics originated in the fatal decision to try to match population growth with more production, instead of limiting population to correspond with resources. Worse, neolithic man sold his primal birthright for a mess of pottage that never fully materialized, because the material gains promised by agriculture proved to be largely illusory. First, numbers soon caught up with increased output. Next, even when food intake was adequate in quantity, it lacked the quality of the extremely varied and healthy diet of the hunter-gatherer. Hence more people than ever before now lived an increasingly marginal existence: the archeological evidence clearly demonstrates that, for the first time in human history, populations began to suffer from perennial malnutrition. And when crops failed, as they often did, men and women starved in large numbers—again, something new in human history. Finally, greater population density made these undernourished populations vulnerable to epidemic disease, which had rarely troubled dispersed primal groups; and a less vigorous way of life also made them susceptible to degenerative diseases unknown among their primal ancestors.

In the end, the decision to take up agriculture was, as medical anthropologist Jared Diamond says, quite possibly "the worst mistake in the history of the human race." Diamond describes how the process nevertheless fed on itself in a classic vicious circle:

> As population densities of hunter-gatherers slowly rose at the end of the Ice Age, bands had to "choose," whether consciously or unconsciously, between feeding more mouths by taking the first steps toward agriculture, or else finding ways to limit growth. Some bands adopted the former solution, unable to anticipate the evils of farming, and seduced by the transient abundance they enjoyed until population growth caught up with increased food production. Such bands outbred and then drove off or killed the bands that chose to remain hunter-gatherers, because ten malnourished farmers can still outfight one healthy hunter. It's not that hunter-gatherers abandoned their lifestyle, but that those sensible enough not to abandon it were forced out of all areas except ones that farmers didn't want.

Unfortunately, as clearly implied in this quote, intensifying one's own production is not the only possible response to ecological scarcity. Indeed, having organized a military force to drive off any primal competitors, why would one not then employ it to seize the lands and bodies of fellow agriculturalists? Although agriculture is not intrinsically evil, adopting it as a mode of production therefore has fateful consequences. Greater production requires an increasingly powerful central authority backed up by an ever stronger military force; it can only be a matter of time before this force is used to wage aggressive war. !n its earliest stages, before this dreadful dynamic had run its course, the agricultural revolution may have allowed a relatively benign and peaceful way of life to flourish for a time, at least in a few favored places. But once the levels of population, wealth, and social differentiation became high enough to make wars of conquest feasible and profitable, limited or ritual conflict, much less live-and-let-live, were no longer realistic options, so organized warfare turned into a way of life.

In sum, the Neolithic Transition was *the* decisive event in human history. The ecological and social forces unleashed by the agricultural revolution ignited a vicious struggle for economic survival, political hegemony, and military supremacy that launched humanity on a tragic trajectory toward civilization. Why tragic? Because, says John Reader,

> in the brief span of time that civilisation has been a feature of human existence, it has not demonstrated any tendency to produce a well-regulated

steady state wherein people are well-fed and secure, generation after generation. Civilisation is distinguished more by its erratic cycles of uncontrolled growth and collapse than by any inherent tendency toward stability. Time and again, it has risen dramatically from the field of human endeavour, then collapsed and fallen. Human ingenuity drives the process. Human inability to impose adequate restraint brings it down. . . . [I]n every instance so far, the uncontrolled growth of civilisation has ultimately thrown up more problems than human intellect could solve.

But there could be no turning back. For better or for worse, the Neolithic Transition revolutionized the terms of human existence. Once the process of acquiring power over man and nature starts, it feeds on itself: increased energy and control lead in a vicious circle to the necessity for yet more energy and control—and so on ad infinitum, limited only by the available resources and technology.

The Ancient Civilizations

Thus arose the civilizations of antiquity, societies that carry the dynamic of the Neolithic Transition to its logical conclusion. Natural resources and human labor are now socially organized to produce economic wealth and military power: primitive agriculture gives way to large-scale intensive cropping dependent on irrigation; villages turn into cities and towns peopled by traders and artisans; and occasional skirmishing becomes more or less perpetual war fought by professional soldiers. These defining features of ancient civilization all but impose its characteristic political organization: a semi-divine warlord-king with near absolute power; a small class of officers and officials who serve as his lieutenants; and a mass of slaves, serfs, or subjects owing absolute obedience to those above them in the hierarchy. Almost all vestiges of the primal ethos and way of life have been extinguished or perverted.

In an equally nefarious development, the shaman turns into a spiritual king, a high priest who stands at the apex of a sacerdotal hierarchy paralleling the political and military hierarchies. Ordinary people no longer have a natural right to direct participation in the sacred mysteries: this is the prerogative of the priests, for they alone possess a divine mandate to instruct and rule the people in the name of the gods. But even the priests have lost the shaman's easy intimacy with the spirits. Indeed, they no longer get their spiritual guidance directly from the source, but from the word and the law—that is, from religious ideology, which now begins to crowd out or even preclude the direct experience of the sacred. Thus doctrine replaces experience, and organized worship replaces mystical participation: spiritual life, too, is perverted, and humanity's fall from primal grace is complete.*

The ancient civilizations are therefore the antithesis of primal liberty, equality, and fraternity. From direct social participation on a rough basis of equality, man falls into hierarchical politics; from the simplicity and ease of primal union with the cosmos, man falls into hierarchical religion. And so the enduring pattern of civilized life was laid down: centralized power based on a standing army, a system of tax collection and labor conscription that siphons wealth upward, the intensive exploitation of nature (and the first serious environmental problems), and a religious ideology enforced by a priestly class.

One aspect of that religious ideology deserves special attention. To the shaman, the primal power is sexual in nature, for it is the union of Mother Earth and Father Sky that gives life to us all. So both the light and the dark powers, the male and the female forces, are equally necessary and equally honored. But kingship, perpetual war, irrigation, and priestly religion overthrow this balance: to a greater or lesser extent, the Sky God and the male role are exalted over the Great Mother and the female role, both spiritually and socially. The religions and cultures of the ancient civilizations are therefore one-sided—or "patriarchal," to use the favorite epithet of modern feminist critics. But what is repressed in consciousness does not go away; it instead returns in an unhealthy guise. Civilization's repressive one-sidedness thus becomes a root cause for much of the alienation, destructiveness, oppression, and violence that have shadowed human history.

During the so-called Axial Age, various messiahs attempted a spiritual transformation of ancient civilization: they tried to assuage its severity and restore its balance. Unfortunately, the teachings of Buddha, Jesus, and the other great sages of this era were soon corrupted into religious ideology and renewed justification for hierocracy and autocracy, so the attempt to reform ancient civilization failed. Yet their call for a return to the original source of sacred knowledge and to a life of nobility and simplicity in harmony with a deeper spiritual reality has never been forgotten either: the lost possibility of wholeness and meaning exemplified in their lives and teachings has continued to haunt civilized man.

---

*This fall is symbolized in the Judeo-Christian tradition by Adam and Eve's expulsion from Eden. That it really was a fall is revealed by the word *religion*. From the Latin *religare*, it means "to link again," so its function is to *reconnect* humanity with the sacred power lost when humans abandoned the simplicity and ease of primal life, seen in retrospect as "paradise."

Another attempt to reform ancient civilization took place in Greece. Although Greek civilization had much in common with the other ancient civilizations, it was also the great exception in important respects. In the rest of the antique world, religion and politics were all but inseparable. But in Greece, we see the first real attempt (in the West) to distinguish their differing functions in society and to apply human reason to social problems. The Greek polis, or more particularly Athens, thus became the place where politics as we know it was invented.

Whatever their differences, which were considerable, Greek thinkers like Plato and Aristotle nevertheless shared a common perspective: they believed that politics was not given by the gods but subject to human control; and that the goal of politics was to foster a good and noble way of life. In other words, politics existed and justified itself only as a means toward better and wiser human beings, so the job of the polis was to educate the citizens in wisdom and virtue. But education meant something other than indoctrination: wisdom and virtue were to be achieved not through blind adherence to religious doctrines inherited from the past or through political obedience to ideologies imposed from above but, instead, through personal participation in the common life of the polis, for this would foster the self-development of the citizen.

The Medieval World

Unfortunately, Greece's glory was short-lived, and the effort to liberate at least a small elite from religious ideology and political autocracy ultimately failed. (At least in the short term: the eventual rediscovery during the Renaissance of the noble ideals and dazzling achievements of Athenian thought set the stage for the modern era and for the eventual emergence of the liberal paradigm.) Although Macedonian and Roman imperialism spread Hellenic culture from Ireland to Afghanistan, it also entrenched the hierarchical politics of the ancient world more firmly than ever.

The later political triumph of Christianity made matters worse, because the ideological struggle for control of the newly established church was won by hardliners like Augustine. According to Augustine, the secular ruler's role was to be God's hangman on Earth (a sentiment echoed later by Martin Luther). Following Constantine's conversion, therefore, the Roman state became an enforcer for a church whose theological and political claims were all-encompassing, a pattern that continued into medieval times.

It is important to acknowledge the great cultural and technological achievements of the Middle Ages: they constituted the matrix and foundation of the modern way of life. Nor can one deny the great civilizing influence of the medieval church. Indeed, as we shall see later, the moral legacy of the Middle Ages was indispensable to the success of modern political economy. Unfortunately, it was not the virtues but the vices of the medieval church that decisively propelled political thought in a radically new direction.

The first problem was that a worldly, political church lost much of its spiritual prestige by becoming venal and corrupt. The result was that many persons of good will (and deep religious sentiment) came to abhor established, clerical religion and so began to dissent from it.

However, the medieval church could not tolerate dissent. Indeed, a characteristic figure of the Middle Ages was the Inquisitor, whose role was to exterminate by force all opposition to the religious monopoly and political position of the church. The Inquisitor is a tragic figure in the true Greek sense. He aims at holiness, but by trying to enforce a narrow and prejudicial standard of religious virtue and to eliminate all purported infidels, heretics, and witches, he becomes an agent of cruelty and destruction. Instead of peace, he brings the auto-da-fé.

But dissent flourished despite the Inquisition, and the Protestant Reformation split Christendom into warring camps, all of them claiming divine sanction for their beliefs. Hence theological zeal combined with dynastic ambition and political expediency to drench Europe in blood. For all its undeniable virtues and glories, medieval religion was therefore the author of discord and death.

The Birth of Liberal Polity

Because organized religion seemed bent on destroying the polity through internecine strife, some thinkers naturally began to question the identification of politics with religion and to explore ways of extricating the state from the role of God's hangman. Niccolò Machiavelli took a major step in this direction by distinguishing between political and religious virtue: politics, he asserted, is about seizing power in this world, religion about preparing for the next, and confounding the two enterprises brings chaos. However, it was Thomas Hobbes who became, in Karl Marx's words, "the father of us all" by proposing that politics be severed completely from religion and traditional morality.

Looking back at the horrors of the Inquisition, Hobbes saw that spiritual truth could not be imposed by political means and that attempting to do so would lead to a massacre of innocents. Remembering the just-ended bloodbath of the Thirty Years' War (1618–1648), during which Protestant and Catholic armies had vainly tried to win theological supremacy by force of arms, he concluded that basing politics on a particular standard of religious virtue was a prescription for fratricide, both within and between polities. And examining the theological justifications offered for the competing standards, he found only hot air, assertions of truth that could never be proved by reason or evidence and so would always tempt men to prove them by the sword.

Politics must therefore renounce its moral vocation. The aim of politics, said Hobbes, is not to make "the citizens . . . doers of noble things" but, rather, to "furnish [them] with all good things." In other words, do not try to make men and women good; make them reasonable instead. Give them the freedom to pursue their own happiness, but set up governments as policemen to keep the resulting struggle for advantage within tolerable bounds—bounds that could readily be discovered by human reason, provided that speculative theology were replaced by mechanistic science.

As if abandoning morality as the ground of politics were not sufficiently radical, Hobbes also rejected the traditional view that man is a naturally social being. He embraced individualism instead. To return briefly to our historical account, the individual as we know him is a modern invention—in fact, one of the great achievements of modernity. In tribal societies, individuality is by no means absent, but tribal members are so psychically attuned to their community and surroundings that they tend to merge with them. In ancient and medieval civilization (with Greece being the exception), only a few at the very top of the social pyramid could be said to have possessed individuality; the large mass of the people at the bottom simply did not count, except as sheep count to the shepherd.

Western political philosophy before Hobbes naturally reflected this overwhelming social reality. Theorists assumed as a matter of course that men and women were social beings by nature and that the community must necessarily take precedence over the individual. But the Renaissance and its aftermath brought a sea change to European society, creating conditions that gradually made people more aware of themselves as individuals—a change symbolized by the famous *Cogito ergo sum* of Descartes, which made the thinking *self* into the cornerstone of philosophy. Hobbes had the prescience to recognize, and the temerity to ratify, this change: he grounded his political theory on the isolated, asocial individual instead of on the community.

By liberating politics from the theological justification of rule and individuals from communally enforced virtue, Hobbes became the intellectual founder of modern political life in all important respects. As we shall see in the next chapter, where we examine his ideas in greater depth, from these bold steps eventually followed all the characteristic features of liberal polity—rule by contractual consent of the governed, religious toleration and the separation of church and state, the redefinition of the good life in material terms, and the role of the nation-state as provider of worldly satisfactions, to mention only the most important. Of course, the liberal paradigm of politics did not spring full blown from Hobbes; it was given its final shape by the thinkers who followed in his footsteps (especially John Locke, although he often receives more credit than he deserves). Moreover, it took the entire intellectual movement that we call the Enlightenment to complete the overthrow of religion and to install reason (in the narrow form of rationality) as the sole guide for human affairs. But it was Hobbes who, by standing two millennia of political thought on its head, sired modern politics and became thereby "the father of us all."

Looking Beyond Amoral Individualism

Hobbes's liberation of politics from virtue and individuals from community produced much that was necessary and positive for human evolution. We need hardly elaborate the great (but not necessarily unique) achievements of the liberal paradigm of politics: juridical equality, civil rights, religious toleration, freedom of thought and speech, governments that are ultimately answerable to the people, widespread increases in standards of living (at least in those societies where the liberal paradigm has been long and thoroughly applied), great advances in scientific knowledge and technological power, and so on. Yet, as we have already seen with respect to ecology and as we shall explore in some depth in the chapters to come, this litany of progress is very far from being the whole story, for both nature and man suffered huge losses under the new dispensation.

Of course, all political paradigms contain inherent contradictions and therefore generate problems that must be solved. The job of the statesman, as opposed to the mere politician, is to preserve the paradigm by dealing effectively with these problems. However, if political wisdom and skill are lacking or if the contradictions are very deep, small problems eventually coalesce into a large problematique that challenges the old paradigm. At this point, mere reform, however well conceived, no longer suffices and may even make matters worse, so pressure builds up for a fundamental change in regime.

This is, I will argue, precisely our predicament. Because the basic premises of the liberal paradigm are intrinsically self-destructive, it has spawned deep and intractable problems that are propelling us toward political succession, toward a fundamental change of regime just as radical as that introduced by Hobbes when he sired modern politics. In brief, the politics of amoral individualism has failed. In consequence, while conserving many of its important features, we now seem obliged to transcend the liberal paradigm. That is, we must restore the moral or spiritual context of politics, finding some way of making politics once again rest on virtue (rather than on mere self-interest) without at the same time resurrecting the intolerance and oppression associated with almost all forms of religious politics, ancient or modern. Then, as a corollary, we must restore the lost balance between individual rights and community interests, finding some way of upholding the common good without at the same time subjecting individuals to the age-old evils of hierarchical politics. In other words, the challenge is to find a way of going beyond amoral individualism without also losing the individual along the way.

Suggesting that liberal politics has failed and that we therefore need to restore both political virtue and communal bonds will shock many readers, for among the dirtiest words in the lexicon of contemporary liberalism is *values* when it is used to mean something higher than personal preference. What I propose will tend to be seen as a reactionary desire to do away with individual freedom of conscience and action—and hence to threaten what we are most strongly attached to in the liberal paradigm.

Such a fear arises in part from a basic confusion among today's liberals about the nature of so-called values and their role in human life. First, that we now use the word *values* (whose literal meaning is "monetary or material worth") to denote ideals, standards, mores, or principles reveals the depth of the economic bias and moral disarray in modern civilization. Second, as we shall learn below, the founders of the liberal paradigm and of the American republic relied *explicitly* on what we now call "higher values"—that is, on the presence of a moral code grounded ultimately in religious sentiment. Finally, values are not socially dangerous in and of themselves: after all, we call a person who lives without scruple or principle a "sociopath," and a society without moral standards is inconceivable because cultures are defined precisely by their "norms." So the issue is not whether we will have collective values, but what kind they will be. And how they will be manifested: in an oppressive political ideology or an uplifting moral code? In this light, the political task is not to shy away from values but, rather, to establish, and then maintain, a principled basis for governance.

But now we begin to anticipate the Conclusions, so let us turn to the main argument in Chapter 1 to see how we are being driven by the contradictions of the liberal paradigm toward the twin outcomes of anarchic self-destruction, partial or total, and totalitarianism, more or less benign. It will then be clear why a fundamental change in regime is not an option but a necessity.

I

Moral Entropy

Nearly every respectable attribute of humanity is the result not of instinct, but of a victory over instinct.

—John Stuart Mill

Capitalism creates a rational frame of mind which, having destroyed the moral authority of so many other institutions, in the end turns against its own: the bourgeois finds to his amazement that the rationalist attitude does not stop at the credentials of kings and popes, but goes on to attack . . . the whole scheme of bourgeois values.

—Joseph A. Schumpeter

Despotism may govern without faith, but liberty cannot. Religion is much more necessary in the republic which they set forth in glowing colors than in the monarchy which they attack; it is more needed in democratic republics than in any others. How is it possible that society should escape destruction if the moral tie is not strengthened in proportion as the political tie is relaxed? And what can be done with a people who are their own masters if they are not submissive to the deity?

—Alexis de Tocqueville

THE LIBERAL PARADIGM OF POLITICS IS MORIBUND. Liberal politics has become an increasingly naked struggle for power played out in a media arena before an electronic mob. The politically active and aware continue to maintain, at least in public, that new policies and new leadership can restore political health, but private suspicion that we may be slouching toward ungovernability, or perhaps worse, is growing. Many have given up on politics completely. The question posed by Alexander Hamilton in the first paragraph of *The Federalist*—"whether societies of men are really capable or not of establishing good government from reflection and choice, or whether they are forever destined to depend for their political constitutions on accident and force"—has now reemerged to confront the current generation of Americans with stark clarity.

What brought us to this pass is abundantly clear: the liberal paradigm of politics unleashed human will and appetite, but provided no countervailing source of moral principle strong enough to preserve society from their ravages over the long term. Liberalism is therefore based on intrinsically self-destructive principles. Only extraordinary historical circumstances, now radically altered, and an inherited morality, now seriously decayed, have enabled it to survive thus far. Let us examine the theory of liberal politics to see why its basic premises are self-destructive and how its inner contradictions tend to bring about its eventual demise. (We can then go on, in the next chapter, to use the American case to illustrate liberal self-destructiveness in practice.)

Hobbes's Philosophical Revolution

Before Hobbes, political theorists generally followed Aristotle in taking the innate sociability of the human species as axiomatic: man is by nature a "political animal" who cannot exist, much less be fully human, outside the polis. And the polis is no mere alliance of self-interested individuals to be entered and left at will but, rather, is a tribe writ large, a community given by nature that is united by common blood and shared ideals. In other words, the political community just *was*, so premodern theorists did not have to explain or justify its existence, only its proper form. And whatever its form, the community and its needs preceded the individual and his rights; indeed, in this older, communitarian way of thinking about politics, there really was no such thing as the individual and his rights as we understand them.

Hobbes broke radically with this tradition. He posited instead a "state of nature" in which men and women exist as atomistic individuals owing little or nothing to others or to any higher power. In this presocial state, they have a natural right to indulge their passions in whatever way they can; and the lack of a higher authority or community structure leaves them completely free to do so. But the result is bound to be a free-for-all, a "war of every man against every man," in which survival is at stake and power is all that counts. Nor can there be any end to the struggle, "because [a man] cannot assure the power and means to live well, which he hath at present, without the acquisition of more." Hence, said Hobbes, there is in the state of nature a "perpetual and restless desire of power after power, that ceaseth only in death."

Fortunately, although passion predominates, men and women also possess reason. And reason tells them that life in the state of nature—an anarchic chaos of conflicting will and appetite—is bound to be "solitary, poor, nasty, brutish, and short." To escape this fate, they should agree to give up their natural right to "do anything and have anything" and place themselves under a commonwealth ruled by a "sovereign," preferably a monarch. This willing surrender of all their private power to a public sovereign in accordance with the "laws of nature" revealed by reason constitutes the famous "social contract." Once private force has been converted into public power, the sovereign makes and enforces rules that permit and even encourage individuals to seek their own selfish ends— but now peacefully, within a framework of laws that preserve both public order and private rights.

Men and women therefore get the advantages of the state of nature, primarily the opportunity for self-gratification, without the corresponding disadvantages. But to get them they must grant absolute power to the sovereign, for this is the inescapable price of the social contract: "Covenants, without the sword, are but words, and of no strength to secure a man at all." Besides, living in an orderly commonwealth brings positive benefits that more than make up for the loss of political rights— "convenience," "commodious living," and progress in the arts and sciences, or what we would today call economic development. In any event, political rights are not that important, for although the sovereign's power is absolute, its role is quite limited (at least in theory): it is to make laws that keep individuals from harming one another or disturbing the peace, but that leave them otherwise free to pursue private ends.

Hobbes's state of nature and social contract are, of course, anthropological and historical fictions, and we must not suppose that Hobbes took them for fact.* They were instead the basic elements of a new theory intended to resolve the crisis of his time—a crisis that was at heart

---

*All previous social systems (up to and including the most "primitive" bands of hunter-gatherers) were organized on some basis or other—kinship, religion, an aristocratic ideal—that made them places where life was *not* "solitary, poor, nasty, brutish, and short." In other words, except during brief periods of anarchy, human beings have never lived in a Hobbesian state of nature. In the Europe of the mid-1600s, however, long-standing trends were eroding the basis of social organization and threatening to produce political breakdown. Thus Hobbes's image of the state of nature is largely a projection of his fears for the future, not a description of the anthropological or historical past. On the other hand, the idea of the social contract does contain a kernel of anthropological truth: in primal societies, says Claude Lévi-Strauss, "power both originates in consent and is bound by it."

political, although it took the outward form of religious warfare. Because
the Protestant church was a man-made institution, its basic principles
and mere existence challenged not just the Catholic church but every
form of authority not based on reason and consent—especially that of
the kings who ruled by divine right. There could be neither peace nor
stability until this challenge to royal authority was squarely met.
Hobbes's philosophical genius consisted in inventing a political myth,
the social contract, that explained and justified the king's rule in Protestant terms.

The brilliance and daring of Hobbes's solution is astonishing: he
turned reason and consent, the very grounds of the challenge to royal authority, into an argument for strong sovereignty—that is, for monarchy
given the prevailing conditions. But this solution also turned the world
upside down and raised disturbing questions. Was it really necessary to
go to the extreme of overthrowing the familial and communal basis of
politics altogether? And even if some new political myth or fiction were
now needed, why hypothesize isolated, asocial individuals, contrary to
the historical and anthropological fact of biosocial man, unless this is the
conclusion you want to reach? Indeed, is there not a serious danger that
such a hypothesis will become a self-fulfilling prophecy? Especially if
you get rid of religion and allow or even encourage men and women to
pursue their own selfish ends? What follows will argue that this is precisely what has occurred. Hobbesian politics has created a society populated by amoral men and women who are prey to "a perpetual and restless desire of power after power."

The problem resides in Hobbes's deeply asocial assumptions. As there
is no natural or preexisting political community, and men and women are
not civil by nature, a political community must be artificially constructed: "By art is created that great LEVIATHAN called a COMMON-
WEALTH." But the motives for joining the commonwealth are purely negative: fear of violence on the one hand and a realization that "the
contentments of life" can be obtained in no alternative way on the other.
The Hobbesian polity is therefore a necessary evil, to which individuals
give only grudging consent. The sovereign's role is also essentially negative: in the absence of any higher moral standard or any purpose for politics beyond the satisfaction of private desire, the sovereign simply preserves public order with laws that check excessive displays of will and
appetite. If people within a commonwealth behave well, it is because a
secure and well-ordered existence allows the better and more reasonable
side of human nature, otherwise dominated by the passions, to come to
the fore. But this appearance of civility is deceptive. Hobbesian society is

always only one step removed from the state of nature, and the passions that fuel the war of all against all smoulder within each human breast, ready to flame up again the moment public authority falters.

The core premises of Hobbesian polity thus incline it toward self-destruction. It is a mere collectivity of individuals who are by nature selfish and passionate; who exist as social atoms, lacking any natural ties of sociability or affection; and who possess a natural right to do anything and have anything. In addition, they are essentially untouched by compassion or an innate moral sense. Reason does indeed tell them to behave in accordance with the "laws of nature"—but these laws are *prudential*, not moral. That is, they are justified as necessary for the individual's self-preservation. Moreover, whatever their moral status, they are practically compelling *only when enforced in a commonwealth*. To put it another way, they are clauses in a secular contract that holds only as long as the contracting parties receive the promised advantages.

To be specific, the laws of nature ordain that "every man . . . ought to endeavour peace" and "be contented with so much liberty against other men, as he would allow other men against himself." However, every man also has an overriding right of self-defense in which "he may seek, and use, all helps, and advantages of war" once the peace is disturbed or his vital interests are threatened. In addition, although the theory requires that individuals obey the sovereign's laws once the commonwealth is established, the basis of obedience in practice is, again, prudential: awareness of the benefits of civil society and fear of the consequences of disobedience. In practice, therefore, one is largely free to do whatever one can get away with. Worse, although most individuals are reasonable and inclined to live at peace, a greedy, ambitious, and unreasonable few will always stand ready to embroil the whole society in a vicious circle of competitive self-seeking. In sum, human relationships are fundamentally adversarial, and the sword of Leviathan is all that prevents the unspeakable misery and violence of the state of nature from erupting anew.

To use a mechanical metaphor, Hobbes's polity is like a giant steam engine that lacks a natural governor. It therefore threatens to run faster and faster until it flies apart. (A modern systems engineer would say that it is dominated by positive feedback or a tendency to enter a runaway mode.) But individuals have just enough wit to realize this, and so they agree to clamp a governor on the political engine: an all-powerful Leviathan that overawes them and contains their steamy passions with laws. Now governed by the negative feedback of the sovereign, the engine chugs along within tolerable limits, leaving individuals free to indulge themselves without fear of causing an explosion.

Although Hobbes did not himself use this metaphor (because New-comen had yet to build the first working steam engine), he might well have delighted in it, because his conception of politics was fundamentally mechanical. The basis of the old politics was belief; of the new politics, structure. The problems of government can be solved with good engineering—that is, "scientifically," for "the skill of making and maintaining Commonwealths consisteth in certain rules, as doth arithmetic and geometry." Hobbes had, in effect, invented a politics for the coming machine age. The Madisonian preoccupation with the machinery of constitutional government so characteristic of the United States is therefore at bottom Hobbesian (which is not to deny the more direct or proximate influence of Montesquieu's doctrine of checks and balances). And the modern administrative state, a governmental machine for satisfying the material aspirations of the people, is also fundamentally Hobbesian. Hobbes is indeed "the father of us all"—and of American politics above all—to a much greater extent than is commonly realized.

To sum up, by abandoning natural community as the foundation and virtue as the end of politics, Hobbes was able to dispense with divine right and reestablish monarchy on secular grounds. So he overthrew tradition only to uphold it. This won him few friends: potentates hated losing the God-given right to instruct and rule the people; and the newly restive plebs were not pleased with a theory of politics that left the crown in undisturbed possession of absolute power. Nevertheless, the brilliance of his philosophical revolution overwhelmed all opposition: like it or not, later theorists had to adapt to, if not adopt, the new way of thinking about politics invented by Hobbes.

Locke's Bourgeois Politics

John Locke thus began his theory of politics with man in the state of nature making a social contract. But in *Two Treatises of Government* (1690), Locke turned Hobbes on his head by using the latter's premises to justify bourgeois political liberty. This reversal made him a genuinely great political thinker in his own right and the author of the liberal paradigm as we know it. Nevertheless, Locke's theory incorporated Hobbes's mode of reasoning and almost all of his basic assumptions. His originality and historical importance are due to three major corrections of Hobbes that allowed him to slip a velvet glove over the mailed fist of Leviathan and recast a conservative doctrine supportive of monarchy into a revolutionary argument for representative democracy.

Hobbes's assumptions were extreme. First, the good things of life are so scarce in the state of nature that an all-out power struggle to obtain them is inescapable. Second, human beings, although capable of reason, are incorrigibly passionate. Third, there is no intermediate possibility between the absolute anarchy of the state of nature and the strict order of the commonwealth. From the extremity of these assumptions follows relentlessly the extremity of Hobbes's conclusion that there must be an all-powerful, unitary sovereign to control human passions and forestall political chaos.

Locke relaxed all of these assumptions. First, he took the New World as his model for the state of nature: originally, "all the world was America," a vast and inexhaustible commons begging to be appropriated. Since nature is fundamentally abundant, a sufficiency is available to all who will work—if not here, then just over the horizon. There will still be conflict, because men and women are creatures with a surfeit of passion and a deficit of reason, but not the all-out conflict of the war of all against all. Thus, although a sovereign power is still essential, it need not be an implacable Leviathan. In fact, said Locke, a government more like a night watchman to keep the peace, or a referee to ensure fair play, will do.

Second, this relatively sanguine political conclusion was reinforced by Locke's more sanguine view of human nature. Not only is there a "natural harmony of interests" among human beings, but, except under extreme conditions, the conscience and reason of the average man suffice to keep his passions in check. So not only are the good things of life relatively abundant, but most people will behave decently most of the time. Extreme political measures are, again, unnecessary: limited government can easily maintain order.

Third, in his most decisive and telling correction, Locke rejected Hobbes's all-or-nothing alternatives of anarchy or autocracy. Instead, said Locke, the social contract occurs in two stages. First civil society is founded, and *then* its members agree to establish a commonwealth. Adding this extra step makes all the difference: once formed, civil society constitutes a permanent bulwark against the anarchy of the state of nature; and living in civil society tames the passions of its members. In short, society, not polity, bears the main burden of maintaining order. A ruling power is still needed as the ultimate guarantor of the social contract, but not as the first line of defense against anarchy. The ruler can therefore get along with less than absolute powers; and changes in government can occur without bringing on chaos. Indeed, said Locke, the members of civil society have both the right to choose the form of sovereignty that best meets their needs and to rebel against governments that usurp the people's rights.

Locke should not be misunderstood as calling for weak government. Men and women are passionate; material goods are always scarcer than human wants; and civil society needs the backing of the ruler's sword. Strong government is therefore essential, and Locke grants rulers all the power they need to direct the individual to his "proper interest" and to compel him with laws that "preserve and enlarge freedom." Nevertheless, thanks to his more sanguine view of both the state of nature and human nature, as well as his ingenious modification of the social contract, Locke was able to argue for government by continuing consent of the governed in place of Hobbes's one-time consent followed by autocracy. From this revolutionary idea eventually followed "the rights of man" and the whole history of modern political development, especially representative democracy.

Locke's theory of private property also had revolutionary political and economic implications. Although Hobbes had in effect invented political economy by making material satisfaction the end of politics and economic development the task of the sovereign, he established only the basic direction. It was left to Locke to become the founder of modern political economy by making private property the basis of liberal politics.

Locke elaborated and extended Hobbes's right of appropriation within the state of nature. In the superabundance of the natural state, men and women create property by applying their labor to an unclaimed part of the commons, which then becomes theirs. And what one man takes from nature harms no one—"since there was still enough, and as good left; and more than the yet unprovided could use." Once appropriated, this primal property is then passed on in an unbroken chain of succession to the current generation. Of course, with the introduction of money, property begins to change hands, and the rough equality of the state of nature is replaced by the sometimes harsh inequality of civilization—but this outcome does not, according to Locke, change the principle or call for different rules. In any event, the existence of "America" makes the issue of inequality moot, for anyone not happy with the current distribution of property in Europe can light out for the New World and appropriate land from the American commons.

Locke's justification of property rights flies in the face of history. Whatever its hypothetical origin in the state of nature, actual title was almost certainly based on conquest or seizure. Ironically, America, the very case that Locke used to make his point, demonstrated this: the Europeans took the land from the Indians. In fact, during his own lifetime English landlords were aggressively enclosing—that is, expropriating—the lands that had for centuries been the communal property of agricultural laborers. Moreover, by extending the right of accumulation into a money economy, which allows one to employ "servants" or to put money out at interest and thereby acquire property indirectly, Locke resorts to an intellectual sleight of hand that radically extends the idea of "individual" appropriation from a "commons." And his beautiful theory is again contradicted by an ugly fact: in America, "property" was created with slave labor. So Locke's reasoning may well justify usufruct under the special conditions of the state of nature, where appropriation of the commons by individual labor harms no one, but it does not necessarily justify ownership, much less for all time. And the farther away from the state of nature, the less persuasive "first come, first served" in remote antiquity seems, especially in a money economy erected on a foundation of conquest and slavery. Besides, ecological scarcity renders Locke's argument untenable in its own terms: without the free commons of "America" as a safety valve, those lacking property have nowhere left to turn and are likely to be pauperized in perpetuity.

In other words, like the social contract itself, Locke's property doctrine is a political myth—but one that is critically important to his theory as a whole, because economics in general and private property in particular are the basis of the Lockean political order. Not only is material satisfaction the end of politics (with political rights being an indispensable means toward this end), but the process of acquiring property fulfills a vital political function. Instead of fighting over religion, the people unite to conquer nature and enrich themselves. And once they are sufficiently rich in goods, they will wish to enjoy their prosperity in peace. Ergo, government is needed only to administer the division of the spoils. In the liberal scheme of things, then, political ambition and personal libido are sublimated into a drive for wealth instead of power or dominance, and economics becomes a surrogate for politics, a channel for all the passions that might otherwise be directed into social conflict.

More important, Locke makes proprietorship all but synonymous with citizenship, essentially restricting political participation to the propertied class. In part, making wealth a prerequisite for participation was simple realism. In the seventeenth century, without "estate," or a sufficiency of property, political liberty per se was hardly meaningful: it was the possession of property that made it possible to develop one's mind and personality for public life and that afforded the independence, leisure, and social position necessary for participation. In addition, Locke believed that the very ownership and management of property inculcated habits and virtues essential to the political class—initiative, enterprise, thrift, prudence, responsibility, and, above all, enlightened self-interest. Indeed, someone without a real stake in society, in the concrete form of property ownership, could not really be trusted with political power.

For Locke, then, life, liberty, and estate are deeply interrelated, and the word *property* summarizes and encapsulates a whole range of important political and social goods. The security of property is therefore of paramount importance, and the primary duty of a Lockean sovereign is to replace the free-for-all of the state of nature with a well-ordered and well-enforced set of rules guaranteeing property rights: "Government has no other end but the Preservation of Property." Locke is thus the root philosopher of the emerging capitalist order: he completes the economization of politics begun by Hobbes, makes private property the dominant political principle, and lays the foundation for modern political economy.

Smith's Market Economics

Adam Smith completed the revolution in political economy foreshadowed in Hobbes and prepared by Locke. In *The Wealth of Nations*, published in 1776, Smith proclaimed the doctrine of the "invisible hand" to explain and justify a market economy. He thereby earned a place in intellectual history as the man who allegedly legitimated selfishness. And Smith indeed argued that self-interest makes the world go round: "It is not from the benevolence of the butcher, the brewer, or the baker, that we expect our dinner, but from their regard to their own interest." Nor is this a problem, for in pursuing his own economic interest, a man is "led by an invisible hand to promote an end which was no part of his intention"—namely, the general economic welfare. Smith therefore urged economic liberty: "Every man, as long as he does not violate the laws of justice, is left perfectly free to pursue his own interests in his own way, and to bring both his industry and capital into competition with those of any other man, or order of men." By inducing the state to cooperate with rather than dominate the economic process, Smith became the intellectual father not just of the market system and free trade but of modern political economy as we know it.

Yet Smith was deeply ambivalent about economics. On the one hand, he was a realist who understood that the radical changes already wrought by the Commercial Revolution were irreversible and that the transformation about to be wrought by the nascent Industrial Revolution was irresistible. He also saw that aristocratic mercantilists were distorting and hindering the economic process by trying to maintain rigid political control of the market. He therefore urged economic liberation: leaving individuals free to pursue "opulence" was the best way to foster social progress and increase the national wealth.

On the other hand, before turning his attention to economics, Smith was a major figure in the "moral sentiments" school of philosophy that was one of the ornaments of the Scottish Enlightenment. And when he put on his moral philosopher's cap, Smith found that wealth was inextricably linked to inequity and injustice: "Wherever there is great property, there is great inequality. . . . The affluence of the rich supposes the indigence of the many." Moreover, as a believer in the classical model of virtue, which enjoined a heroic command of the self, he opposed the self-indulgent values of economic man. So Smith denigrated riches and strongly recommended moderation: let a man be content with little, with a cottage instead of a mansion. He also exhibited a republican disdain for mere commerce (knowing all the while that his standards and attitudes were passé). Thus, despite his central role in fostering economics both as an activity and as a theoretical pursuit, Smith was paradoxically anti-economic at heart, anticipating in his own work much of the later critique of bourgeois political economy. Those who use him to justify unrestrained greed and absolute economic freedom both misunderstand and misrepresent him—to the point of slander. If he legitimated selfishness in the economic sphere, he also knew that it had to be kept firmly in check both by government, whose duty it was to uphold "the laws of justice," and by society, whose duty it was to assert moral principle and foster civic virtue.

In the end, Smith's position resembles that of Locke: the "moral sentiments" embodied in civil society would suffice to keep economic self-seeking within appropriate bounds. Yet he no longer had the latter's certainty that this would always be the case. Writing almost eighty years after Locke, Smith could already see disquieting signs of moral erosion. He noticed, for example, that the industrial division of labor tended to degrade the worker: unlike the artisan of yore, who was often his own master and was responsible for a whole piece of work, the hired hand in a mill or factory had no autonomy and performed one minute and repetitive operation all day, every day, inevitably causing his faculties to atrophy. Indeed, Smith discerned, even in his own time, a general erosion of the spirit and vigor of the common people. In consequence, his view of the industrial future was gloomy: "All the nobler parts of the human character may be in great measure obliterated and extinguished in the great body of the people." Nevertheless, despite these concerns, Smith, like Locke before him, relied ultimately on civil society to uphold morality and contain self-seeking.

Unfortunately, he failed to appreciate the extent to which market free-dom would vastly increase the burden on society. Following Hobbes, Locke had proposed that politics be governed by enlightened self-inter-est rather than moral principle. Now Smith wanted to abandon the eco-nomic sphere to self-interest as well. This left the defense of virtue and morality to civil society alone. But was it equal to the task? Even Smith was not so sure—and the real challenge to society still lay ahead, for in 1776 the bourgeois class had just begun to acquire the political power to put his ideas into effect.

Marx's Paradoxical Critique

Putting the matter in this way leads us naturally to Karl Marx's critique of bourgeois political economy. Marx is, of course, justly famous as the author (with Frederick Engels in 1848) of the revolutionary *Communist Manifesto*. But what is not often appreciated is how much of the basic structure of liberalism Marx in fact accepted. Indeed, writing a century and a half after Locke and seventy years after Smith, Marx does not even bother with the state of nature or the social contract and other funda-mentals. Instead, he simply acknowledges the paternity of Hobbes and takes liberal political economy as given. In fact, the irony of Marx is that he criticizes the bourgeoisie in terms that are essentially bourgeois: he makes economics *the* explanatory force and thus takes Hobbesian mate-rialism to its ultimate limit—surpassing not only Locke but even Smith! And he also claims to be more skeptical, rational, and scientific—that is, truer to the intellectual ideals of the Enlightenment—than his liberal predecessors. But although Marx accepted the basic premises and mode of reasoning of liberal political economy, he could not accept what the bourgeois revolution had wrought, for it had overthrown the autocracy of kings only to establish a tyranny of property.

Marx began his critique by celebrating the epochal achievements of the bourgeoisie. The bourgeois revolution had vanquished the old regime and banished the superstition and arbitrary rule of the Middle Ages; it had also launched a scientific conquest of nature that had already en-riched humanity enormously and might one day abolish scarcity entirely. Thus the bourgeoisie had thrown off the shackles of premodern society and liberated vast human and material energies—inaugurating a new phase of history that was exhilarating, dynamic, creative, progressive, and full of promise for a better future.

But this promise could not be fulfilled as long as the bourgeois class remained politically ascendant. Having "pitilessly torn asunder" the medieval order, capitalism had all but destroyed community itself, thereby causing unspeakable suffering. Worse, while enriching and empowering a small class of exploiters, the market turned men and women into commodities. Most people were therefore worse off under liberalism: they had lost the security and closeness of organic community, while obtaining few advantages from the liberal order. On the contrary, they were more ruthlessly exploited than ever before, especially if they had the misfortune to be colonized. In brief, capitalism was in its very essence a system of human exploitation, so bourgeois "freedom" was a mockery for all but the fortunate few.

The Marxist critique exposed the great contradiction of Lockean politics: if the basis of the political order was to be proprietorship, which gave men and women a concrete stake in the society and taught them virtue and prudence, what was to be done with a large and seemingly permanent class of propertyless wage earners? To this question, said Marx, there could be but one possible answer: universal proprietorship. Writing in the aftermath of the American and French Revolutions, Marx accepted Locke's terms but went him one better: let there be no more aristocracies, either of blood and land or of capital and trade (nor, ultimately, even of merit); let there instead be equality of estate for all, for this is the precondition of genuine and universal freedom. Since equality cannot result from laissez-faire economics or electoral reform within a bourgeois polity, but is possible only when economies are collectively owned and centrally directed, capitalism must be overthrown and replaced by socialism, which will complete the task begun by liberalism. Under the aegis of the famous "dictatorship of the proletariat," socially directed production will eventually abolish natural scarcity; and the resulting superabundance will cause the state to "wither away" into a mere utility like the post office.

In urging dictatorship, Marx is faithful to his philosophical sire. Locke's republican influence dominated in Britain and North America, but most Enlightenment theorists on the Continent tended to side with Hobbes in believing that benevolent despotism was the safest and most efficacious way of bringing about social, economic, scientific, and technological progress. And without such progress, mere political liberation was not really meaningful. In any event, said Marx, until the final victory over the forces of capitalist darkness, class war requires the absolute sovereignty of a proletarian dictatorship.

At the same time, Marx, as much biblical prophet as political philosopher, broke decisively with Hobbes and the Enlightenment mainstream by bringing religion back into politics. The Marxist sovereign has the duty not merely to provide "the contentments of life" but also to abolish material scarcity entirely, for only total abundance will end the class domination and social oppression that has marred all previous history. When this overweening objective is joined to the general Enlightenment drive for social perfection, the result is an ideological crusade for an earthly paradise—in effect, a secular religion. By resurrecting the eschatological element that Hobbes had tried to exclude from politics, Marx unleashed a new era of quasi-religious warfare, both within and between states.

Marx therefore heightens the contradictions of liberalism instead of alleviating them. The basic image of man—individualistic, materialistic, hedonistic—is not essentially different. A Hobbesian power struggle leading to the domination of one class is thus inevitable. The only long-term solution is the abolition of scarcity: by recovering the cornucopian abundance of the Lockean state of nature, the struggle for dominance can be undercut without needing human beings to be any better than they are and without having to resort to traditional religion, which is always a mystification, or to morality, which is simply a rationale for a particular kind of class rule. In effect, abundance is the substitute for morality, so the conquest of nature as the means to abundance is even more of an article of faith for Marxists than for Lockeans.

In the meantime, however, only a proletarian Leviathan can organize the grand march toward utopia. And although the eventual goal is communism—a fraternal order of "from each according to his ability, to each according to his needs" (as in most primal cultures)—the best that can be expected along the way is a revolutionary solidarity of the oppressed against the oppressors and a revolutionary morality of expedient means toward the end of proletarian victory. In short, although benign in theory, Marxist politics are in practice starkly Hobbesian: the exigencies of the class struggle justify iron rule in quasi-perpetuity. What is worse, this rule is based on a utopian ideology that is as much of a mystification and a rationale for the domination of a particular class as any traditional religion. As a political doctrine, Marxism therefore combines the authoritarianism of Hobbes with the very worst aspect of premodern politics: the religious element that Hobbes tried so hard to get rid of.

The Contradictions of Hobbesian Politics

We have examined the basic premises of liberal polity as they were first set forth by Hobbes himself. We have also seen how Locke, the founder of the liberal paradigm of politics as we know it, retained Hobbes's premises but moderated his conclusions. And how Smith expanded the liberal paradigm to include economics. Finally, we have seen how Marx embraced both Hobbes's premises and his authoritarian conclusions, rejecting only his liberalism. Our task now, both in this chapter and in the rest of the book, is to expose the very deep contradictions of a way of life and a system of politics based on Hobbesian premises, with particular reference to the classical liberalism of Locke upon which American politics is based.

First and foremost, as argued in my *Ecology and the Politics of Scarcity*, Hobbes's premises are fundamentally anti-ecological. His "commodious living," Locke's "estate," Smith's "opulence," and Marx's "communism" all require that nature provide and keep providing for man's continually escalating material demands. Hobbes's originally modest aim of fostering the conveniences of life in the commonwealth eventually swells into Marx's immodest aim of abolishing scarcity—a utopian goal eventually embraced by the followers of Locke and Smith as well—so that the practical efficacy and even the moral validity of modern politics comes to depend crucially on creating economic wealth by exploiting the supposed cornucopia of nature. But nature cannot support such inflated demands: the myth of cornucopian abundance is false, and the penalty for transgressing ecological limits is self-destruction. In brief, Hobbesian politics in all its forms exploits and destroys nature, so it must be rejected on ecological grounds alone.

The political contradictions are equally grave. The Hobbesian commonwealth is but a step away from the state of nature. In theory and in practice, it is a vicious circle of conflict and oppression waiting to happen, so an all-powerful Leviathan is essential simply to keep the peace. That a state with absolute powers is indispensable was the conclusion not of Hobbes alone but also of Marx and other Continental thinkers. Despite its theoretical liberalism, therefore, the fundamental tendency of Hobbesian politics in practice is not to limit state power but, instead, to concentrate it and make it more effective: in no other way can the state guarantee internal security, survive in the Machiavellian rough and tumble of international politics, and also fulfill its positive duty to promote economic and social well-being.

Locke was the great exception, embracing the premises but rejecting the conclusions. Complaining that handing people over to an autocratic lion was a poor way to protect them from foxes and polecats, he instead made the sovereign into a zookeeper whose job is to prevent the animals from preying on one another. In place of Hobbes's Leviathan, Locke therefore proposed what is usually called "the night-watchman state," whose role is strictly limited to keeping the peace.

As we have seen, he accomplished this feat by relaxing three of Hobbes's key assumptions. First, he made nature more abundant. Second, he made people nicer. Third, he made society prior to polity. Ergo, no Leviathan. The brilliance of Locke's theoretical legerdemain and the enormous success of his ideas in the real world are beyond dispute. But he accomplished less than he claimed, for the Hobbesian lion was not permanently tamed, only temporarily caged—there to stay only so long as these assumptions remained valid, for if not, then he runs loose again.

In fact, every one of Locke's arguments for the zookeeper state is seriously flawed. First, nature is less abundant than even Hobbes believed (and the existence of ecological scarcity only strengthens the argument for a powerful sovereign). Second, even if men and women are less passionate and more reasonable than Hobbes made them out to be, this point is hardly decisive. The force of Hobbes's argument does not depend, as many mistakenly believe, on the fundamental depravity of human nature. Hobbes never said that men and women are intrinsically evil, only that passion dominates reason, which was not disputed by Locke; and that the greedy and ambitious few will always embroil the rest in a deadly power struggle, which was not directly rebutted by Locke. In fact, Locke agreed that Hobbesian conditions would bring out the worst in human nature: he acknowledged the international arena to be a state of nature that reduced men to preying on one another, just as Hobbes contended. In other words, Locke conceded Hobbes's essential point: put human beings in a tight enough spot, and passion will overwhelm reason. (This is why ecological scarcity has such serious political implications: it threatens to inflame passions and bring out the worst in human nature.) But, said Locke, and here we come to his third point, except in international relations circumstances are never as dire as Hobbes makes out. Why? Because of society, which curbs the passions and binds men and women together in a stable moral community. That Locke again exempts the international arena, precisely because it is not a "society," reveals both his closeness to Hobbes and the depth of his reliance on a preexisting civil order. In effect, Locke resurrects the natural community denied by Hobbes and makes his nonauthoritarian political doctrines entirely dependent on it.

We have now come to the crux: what distinguishes Locke from Hobbes and justifies the benign and limited politics of classical liberalism is the existence of civil society as the guarantor of stability and morality. But modern politics has been erected on a *premodern* foundation. Why? Because the civil society upon which Locke rests his case for limited government is a legacy of the Middle Ages—of an era governed by a philosophy and way of life radically different from that of modernity, one that regarded will and appetite as dangers to be combated rather than passions to be indulged. By contrast, liberal theory and practice are concerned almost solely with the expedient means toward individual self-expression and self-gratification, not with controlling the human passions or sustaining, much less creating, a moral community. To use the image of Spanish philosopher Miguel de Unamuno, modern civilization is guilty of "spiritual parasitism": it has relied on Christian virtues while scorning the faith that created and nourished them.

But parasites drain the life from their host. Hence the free play of individual selfishness within the liberal polity has steadily vitiated the very civil society upon which it utterly depends. In effect, just as modern economies based on the premises of Hobbes consume the ecological capital of all the ages, so liberal polities destroy themselves by devouring their own moral capital, the fund of fossil virtue they have inherited from the premodern past. In sum, because liberalism tends ever and always toward moral entropy, it is rapidly exhausting the moral legacy upon which its doctrines and practices are grounded.

Moral Entropy Destroys Civil Society

The intrinsic amorality of liberalism was immediately grasped by the Marquis de Sade, who carried Hobbes's emancipation of the human passions from traditional moral restraint to its logical conclusion: all is now permitted. In *Juliette*, published in 1797, de Sade says that "self-interest . . . is the single rule for defining just and unjust." It follows that morality is a fiction: "There is no God in this world, neither is there virtue, neither is there justice; there is nothing good, useful, or necessary but our passions, nothing merits to be respected but their effects." So de Sade was not merely a libertine and a pornographer: he was a genuine Enlightenment *philosophe* and an authentic (albeit perverted) liberal, whose folly and tragedy consisted in trying to advance the cause of sexual liberation too far in advance of its time.

Although a civilization living on fossil virtue, like a family living on borrowed money, must eventually exhaust its moral resources, inertia is a powerful force in human affairs. It has therefore taken the world almost two centuries to catch up to de Sade. To be sure, by the end of the nineteenth century more and more people had come to understand—either with horror, as in the case of Dostoyevsky, or with at least partial approbation, as in the case of Nietzsche—that they were living in a fundamentally amoral civilization in which the Sadean conclusion was inescapable:

God is dead, so all is permitted. However, a deeply rooted social and moral legacy is not readily destroyed, so the triumph of liberalism has occurred only in our own time.* Let us trace out in more detail exactly how and why Locke's civil society has succumbed to moral entropy, pushing us to the brink of a social and political debacle.

By *society*, Locke meant family, school, and church, plus the whole web of personal and economic relationships in which men and women were embedded, along with all the customs, habits, and mores accompanying these institutions and relationships. All this together constituted an autonomous social order that was, according to Locke, essentially independent of the political order. Society thus had more than enough weight to counterbalance the Hobbesian tendencies of the latter. In addition, by inculcating reason and virtue and also by punishing dissent and deviance, society moderated self-seeking behavior and the struggle for advantage within the social order itself. But Locke was wrong. The civil society of his age was not independent and could not stand alone: it was an ephemeral legacy subject to erosion, not a permanent bulwark against the baneful forces of human passion.

Locke's biggest blind spot was economics. Although he was one of the founders of modern political economy, he did not foresee its eventual consequences. But by basing politics on property he laid the foundation for Smith's market economics and the whole course of modern economic development. And whatever civil society's putative independence from the political sphere, it could not withstand the impact of economic and technological change (as, indeed, Smith had feared might be the case). Moreover, Locke also failed to foresee that politics itself would lose its independence—and thus its ability to control events and to limit the effect of economic forces on society. In short, amoral self-seeking soon dominated both economics and politics, leaving civil society as the sole repository and guardian of traditional virtue. Utterly beleaguered, it could not for long withstand the assault: society disintegrated as economic forces began to tear apart its basic fabric.

The destruction of civil society by the market system will be the focus of Chapter 3. But for now, suffice it to say that economics is governed by

---

*At the same time, we should not underestimate the rapidity with which society can collapse once it becomes demoralized. As pointed out by Will Durant, "From barbarism to civilization requires a century; from civilization to barbarism needs but a day." Society depends *crucially* on near-universal assent to its norms: if its members defect from these norms en masse, or if its fabric is destroyed, whether by calamity or by the actions of a small but determined minority, then chaos quickly ensues. (See, for example, Thucydides' tragic account of the fall of Athens.)

Gresham's Law: lower values tend to drive higher ones out of circulation. Social man, whose life was dedicated to being, was gradually displaced by economic man, whose life is based on having. And once economic man had been created, at an enormous cost in human misery, then the values of selfish acquisition and possessive individualism rapidly and inexorably drove out all others.

Even religion no longer provided unquestioned moral support for individual virtue. Eternal verities and absolute morality did not survive the Reformation: a faith that is made by man can be changed by him, or even be abandoned altogether. In a development that would have utterly dumbfounded Locke himself, the Protestant church began to condone and even bless greed, envy, and pride—in fact, all the Seven Deadly Sins except sloth. The predominant thrust of Weber's famous "Protestant ethic"—which all but dispensed with traditional virtue in favor of the "virtues" critical for economic success, such as industriousness and delayed gratification—was therefore to invest bourgeois acquisition and possessive individualism with divine favor. So religion gradually ceased to be a check on individual selfishness and instead began to condone it.

The loss of the moral support provided by traditional religion inevitably foreshadowed an eventual decline in morality itself. Although the original liberals criticized allegedly archaic moral codes and the religious superstitions that supported them, they nevertheless continued to uphold the idea of morality itself. And liberals also continued to behave with great propriety until comparatively recently. The Protestant ethic may not have been much of a moral code by previous standards, but, it was never a mere license for self-enrichment and self-aggrandizement: it spiritualized them by making wealth and power a function of rectitude. In other words, the Protestant ethic insisted that they be earned through firm self-control and strict social observance. The result was the much-derided bourgeois—prudent, thrifty, hard-working, law-abiding, decorous, conformist, stolid, stuffy, and smug. Admirable or not, the bourgeois became the proverbial pillar of Lockean society, precisely because he knew the difference between "liberty" and "license" and therefore understood the necessity to preserve the social order from excessive will and appetite.

It is now fashionable to deride bourgeois morality, especially that of the Victorian era, but it was never merely hypocritical. Moreover, hypocritical or not, it did indeed exact outer conformity to a high standard of personal conduct. The Victorian gentleman who replaced the old-style burgher was, as the name plainly states, expected to be the soul of gentilesse—kind, courteous, moderate, refined, gracious, and well behaved almost to a fault.

But the Victorian age was the last hurrah for bourgeois morality: by its close, both the moral legacy of the Middle Ages and the Protestant ethic that had partially supplanted it had weakened to the point where they no longer effectively restrained or channeled the passions. The moral climate of Western civilization therefore shifted dramatically at the beginning of the twentieth century. This change in mores was epitomized by the famous Bloomsbury group. As one of its most prominent members, the great economist John Maynard Keynes, later said, "We repudiated entirely customary morals, conventions and traditional wisdom. We were, that is to say, in the strict sense of the term, immoralists." These "immoralists" pioneered the way for the rest of us. So the death of traditional religion had precisely the consequence foreseen by de Sade, Dostoyevsky, and Nietzsche: a society in which all is permitted.

In the context of this new moral climate, bourgeois man (and I will get to bourgeois woman in a moment) was no longer content with mere political and economic liberty. He began to clamor for social and psychological freedom as well—that is, for "liberation" from the inner repression involved in submitting to the demands of "civilization." Twentieth-century history is thus the record of how the "immoralism" of the avant-garde spread to the common man. Indeed, it is the chronicle of an orgy of "desublimation"—an explosive release of hitherto repressed fantasies and desires, along with a resolute rejection of the social conventions that presumed to control or forbid their expression. The result is a society in which it is more and more the case that anything goes—including behavior formerly thought to be utterly pathological, such as sadism and masochism.

In retrospect, it seems surprising that liberal thinkers could be so blind to the dangers of moral entropy. This shortfall was due largely to their faith in reason in general and education in particular. Indeed, for Locke, education and civil society were almost synonymous. But education in Locke's time (in fact, for some time to come) consisted of humane learning designed to inculcate virtue and form character. Locke's own educational proposals show that he wished to create an elite class of citizens whose self-interest would always be enlightened—in other words, a natural aristocracy dedicated to the preservation of civil society and qualified for rule by virtue and merit. He could not therefore imagine a time in which education would cease to be a promoter of self-restraint and become an instrument of self-seeking.

What Locke and other Enlightenment thinkers failed to see was that "reason," the dominant educational principle of the new era, was a sword that could cut two ways. On the one hand, within the context of education for character, reason could indeed foster a self-interest that would be enlightened rather than depraved. But in a different context, reason could easily decay into a narrow rationality that debunks all values higher than individual wants and becomes a mere calculus of means toward selfish ends—which is exactly what happened. As Schumpeter points out, once the "rational frame of mind" has destroyed all other forms of "moral authority," it "goes on to attack . . . the whole scheme of bourgeois values." So "the rational attitude" subverts not just traditional religion and morality but all fixed standards and moral principles, including the Protestant ethic. In the end, reason ceased to restrain will and appetite and began instead to encourage their expression.

The increasing rationalization of society (to be discussed in depth in Chapter 6) thus made education a vehicle for the subversion of all moral principle, including the very reasonableness that Locke believed would be its fruit. The result was, as Edmund Burke lamented, the rise of a new class of "sophists, economists, and calculators"—economic men uninhibited either by tradition and morality or by reason in the Lockean sense and therefore incapable of putting aside self-interest in favor of some larger conception of the common weal. The further result, foreshadowed by the Bloomsbury "immoralists," has been a radical devaluation of so-called values themselves to the status of mere personal preferences. In short, education for character and public spirit was slowly replaced by education dedicated to instilling the attitudes and aptitudes of economic man.

The decay of reason threatens not only education, and therefore society, but polity as well. Locke made political freedom depend explicitly on reason: "The *Freedom* then of Man and Liberty of acting according to his own Will, is *grounded on* his having *Reason*, which is able to instruct him in that Law he is to govern himself by, and make him know how far he is left to the freedom of his own will." Ergo, men and women who are *not* reasonable must be governed primarily by force, just as Hobbes maintained.

Moreover, in the absence of revealed truth, the decay of reason effectively destroys the ability to make moral distinctions. All that is left is mere rationality, which does not suffice for making important social decisions. Hence we now lack any principled basis for making public policy in many areas—especially on issues that raise, at least for some people, important moral questions. And where there is no principle, power decides. The decay of reason therefore compounds the social problems caused by the decline of religion and, as we shall see later, fosters a politics of mere expediency.

In this fashion, the moral entropy that is intrinsic to the liberal order has steadily eroded both the moral legacy of the Middle Ages and the bourgeois rectitude of the Protestant ethic. The upshot is that the morality of liberal society (if we can call it that) becomes increasingly egotistical. Everything is evaluated in terms of costs and benefits to ego, even the most intimate personal ties, and there is little left to hold together basic social relationships, much less Locke's civil society. A vicious circle of decay in both morals and mores is propelling us toward a social collapse whose details—crime, broken families, drug addiction, and the like—are so well known as to require neither documentation nor discussion. However, a brief look at two aspects of the vicious circle will further illuminate the general point.

With respect to crime, for example, the principal duty of the liberal state is to keep the peace by suppressing deviant behavior. As we all know, however, the night watchman has fallen down on the job: despite prisons packed to the rafters with criminals, there are even more out prowling the streets. How could it be that the liberal state of today—especially in the United States, but increasingly in other modern polities as well—is failing to perform its one essential function?

Leaving aside all sociological complexities, the answer is that crime is the logical consequence of abiding by Hobbesian premises. When all members of the society live to satisfy their appetites, they are thrown not only into a fierce competition with each other for access to the sources of satisfaction, but also into a Sadean moral wasteland in which that satisfaction is the ultimate and only value. Eventually all that restrains them is fear of the watchman's club—and when that ceases to intimidate, crime flourishes. Those who take to a life of crime in today's inner cities are simply good Hobbesians: if the sovereign does not provide enough of the necessary and appropriate conveniences of life, then you owe the state and society neither loyalty nor obedience. As Hannah Arendt put it, "Hobbes foresees and justifies the social outcasts' organization into a gang of murderers as a logical outcome of the bourgeoisie's moral philosophy." The practical effect of Hobbesian polity is therefore paradoxically to encourage just the kind of lawless violence that it is supposed to prevent, because living by liberal premises over the long term fosters a vicious circle of antisocial behavior that tends toward the state of nature and the war of all against all.

However, family breakdown is the most serious manifestation of the vicious circle. The disintegration of the little society of the family is a truly ominous development, foreshadowing the ultimate collapse of the larger society that depends on it. The basic social task is to civilize children: "Nowhere," says Robert Edgerton, "have adults found it necessary to teach their children to be selfish, greedy, angry, stubborn, envious, or disobedient; instead, they search everywhere for means to limit or eliminate these characteristics in their children." Unfortunately, today's adults are failing. As a consequence, society is overwhelmed. Public institutions can cope with dysfunction when it is the exception, but not when it is the rule. Besides, recent experience shows that social programs cannot compensate for family failure: what children are not taught at home they are very unlikely to learn elsewhere. Schools, for example, cannot by themselves civilize each new cohort of barbarians. Nor can an army of social workers, however dedicated, make up for parental neglect.

To put it more formally, the family is the primary arena in which ego learns to moderate its narcissistic demands and harmonize itself with some larger social entity: loyalty, integrity, responsibility, self-control, and the like are all learned primarily in the family setting. In other words, the family is where we acquire civility, the ability to live constructively and well in civil society. If the family fails to model and inculcate civility or to bind the child to the community, then society is no longer a bulwark against selfishness, becoming instead a mere arena for it—a place where fundamentally amoral and asocial beings struggle for personal advantage with little or no regard for the welfare of others, much less the public good. The decay of the family thus portends a bleakly Hobbesian future.

This provides the appropriate context for the promised discussion of bourgeois woman. To get right to the point, feminism heralds the final collapse of civil society and hence liberal polity. Women's liberation means precisely what it says: women now want to be just as "liberated" as men, just as "free" to pursue their own selfish ends. To obviate any possible misunderstanding, I am neither blaming women for deciding to play by men's rules—given the economic conditions and moral climate created by generations of male self-seeking, they really had little choice—nor am I suggesting that some reactionary status quo ante be restored. I am merely reporting the social and political consequences of women becoming good liberals looking out for Number One in the great marketplace of life. For the fact is that, whereas men long ago abandoned the family for the marketplace, women until very recently upheld both family and civil society by *not* living according to Hobbesian premises: men lived for money or power, women for love.

The role of woman in bourgeois society was therefore utterly anomalous. Putting aside all ambition for herself, she was to be the gentle custodian of traditional virtues, the warm champion of the heart against the head, and the loving incarnation of home and hearth. And in so being, she provided the social and emotional glue that held together a society otherwise given over to self-interest. This meant, of course, that she was largely excluded from public affairs—if not by law, then by custom and practice—so that she could devote all her energies to nurturing private life. (We should not forget how recently women won the franchise: 1920 in the United States but as late as 1971 in Switzerland.)

Today, however, the situation is quite different. The usual way of putting it is to say that women have escaped an anomalous and inferior status to take their rightful place in the modern world. But it would probably be more accurate to say that capitalism has finally succeeded in incorporating the last major class to resist the blandishments of the market system. In consequence, as increasing numbers of women (especially elite women) embrace economic values and attempt to live life in imitation of liberal men, positive feminine values are diluted and negative masculine values reinforced, with harmful consequences both to society and to the women themselves. Indeed, the sum of gains to individual women (again, mostly elite women) from increased wealth, status, and power may well be outweighed by the long-run social costs of women's liberation—for women probably have more to lose than men from further social decay in America, where the level of crime and personal violence is already appallingly high and where the level of support for the health, education, and welfare of children is dismayingly low. The women's liberation movement therefore epitomizes the tragedy of liberalism in general: individuals get what they want—the satisfaction of private desire—but only by destroying their natural and social environments.

In sum, women formerly devoted themselves to resisting moral entropy: they tended our inherited moral capital and thereby preserved the civil society that is absolutely indispensable to the success of the liberal polity. But now that they are no longer willing to make that sacrifice, both civil society and liberal polity are in jeopardy, and the future is, once again, bleakly Hobbesian. Feminism thus completes the work of demolition begun by economics, irreligion, amorality, unreason, and egotism: it delivers the coup de grâce to Lockean society.

More positively, however, the feminist movement also works to revive the erotic and life-centered values traditionally associated with the female sex. (And this I support completely: what might be called "deep feminism"—that is, restoring the lost primal balance between female and male—is probably the sine qua non of a humane future.) Moreover, the work of feminist authors has justly challenged outmoded ideas and archaic attitudes, obliging us to consider human history in a new light.

(In fact, I have relied on their work at critical junctures in my own argument.) But political feminism is another story, for when women devote themselves to "gender politics" within the pluralist arena, they not only take on the "patriarchal" or negative male values characteristic of that arena but also contribute to the factional excesses to be analyzed in the next chapter. In addition, doctrinaire or ideological "gender feminism," which is criticized by many feminists as well, is just as pernicious as all the other "isms" that have plagued the modern era: making "patriarchy" *the* fundamental category of social analysis does scant justice to the depth and complexity of our cultural predicament, which can hardly be explained by the simple opposition of male and female. As Doris Lessing points out in the Preface of *The Golden Notebook,*

> I don't think that Women's Liberation will change much, though—not because there is anything wrong with their aims but because it is already clear that the whole world is being shaken into a new pattern by the cataclysms we are living through; probably by the time we are through, if we do get through at all, the aims of Women's Liberation will look very small and quaint.

Like environmentalism, therefore, feminism is really a symptom of the breakdown of the old order and a metaphor for an impending cultural transformation: an evolution toward greater and more inclusive consciousness that entails the return of older repressed values in a new guise and their synthesis with the best modern ones to produce a new paradigm of politics more compatible than liberalism with the ecological and human requirements of the twenty-first century. (It is toward such a synthesis that the Conclusions will point.) In short, gender feminism is a big part of the problem, but deep feminism may be an important part of the solution.

To conclude this brief discussion of moral entropy, we must understand that narcissism and egotism are *fundamental* to liberalism. For all its noble intentions, its inner logic as a political and social doctrine is absolutely clear, even though few yet dare follow the logic to its licentious Sadean terminus. Liberalism means exactly what it says: *liberation* of the self from all social or moral restraints except the necessity to keep the peace. Liberal society is therefore, as Keynes openly acknowledged, frankly immoral. When push comes to shove, it means getting what one wants regardless. If behavior in accordance with this principle has become contradictory and pernicious, then it is the principle itself, not the behavior, that must be called into question, because moral entropy is intrinsic to a liberal polity based on Hobbesian premises.

The Tragedy of Modern Politics

The drama of modern politics is a tragedy in which the hero, his supposed enlightenment being but another name for hubris, has become the author of his own impending doom. Alfred North Whitehead attributed to natural law a tragic quality because, like the ancient Greek dramas, it exhibits a "remorseless working of things" against which it is useless to struggle or protest. The hubris of Hobbes and his intellectual heirs was to ignore entropy, a fundamental natural law that applies to social as well as physical systems (albeit with nowhere near the same degree of mathematical rigor). They thereby set in motion a tragic dynamic, a vicious circle that has produced social breakdown and a looming political debacle.

Social systems and natural systems are not essentially different. Both must combat the ever-present tendency of complex systems to break down by using a constant input of energy to maintain their stability. In natural systems, the energy is physical: in the final analysis, the structures of life are maintained against the tug of entropy by a continuous infusion of solar energy. In social systems, however, the source of energy is as much moral as physical: in the end, societies are held together by virtue and civility, by a shared ethos or civic religion that fosters relatively public-spirited behavior. Without such behavior, a polity is fated to a more or less rapid descent into moral entropy and social chaos. Here, for instance, is Nadezhda Mandelstam's description in her memoir *Hope Against Hope* of how one particular virtue became extinct:

> There were once many kind people, and even unkind ones pretended to be good because that was the thing to do. Such pretense was the source of the hypocrisy and dishonesty so much exposed in the realist literature at the end of the last century. The unexpected result of this kind of critical writing was that kind people disappeared. Kindness is not, after all, an inborn quality—it has to be cultivated, and this only happens when it is in demand. For our generation, kindness was an old-fashioned, vanished quality, and its exponents were as extinct as the mammoth. Everything we have seen in our times . . . has taught us to be anything you like except kind.

In deliberately setting up polities to exist without virtue, if not in spite of it, Hobbes and his followers were trying to evade a law of politics, if not of nature. Temporary success there might be—due both to the wealth of inherited moral and biological capital and to the increase in technological power—but in the long run the failure to account for and combat moral entropy would became liberalism's nemesis: not only kindness but all the other virtues necessary to social and political life are slowly becoming "as extinct as the mammoth."

Hobbes's failure is ironic. He saw very clearly that religious politics is bad politics: upholding the official faith (or the party line) requires squashing or exterminating heretics and dissidents. In other words, enforced virtue is a contradiction in terms: right depends on might. To adapt the immortal words of Chairman Mao, all religious politics grows out of the barrel of a gun. Whatever morality it claims to possess is therefore annihilated by its intrinsic violence: virtue dies upon the stake along with the heretic or is entombed in the gulag along with the dissident.

But Hobbes's proposed remedy also substitutes power for virtue, albeit in a different fashion. Hobbesian politics is parasitic: it feeds off a reservoir of fossil virtue that it inherits and does nothing to sustain, much less replace. The available moral energy therefore dwindles, and the sovereign is obliged to make up for this loss by supplying more and more political power. It is just as de Tocqueville's epigraph predicts: because "despotism may govern without faith, but liberty cannot," the "political tie" must become stronger whenever the "moral tie" is relaxed. The inexorable tendency of all forms of polity based on liberal premises, as Hobbes himself made explicit, is thus to compensate for the decline in the civic virtue of the individual by increasing the political power of the state—the story of modern politics in a nutshell. In short, all forms of Hobbesian polity, supposedly liberal or not, are ultimately authoritarian (an issue to which we shall return in Chapters 7 and 8).

Shifting the scientific metaphor from thermodynamics to cybernetics, we find that systems or cultures whose subsystems are not closely coupled by negative feedback loops are inexorably drawn into a regime of positive feedback that destroys them. The steam engine, the implicit model of the Hobbesian polity, illustrates this clearly: without a governor, it will run away and explode. Precisely because it is mechanical, however, the steam engine is a bad metaphor for society, which is not a machine but rather a complex system requiring *decentralized* control—in other words, a virtuous people instead of an omnipotent ruler. A sovereign with absolute powers is therefore a poor substitute for a well-behaved and law-abiding citizenry. Indeed, to maintain even a semblance of centralized control, especially in difficult or threatening circumstances, such a top-down sovereign must resort to crude and heavy-handed measures—stifling regulations, punitive laws, secret services, and other equally vicious forms of governance. In the end, Hobbes's putative solution to the problem of religious politics is false, for it changes neither the dynamic nor the outcome: whether a regime's standard is absolute truth or no truth at all, the basis for social cohesion is still political force. The modern Leviathan and the premodern Inquisition are two sides of the same coin.

It would appear that there are quasi-natural laws governing politics that cannot be repealed by human will or evaded by human cleverness. Flouting these laws, as Hobbes and his heirs tried to do, sets in train a "remorseless working of things" that brings tragedy. There is only one possible basis for a good politics: wise and virtuous self-limitation arising out of a genuine moral vision. As Madison said, "To suppose that any form of government will secure liberty or happiness without any virtue in the people, is a chimerical idea."

But we need to understand this political imperative practically as well as theoretically, so let us now turn to the specifics of the American case. Moral entropy has made its greatest inroads in the United States.*Not even the most secular and prudential aspects of the Protestant ethic— hard work, delayed gratification, foresight, and the like—have escaped erosion. In fact, more and more of America's youth have turned against traditional values, not just in the increasingly feral inner cities but even on elite university campuses. America thus exemplifies the process of growing barbarization that is pushing us toward a Hobbesian future.

---

*Moral chaos is, of course, greater elsewhere. An example is Russia, where civil society was wantonly destroyed by Lenin and his heirs, leaving a legacy of utter demoralization that is probably the greatest obstacle standing between the long-suffering Russian people and a better future. Many countries of the South are in a similar position: colonization undermined the old order without successfully installing a new one, so anarchic kleptocracies have proliferated. But these are not examples of moral entropy. Nevertheless, by showing what happens when civil society is destroyed, they illustrate the dangerous terminus toward which we are headed, albeit by slow decay rather than sudden shock. A contrary example also suggests that moral coherence is critical to economic or social success. East Asia's escape from the trap of underdevelopment is due largely to a "Confucian ethic" that creates a strong civil society and fosters a character structure conducive to economic growth and social progress.

2

ELECTRONIC BARBARISM

Civilisations as yet have only been created and directed by a small intellectual aristocracy, never by crowds. Crowds are only powerful for destruction. Their rule is always tantamount to a barbarian phase. A civilisation involves fixed rules, discipline, a passing from the instinctive to the rational state, forethought for the future, an elevated degree of culture—all of them conditions that crowds, left to themselves, have invariably shown themselves incapable of realizing.

—Gustave Le Bon

Your Constitution is all sail and no anchor. . . . Either some Caesar or Napoleon will seize the reins of government with a strong hand; or your republic will be . . . laid waste by barbarians in the twentieth century as the Roman Empire was in the fifth. . . .

—Thomas Babington Macauley

This time however the barbarians are not waiting beyond the frontiers; they have already been governing us for quite some time.

—Alasdair MacIntyre

As we have seen, the New World was central to Locke's thought, both as concept and in actuality: it exemplified the cornucopian physical abundance that made liberal polity feasible. America was also a tabula rasa, a place to throw off tradition and make a fresh start. It was therefore the ideal place to put the new political ideas into effect. In fact, independence and its constitutional aftermath merely ratified a political and social revolution that had already occurred in the hearts and minds of the colonists, and a *novus ordo seclorum* relatively unencumbered by the dead weight of the past took root in the virgin soil of the New World.

At the same time, however, this "new order of the ages" was a deeply traditional Lockean society—different from that of the mother country, but just as strong. And social strength was the basis of political success: "The early settlers," said de Tocqueville, "bequeathed to their descendants the customs, manners, and opinions which contribute most to the success of a republic."

Moreover, the new political order was created and directed by a close-knit group of disciplined, learned, prudent, and public-spirited individuals—that is, precisely the kind of "small intellectual aristocracy" Le Bon said is necessary for a civilized politics. In addition, colonial society was fundamentally conservative. The so-called American Revolution was, in fact, a *rebellion*, reluctantly undertaken only after much brooding and many efforts to obtain a redress of grievances. Thus it was fought not to overturn colonial society but only to overthrow royal authority. Nor did the American aristocracy ever abandon its cultural and philosophical allegiance to the mother country or to European civilization in general. In fact, the Founding Fathers exemplified (and were seen by their European contemporaries as exemplifying) the best of Enlightenment civilization, combining philosophical learning and high principles derived from natural religion with practical reason and political skill.

The United States therefore began its independent political career as a virtuous republic supported by a strong and conservative society and animated by the highest ideals of the age. Its institutions were rooted in a coherent political and moral philosophy—drawn not from Locke alone but from many different sources, especially the Scottish Enlightenment. And its affairs were directed by a class of natural aristocrats who put the stamp of their own learning and character on the whole society.

The Demise of the Virtuous Republic

That American political institutions were deeply and self-consciously rooted in morality and religion is little understood and less appreciated today. However, as Madison's words cited in the previous chapter show, the Founders took it as given that a polity "without any virtue in the people" was "a chimerical idea." Indeed, said John Adams, the new Constitution was designed "for a moral and religious people," an accurate description of the early Americans. Unfortunately, however, the Federalists, who won the constitutional battle to shape the American future, shared Locke's blind spot: rejecting the warnings of the anti-Federalists, they refused to acknowledge that the virtue they took for granted could be the victim of their own policies.

Alexander Hamilton exhibited this blindness in its characteristically American form. Faithful to the spirit of Hobbes, Hamilton and his fellow Federalists constructed a constitutional machine to combat *political* tyranny with *political* checks and balances—a machine so cunningly designed, they believed, that it would never generate enough power to oppress the people. In fact, however, as their opponents complained, the machine had the potential to become very powerful indeed. And the anti-Federalists were right: all that they feared and predicted—the political eclipse of the sovereign states, the dictatorship of the federal courts, a national-security state, and an imperial presidency—has slowly but surely come to pass. Moreover, like Locke, the Federalists did not understand that a polity based on self-interest could undermine the society on which it ultimately depended; or that economic and technological change could subvert the constitutional machinery they had devised. With Hamilton leading the way, the Federalists therefore committed the new republic to a course of development that would rather quickly erode the republican virtue of the early Americans and fundamentally alter the character of their political institutions.

Leaving institutions aside for the moment, let us focus on mores. Hamilton wanted the new nation to promote commerce and manufacturing, so his vision led in the direction of urban complexity and national power, which implied strong government and elite rule. He was vigorously opposed by Thomas Jefferson, who instead favored agrarian democracy as the best way to prevent tyranny and preserve the republican spirit of the people. Jefferson's vision thus led in the opposite direction—toward rural simplicity and local power, both of which would foster popular rule (albeit under the tutelage of a class of natural aristocrats who would do most of the actual governing). Upon gaining their independence, the American people therefore confronted a fateful choice between two very distinct images of the future, each entailing radically different political consequences. To borrow the metaphors of Leo Marx, it was a choice between the Hamiltonian machine and the Jeffersonian garden. But Americans would not choose between the machine and the garden: instead, they responded in character by evading the issue and trying to have it both ways.

The result was a Hamiltonian machine run as if we still lived in a Jeffersonian garden, so we got the worst of both worlds. Americans embarked on all-out economic expansion along the lines desired by Hamilton, and power began to be concentrated and centralized in exactly the ways that the anti-Federalists had feared. Indeed, Jefferson himself promoted Hamiltonian ends during his presidency—by negotiating the

Louisiana Purchase and dispatching the Lewis and Clark Expedition, among other things. Ever the realist, Jefferson understood that a purely agrarian economy would leave the new nation perpetually dependent on the trade and industry of Europe, so local autarky had to be sacrificed to national autonomy. Similarly, national power had to be extended across the continent both for security reasons and to provide land for a growing population.

In the end, Jefferson's vision of yeoman citizens in small ward republics was eclipsed in the pell-mell drive to seize, settle, and develop an "empty" continent—but his fundamentally democratic spirit endured. In fact, Jeffersonian populism decisively defeated the elitism represented by Hamilton. Americans therefore "chose" a contradictory and potentially explosive mixture of Hamiltonian development, without the aristocratic social controls needed to keep it within appropriate bounds, and Jeffersonian democracy, without the agrarian social setting required to make it work. The epigraph by Macauley perfectly describes the result: a politics that was "all sail and no anchor."

This development boded ill for the future. Although the United States was thriving when de Tocqueville wrote *Democracy in America* in the mid-1830s, he nevertheless sensed trouble ahead, for American democracy was rife with contradictions. The most important of these was that between equality and liberty, a struggle he feared might eventually result in the demise of liberty at the hands of equality. And this conflict between the democratic and liberal principles is indeed at the root of nearly every difficult problem or controversy in American politics, from the clash between Jefferson and Hamilton to today's battles over affirmative action.

Another worrisome contradiction observed by de Tocqueville was the tendency for Americans to oscillate between apathy and activism. On the one hand, they withdrew into "small coteries" of the like-minded and let the larger society fend for itself; on the other, they threw themselves into fervent participation in voluntary associations of all kinds, including political associations. And although this "art of association" was essential to American democracy, fostering the social and political cooperation that made it work, it also produced a "confused clamor" of "a thousand simultaneous voices demand[ing] the satisfaction of their social wants." In the long run, such a schizophrenic, all-or-nothing approach to politics might propel American democracy toward a tutelary state tyrannized by an oppressive majority. Or, in blunter language, toward mob rule, the classic fate of democracies.

Yet American democracy was undeniably successful despite these and other contradictions. What made it so, said de Tocqueville, was a powerful civic religion: the contradictions were contained, at least for the present, by the mores or "habits of the heart" that the American people had inherited from the founding generation. But he also noted that it was a question of so far, so good, because these very mores were now threatened by the social changes resulting from the democratic ethos itself.

De Tocqueville observed, for example, that in America, much more than in Europe, "morals are the work of women." American men were so preoccupied with getting on that it was left to women to preserve and instill the all-important "habits of the heart." Unfortunately, American women were also beginning to demand and get a "democratic education" that, according to de Tocqueville, made them too much like men and thus tended to disqualify them for this critical social task. (In effect, American women were even then beginning to abdicate the moral guardianship of the liberal political order.) In this and numerous other ways, American democracy attacked its own moral basis: selfish individualism was rapidly eroding the inherited "customs, manners, and opinions" needed for republican success, raising questions in de Tocqueville's mind about the future.

In fact, as we now know, the age of Jackson that he so brilliantly described was in many respects the high point of American democracy. A few decades later, in the aftermath of civil war and rapid mechanization, American society was transformed from rural to urban, agrarian to industrial, and local to national. And with so-called modernization came the social breakdown and moral entropy described in the previous chapter: physically and psychologically uprooted, men and women were no longer members of a moral community, but mere components of an amoral mass society. Thus perished de Tocqueville's "habits of the heart." ·

The story of modernization is well known and needs no further elaboration at this point. What is not so well understood, however, is the degree to which the pace of change has accelerated dramatically in recent years. That is, although the destruction of Lockean society in America began with the achievement of independence and has continued steadily ever since, *most of the damage has occurred since World War II*. Many people who are still middle-aged spent their earliest years in a physical and social milieu that would have seemed reasonably familiar to de Tocqueville, despite substantial technological changes. But given the extent of modernization between the 1830s and 1930s, how is it possible that so much of de Tocqueville's America survived largely intact until comparatively recently?

The answer has three parts. First, there are enormous lags in social systems. Thus the passage of the older generation is usually necessary for new ideas and practices to become fully accepted or implemented. More important, even major technological or demographic changes—for instance, the introduction of the automobile or the decline of family farming—have a delayed impact. In fact, society is more affected by delayed and indirect change than by direct, first-order change: the automobile began as a simple replacement for the horse and carriage, but it eventually remade the city in its own image and created a new kind of civilization. In short, most of the consequences of economic and technical development during the first half of the century did not have their full impact until after World War II.

Exponential growth is the second major reason why the postwar era is radically different. Technicalities aside, this is growth that feeds on itself: each new increment adds to the base from which further increase will occur, as when interest compounds in a savings account. The implications of such compounding are momentous. If long continued, exponential growth produces quantities that are prodigious: after twenty doublings an initial quantity is a million times larger. Since a quantity doubles in approximately ten years at a 7 percent growth rate, and since each doubling (as the term denotes) multiplies all that has gone before by two, it should be obvious why the later stages of the growth process have very different implications from the earlier ones. Not only are the numbers so much larger, but these larger quantities engender qualitative change. To illustrate, consider the United States, which, despite having a relatively low rate of population growth today, added almost as many people to its population during the 1980s (approximately 22 million) as lived *in the entire nation* in 1850 (roughly 23 million). And this sizable group of newcomers can no longer be sent out to an expanding frontier, but must instead be accommodated within an existing physical and social milieu that is already fully occupied. Thus not only have the quantities of everything grown much larger during the postwar period, but they have also had, and will continue to have, a far greater impact on the quality of our lives.

Third, the rate of change has accelerated. The postwar era has been one long, gigantic boom of growth, innovation, and social transformation, dwarfing everything that came before. In the last fifty years, from levels that were already high, world population has grown 300 percent, and energy production has increased a mind-boggling 2,500 percent. The same fifty years have also seen Japan go from the abacus to the supercomputer. Indeed, no matter which index of change one chooses, it will show the curve of growth rocketing upward toward the asymptote during the past five decades. In consequence, says energy analyst William Clark, "50 percent of the change recorded in 10,000 years of human history has come in the last half century"—a bit of hyperbole, to be sure, but one that nonetheless suggests the awesome magnitude of change since 1945.

Putting social lags, exponential growth, and accelerating change together gives us a credible explanation of why we only yesterday inhabited the relatively stable, traditional world shown in Norman Rockwell's sentimental paintings of small-town America; whereas we now dwell in an electronic, spacefaring, globalized, media-saturated megalopolis, with all that such a transformation implies—both quantitatively and, more important, qualitatively.

Yet we do not seem to understand just how much has changed, nor how radically. Partly this is because it is notoriously hard for those immersed in social change to see it at all, much less in proper perspective. For example, as we shall see later, television has dramatically altered our social and political milieu, but it has done so by degrees, so we have adjusted gradually and have taken the resulting transformation mostly for granted. Confronted with incremental change, we are like the hapless frog in the famous biology experiment: the water temperature rises so imperceptibly that the poor creature does not realize he is being slowly boiled alive.

As a result, we do not fully appreciate that we have lived through an ecological, social, and technological revolution that has largely vitiated the conditions necessary for the success of the American constitutional system—among them the virtue and religion that Adams and Madison saw as indispensable to the polity they had helped to create. In fact, only the lags spoken of above have preserved us from more radical change. Unfortunately, this also means that an enormous overhang of delayed social and political change looms over what is left of Lockean society. And the end is nowhere in sight: economic globalization and the information revolution are accelerating the pace of growth and innovation and have already begun to effect drastic transformations in our way of life. In other words, the moral entropy and social breakdown of today are probably harbingers of worse to come.

Pluralism Devours Democracy

Moral decline has engendered institutional failure. In essence, efforts by generations of reformers to preserve the original spirit and practice of American democracy from the new socioeconomic conditions hostile to it could not succeed: the revolutionary forces of economic development, technological innovation, and instrumental rationality overwhelmed all opposition. What, for example, has been more politically powerful than the automobile during the last half-century—if political power is defined as the ability to reshape society in a given image? Nothing. Even foreign policy now dances to its tune, because safeguarding our oil supply is of paramount importance.

Moreover, all efforts to reform American politics confront a fundamental paradox: employing Hamiltonian means toward Jeffersonian ends is self-defeating. Using the power of the state to treat the symptoms of social breakdown almost always contributes to the problem that created the need for intervention in the first place. How, for example, can increasing government intervention in private family life, no matter how well intended or well justified by changed social circumstances, fail to undermine further the long-term autonomy and integrity of the family unit? As David Frum points out:

> It really should not surprise anyone that the welfare state has weakened family structures. That is what social programs were meant to do. The family used to be connected by its members' mutual responsibility for child-rearing, unemployment, sickness, old age, disability, and burial. . . . The welfare state was intended to replace those old family functions, and thus reduce the economic importance of the family—which, predictably, weakened the family's stability. . . .
>
> Affection . . . one of the most impermanent and weakest of human ties . . . is now all that holds families together.

Once the process of moral entropy is well advanced, therefore, all supposed cures are likely to be but another manifestation of the underlying disease. Worse, resorting to statist solutions in the name of "democracy" is almost always a sham—because such solutions, successful or not, inevitably make the polity more bureaucratic and less democratic. Agricultural subsidies are a prime example: rather than preserving family farming—their intended, or at least ostensible, purpose—they have promoted a rationalization and collectivization of American agriculture that favors corporate farming. In short, says democratic theorist Robert Dahl, "far from diminishing hierarchy," the effort to protect individuals from economic oppression by erecting a welfare state "has multiplied the number, domain, and scope of hierarchies in American life."

Lincoln's famous definition of democratic government as "of the people, by the people, and for the people" can be used to encapsulate the history of American political institutions. American government was originally of and by a relatively small property-owning elite. However, this situation was generally perceived as serving the interests of the people at large (slaves and Indians obviously excepted): it was a genuine elite, it had led a successful fight for independence, and it had just resolved the new nation's constitutional crisis. But, to simplify greatly, as the founding generation passed away and as economic and social change undermined traditional society, the demand for popular democracy grew apace—leading ultimately to the Jacksonian revolution that enfranchised the common man and instituted government of, by, and for "the people" as then defined (i.e., adult white males).

But the resulting heyday of American democracy was brief. Extending the franchise could not resolve the inherent contradiction between popular democracy and economic development—a problem apparent not only to de Tocqueville but also to many native observers. Lincoln's classic formulation was obsolete even as he uttered it: by the end of the Civil War, the democratic ethos had succumbed to radically changed socioeconomic conditions—partly caused by the war itself, but mostly due to rapid industrialization. A larger and more differentiated population reflecting increasingly diverse interests could no longer express itself politically or be governed except through organizations. Moreover, the triumph of union power over states' rights gradually shifted the locus of government farther away from the average citizen—so that, again, he had to make his voice heard through organizations. In effect, by being forced into organized channels, political participation was bureaucratized; and popular democracy was replaced by pluralism, a political system dominated by organized interests.

Following the great divide of the Civil War, the character of American government therefore changed: it was more and more *of* groups and organizations serving some special interest; *by* a special class of lobbyists, lawyers, and bureaucrats; and thus not really *for* the common man (much less those excluded from the franchise), except in name. Even though "the people" cast the ballots and were the economic beneficiaries of the system, the United States was no longer a democracy in Lincoln's sense. In the six score and ten years since his elegy for the vanishing democratic ethos, government of, by, and for the people has been supplanted first by pluralism (or "interest-group liberalism") and now, in latter days, by "hyperpluralism." To the extent that we are still governed, it is by a tyranny of organized minorities.

From Pluralism to Hyperpluralism

Traditional democratic theory is based on the assumption that both the citizen and those who represent him will decide issues as whole persons, balancing many different interests to arrive at a policy that best accommodates them all. It is not that they are unselfish angels who care only for the common good. Rather, they have so many cross-cutting interests that only stupidity would make them choose policies benefiting one particular interest to the exclusion or harm of all others. After all, a man values every part of his body, and only the necessity to preserve his life as a whole will induce him to sacrifice so much as a toe. As this metaphor implies, democracy is predicated on the fundamental unity of the body politic: individuals are roughly equal in condition, share a common outlook, and want more or less the same things; hence their self-interest and the common interest largely coincide.

In a pluralistic polity, however, the dynamic is reversed. The various groups and classes have less and less in common and tend to see their private ends as apart from or even opposed to the ends of others. They therefore organize themselves to pursue their own particular interest, to the neglect or even detriment of all others. And by contributing heavily, lobbying extensively, and litigating relentlessly, these organized minorities achieve a disproportionate influence on policy outcomes. The result is precisely the kind of corrupt politics excoriated by Rousseau: "The basest interest brazenly adopts the sacred name of the public good . . . and iniquitous decrees whose only goal is the private interest are falsely passed under the name of laws."

Unfortunately, legislators find it virtually impossible to resist organized minorities, not just because they are beholden to them for money, information, access, and support, but also because the essential purpose of a supposedly democratic system is to respond to "popular" demands. Thus lawmakers are easily moved to action or cowed into submission by the intense pressures brought to bear by activists. In other words, without a genuine philosophy of governance or a broad popular consensus on what government is to do apart from satisfying demands, those who most strongly and loudly assert them tend to win all the political battles. Pluralist politics is thus, by its very nature, dominated by an ethos of organized selfishness.

The plight of children in contemporary America is a tragic example of the consequences. As is well documented by economist Sylvia Ann Hewlett, by whatever yardstick one chooses to measure, the physical and social health of children today is significantly worse than twenty years ago. One statistic goes a long way toward providing an explanation: according to Congressional Budget Office estimates for 1995, the federal government spent $7.50 on each person over sixty-five for each $1 on persons under eighteen. (Other observers see the budgetary imbalance as much worse: Peter Peterson makes it $11 in benefits for the old to every $1 for the young, whereas Haynes Johnson puts the ratio at 14 to 1!) Moreover, the cost of medical and social benefits to the former is growing so rapidly that the disproportion will become greater in the future, turning the federal budget into an engine for supporting retirees. Although we may justly pride ourselves on providing well for the aged, this figure suggests that they now command an excessive share of national resources—and that we are sacrificing the future represented by our children to the past represented by our grandparents. Alas, the logic of pluralism almost guarantees such a perverse outcome: children, being penniless and voteless, have no political clout; even young parents struggling to make ends meet have comparatively little; but old folks have the time, money, and incentive to organize effectively, so they wallow in government largesse.

It could hardly be otherwise. Because the whole point of the pluralist game is to milk the system, a Hobbesian dynamic is set up: if you don't grab one of the teats, others certainly will, leaving you hungry but still liable for the taxes that buy the milk. Only a simpleton would hold back, and the resulting scramble turns the political realm into an arena for the pursuit of purely private advantage. In consequence, individuals and groups tenaciously defend or advance rights, often with little regard for whether this discomfits, discommodes, offends, or even outrages others; at the same time, they clamor for benefits, but try to shove off as many of the costs as possible onto others; and they also avoid or even evade duties and obligations.

Little wonder, then, that a pluralist polity has now become mired in a chronic budgetary crisis. The one thing on which both Democrats and Republicans can agree is that their respective constituents have a sacred right to batten on the public purse. But the cumulative effect of trying to satisfy all particularist demands, even if each demand is by itself relatively inconsequential, outruns by far what the people as a whole are willing to support with their taxes. The fiscal crisis exposes the fatal flaw of pluralist politics: as Walter Lippmann phrased it, "When modern states abandoned the Jeffersonian principle of special privileges to none they became committed to the principle of special privileges to all"—an impossibility. In effect, when wealth can be had by voting for it instead of creating it, then democracy begins to devour itself, as happened in ancient times.

Once it takes hold, however, the pluralist dynamic is irresistible: no politician who values his seat dares to bring the gravy train to a halt. As Frum points out, an enormous expansion of "special privileges to all" has recently occurred under the aegis of supposed "conservatives" who oppose the welfare state in principle but truckle to it in practice, because it is the only way to stay in power. What is worse, a ratchet effect—in which the level of entitlement can rise, but never fall—pushes the demand for rights and benefits ever higher and drives the level of duties and responsibilities ever lower. And urging the citizen to perform his duties on the grounds that it is in his self-interest to do so is self-defeating, because self-interest is the source of the problem in the first place. Indeed, as indicated previously, almost all the commonly proposed cures for the ills of liberalism are yet another manifestation of the underlying disease.

More participation, for example, is often put forward as the panacea for our political ills. But this is a singularly inappropriate remedy—unless those who participate do so in a responsible and public-spirited fashion, which is less and less the case. On the contrary, the conditions for genuine democratic participation are no longer present: not only is America a mass society populated by people without either a vision of the common interest or a desire to seek it, but the institutional channels even for mass democracy have largely dried up. For a whole complex of reasons, political parties, which used to buffer government from narrow or excessive demands, have fallen into desuetude. Partly as a result, old-style, broad-based interest groups, such as the National Association of Manufacturers or Americans for Democratic Action, which also served to aggregate and moderate political demands, are no longer important factors either. In addition, the character of de Tocqueville's "voluntary associations" has changed significantly: the Boy Scouts, the Red Cross, the Kiwanis, the PTA, and other broad-based, civic-minded groups are down; but Alcoholics Anonymous, Act Up, the American Association of Retired Persons, the Rainforest Alliance, and other narrowly based or individually focused groups are up. In other words, the negative or even pathological side of "voluntary association" now predominates: when people do not simply withdraw into their well-stocked private "cocoons," they "clamor" for their "social wants" by joining with others to pursue particular interests instead of the public good. Political participation today almost always means joining or supporting a "single-issue constituency," a group that passionately pursues one very specific aim with little or no regard for the interests of others or of the whole. The logic of organized selfishness has therefore arrived at its logical terminus: American politics is an increasingly naked struggle between groups who care about one thing and one thing only—getting what *they* want at almost any cost. So out of pluralism has emerged the contentious politics of hyperpluralism.

The abortion issue is an especially good example. Two opposing political armies, each espousing contradictory principles—one "pro-life," the other "pro-choice"—and each believing totally in the righteousness of its cause, are locked in mortal combat. To this struggle there can be no political solution: the rights being asserted—the "right to life" and the "right to privacy"—are mutually exclusive and irreconcilable. Nor will either army accept anything less than total victory. Even Supreme Court decisions, hitherto the final arbiter of difficult social issues, settle nothing: on the contrary, they only inflame the losing side into redoubling its efforts. Thus even if the polity possessed a genuine moral standard for deciding between the two claims, it could not enforce its decision. In fact, some of the combatants have taken matters into their own hands, so this pocket civil war has begun to generate real, flesh-and-blood casualties. Abortion has thereby turned the American polity into a literal battleground.

But the first casualty in any war is always the truth, so hyperpluralism has inundated the polity in lies and half-truths. The problem is inherent in a liberal polity: because the goal is to satisfy private wants rather than to achieve public ends, all political arguments are likely to be more or less unconscious rationalizations of private prejudice and self-interest (with appeals to the common good thrown in simply as rhetorical camouflage). This tendency is bolstered by the previously noted propensity to withdraw into "small coteries" of the ideologically like-minded, with the result that genuine dialogue among differing groups or viewpoints has become a rare phenomenon in American life. The intense partisanship of hyperpluralism only makes matters that much worse: with politics now seen as a zero-sum game, in which a win by one side is a defeat for the other, confrontation tends to be total. Political discourse, such as it is in liberal society, therefore gives way to propaganda barrages designed to shut up or shout down the opposition. There is not even the pretense of considering other views. And the end justifies the means, so both sides resort to what used to be called the big lie, as when those opposing abortion hold up pickled fetuses and those favoring it brandish coat hangers—visceral symbols that bypass all the political, legal, moral, and emotional complexities of this excruciating issue.

Although not all political statements in a hyperpluralistic polity are as blatantly irrational, even more cerebral arguments for, say, civil rights or free trade or immigration reform are but partisan briefs in an adversarial proceeding focused on political victory, not deliberative truth. Our myth is, of course, that partisan debate in "the marketplace of ideas" will result in good ideas driving out bad. But the actuality seems to be that all mar-

ketplaces, including that of political discourse, are dominated by Gresh
am's Law. So slogans and symbols have driven out reasoned discussion;
and systematic mendacity has largely preempted reasonable argument.
Public discourse in a hyperpluralistic polity therefore generates heat, not
light. In fact, that is its real purpose, for the winners of the political
struggle are those who build the hottest fires under the politicians' feet.

As ordinary citizens come to perceive politics as simply a struggle for
private advantage, they either abandon politics altogether or they join
with others to mobilize the political muscle necessary to extort a desired
outcome from the politicians. The politics of hyperpluralism is therefore
a classic vicious circle in which success by one organized minority only
begets a counterattack by others. In this fashion, not only are more and
more issues politicized than ever before, but the intensity of the struggle
continually escalates.

It is not that single-issue constituencies are a new phenomenon in
American life: the temperance movement that forced the nation into its
noble but disastrous experiment with prohibition is a classic example both
of this style of politics and of the dangers inherent in it. However, such
movements used to be the exception. Now they are becoming the rule.
The basis of pluralist grouping has shifted from economic interests,
which can easily be compromised, to noneconomic values, which cannot—that is, from labor unions and chambers of commerce to abortion
armies and gay activists. In consequence, the level of fundamentalism, fanaticism, and confrontation has risen, spreading a poisonous climate of
bitterness, grievance, and resentment that has already provoked violence.

In this connection, hyperpluralism has turned the American legal profession into an autoimmune disease of the body politic. Obedient to the
spirit of the times, lawyers have begun aggressively employing all their
considerable talent and training to exploit every means abundantly provided by the American legal system in pursuit of victory at all costs—not
always on the merits of the case, but through lengthy and exhausting lit-
igative wars of attrition that have begun to cripple the legal system itself.
Worse, because hyperpluralistic demands are minority demands and
cannot expect to command a legislative majority, at least in their purest
form, the courts have become the favored avenue for pressing them—
with the result that *private* litigants and their lawyers are increasingly determining *public* policy. Of course, it is all in a good cause: civil rights,
defendant's rights, environmental protection, just compensation, tax
avoidance, free enterprise, free expression, welfare rights, immigrant
rights, and so on. In the end, however, it amounts to an unrelenting legal

attack on the legitimacy, vitality, and integrity of the political system: in contemporary America, law threatens to usurp politics.

In sum, thanks to hyperpluralism, the American government is whipsawed by a multiplicity of special-interest groups engaged in a no-holds-barred struggle to dominate public policy. Even areas formerly insulated from the worst forms of partisanship—such as foreign policy or appropriate medical treatment or appointments to the Supreme Court—are now the focus of bloody-minded political activism. We are governed by a tyranny of organized minorities that either extort desired outcomes from elected officials or forbid them to make public policy in many areas; and politics has become a war won by those who hold the feet of the politicians to the hottest fire. Pluralist political theory, while pretending to the authority of "political science," attempts to cloak this unpalatable truth with ideological decency, but the reality is otherwise: "Modern politics," says philosopher Alasdair MacIntyre, "is civil war carried on by other means."

The Nightmare of Factionalism

What is worse, hyperpluralism is taking a new and more menacing turn: toward a growing acceptance or even encouragement of tribal politics. Although the official motto and long-time ideal of the United States is "E pluribus unum," a significant number of the "many" have now decided not to become part of the "one." Rather, on the grounds that the common culture is but the oppressive ideology of white males of European extraction, they have made plain their desire to opt out of it. Thus the goal of integration is on its way to being replaced by that of separation, and ethnic, religious, and cultural fundamentalism has grown into a significant political force. But if major groups within the political community refuse assimilation and insist on their primordial affiliation to race, sex, language, culture, creed, locality, ideology, or lifestyle, then the pluralist political game is all but over. Once this kind of particularism predominates, the cool weighing of interests and the willingness to bargain over them that a pluralist polity requires are swept away by a passionate attachment to ultimate values.

In effect, we are experiencing an upsurge of what the Founders called factionalism—politics as the ardent expression of principles or passions, rather than the reasoned balancing of interests. In the political philosophy of *The Federalist*, especially Madison's pivotal Numbers 10 and 51, it was the thing most to be feared, and our constitutional machinery was largely designed with an eye to preventing it. Now, two hundred years later, we are tending toward Madison's worst nightmare: pluralism is being replaced not only by hyperpluralism based on single-issue constituencies making uncompromising demands, but also by factionalism based on separatist principles utterly incompatible with the traditional spirit and practice of American politics. And various fringe groups, even among the white majority, increasingly assert the principle of nullification: *your* laws are not *our* laws. Madison's machine is therefore breaking down: the old politics of "who gets what, when, how" (to use Lasswell's famous formulation) is being supplanted by a new politics of ultimate or absolute values that cannot be bargained away without betraying one's principles.

The crucial difference between pluralism and factionalism was wittily captured by Jonathan Swift in his satirical account of Lilliputian politics. During Gulliver's sojourn in Lilliput, the burning political issue was how high to wear one's heels, so the king kept his own heels at mid-length, raising or lowering them a fraction to favor first one side and then the other. The crown prince, meanwhile, placated both parties by hobbling about on one high and one low heel. These adroit measures preserved the peace of the realm, because the height of heels is a matter of degree, not definitive choice. Thus each side was open to compromise. Previously, however, the burning question had been where to open soft-boiled eggs—at the big end or the small? Since this is a definitive choice, not a matter of degree, compromise was impossible. Peace was restored only after numerous civil wars between the Big-endians and Small-endians, and the losing faction, its books banned from Lilliput, continued to foment subversion from exile. So pluralism is a politics of more-or-less, in which things can normally be worked out, whereas factionalism is a politics of either-or, in which the opposing sides will always be at loggerheads and may eventually come to blows.

In this light, the demand for "multiculturalism," to the extent that it implies a separation from the common culture rather than a celebration of diversity within it, is an extremely disturbing development. It divides the polity into factions that disclaim any common identity and threatens to bring the concealed civil war of modern politics out into the open. However, all the trends point in the direction of greater primordial attachment: not just in the United States, but all over the world, people are reacting against the thin culture of modernization by reasserting their "roots" and demanding official recognition of their particular language, culture, or lifestyle. And the United States is more vulnerable than most, because neither the myth nor the reality of the melting pot can be expected to survive the destruction of the Lockean society that was all that sustained it. Moreover, given the long and hateful exclusion of African-Americans from the dominant culture, it is hardly surprising that many of them would now wish to return the compliment. But that does not diminish the political threat to the American polity of multiculturalism as currently conceived and practiced.

Some observers profess unconcern, seeing the current upsurge of separatism as a swing in the political pendulum that will soon correct itself, like similar excesses of the past. However, the logic of the previous analysis suggests otherwise: as particularism intensifies, pluralism begets hyperpluralism; as it intensifies further, it begets factionalism and, ultimately, separatism.

Of course, as historian William McNeill points out, the national monocultures of the recent past are the exception: he therefore sees us beginning to drift back from an abnormal state of "barbarian homogeneity" toward the more normal condition of "civilized polyethnicity." Unfortunately, as Lebanon, Sri Lanka, and the former Yugoslavia demonstrate—and such examples, both ancient and modern, could be multiplied extensively—polyethnicity is not without its perils. Without an overarching political structure to contain factional strife, multiculturalism is a recipe for civil war.

Indeed, as McNeill makes clear, the normal state of political affairs corresponding to civilized polyethnicity is empire, for only an imperial authority can prevent such an outcome—not just by exerting power but also by providing a larger and more inclusive culture in which all lesser groups can share and to which they therefore give secondary allegiance. (As our forefathers discovered, confederation, the other available solution to the problem of multiculturalism, is attractive in theory but awkward and unstable in practice; except in unusually favorable circumstances, confederations have not thrived over the long term.) But empires are hardly noted for their practice of liberty and equality: on the contrary, by their very nature they enshrine hierarchy and difference. In other words, factionalism fits both logically and historically with nondemocratic and nonlibertarian politics, not liberal democracy. As John Stuart Mill said in *Considerations on Representative Government*:

> Free institutions are next to impossible in a country made up of different nationalities. Among a people without fellow-feeling, especially if they read and speak different languages, the united public opinion necessary to the working of representative government cannot exist.

In short, because liberal democracy assumes near-universal allegiance to a common political culture, it is fundamentally incompatible with multi-

culturalism; to try to combine the two is to embark on a path whose logical terminus is civil war, followed by imperium.

Yet the American polity is already far gone in this direction. Without a
formal decision—in fact, with no real public debate about the feasibility,
desirability, or ultimate political consequences of multiculturalism—we
seem to have abandoned the traditional goal of assimilation and integration and to have embraced policies that reify and reinforce social and
even racial differences. We are therefore making, if we have not already
made, one of the most important political decisions in our history largely
by default.

In a beautiful example of how private interests increasingly determine
public policy, the universities are slowly ceasing to transmit a common
culture, much less the cultural tradition from which liberal democracy
emerged. But, said Lippmann, "Without this tradition our world, like a
tree cut off from its roots in the soil, must die and be replaced by alien
and barbarous things." What is worse, the universities are in the vanguard of the multicultural movement and seem bent on producing a new
political generation that accepts separatism as a matter of course. On all
too many campuses, the lines of segregation have been deliberately re-
drawn, often creating a kind of voluntary apartheid, as various factions—
racial, ethnic, sexual, political—carve up the little polity of the university
into separate, sovereign fiefdoms. (In a terrible historical irony, some
urban public school systems have also begun moving in this direction—
that is, toward a revival of "separate but equal.") It is now possible for
someone to receive a degree having studied mostly the history and experience of his or her kind. This institutionalization of factionalism mocks
the very idea of a university education—which, as the name implies, is
supposed to lift students out of their own narrow personal world and into
a more *universal* (and therefore less prejudiced) understanding of life.
What is the chance of genuine political dialogue or social peace between
groups if there is no agreed moral framework, no shared language of discourse, and no common sense of destiny—because each group has been
schooled to view the world only through its own particular lens?

This is not to oppose ethnic or gender studies per se. That the history
and life experience of all races, classes, and so on, deserve serious attention at the university level, which they have not always received, goes
without saying. In other words, what is "universal" needs broadening and
redefining in a culture that is less and less European in the traditional
sense. But if there has been cultural bias, our aim should be to correct it,
not to substitute other, even less inclusive biases for it. Still less to abandon the received culture altogether, for the very legal and political princi-

ples being adduced in support of multicultural objectives came out of the European tradition. In addition, as we shall see below, the wisdom and judgment essential to political life come from studying great art, great thought, and great science, which are always universal. It would therefore be tragic if justifiable ethnic pride or bitter racial memories led to a rejection of universal cultural values or to the solipsistic extreme of refusing to connect to some larger human whole, for that way lies barbarism.

Nevertheless, like feminism, multiculturalism is an important political symptom: people are clearly fed up with being ground into social atoms by the destruction of Lockean society. Yet, at this point, we can hardly expect to restore an illusory monocultural past. We shall therefore have to move forward to some more inclusive identity that is multicultural in the true sense. As implied above, however, the question is whether the latter can be achieved without a fundamental change in our constitutional regime—that is, without some kind of overarching imperium to provide unity. Be this as it may, coming to grips with the political consequences of multiculturalism is clearly going to be one of the great political issues of the next century (and not just for Americans alone, thanks to the mass migrations now reshaping the demography of the world).

To sum up, the Americans who once were, in de Tocqueville's phrase, "born equal"—precisely because they had renounced the ethnic, social, and class structures of the Old World—now seem much less inclined to pursue a common destiny. But if groups continue to separate from the common political culture, then social conflicts will become intractable, and an increasingly divided nation will soon become ungovernable. To demand self-determination or special treatment rather than a fair share of the pluralist spoils is, in effect, to secede from the American polity as it was constituted. Factionalism therefore makes manifest the latent civil war of modern politics. To return to our previous image, it enormously increases the pressure inside the political engine, and this must be matched by a proportionate increase in governmental authority, lest the engine fly apart. Thus an increasingly Disunited States of America struggles to escape the horns of the dilemma that multiculturalism presents: avoiding Leviathan while averting a political explosion.

The Death of Citizenship

The deeper meaning of the progression from pluralism to factionalism is that citizenship is all but dead. The split between apathy and activism noted by de Tocqueville has become more extreme, producing increasingly pathological manifestations at both ends of the spectrum and reducing those in the middle to mere consumers in a political marketplace.

The reasons for apathy are not hard to find. Above all, with elections and legislative decisions turning on money, media, and manipulation, not the voice of the people, the common man sees politics as the near-exclusive preserve of well-connected insiders or well-heeled organizations. Many Americans, perhaps the majority, have simply lost faith in the integrity and legitimacy of a political process that is no longer of, by, or for the people in any meaningful sense. Unless galvanized by some issue or cause about which they care very deeply, they therefore drop out. This, of course, sets up a classic vicious circle: the less people participate and vote, the more well-heeled and well-connected special interests dominate; but the more they dominate, the less people participate and vote.

Another serious problem is the complexity of the American electoral process compared to that in other democracies, where citizens vote less frequently and have to make fewer, but more meaningful, choices when they do. By contrast, Americans, with their mania for doing everything "democratically," have to vote on every office from dogcatcher to president, not only in the main election but also in the primaries. Moreover, they confront ballots loaded down with countless local measures and state referenda—many trivial, but some of great moment—written in impenetrable legalese. In effect, they are asked to be amateur legislators, a task for which they lack the time, training, or inclination. (We can therefore forget about increasing political participation: even *voting* has become too onerous for the average American. Significantly, the voting rate is highest among the elderly: not only do they have the time, but their political values reflect the America of yesteryear, when civic spirit was more the norm.) In short, the common man, confronted by a wretched excess of democratic choice—and already doubting the integrity and legitimacy of the process—quite rationally chooses not to vote.

On the other hand, those who are galvanized into action are not acting as citizens either, because they are almost always partisans of some particular interest. They pursue a single issue of intense emotional concern, such as abortion, with bloody-minded zeal; or they conduct raids on the public purse; or they subvert the democratic process by seeking and getting special favors. In other words, they behave exactly contrary to the ideal of good citizenship, draining the life out of the body politic by advancing partial interests at the expense of the whole.

In between these two poles are the great majority of ordinary, well-meaning men and women who might like to participate more actively and who want to do their civic duty as best they can, but who find themselves unable to do so to any significant degree due to the press of other responsibilities and the high cost of participation noted above. In the end, the citizen is obliged to leave politics to the professionals. But surely citizens still have the final say when they go to the polls, turning out the old lot of rascals and voting in the new? In fact, however, even voting is no longer an exercise in citizenship, because the voters inhabit a political environment that no longer jibes with the basic assumptions of democratic theory.

The first problem is that our physical and social milieu is now so grandiose in scale, complex in structure, and isolating in character that confusion and anomie are rife. To be blunt, the putative citizen can no longer comprehend his world well enough to cast an intelligent ballot. The major political issues of our time have become so esoteric that only full-time specialists can hope to understand them. (However, serious disagreement among the so-called experts over nuclear power, monetary policy, military preparedness, and other critical issues hardly inspires public confidence, either in the experts themselves or in the tractability of the problems.) At the same time, the new information technology, whatever its role in undermining repressive regimes elsewhere, has not given the average citizen here more knowledge and control of his environment: on the contrary, it has only increased the velocity, magnified the complexity, and reduced the intelligibility of public life, while further restricting the common man's access to relevant information. As political scientist Langdon Winner says, "manifest social complexity" has been overlaid by "hidden electronic complexity." In addition, the world is now so interdependent that events occurring elsewhere, perhaps even halfway around the world, decisively affect both national and local affairs. Finally, as will be discussed in more detail below, the citizen's information about all of this is filtered through the distorting haze of the media. In consequence, says Winner, "the idea that civilized life consists of a fully conscious, intelligent, self-determining populace making informed choices about ends and means and taking action on that basis is revealed as a pathetic fantasy."

The second problem is that the voter of today has become a passive consumer in a political marketplace. That is, both politicians and policies are now marketed like any other commodity, especially at the national level; and more and more money and expertise are expended to make elections a purely formal exercise, a mere ratification of the success or failure of the candidate's marketing strategy. In fact, probably the most meaningful public act in which the average citizen can be involved today is not casting a ballot but, instead, being selected as a respondent in a so-called public opinion poll, for that is what politicians actually pay attention to. One danger of this mode of politics is, of course, that the consumer will "buy" on impulse and later suffer a terrible case of "buyer's remorse" when he finds that he has bought a "lemon"—the story of recent elections in a nutshell. The greater danger is that the electorate's disillusionment and frustration with an electoral process that is cynically manipulative and that does not seem to offer appropriate or meaningful choices will create an angry and ungovernable crowd in place of a public.

Indeed, it is precisely to this danger that we must now turn our attention, for the third and perhaps most serious problem is that meaningful citizenship has also been extirpated by what is tantamount to a takeover of the political process by the media, especially television. In effect, politics is now a spectator sport: the moral and social vacuum left by the decay of Lockean society has been filled by an ersatz media community. Today's "public" is a mere audience—a dispersed and passive crowd of private consumers responsive not to their fellow human beings but to an artificial, commercial, self-referential, mesmerizing, and specious media environment. But without a genuine public engaged in real deliberation, there can be no politics worthy of the name, certainly not a democratic politics. In essence, Marshall McLuhan's famous "global village" looks to be less and less like a community and more and more like an electronic mob crowded around a media circus.* What is worse, this development seems likely to terminate in the annihilation of political reason, the sine qua non of liberal freedom.

Media and the Destruction of Political Reason

Leaving the special dilemmas posed by television aside for the moment, the problem with living in a media-saturated environment is that the citizen no longer has direct access to important events. Virtually all of his knowledge of the world is secondhand, obtained from sources that se-

---

*However, what follows largely vindicates the core analysis of McLuhan's prescient *Understanding Media*. Misled in part by his unusual presentation, most failed to grasp his basic point. Media are not neutral: "All media exist to invest our lives with artificial perception and arbitrary values," because each medium is itself a "message" that expresses and inculcates a particular brand of consciousness, along with an associated worldview. Thus "we become what we behold." Moreover, each medium constitutes an Archimedean "place to stand" from which the mind can be levered into a particular "tempo or pattern." In this light, "education is ideally civil defense against media fallout," for otherwise one is subliminally governed not only by the values implicit in the medium but also by those who control these "places to stand."

lect, simplify, and distort reality—even if they try hard not to, which is not always the case. In other words, the report is not the reality; it is an artifact of the reporting process. The facts may be accurate as far as they go, but what appears in the media is always a "story" that creates a false sense of verisimilitude when statistics and statements are inflated into reality by the reporting process itself. Thus even if the media do their utmost to represent the world faithfully, the reader imbibes a reality fabricated for him by others. It goes without saying that what appears in the *New York Times* is not a fabrication in the pejorative sense, but the fact remains: media reports are always a hearsay reality that is shaped, if not distorted, by the process that creates it.

Part of the problem is that the media necessarily dissect reality into discrete stories and rarely devote sufficient attention to relating these fragmentary accounts to some larger whole (partly because of lack of space, partly because it does not sell, and partly because the opinion makers themselves do not desire it). Any given story, which may emanate from an interested party, therefore contains only a small part of the total picture, while seeming to stand for much more. And because the spotlight shifts constantly—South Africa yesterday, AIDS today, the budget crisis tomorrow, Bosnia the day after, the ozone layer next week—media reality is a jumble with little or no sense of continuity. Context is also absent: the kind of historical, cultural, geographical, epidemiological, or ecological background needed to comprehend the most important stories of our times is rarely available except in the most serious journals. But knowledge depends critically on continuity, depth, and context, so an ever-changing kaleidoscope of stories, each constituting a kind of half-truth, provides only partial understanding—the little knowledge that is proverbially more dangerous than none at all, because it creates the illusion of knowing.

In other words, given the way in which media reality is constructed, its veracity or authenticity would always be questionable to some degree even in the absence of bias. But the media are, in fact, deeply biased toward the ephemeral: the very word *"journalism"* reveals that it is about *today's* happenings. So elections and the like are extensively covered; but long-term trends and institutional structures get much less attention; and the still deeper philosophical or ideological level of reality receives practically none. Unfortunately, this defect ensures that some of the most important stories will be underreported, if not unreported, until they reach a crisis point and at last become "news"—by which time it may be too late to do much about them.

In addition, the notorious predilection of the media for the sensational—for what is new, unusual, bizarre, illegal, menacing, and destructive—may give audiences the stimulation they crave, but it hardly provides a profound or balanced portrait of reality. (This is the opposite side of the coin to the problem of underreporting mentioned above: the ozone hole is headline news, because the media cannot resist a story about the sky falling; but creeping habitat destruction is not, even though it is the greater long-term ecological threat.) A succession of crises, threats, and emergencies therefore crowd the front page—appearing out of the void, making headlines for a while, and returning again to the void—leaving too much of the rest of the paper to be filled with fad, glamor, celebrity, scandal, sex, and violence.

Unfortunately, a preoccupation with trivia is not a trivial matter: a tight focus on inside dope and inside dirt tends to obscure the real meaning and import of serious matters. Worse, focusing on conflict for its own sake turns politics into a melodramatic struggle between heroes and villains (identified for us by the media) or even into a running soap opera (in which the evil deeds and dark secrets of the high and mighty are exposed by the media). And elections become horse races: who wins and how, not what they stand for, are the main focus. So the substance of politics is lost in a preoccupation with personality and drama. Worse, the media's preference for scandal over substance has contributed greatly to the loss of faith in the democratic process: so much dirty linen has been washed in public in recent years that a miasma of cynicism and disrespect now hangs over the political process. And it is, says James Fallows, a vicious circle: "By choosing to present public life as a contest among scheming political leaders, all of whom the public should view with suspicion, the press helps bring about that very result."

In effect, the media have become one of the most corrosive of Lippmann's "acids of modernity," destroying what is there without putting anything worthwhile in its place. And no improvement can be expected: not only does scandal sell, but a trendy approach to the news glorifies the role of those who report and thereby establish the trends. In other words, treating the world as a media event has elevated the media to power: they are now the ultimate arbiters of our cultural and social reality and, hence, among our most important political actors.

This brings us to the third and most dangerous form of media bias. Not only are the media political actors in their own right with their own interests to defend and advance, but they are also the primary means by which political interests in our society are expressed, so all the other political actors exert their utmost to make their own definition and interpretation of "the news" prevail. More generally, they try to influence the media's basic mindset, so that their particular concerns, problems, and perspectives dominate the national agenda. They could hardly do otherwise, for, as David Hume pointed out in *Of the First Principles of Government,*

nothing appears more surprising to those who consider human affairs with a philosophical eye than the easiness with which the many are governed by the few. . . . When we inquire by what means this wonder is effected, we shall find that, as Force is always on the side of the governed, the governors have nothing to support them but opinion. It is, therefore, on opinion only that government is founded, and this maxim extends to the most despotic and most military governments as well as to the most free and most popular.

In this light, it is hardly surprising that American politicians have turned into "media whores" or that a new class of media manipulators and pundits has emerged to "spin" the story before it is reported and then to "analyze" it afterward, all with the aim of making "the news" reflect the viewpoint of particular political actors. So what eventually emerges in the media is the outcome of a frankly political struggle to mold public consciousness. But some participants in this struggle are obviously more equal than others. In particular, because they depend so heavily on official sources, the media tend to present an official view of reality. Conversely, those outside the "mainstream," as defined by the media, lack "credibility" and cannot get a hearing (or are even held up to ridicule). Both in form and content, therefore, "the news" is always a political construction—one-sided at best, partisan at worst.

In sum, in today's mediated world, the citizen's understanding is based not on his own sense experience but on hearsay—on a plausible but skewed or even deceptive secondhand account constructed for him by others who have an ax to grind. The media's boast that the common man is better informed than ever before is false: he is only swamped in data, from which he derives but little information, even less knowledge, and virtually no wisdom; and this little information and less knowledge, even when they are reasonably accurate, are not really his in any meaningful sense. That the quality of the hearsay obviously differs radically between the *New York Times* and the *National Enquirer* does not change the principle: the so-called citizen lives in a virtual reality created for him by the media.

Television makes matters much worse, because its version of virtual reality is far more convincing: it all but expropriates the viewer's consciousness. Television is not an informative medium at all, but a dramatic one: it transmits images, not ideas; it evokes emotions, not thoughts; and it arouses passion, not deliberation. Indeed, at its worst, it is frankly inflammatory. Moreover, all the media problems mentioned above—selectivity, discontinuity, superficiality, and the like—are exacerbated by television. In fact, because it portrays the world in ever smaller "bites" of sound and image, television creates what is tantamount to a cartoon of reality. Conceived and executed by a great artist, such a cartoon might convey some essential truth; in the hands of lesser beings harassed by deadlines and driven by ratings, it is just a caricature.

It is, moreover, a caricature that is grossly distorted by commercialism: the purpose of television is to lure a mass audience with mass entertainment so that mass advertising can promote mass consumption. In effect, not just the advertising but most of the programming, too, are propaganda for commodities—that is, for a vision of life in which what you possess or consume determines your worth and happiness. And because the ultimate sin is to bore the audience, even news programs are show business—designed to amuse and beguile, not to inform, and "packaged" accordingly. (Indeed, news events are sometimes dramatically "re-created" by the major networks.) In effect, television news is a commodity sold to viewers like any other product. At best, therefore, television caricatures and trivializes social reality; at worst, it deliberately manipulates or even inflames the emotions of the viewer and fosters an addiction both to consumerism and to the medium itself.

The point is not simply to inveigh once more against the crass commercialism of television, nor to lament in elitist tones its aesthetic poverty. Rather, it is to point out that a media environment increasingly dominated by television qualitatively transforms the relationship not just of the individual to the world but, more important, of the citizen to the polity. Reading is active: the reader translates printed words on a page into mental images, which takes imagination and thought. Viewing television is passive: the viewer absorbs ready-made images, which takes neither thought nor imagination. Because reading exercises the mind, whereas television entrances or even stupefies it, citizens no longer deliberate but instead respond to events with raw emotion. Television is therefore antithetical to the traditional understanding of politics and citizenship in the liberal tradition.

We have come through a two-stage media revolution during the past two hundred years: initially, from mostly direct participation in local life, which provided firsthand knowledge of persons and events, to mostly indirect involvement in national life, with print media serving both as the source of secondhand information and as the arena for public discourse; then, in the postwar era, from this indirect but still active involvement via print media to the passive consumption of images. The average citizen now lives in an increasingly artificial world—a virtual reality fabricated by a medium that does not allow for public discourse in the traditional sense, both because it is dramatic rather than deliberative and because it does all the imagining and thinking for him. Bluntly put, images are inflicted on an iconographically naive public by clever experts whose purpose is to amuse, beguile, distract, entice, and manipulate rather than to inform or elevate. The result is a passive and stupefied populace lacking the capacity for political reasoning.

That the public has in recent years become more distrustful and critical of TV news matters little, because the damage has already been done and the vast majority continues to watch rather than read. The consequences are disastrous: since our constitutional arrangements are predicated on the assumption of rational public discourse, with all that this implies in terms of literacy and popular knowledge, the polity is floundering or even foundering in a media environment hostile to its basic principles.

Specifically, television has made a travesty of the democratic process. Citizens attempt to choose their political representatives on the basis of the deceptive secondhand information channeled to them by television, but media bias is overlaid and amplified by the machinations of the politicians, who naturally employ all the manipulative means developed by a commercial society to sell themselves to a mass audience. And since doing so obviously requires the wherewithal to buy the means of persuasion, money is more than ever the decisive factor in winning and keeping political office. (One implication is that incumbents are given a virtual lock on office, because they can normally raise far more money than any challenger; incumbency also provides precious media visibility and all-important "name recognition" for free.)

Worse, television politics demands not statesmanship but public relations or play acting. To be sure, dramaturgy has always been an important part of political leadership: to attract and inspire followers, leaders must project charisma and have a good sense of political theater. Television, however, has turned dramaturgy into pandering. Since what sells is not the steak but the sizzle, politicians adopt whatever posture is needed to seduce the fickle audience. In effect, television obliges politicians to practice demagoguery: in a medium built for images, reasoned discussion of issues and ideas bores viewers stiff; but subtle appeals to popular emotion and prejudice strike home. Hence media "positioning" all but replaces politics in the traditional sense: "Modern campaigns," says reporter Marc Sandalow, "have degenerated into a distasteful theater of the bizarre."

Moreover, because audiences are now habituated to television's frenetic pace, their attention span is so short that politicians must get their message across within seconds, lest the people exercise their democratic right to change channels by remote control. Political campaigns therefore consist of brief "spot" advertisements deliberately crafted to hit below the belt. In consequence, reasoned debate is no longer a part of electoral campaigns: it has been all but superseded by "negative campaigning" that attacks the opponent's fitness and character or by "attack ads" that cast his ideas in a prejudicial light.

More generally, four decades of television seem to have fundamentally transformed the consciousness of the American public, especially the younger generation. In 1968, according to journalist Kiku Adatto, the average sound bite in network newscasts lasted 42.3 seconds; in 1992, a mere 8.4 seconds. But to perceive the world in less than ten-second sound and image bites is to begin to think in the same fashion: anything long, boring, difficult, unpleasant, or complicated becomes intolerable. And all sense of perspective disappears: on television, where the time is always now, the political score is kept on a weekly or even daily basis, and "instant analysis" of the problem of the day takes the place of real reflection. Even newspapers and newsmagazines have had to accommodate this radically shortened and attenuated attention span by making stories briefer and by employing bright colors, splashy graphics, and other attention-grabbing techniques borrowed from television. However, the print media are probably fighting a losing battle. Not only are there many complete illiterates who cannot read at all, as well as a large number of functional illiterates who cannot read anything complex, but also a still larger number of poorly educated aliterates, especially among the younger generation, who no longer read in the old way: they have not been trained to do so, and their thinking habits have been corrupted by television. In short, "vidiocy" is rampant.*

To illustrate how radically television has transformed public discourse, consider the way in which it deals with environmental problems: no te-

---

*Although the problems of American education have many causes, the transformation of the rhythm and texture of the students' minds by television is certainly one reason why achievement at every level has declined. For example, the written vocabulary of the average elementary school student today is less than half what it was in 1945; and university teachers report a marked decline in analytical skills among their students in recent years. A genuine education is of necessity a long, difficult, complex, and sometimes boring process whose ideal outcome is the ability to see issues in context, depth, and perspective—none of which is compatible with a short attention span, an overwhelmingly present orientation, or a desire to be entertained. In other words, a real education demands a character structure entirely opposed to that of the media milieu, which has become the mainstream culture. Parents and teachers who want a real education for the young must

dious explanations of the dangers of pollution but, instead, shots of oil-soaked birds gasping for breath; no long-winded sermons on the sacredness of life but, instead, pictures of baby seals being clubbed to death. All the boring complexities of ecology, economics, morality, and the like are simply bypassed, as the emotional reaction to the image overwhelms thought about the problem revealed by it. Thus, whereas images can indeed point to problems and stir up passions, they cannot elucidate the complexity of the issues involved or clarify the value conflicts they contain; nor can they point the way to reasoned solutions.

Moreover, the most important stories simply cannot be told in images. There is, for example, no dramatic way to show the long-term impact of extirpating large numbers of seemingly unimportant species or of running persistent budget deficits: one must *think through* the likely consequences. Nor can one picture the insidious growth of state power in our time, because this kind of understanding requires historical context and deeper reflection. So political scandals like Watergate and Irangate are played as soap opera, rather than as what they really are: symptoms of the polity's transformation into a national-security state governed by *raison d'état* and an imperial presidency. In the end, we get only what television can provide—the superficial drama of events—so the polity is effectively deprived of the kind of information it needs to understand or solve its problems.

In fact, the long-term effect of television is to undo the work of civilization. As Oswald Spengler pointed out, "the liberation from the visual" is one of civilization's great achievements, because it permitted higher-order thought. Television, however, mimics experience so effectively (relative to print media) that it all but drives out thought: viewers mistakenly believe that they have been magically transported to the scene and are emotionally gripped rather than mentally stimulated. In addition, advertising is basically about magical self-transformation, so the effect of adspeak is to encourage magical thinking in general—that is, to make our minds more primitive (in the pejorative sense). Moreover, the ultimate effect of a flood of brief images is to wash out the sense of past and future and to induce an overwhelming present orientation—which is, again, to make our minds more primitive. Finally, if the goal of civilization is greater consciousness, a position held in one form or another by virtually everyone from Plato to Freud, then television is indeed the

---

therefore fight the media for their hearts and minds. But it is hard enough to raise children *in accordance with* the dominant culture; to try to do so *against* that culture is nearly impossible. And the worst is probably yet to come: when today's media-saturated youth become parents in their turn, will they even make the effort?

enemy of civilization: to use Freudian language, it fosters more Id and less Ego, more unconscious emotional reaction and less of the reality principle. In effect, television is psychoanalysis in reverse. Thus not only has the polity been deprived of the information it needs to understand or solve its problems, but it is even beginning to lose its ability to think constructively about them. We are making political decisions on the basis of a "reality" that is increasingly unreal.

The gap between image and reality exists in large part because media reality is self-referential. While "the news" may seem to originate in external events, much of what appears in the media, especially about politics, is actually a commentary on or a reaction to what has already appeared, with the actors and the reporters monitoring their performances and adjusting their behavior accordingly. What is worse, says political scientist Thomas Patterson, "journalists have . . . hijacked the news," because on network television "the news focuses more on the journalists than the people they cover." In effect, "coverage" largely replaces the events themselves, as journalists spend much of their time promoting themselves or chasing their own tails, especially on "big" stories like celebrity trials and political campaigns. To reiterate, media reality is a hall of mirrors in which we see reflected mainly the media process itself—and yet this mere spectacle is now our reality, because we have "become what we behold," just as McLuhan predicted.

The upshot, says Daniel Boorstin, is that we live in a state of "national self-hypnosis" and a "thicket of unreality" made up of "pseudo-events." Because of this "contrivance of experience" in which the vivid images proffered by television mostly overshadow pale reality, Lincoln's famous maxim that "you can't fool all of the people all of the time" no longer holds. To use an all-too-appropriate contemporary barbarism, not only Lincoln's words but reality itself have been rendered "inoperative" by the rise to predominance of the visual media, which are capable of creating a virtual reality that is more persuasive than the real thing. So we live in a largely imaginary or even fantastic political reality in which most action is purely dramatic or symbolic—not meant to accomplish anything real, but only to manipulate the images, because they are all that count anymore.

To conclude this discussion of the media circus (and link it to the previous discussion of factionalism), we profess to be ruled by the voice of the people—or public opinion. But a genuine public opinion does not exist today, because we only form *opinions* by confronting the ideas of others; before that, all we have are private *prejudices*. Without some form of active and reasoned public debate, there is no public opinion at all, only a congeries of private prejudice—a public mood at best. It is this volatile and fluctuating mood that our vast polling apparatus measures and reports back to us as "public opinion." And what purports to be public discourse in the print media today is more like an exchange of partisan missiles by warring political factions than a reasoned effort to arrive at prudent public decisions. Real policy debate is largely confined to small groups of specialists whose deliberations are carried out, if not actually in secret, then in semi-private, and followed only by a tiny minority. In effect, we now have a polity without a public, because "the people" are increasingly fragmented into many separate and mutually exclusive universes of private discourse.

This is why the various proposals to use interactive television to create an "electronic democracy" or "cyberdemocracy" are ill-conceived and dangerous. The unbuffered prejudices of a populace mesmerized by media seem more likely to produce a politics of "accident and force" than of "reflection and choice." In other words, junking Madison's checks and balances for a "hyperdemocracy" in which the masses represent themselves directly will simply give free rein to popular "passions" and encourage the "mischiefs of faction." In general, any attempt to make the polity more democratic when the society no longer fulfills the necessary conditions for representative democracy, much less direct democracy, are doomed to failure. What is worse, they perpetuate the denial of reality that is one of the chief obstacles we must overcome.

To sum up, the media circus is dedicated to what the pioneering advertising genius Edward Bernays frankly called "the engineering of consent." The modern media are fundamentally opposed to our political ideals and institutions, which are those of *citizen* democracy. They instead foster a *consumer* democracy that is democratic in name only—a travesty of representative government. To put the point more generally, representative or liberal democracy is obsolescent, if not already obsolete, because its characteristic institutions do not fit contemporary socioeconomic conditions: moral entropy, factionalism, and now media politics contradict it root and branch. The media takeover of the political process is tantamount to a change of regime—that is, no mere change in the *form* of democracy but, instead, a shift to an antidemocratic polity in which the average citizen has been rendered "inoperative" for all practical purposes. The media may boast of their role in subverting old-style totalitarian regimes dependent on propaganda and the secret police, but they fail to see how, by participating in "the engineering of consent," they are contributing to a more insidious form of social control of the kind presaged in Aldous Huxley's *Brave New World*. After all, those who live under overt totalitarian rule are fully aware that they are being lied to and can suspend belief; but the so-called citizens of an allegedly free society who have been lulled into taking a specious or even deceptive media reality at face value are likely to believe that they are reasonably well and truthfully informed when they are not. Who is the worse off? Indeed, historically, the manipulation of emotions and symbols from above has been associated with a policy of bread and circuses and with one or another type of imperial rule. "Spectator participation in media-fantasies," says historian William Irwin Thompson, "is a return to the peasant's illiterate participation in . . . medieval pageantry": as long as television remains the dominant form of communication, we will have a "polity of mediocrity" based not on laws or institutions but, instead, on a magical manipulation of a mesmerized "electropeasantry" by charismatic leaders and their hired "imagineers." This, then, is what the media's expropriation of reality and destruction of political reason have wrought: they have turned the people into an electronic mob, so the true prophet of the televisual age is not Marshall McLuhan but Gustave Le Bon.

The Electronic Mob

De Tocqueville praised the Americans of the founding generation for their independence of thought and ability to discuss difficult issues with civility and intelligence. But, like the virtuous republic itself, the high political and intellectual standards established by the Founders failed to survive their demise. The American Age of Reason was an aristocratic flash in the pan lasting only a generation or two: "Its ideas were soon repudiated," said Herbert Schneider, "its plans for the future were buried, and there followed on its heels a thorough and passionate reaction against its ideals and assumptions." Jackson's election symbolized the victory of the egalitarian over the aristocratic principle, with all that such a shift implies. By de Tocqueville's time, therefore, elevated political discourse was but a dim memory: "I know of no country in which there is so little independence and real freedom of discussion as in America." Lacking standards of their own derived from tradition, religion, education, or philosophy, most Americans no longer seemed to possess the wherewithal for independent thought. In consequence, they were simply overwhelmed by majority opinion, by what de Tocqueville called the "enormous pressure of the minds of all upon the reason of each." Worse, the majority now stood in judgment over the individual and was quick to inflict "obloquy and persecution" on deviant opinions. In the end, only the strongest personalities could resist the pressure to conform to the views of the multitude.

To make a long story short, what de Tocqueville observed then was the emergence in its peculiarly American form of the phenomenon that his compatriot Le Bon would later call "the crowd" in his sociological classic of that name. In crowds, said Le Bon, independent minds are submerged in a collective mind that brooks no dissent; emotions are intensified at the expense of intellect; and simple ideas, striking images, and repeated slogans drive out deeper thought. Already, in de Tocqueville's day, even before the rise of mass society, the American public had begun to decay into a democratic crowd. What we observe today is the hyperdevelopment of this phenomenon—but now exacerbated by television, because images are the mental currency of crowds and pander to all their worst characteristics. "A crowd thinks in images," said Le Bon, "and the image itself calls up a series of other images which have no logical connection with the first . . . [and so] crowds have a hard time distinguishing between reality and illusion."

Hence the American people are no longer a democratic public, but an electronic mob that reacts to events in the media arena by ricocheting from issue to issue, personality to personality, emotion to emotion without ever really understanding or reflecting upon what it is seeing. But turning democratic politics into the equivalent of a Roman circus entails very serious dangers. Historically, as pointed out by Le Bon, "crowds are only powerful for destruction," and "their rule is always tantamount to a barbarian phase." What this means in practice is that the mob, by reacting angrily against what it does not like, can prevent public actions, but it cannot provide sustained popular support for constructive measures. This is precisely the condition of the American polity today: no real sacrifices can be exacted, and no real initiatives taken, because to do so would risk rousing the mob.

In insisting on the barbarism of the crowd, Le Bon is not being merely "elitist." From ancient times, thoughtful observers have made the health of the polity, especially a democratic or republican polity, dependent on what we now call a liberal education, precisely because such an education inculcates habits of mind conducive to prudent political decisions. As Jefferson said, "If a nation expects to be ignorant and free, in a state of civilization, it expects what never was and never will be." And we saw in the last chapter that such an education is indispensable for liberal polity, because it is reason, and reason alone, that makes personal liberty possible. Moreover, and more generally, because our sensibilities are bound to be formed by what we see and hear predominantly, "an elevated degree of culture" and a good politics are also inextricably linked. Both involve the exercise of *judgment*—that is, the aesthetic task of weighing good and bad, rather than the rational task of assessing facts and logic. Reflecting on his experience as president of the Czech Republic, Václav Havel makes this explicit: "I have discovered that good taste is more useful here than a post-graduate degree in political science."

A good politics is therefore dependent on a high level of education and culture, both in the politician and in the polity as a whole. Passive consumers of commercial mass culture cannot be expected to acquire the ability to ponder issues or imagine alternatives in any sphere of life—not even in daily living, much less politics. How likely is it that a mass of individuals immersed in a media environment that turns world affairs into soap opera writ large will support thoughtful, prudent public-policy decisions, such as those needed to sustain a long-term foreign policy? In short, to destroy culture is to destroy politics: a crowd awash in kitsch and entertainment or steeped in sex and violence will lack not merely good taste but also the faculty of judgment essential to any good politics—especially a democratic politics.

This point was explicitly recognized by the Founders. Next to faction, or perhaps even ahead of it, they feared "the mob" and its destructive potential. That this fear reflected a regard for their own property and position is undeniable, but we would be in error to consider it the only, or even the major, ground of their concern. They simply understood very clearly that the political system they were establishing depended upon the existence of a genuine public—a people who were not only virtuous, reasonable, and moderate, but also willing to eschew factionalism and to accept the existence of some kind of authority, both moral and political. In addition, they had to share a common frame of reference within which to deliberate. Lacking these characteristics, a people are not a public but a mob—and no mob could be trusted with political responsibility, lest the new polity suffer the fate of Athens and Rome.

There were, of course, important differences among the Founders about the political capacity of the common man. Some, perhaps most, were frankly elitist, believing that the potential for political excellence is confined to the few. Others, such as Jefferson, although equally insistent upon the necessity of a natural aristocracy for effective rule, were more optimistic about the educability of the people: "If we think them not enlightened enough to exercise their control with a wholesome discretion, the remedy is not to take it from them, but to inform their discretion with education."

History has not been kind to the optimists. De Tocqueville was only the first among many to point out the shortcomings of the American public. And repeated studies by contemporary social scientists have shown that the so-called active and informed public (using a quite generous definition of "informed") constitute only about 3 percent of the population. The rest languish in blissful ignorance of public affairs. What this suggests is either that the people at large are not as educable as the optimists assumed or that our vast educational establishment devoted to rationalistic and technological ends is churning out barbarians rather than citizens—that is, people incapable of acting as members of a genuine public and fit only to be part of a crowd. (To repeat an earlier observation, the education that was supposed to preserve Lockean society has only hastened its destruction.) We are therefore left with the eternal question about democratic polity: Does the decline of the original American public first into a democratic crowd and now into an electronic mob demonstrate that "the people" are not fit for self-government—or does it merely indicate that genuine democracy and republican government require radically different principles from those found in self-destructive liberalism?

As a practical matter, however, both the question and the answer are moot. The electronic mob is already with us, so we cannot escape the political threat that it represents. As Lippmann expressed it, "These masses without roots, these crowds without convictions, are the spiritual proletariat of the modern age, and the eruption of their volcanic and hysterical energy is. . . . the chaos in which the new Caesars are born."

Slouching Toward Barbarism

This and all the other challenges to governance described above fall upon a polity singularly ill-equipped to meet them. Even as they struggled to overcome the defects of the Articles of Confederation, the Founders were deeply ambivalent: they wanted a more effective, unionist central government, but they also feared tyranny, so they loaded their new constitutional machine down with multiple constraints on the exercise of federal power. The result of this ambivalence was what Richard Hofstadter rightly called a "harmonious system of mutual frustration," a polity with built-in propensities toward ungovernability. Indeed, by European standards Americans hardly had a government worthy of the name—witness Macauley's belief that the Constitution was "all sail and no anchor." Even contemporary observers are often astonished by the ineffectuality of American government: "By contrast with all other great nations," says British historian J. R. Pole, "the United States appeared to live by a Constitution which made it virtually impossible for the government to govern, not in the sense of exercising arbitrary power over individuals, but in the ordinary sense of deciding what questions required prior national attention, and what means were appropriate to achieving the required objects."

Hamilton's great hope for the new republic—that it be governed by "reflection and choice" rather than by "accident and force"—thus appears in retrospect more like rhetoric than realism: policies based on reflection and choice are not the most likely outcome of a harmonious system of mutual frustration. Nevertheless, given the social conditions then prevailing, the Founders could reasonably expect that the federal system they had devised would govern adequately.

The enormous worldly success of the United States notwithstanding, this expectation has not always been fulfilled, as Pole's words suggest. And the problems have become worse over time. Many political scientists believe that the United States is now mired in an intractable "crisis of ungovernability" caused by excessive political demand on a weakened governmental structure, which can no longer resist the immoderate and growing claims on its resources. As a result, even routine functions of government, such as passing a budget, have become draining political ordeals that leave little energy or enthusiasm for anything more ambitious. But political paralysis is only a superficial manifestation of a deeper problem: the failure of the American constitutional system.

In a mere two centuries, we have created a polity that represents the worst nightmare of the Founders, even the most democratic among them. There is hardly any virtue in the people; rights are exalted and duties neglected; the polity is riven by factional struggle; the citizen is an apathetic and disillusioned political consumer; the public is an electronic mob; and politicians are therefore demagogues by force of media circumstance, if not predilection. The upshot is that we are now "governed" precisely by accident and force. How else to account for the way in which we have allowed the automobile to dictate our cultural arrangements? Or for how multiculturalism is just happening to us without any real debate, much less a formal vote, on its momentous political implications? And to the extent that political outcomes are not the result of accident, they hardly result from reflection and choice but, rather, from the power plays of officials and interest groups who force their private agenda on the public. It is a credit to the adaptability of the system and the dwindling residue of civility among the American people, who still hear the faint echo of their ancestors' "habits of the heart," that we continue to muddle through rather than lapsing into total ungovernability— but time is running out.

In fact, we are rapidly creating the objective conditions for a radically different kind of polity. A large, complex, and demoralized society riven by uncompromising factions and peopled by an electronic mob moved by slogan and emotion in response to a media circus is not going to be governed democratically for very much longer, unless by a kind of tutelary or imperial democracy. As argued in later chapters, we are in fact groping our way toward a despotic "solution" to the current crisis of governance: the end of all our muddling through seems likely to be Leviathan.

In conclusion, "liberating" men and women has a tragic outcome: the long-term effect of embracing Hobbesian principles—that is, of rejecting community and virtue as the basis of the political order—is to corrupt the mores upon which *any* social and political order is founded and thereby to degrade the people into a mere crowd. Thus the conditions for genuine freedom are destroyed, leaving a moral and political vacuum that can be filled only by Leviathan. And neither government nor civilization itself can long survive the reign of a demoralized mob, which is "always tantamount to a barbarian phase." Despite its original liberalism, Hobbesian politics therefore terminates in barbarism. MacIntyre's summary judgment is brutal but exact: we are not waiting for the barbarians; we *ourselves* are the barbarians who "have already been governing us for quite some time."

3

PREDATORY DEVELOPMENT

A bull contents himself with one meadow, and one forest is enough for a thousand elephants; but the little body of a man devours more than all other living creatures.

—Seneca

What we call progress is a mysterious marriage of creativity and plunder. Civilization has flowered when human beings have devised ingenious new ways to organize production and social life, but such organization has usually been accomplished with stolen goods. . . . Undergirding [its] extraordinary achievements in art, philosophy, literature, and statecraft [are] military power and conquest.

—Richard J. Barnet

Men and women are free to choose anything in economic societies—except to opt out. The ultimate treason is to prefer to neither produce nor consume wealth. Cultures that do not believe in economics must be developed out of existence. Roads, schools, and hospitals are the preferred weapons of destruction.

—Susan Hunt

WE TEND TO THINK OF ECONOMIC DEVELOPMENT as an almost unmitigated good. Indeed, according to the liberal creed, it is the indispensable precondition of "progress" and contains the solution to virtually all human ills: whatever its transitory difficulties or failures, it will eventually lead us to a kind of utopia in which all human wants are satisfied. This faith is common to all forms of modern political economy, whether it goes by the name of liberal or socialist. Hence economic development is the raison d'être of all modern states.

Although a heretical few have always questioned the equation of industrial might with civilized progress, primarily on spiritual or aesthetic grounds, it is only in recent times that more voices have been raised in opposition, but now primarily on environmental grounds. Both critiques miss a fundamental point: economic development and civilization are synonymous. Modern economic development is merely an intensification and amplification of a process that began when human beings abandoned the "original affluent society" of the hunter-gatherer for the radically different way of life of the cultivator, setting in motion the process that led naturally and inexorably to the civilized state. Thus the Industrial Revolution replays the original tragedy of civilization by repeating the "mistake" of the Neolithic Transition—that is, choosing to intensify production rather than to limit human numbers and wants. In this light, a genuine critique of modern political economy must begin by pointing out that not just industrial civilization, but civilization itself, is the outcome of a millennia-old process of predatory development destructive of all preexisting natural and cultural forms. To amplify Seneca's epigraph slightly, when man left the meadow and forest for the city, he had perforce to ransack the Earth to gratify his burgeoning desires, and so his "little body . . . devours more than all other living creatures." Destruction is therefore not an unfortunate by-product of "progress" but its very essence—and the greater the progress, the greater the destruction that can be expected. This is the story of modern economic development in a nutshell.

The Four Great Ills of Civilization

To pick up where we left off in the Introduction, human beings did not so much choose civilized existence as find themselves obliged to adopt it because of ecological scarcity and military conquest, threatened or consummated. So civilization in general and economic development in particular have always been associated not with diminished scarcity but, rather, with its increase (a paradox we shall explore in greater depth in Chapter 5). Moreover, civilization, militarism, and economic development arose together and can be said to be identical—merely different aspects of a single process in which the extraction of more matter and energy from nature necessarily involved political control, military "protection," and economic exploitation of rural peasants by urban lords. Barnet's judgment is exact: the basis of civilization, especially "high" civilization, is "stolen goods"—but in a far more pervasive and profound sense than he seems to imply, so let us examine briefly what gets stolen when human beings become civilized.

The anarchist philosopher Pierre Proudhon once said, "Property is theft." He might as well have said, "Civilization is theft," because all civilized existence is based on man stealing either from nature or from his fellow men, directly or indirectly. That man robbed nature to make civilized life possible was known even to the ancients. Plato, for example, noted in his *Critias* that Athens had stripped the flesh from the landscape of Attica: "What now remains compared with what then existed is like the skeleton of a sick man, all the fat and soft earth having wasted away, and only the bare framework of the land being left." Having used up most of its local resources, Athens then had little choice but to engage in trade, which in turn led directly and ineluctably to empire. Athens is thus the paradigm: once a metropolis has consumed its ecological core, it must turn to looting its periphery.

Modern scholarship has demonstrated that the rise and fall of all ancient civilizations were deeply affected, if not determined, by such ecological factors as deforestation, salinization, and desertification: the ancient Mesopotamians, Egyptians, Greeks, and Romans, as well as the Mayans of the New World and successive dynasties in India and China, were all deeply implicated in a sometimes fatal process of ecological degradation and destruction. And the destruction did not stop at home but was extended abroad through a process of imperialistic expansion and exploitation that brought Nubian gold to Egypt, the cedars of Lebanon to Carthage, the lions of Africa to Rome, and slaves from everywhere to all of ancient civilization. Rome, in particular, ruthlessly mined captured provinces for their human and ecological wealth. In brief, the early civilizations demanded more from nature than nature freely offered, so they had to pursue policies of exploitation, conquest, and enslavement.

The vast majority of humankind therefore paid for civilization in lost political freedom and socioeconomic equality, stolen from them by what Lewis Mumford called the "megamachines" of antiquity: small coteries of kings, priests, scribes, and nobles who subjected large populations to political domination and economic oppression. In fact, by looking carefully, we cannot fail to see that the great monuments of antiquity we travel halfway around the globe to admire were built not out of mortar and stone but, as Pablo Neruda said of Machu Picchu, out of blood and bone. Indeed, ancient philosophers such as Aristotle acknowledged—out of realism, not lack of humanity—that the ultimate basis of civilized life was slavery, the theft of a man or woman's very life. For it was slavery that produced the economic surplus necessary to give the citizens of the polis the modicum of wealth and leisure they had to have to participate fully and creatively in public life.

To sum up, whatever civilization's many achievements and benefits, which are incontestable, they have always been accompanied by four great ills: the careless overexploitation of nature, organized violence directed at outsiders, political or religious tyranny exerted over insiders, and gross socioeconomic inequality, if not outright slavery. The advantages of civilization were therefore purchased at a very high price, especially for those at the bottom of the social pyramid: the edifice of ancient civilization rested on a base of infamy and crime.

The Enlightenment "Solution"

This much was apparent to Enlightenment thinkers. They saw that tyranny and slavery, or inequality and exploitation tantamount to slavery, had marked all previous civilized existence, and they proposed to abolish them. However, they did not promise to cure all of the four great ills of civilization. On the contrary, they proposed to remedy only two of them, political tyranny and socioeconomic oppression, *precisely by worsening the other two*—that is, by intensifying the exploitation of nature and, at least implicitly, expanding the range and scale of conquest and colonization.

Reduced to its essence and stripped of all nuance, the economic program of the Enlightenment was quite simple: to do away with premodern tyranny and inequality through what we have come to call economic development. By turning government into an engine for facilitating capital investment, technological innovation, and the exploitation of new resources, especially in the colonies, both trade and manufacture would grow continuously. The result would be hitherto unimaginable levels of productivity and wealth. In addition, redirecting the aim of government to the promotion of Hobbes's "contentments of life" would transform its very nature: from being an oppressor, government would become a benign overseer permitting and even encouraging individuals to accumulate "property." Property would in turn establish the basis for individual civil rights, political participation, and personal happiness. By becoming sufficiently wealthy, societies could afford to mitigate, if not eliminate, the worst aspects of inequality and oppression. At the very least, any remaining disparities of wealth, status, and power could be justified as fair, because they would arise from differences of talent and character, not mere accidents of birth. This, in brief, is the vision that underlies modern political economy and justifies its core institutions—to wit, Locke's night-watchman state to guarantee "property" in all its aspects and Smith's program for the creation of "opulence" through freedom of trade and manufacture.

This recipe for progress has seemingly been a huge success. In those parts of the globe that have implemented it fully, premodern tyranny has indeed been overthrown, and a kind of opulence created. In consequence, the now-opulent urge the still-indigent to adopt liberal political economy as rapidly as possible, so that they too can be rich and free. Nevertheless, certain questions arise. First, could it be that new forms or possibilities of tyranny have emerged simultaneously with the abolition of the old? In much of what follows (especially Chapters 7 and 8) I will argue that this is in fact the case. Next, could it be that the opulence we enjoy is in some sense false or even fraudulent—and has, moreover, been acquired at an enormous personal and social cost? In the remainder of this chapter and the two that follow I will try to show that economic development has become contradictory and self-defeating (even in its own terms) as a means to human satisfaction. Finally, could it be that the dependence of modern political economy on expanded ecological and military violence is no longer tolerable? The evidence for the affirmative would appear to be compelling. In short, the Enlightenment "solution" now seems fatally flawed.

To appreciate the depth of this failure, we must go back, as always, to our philosophical roots—to Hobbes as the founder of modern political economy. The genius of Hobbesian polity is that it transforms political conflict into economic competition: instead of fighting over irreconcilable matters of principle such as religion, men and women contend in the marketplace for carnal satisfaction under the aegis of a powerful but dispassionate and supposedly benign sovereign that facilitates their pursuit of earthly happiness. However, the effect of this arrangement is simply to transfer the drive for power into the economic realm—leading to the conquest of nature, to commercial aggression against other nations and peoples (backed up by military force when necessary), and to an undeclared war on organic community (and therefore on the great mass of people within the nation) by those who control the political and economic machinery.

In other words, Hobbesian political economy intensifies and magnifies the fundamental power drive characteristic of civilization itself. Far from transcending the state of nature by adopting Hobbesian principles, modern man has institutionalized it: modern political economy causes man to war against nature, against his fellow men, and against organic community in ways that we shall spend the rest of this chapter exploring. This was not, of course, the outcome intended by the principal authors of modern political economy, for they were deeply moral thinkers. But by leaving ecological and military violence out of their account and by not understanding the fragility of the society upon which all of them relied, directly or indirectly, to foster moral restraint, they effectively gave free rein to those who would deploy the new economic and military means to seek individual and national advantage. So the Enlightenment's purported cure was but a new and more virulent form of the disease.

An Absolute Dominion over Nature

Although man has long exploited nature to support civilized existence, causing thereby all manner of ecological harm, exploitation in modern times has escalated in scale and intensity to become a virtual war against nature almost everywhere on the planet. "War" is not much of an exaggeration, for the propagandists of so-called progress openly flaunt their goal: an absolute dominion over nature by all available technological means. The influential futurist Herman Kahn, for example, foresaw—or, more accurately, extolled—a world in which man is everywhere numerous, everywhere rich, and everywhere fully in control of the forces of nature. In other words, modern civilization still rests on slavery—but now of nature rather than of man. Thanks to improved technology, we have been able to harness natural forces and thus replace draft animals and human beings with "energy slaves."

Apart from certain political and moral consequences to be discussed later, the well-known problem with all forms of slavery is that the masters tend not to value the slaves' welfare very highly, either in theory or in practice. Obliged to come up with a moral justification for an economic necessity, Aristotle argued that slaves are somehow inferior "by nature," so they could be licitly exploited in the service of the polis. This rationale for chattel slavery survived until the middle of the last century. And a similar and equally suspect rationale (to be explored in depth in Chapter 6) is used to justify the energy slavery of today: the Earth is dead matter, an assemblage of mere resources that humans can exploit with impunity.

Although civilization by its very nature involves ecological damage, the toll on natural systems resulting from modern energy slavery borders on the grotesque. Building on the discussion in the Introduction, let us compare the two poles of the development process: modern megalopolis and the traditional rice farming communities of Southeast Asia. In ecological terms, megalopolis is a voracious parasite that wastefully appropriates vast quantities of its earthly host's resources for its own use and returns nothing except toxic wastes—behavior not likely to promote long-term survival. By contrast, the rice farmers of, say, Bali live more like careful symbionts who know that their host's welfare is identical with their own; they take from nature only a perennially sustainable yield, while returning to the land what it needs to continue to yield in the future as it has for centuries in the past—for example, by scrupulously recycling soil washed down by irrigation. To understand the ecological impact of megalopolis in depth would require lengthy exposition, but one statistical comparison suggests how radically different the two ways of life are: traditional rice farmers typically get a 15–1 yield on their energy investment, although much higher yields (up to 50–1) are sometimes attained; but modern industrial farmers get a *negative* 1–10 energy return, because to grow and harvest one calorie of food energy typically requires an investment of about ten calories of fossil-fuel energy. From this it can be seen that Bali is about a hundred times more efficient ecologically than megalopolis—or, conversely, that the latter is at least two orders of magnitude more ecologically destructive. This is the hidden, but very real, cost of energy slavery.

The economic and social consequences of such radically different ecological modes of existence are equally profound. The Balinese structure their social and religious life around their connection with and obligation to the natural forces that produce their food. By contrast, megalopolis is psychologically disconnected from nature, to the point that most of its inhabitants neither know nor care where their daily bread comes from. This lack of connection causes pathological behavior. For instance, in large part because it is not grounded in ecological reality, the monetary system of megalopolis has come to be very tenuously related to or even totally decoupled from the real world that it is supposed to track. Little wonder, then, that modern economies more and more resemble casinos in which one gets rich by financial legerdemain rather than by tangible production.

But if money is all that matters, the Earth matters not at all. Megalopolitan economies therefore turn into agents of ecological destruction. Indeed, the so-called laws of economics all but compel them in this direction, so they systematically overexploit resources in ways that are economically rational but environmentally and socially damaging. For example, because a bird in the hand is worth two in the bush—an illustration of the phenomenon known to economists as "discounting the future"— the long-term ecological health of the planet has little or no market value today. It is perfectly "rational" to drive, say, whales to extinction, because the profits can then be plowed into some new scheme of exploitation, such as cutting down a primeval forest. In other words, conserving resources for a sustained yield is not as profitable as cleaning them out and investing the ill-gotten gains. Precisely to the extent that they behave "rationally," economic actors of all ideological persuasions will therefore consistently and seriously undervalue and overexploit natural resources—whether flow resources, like forests, that could be cropped on a sustained-yield basis in perpetuity, or stock resources, like petroleum, that exist in a fixed quantity.

Seemingly compelled by such logic, we in megalopolis appropriate nature as a mere resource and turn it into commodities and toxins; whereas the Balinese receive the Earth as a precious gift and with careful labor turn it into sustenance for body and soul, into the basis for a way of life widely admired for its aesthetic and spiritual depth. This is not to idealize the Balinese, whose culture, like all cultures, has its shadow side; moreover, in recent decades they too have been increasingly drawn into the world economy and thus into a closing circle of ecological self-destruction. Yet the gap between the two modes of existence is manifest: one culture tries to cooperate with nature, the other wars on it. Moreover, as we shall see in the next chapter, the corollary of ecological destruction is ceaseless consumption. We thus risk sharing the pitiable fate of Erysichthon, a mythological king of Thessaly who plundered a grove sacred to Demeter: as a punishment, the goddess cursed him with an insatiable appetite, so that after ravenously consuming all else around him, including his own family, he had finally to devour himself.

A Political Economy of National Power

An escalated war against nature provided the economic basis for the rise of the nation-state and its subsequent imperialist career. No sooner had the nation-state consolidated its domestic power—using the superior weaponry and resources that were the product, if not the very aim, of the development process—than it turned its armed might outward toward empire. What Barnet calls "the mysterious marriage between creativity and plunder" characteristic of civilization is nowhere better exemplified than by the rise of the West to political and economic hegemony over the planet during the past five centuries. Barnet's continuation to the epigraph sums up the historical record:

> The industrial revolution and modern imperialism—an organizational system for selectively integrating non-European economies into an international capitalist order by force—fed on each other. Without the energy and power so swiftly generated in the industrializing economies, the military power to subjugate whole continents would not have developed. Without the cheap and easy access to raw materials on other continents, the industrial expansion and the extraordinary enrichment of the beneficiaries of im-

perialism would not have taken place. Indeed, reaching for the resources of distant lands was indispensable for the triumph of the technology of terror that has marked the last five hundred years.

This "reaching for the resources of distant lands" was not facultative but utterly obligatory. Despite rapid improvements in the means of production, the agglomeration of large populations in the new industrial towns soon overtaxed local resources. As has been true throughout history—recall the commercial and imperial career of Athens—the industrializing nations therefore had little choice but to extend their ecological reach outward, a process epitomized by the economic historian Karl Polanyi:

> To effect this change [to an international resource base] was the true meaning of free trade. The mobilization of the produce of the land was extended from the neighboring countryside to tropical and subtropical regions—the industrial-agricultural division of labor was applied to the planet. As a result, peoples of distant zones were drawn into the vortex of change the origins of which were obscure to them.

By appropriating foreign resources, the European nations gained enormous wealth and power, becoming thereby economically "developed" and politically dominant. In effect, the wealth race and the arms race are identical, merely two sides of the same coin: economic and military power have worked together to render the industrializing nations rich and powerful, and the pre-industrial lands poor and subordinate, whether or not they were actually colonized. "Development" for the few has thus implied and engendered the complementary state known as "underdevelopment" among the many. With his usual gift for cutting through cant, George Orwell made this explicit: "We all live by robbing Asiatic coolies, and those of us who are 'enlightened' all maintain that those coolies ought to be set free; but our standard of living, and hence our 'enlightenment,' demands that the robbery shall continue."

That free trade was fundamentally imperialist in aim was made equally explicit in *The Wealth of Nations*. As the title indicates, Adam Smith's philosophy of economic development is first and foremost about national wealth; next, it is about the enrichment of the trading and manufacturing classes; lastly, if at all, it is about improving the welfare of the common people (although Smith clearly intended this end). Indeed, not only did Smith devote a chapter of his classic work to the military advantages to be derived from economic development and free trade, but he also urged the British government to expand its empire by seizing colonies from "the Falklands to the Philippines." Thus, although the spirit of free trade is significantly different from mercantilism in important respects, it represents but an improved means to the old end of national power.

Moreover, industry, trade, and war were all but synonymous until quite recently. As late as the early nineteenth century, for example, merchant ships were armed. In fact, they were often supplied with letters of marque that made them naval vessels in all but name, so the line between business and buccaneering was notoriously unclear. As William McNeill points out, there has been a characteristic "oscillation between raiding and trading" in history, and the modern European merchant class was formed when pirates, confronted by improved local defenses and growing difficulty in disposing of their booty, decided to go straight. In short, says McNeill, traders are "reformed pirates," and "the central and essential psychological and institutional forms of north European urban life were shaped in the chaotic age when piracy transmuted itself into trade." The origins of modern industry are also military: the prototype of the factory was the arsenal, specifically the famous Arsenal of Venice that mass-produced warships and armed merchantmen for that imperialist city; and the necessary coordination of work among the specialists within factories was accomplished by regimentation—that is, by officers at the top of the chain of command giving orders to the rank and file at the bottom. And, like trade, industry too is a kind of reformed piracy, as evidenced by the popular name for the great moguls of the Industrial Revolution: "robber barons." In effect, trade and industry are sublimated predation, and the distinctive feature of modern political economy is that the state is in cahoots with the predators: as we shall see below, the Industrial Revolution resulted when the state, unable to lick the reformed pirates, decided to join them instead.

In this light, it should not surprise us that the fruits of economic development have often been used mostly to aggrandize state power rather than to make populations better off. The case of Japan shows that there is no necessary connection between national wealth and popular welfare. The slogan driving Japanese modernization until its defeat in World War II was "rich country, powerful military," so the people remained poor and subservient as the nation grew rich and powerful. And the renunciation of military power in the postwar era did not in any way alter Japan's focus on *national* wealth. On the contrary, its tacit goal is trade supremacy based on technological development fueled by a high savings rate—and if the Japanese people have to live in "rabbit hutches" and suffer other serious disamenities to achieve this end, then so be it. The case of the now-defunct Soviet Union is even more compelling: in effect, Leonid Brezhnev and his ilk were simply not concerned with popular welfare—

except as this somehow redounded to the power, wealth, and glory of the state. So the U.S.S.R. was a military superpower and an imperial hegemon, but the basic necessities of life, if obtainable at all, could be procured only through finagling or endless hours of queuing. Ironically, consumers in impoverished Third World countries were significantly better off: provided they had even a little money, they could at least buy shoes.

To sum up, from the beginning of civilized existence, economic development and warfare have always been linked, but Hobbesian political economy strengthens the linkage. Intensified economic development in the service of a stronger and more centralized nation-state must lead to heightened economic and military competition—and thus to an arms race, as well as to a structure of international dominance that reflects economic and military power. Consumer goods and other economic benefits for the masses, if they accrue at all, are a by-product. But if economic development as we know it tends to engender war, then the solution to the military problems of our age will require something much more comprehensive than arms agreements—to wit, a new form of political economy not based on the Hobbesian premises that fuel a perpetual struggle for economic and military advantage.

A War Against Household and Community

If the ecological destruction and militarism of modern times are simply intensifications of phenomena that date back to the origin of civilization, the modern extirpation of household and community via economic development is without precedent. It is difficult for us to recall how recently what we now call economics was invented. Although Hobbes articulated the fundamental worldview of modern political economy in 1651 (the footing upon which Locke in 1690 and then Smith in 1776 later erected its basic institutions), David Ricardo's *Principles of Political Economy and Taxation*, first published in 1817, is generally regarded as the founding work of modern "scientific" economics. Thus this "science" is less than two hundred years old. Yet we have already almost forgotten the preceding two-thousand-year-old tradition of *household* economy supplanted by the new *political* economy. The contrast between the two modifiers tells the story in a nutshell: the household economy, whose matrix was organic community, was destroyed by a market system organized by the modern nation-state, whose domestic and international power base resides in forced economic development along capitalist lines.

To elaborate, from the time of Aristotle until the end of the eighteenth century, the word *economy* conjured up the image of a busy household:

the Greek word *oikonomia*, from which we get our *economics,* means "household management." (*Oikos*, or "household," is a root that also gives us *ecology*, the science of the earthly household.) Hence Aristotle, who was the first to treat the subject systematically, distinguished very carefully between householding and moneymaking—or production for *use* versus production for *gain*—and maintained that the latter must be a mere accessory to the former. Why? Not so much because gain was morally wrong (the position taken by later Christian thinkers) but, rather, because it was "not natural to man." That is, if men and women value the pursuit of gain in the marketplace over the autonomy and health of the household, then they will inevitably destroy the organic community of the polis, which is the *natural* basis of human existence. Furthermore, in pursuing gain outside the household, individuals become instruments or agents of others' desires and conceptions, not autonomous authors of their own lives.

Autonomy is the key word. Aristotle and other antique thinkers concluded that there was an intrinsic conflict between autonomy and affluence: one can live independently, or one can live opulently, but not both. Wealth may give one an abundance of choice in the marketplace, but such affluence is illusory, because it is dependent and conditional; real freedom comes from autonomy gained through self-sufficiency (or "autarky," which means nondependence, not social isolation). This position was championed in modern times by Rousseau and Jefferson. In his *Notes on the State of Virginia*, the latter made "those who labor in the earth . . . the chosen people of God" not because there is something intrinsically holy about agriculture, but because those who do not win their own subsistence as husbandmen are doomed to "depend for it on casualties and caprice of customers. . . . [which] begets subservience and venality, suffocates the germ of virtue, and prepares fit tools for the designs of ambition." The Jeffersonian tradition therefore follows Aristotle in urging a household economy, because autonomy is the prerequisite for genuine freedom; monetary gains derived from the manipulation of real property or paper wealth are, by comparison, a mess of pottage.

From this perspective, it naturally follows that land and labor are not commodities to be sold like potatoes but, instead, social relationships that are priceless precisely because they are the essential pillars of the household economy. Similarly, the goods obtained from exchange are important—but strictly ancillary to the household economy, never its mainstay. Indeed, for our ancestors, a market was not a vast impersonal system governed by an invisible hand but a bazaar—a literal market*place* where sellers and buyers met face to face to exchange goods as well as news, sociability, even offers of marriage. In short, before the revolution begun by Hobbes and completed by Ricardo, *oikonomia* was part and parcel of a much larger ethical and political conception of human life, not an independent sphere that determined it.

Upon this stable and enduring economic order fell the cataclysm described by Polanyi: organic community was demolished by the Industrial Revolution, "an economic earthquake which transformed within less than half a century vast masses of the inhabitants of the English countryside from settled folk into shiftless migrants." By turning land and labor, the twin bases of the household economy, into mere commodities, the market economy became "a short formula for the liquidation of every and any cultural institution in an organic society." Anything that competed with the contractual relationships demanded by the market system for the allegiance of the individual had to be destroyed: all "noncontractual organizations of kinship, neighborhood, profession, and creed were to be liquidated." In consequence, the uprooted rural masses were not simply thrown out of work, but, far worse, they lost everything that was most important to them—their connection to the land and nature, their ties to kith and kin, their attachment to custom and tradition, their rich folk culture, and, ultimately, their entire spiritual orientation.

Marx and Engels's description in *The Communist Manifesto* echoes Polanyi:

> The bourgeoisie cannot exist without constantly revolutionizing the instruments of production, and with them the relations of production, and with them all the relations of society. . . . [and so] uninterrupted disturbance of all social relations, everlasting uncertainty and agitation, distinguish the bourgeois epoch from all earlier ones.

The outcome of this overthrow of "social relations" was the infamous cash nexus—"no other bond between man and man than naked interest, than callous cash payment"—as a basis for "open, shameless, direct, naked exploitation" no longer concealed by "religious and political illusions." Human beings thus became commodities to be obtained as cheaply and carelessly as possible, a degradation epitomized by child labor.

Nevertheless, despite such conditions, "social relations" were, at least by current standards, still very much alive at the time Marx and Engels wrote. Reciprocity, responsibility, and social spirit were still strong. The bourgeois character structure described by Weber still dominated: work, save, and *then* enjoy. Peoples' expectations of material wealth and social entitlement were still limited. Men and women still looked to family, friends, work well done, and religion—that is, to their personal relations and inner life, rather than to external goods—for their primary satisfactions in life. In other words, the process of moral entropy had barely begun, and both community and virtue still flourished. By comparison with the old order, however, the transformation of life and culture wrought by the Industrial Revolution was indeed cataclysmic, and Marx and Engels correctly identified the new instruments and relations of production that were creating the cataclysm and that would eventually ensure the triumph of the cash nexus.

While Polanyi and the authors of *The Communist Manifesto* might be impeached as biased, there is in fact no real disagreement among historians of the period about the devastating impact of the Industrial Revolution. Nor does Polanyi use the word *liquidation* lightly or carelessly. He argues convincingly that the suffering and misery were the doing not so much of particular evil capitalists (although they certainly existed) but, instead, of a market system deliberately inflicted on a defenseless people in the full knowledge that it would foment an "uninterrupted disturbance in all social relations" and drive them into the toils of the cash nexus. In this light, *liquidation* seems exact: organic community was killed with malice aforethought.

In fact, what was done to the common people of England during the Industrial Revolution differed in degree, but not in kind, from the forced collectivization of peasants in the Soviet Union during the 1930s: Stalin drove millions of people off private plots and onto huge collective farms, at the cost of millions dead due to starvation or execution; in less than a decade, he destroyed an entire fabric of social relations and reduced the former "masters of the land" to mere servants of the state worse off than the serfs of yore—stripped of their religion, their traditions, their very will. Although the process of liquidation was more subtle and less brutal in the West, it was just as thorough in the long run and almost as traumatic in its immediate effects. Certainly the uprooted villagers of England did not experience what happened to them as an emancipation from the fetters of feudalism. On the contrary, they lost their traditional rights and their secure place within the old order, but without acquiring any new legal and political rights or other advantages within the new one. If they were not actually enslaved by the state, they were nevertheless ruthlessly dispossessed and left to wander the land at the mercy of market forces. In brief, the arrival of liberalism brought liquidation and wage slavery, not liberation, to the common people.

The ideological opponents of Marx and Engels, then and now, have always maintained that the fruits of development would eventually "trickle down" to the masses and lift them out of the "idiocy of rural life," so that they would one day become wealthier than the aristocrats of old. In other words, capitalism may have brought wholesale destruction—but it was, in Joseph Schumpeter's memorable phrase, "creative destruction," because in the long run the costs of development would be repaid, and the inevitable early inequities moderated, if not eliminated altogether. (In fact, Marx himself espoused a variant of this theory: the agony of industrialization would eventually be requited, because a socialist revolution would overthrow the bourgeois class and usher in the communist utopia.) Unfortunately, "trickle down" has not worked to the extent hoped for; we are still far from a mature steady state in which all are well satisfied. In fact, the process of "creative destruction" seems to be endless: the pace of change and transformation has only accelerated in recent years.

The Crucial Role of the State

Although the role of the state in effecting this transformation was less direct in Britain than in the Soviet Union, it was just as crucial. Polanyi likens the market system to a giant millstone that inexorably ground organic community into its constituent social atoms. But the mill had first to be set in motion by creating the preconditions for a market economy, the engine that moves the system. Hence the necessity for the liquidation: as long as the potential workforce remained embedded in the old fabric of social relations, the millstone would not turn and the putative laws of economics could not take effect. After all, as long as men and women still belonged to a living community, they were in no danger of starving or freezing to death; if they worked in the factories, it was only for pocket money, not essentials, and they quit as soon as they had enough. Factory owners were therefore plagued by high turnover and labor shortages—a situation paradoxically worsened by paying higher wages, because this just enabled workers to earn pocket money faster. It was thus essential to the success of the market system that the so-called laws of economics be made enforceable—in other words, that the common people be uprooted and turned into "shiftless migrants," economic men and women for whom a cash wage was a matter of life or death.

But the members of organic community naturally did their level best not to be ground down into social atoms destined for the "dark Satanic mills"; they clung tenaciously to the old ways appropriate to the household economy. In the end, they had to be forcibly separated from it by premeditated acts of state—by public policies that facilitated the liquidation of organic community. As the liquidation proceeded, the millstone started to turn, and the so-called laws of economics began to operate: like it or not, with no one else to shelter and feed them, the dispossessed villagers had to toil in the mines and factories. Thus was a two-thousand-year-old tradition overthrown by deliberate human action.

Many will find it incredible that the Industrial Revolution had to be inflicted on the people of Britain. Surely, human nature being what it is and the laws of economics being what they are, then economic development along modern lines was natural and inevitable and would not have to be imposed on anyone. Unfortunately, neither of these assumptions is correct. Although there appears to be a basic human nature that endures across all ages and cultures, our current conception of man's nature was not issued to us by the cosmos: it was inherited by us from Hobbes and his followers. And Hobbes's portrayal of natural man was anything but, for as Hannah Arendt pointed out, he depicts "man as he ought to become and ought to behave if he wanted to fit into the coming bourgeois society." The Hobbesian tradition's unflattering portrait of human nature is therefore more prescription than description.

Be this as it may, the inability of factory owners to attract a reliable workforce by paying higher wages demonstrated that the creature we call "economic man" did not exist prior to the Industrial Revolution. Indeed, Aristotle and Ricardo do not even agree on the *subject* of "economics," much less on its "laws"! These so-called laws were invented by Ricardo and his followers to make sense of, and find practical solutions to, the social disintegration and other problems created by the introduction of market economics in the first place. Like "economic man," therefore, the "science" of economics is a product of the Industrial Revolution—and modern political economy is the ideology that first called both of them into being and then justified them after the fact.

The adoption of this new ideology and its imposition on society profoundly transformed the nature of the state. Civilization depends on the expropriation of a surplus from the basic producers. In all previous ages, political authorities extracted the surplus directly—for example, by conscripting labor or requiring vassals and subjects to pay tribute, either in cash or in kind. The market system, by contrast, largely substitutes indirect economic sanctions for direct political coercion. The capitalist economic machine does the dirty work of extracting the surplus, and the state takes a cut as a reward for fulfilling its critical function under the new dispensation: the enforcement of property rights. What this means in practice was succinctly stated by Adam Smith: "Civil government, so far as it is instituted for the security of property, is in reality instituted for the defence of the rich against the poor, or of those who have some property against those who have none at all."

Naturally, the premodern state and its aristocratic elites at first resisted the new ideology, seeing it as a threat to their political prerogatives, social standing, and cultural ideals. They therefore allied themselves with the common people against the rising bourgeois and struggled against the market forces that were destroying the old way of life. Only when these elites became convinced, by the arguments of Smith and others, that national wealth and state power, along with their own perquisites, would in fact be enhanced under the new dispensation did they begin to throw their weight fully behind the capitalists and adopt the new political economy as their own. The policy of deliberately liquidating organic community followed as a matter of course.

In addition to changing its nature, the state had to become stronger—not more coercive but more powerful and, above all, more "rational" in the Weberian sense. Inflicting economic development on a recalcitrant populace was a much larger and more complex political and social task than any ever attempted by the premodern state. The Egyptian pyramids, the Roman aqueducts, and the citadel of Machu Picchu were extraordinary feats of engineering and social organization, and much political skill was required to achieve them, but the task of revolutionizing traditional society and fostering economic development was far harder. To build the institutions of the modern nation-state and market system, the instrument of government had to be made more capable, efficient, and penetrating. Hence, exactly as foreshadowed in *Leviathan*, the power of the sovereign state has grown enormously in modern times.

Moreover, by its very nature, economic development necessarily benefits some at the expense of others—making the rich richer and the poor poorer, especially during the takeoff phase. Bluntly stated, the enrichment of some absolutely requires the impoverishment of others, at least temporarily. Indeed, development as we understand it occurs only when the benefits can be segregated from the costs, for *profit is precisely the excess of benefits over costs*. To put it the other way around, if all the costs were fully and fairly counted, and all shared equally in both costs and benefits, then development would not take place (or would take place only in a radically different form). In a market system, the state and a well-placed minority receive most of the benefits of economic development, whereas the people at large suffer most of the costs. So development creates political resistance that must be overcome by a more powerful state—that is, through coercion, however legal.

In consequence, our received idea of the Industrial Revolution—that it was a "gradual and spontaneous emancipation of the economic sphere from governmental control"—is simply false. "On the contrary," continues Polanyi, "the market has been the outcome of a conscious and often violent intervention on the part of government which imposed the market organization on society for non-economic ends." In short, to use Marxist language to make a point contrary to Marx, the *state*, not the private capitalist, was the true expropriator, and increased national and state power was both the end and the means of this expropriation.

This is one powerful reason, among many others, why the Marxist solution to the problems of Hobbesian political economy has failed so badly: by appealing to the original agent of expropriation for salvation, it puts the fox in charge of the chickens. Seizure of the means of production by the state does not alter the fact of expropriation; rather, it simply replaces one class of exploiters, the monopoly capitalists and their political lackeys, with a "new class" of apparatchiks and commissars, such as the corrupt *nomenklatura* that ran the former Soviet Union. (This is not to exonerate the capitalist, only to locate him correctly within the politics of development.) In other words, if the problems of liberal political economy result from using state power to inflict economic development on a recalcitrant populace, then the solution to those problems can hardly depend on the exercise of that same power, no matter how exercised or by whom; it must instead involve a radical transformation of the modern nation-state itself, probably requiring a substantial dissolution and devolution of its power.

Development as Cultural Genocide

Much of the preceding will seem strange to Americans, who have always associated economic development with increased freedom and prosperity, not exploitation and misery. But the American perspective on economic development is exceptionally sanguine, precisely because we did not suffer most of the agonies that attended the Industrial Revolution in Europe. In the first place, the early Americans were already uprooted migrants who had come to the New World to better themselves socially and economically. Nothing astonished European observers such as de Tocqueville more than the incredible restlessness of the American—his readiness to pull up stakes at the drop of a hat and move elsewhere in search of greener pastures, perhaps several times during the course of a lifetime. Because the early American was already an "economic man" with his eye on the main chance, Lockean property rights and the individual pursuit of happiness were enshrined in our basic laws. Thus the legal framework of bourgeois political economy, achieved in Europe only after a long and bruising political struggle, was part of the American foundation. In addition, not only was there no long-established and settled society, but the land itself was unoccupied—except by the Indians, who did not "use" it to become rich, and who therefore did not count. In other words, in America, unlike Europe, a preexisting social order and physical infrastructure did not have to be dynamited to make room for the new one: the natural, social, legal, and psychological preconditions for a market economy were already in place; and Americans were already thoroughgoing Hamiltonians dedicated to self-enrichment through economic development—a characteristic that, again, struck European observers forcibly (but not always favorably). In short, Americans were spared most of the trauma of development experienced by Old World populations.

The most important and obvious exceptions to this statement were, of course, the African slaves and Native Americans who bore the brunt of development throughout the Americas. The poignant history of one Indian tribe, the Cherokee Nation, well illustrates not only the extent of this suffering but also the terrible propensity for cultural genocide that animates modern political economy. Long before the arrival of the white man, the Cherokee were settled agriculturists with well-developed social institutions. After some initial difficulty and conflict, they were able to accommodate to the white presence in ways that preserved their cultural and political integrity: the great chief Sequoyah invented a syllabary that made them literate, and the tribe adopted a republican form of government complete with elections and a written constitution. As a result, their national autonomy and special "civilized" status were recognized by both Congress and the Supreme Court. Alas, none of this could save them once gold was discovered on their territory: legality and humanity were swept aside, and in 1838 the Cherokee were forced to walk the infamous Trail of Tears, a winter death march from the Carolinas to a barren reservation in what is now Oklahoma, during which a third of the tribe perished.

Once there, those who had managed to survive the journey's terrible hardships nonetheless began to thrive in these new and unfamiliar surroundings. Unfortunately, their manner of thriving was not pleasing to the white man: they continued to hold their land in common, to preserve their ancient customs, and to maintain their tribal cohesion and identity. Such perversity could not go unpunished.

After visiting them as head of a congressional commission investigating Indian land tenure, Senator Henry L. Dawes pronounced this sentence upon the Cherokee: "They have got as far as they can go, because they own their land in common. . . . There is no selfishness, which is at the bottom of civilization." They must therefore be "civilized" by force: the community that had sustained them through bitter injustice and appalling adversity would have to be liquidated by destroying its institutional basis—that is, by legally proscribing communal land tenure.

Upon returning to Washington, the senator did just that, sponsoring the bill that in 1887 became the Dawes Act. This law extinguished tribal title to the land and assigned it to individual Indians. Although ostensibly designed to benefit the red man (according to the white man's lights), the true purpose of the law can be discerned in Dawes's words: it was intended to destroy the Cherokee and other tribal societies by forcing them to play by Hobbesian rules, whether they wanted to or not.

Of all the acts of cruelty and injustice visited upon Native Americans, none more than this one seems quite so gratuitous and mean-spirited or so clearly illuminates the totalitarian impulse at the heart of the economic development process. The mere existence of a group of human beings who would not obey the "laws" of human nature and economics ordained by the white man was an affront—an affront that could not be tolerated, because selfishness is "at the bottom of civilization."

The Fate of the American Farmer

Naturally, the white man could not escape the costs of economic development entirely. As we saw earlier, moral entropy and community breakdown have been prominent features of the American experience, especially in the postwar era. But certain groups have suffered disproportionately—for example, family farmers, who lost both their livelihood and their distinctive way of life.

Although early America was a Jeffersonian paradise for the small farmer, by the middle of the twentieth century it had become more like a Hamiltonian hell—and this despite a concerted effort by successive administrations to save family farming from extinction. The fundamental problem of the farmer (or any primary producer) is that he sells cheap and buys dear: he is paid pennies at the grain elevator for what eventually becomes a dollar's worth of bread once the cost of storage, transport, processing, and so forth, is included in the price; conversely, fertilizer that goes for pennies at the factory gate costs him a dollar at the general store. Lacking market power and battened on by a host of necessary but parasitical middlemen, the farmer thus receives relatively little recompense for his risks and labors. To use the language of economics, his "terms of trade" are poor in good times and catastrophic in bad. In addition, farmers as a class cannot improve their income in a market economy by becoming more productive, because the greater the production the lower the price. They must therefore run ever harder just to stay in the same place, and the least productive are slowly but inexorably driven off the land. Thanks to these two interlocking vicious circles, the less the farmer produces for his own subsistence, and the more he produces for the market, the worse off he is in the long run. In the face of this brute fact, government farm programs have only slowed the attrition and drawn out the agony, while creating a bureaucratic monster that centrally plans American agriculture.

Ironically, this bloated, labyrinthine, and expensive attempt to save the small farmer closely resembles the effort by concerned British statesmen to prevent the pauperization of the English villager during the early stages of the Industrial Revolution—and has about as much chance of succeeding, given our basic commitment to the market. In fact, irony piled upon irony, subsidies and price supports have mostly benefited not the small farmer but, instead, a handful of big or corporate farmers—that is, those engaged in agribusiness, which consists largely in harvesting government largesse.

One need not be a complete cynic to suspect that this may have been the whole point of the exercise: to use the pork barrel to ensure the triumph and profitability of corporate agriculture, while pretending to foster family farming. Be this as it may, with the virtual disappearance of the small-hold farmer and of the rural communities he once supported, American agriculture has changed from a way of life that supported hard-working and self-reliant families, while still making an important economic contribution, to a purely market-driven (and government-dependent) business run on industrial lines primarily by and for a few rich individuals and corporations. The family farmer is therefore an endangered species: those whom Jefferson considered to be the backbone of American democracy have had their land and livelihood swallowed up by the market system.

Paradoxically, the only small-hold farmers who have managed to thrive in the age of agribusiness are the traditionalists (mostly members of religious sects) who have resolutely refused to adopt the high-energy, high-debt style of "scientific" agriculture touted by agronomists and government agents. They have instead stood by the "old-fashioned" mixed-farming methods and produced for their own subsistence, not for the market. This incongruous fact is extremely revealing: if most of those who listened to the agricultural "experts" have had to sell out and move to the cities as members of the urban proletariat, whereas those who resisted modernization and put their social values first have survived and even thrived, what does this say about so-called modern agriculture? That it is a recipe for self-destruction. Draft horses are not necessarily more righteous than tractors—or even economically superior, although in the solar energy economy of the future this may be true once again—but allowing the market to dictate basic social decisions is folly, because it eventually destroys farming as a way of life, no matter how much it improves the individual farmer's "standard of living" in the interim.

The history of farming in America is therefore a paradigm of the development process and reveals its true nature. As Polanyi said, it is a millstone for grinding human communities down into social atoms. And avoiding this fate is well-nigh impossible (which is why even the Japanese and the Europeans, who have tried very hard to shield their smallhold farmers from market forces, have had only limited success). The Amish farmer with his seemingly ridiculous horse and buggy suggests just how heroic a commitment to one's "old-fashioned" values may be necessary to resist the siren call of development in a society hellbent on modernization, no matter how "free" it is in theory.

Indeed, the seductive promise held out by modern political economy—greater "affluence" with less toil—has proven to be both irresistible and addictive. But even if this were not true, modern economic development is a package deal: although there may be no strict institutional compulsion to buy the whole package, it is not ordinarily possible to get the few things one really wants from a market economy without becoming thoroughly entangled, with the Amish and other traditionalists being the exceptions that prove the rule. For example, because farming with horses is harder than with tractors, most farmers were happy to make the switch; but going into debt to buy machinery makes a larger cash income indispensable for paying back the loan, buying parts and fuel, and so on. Thus, to the extent that they adopted the new methods and produced for the market, small farmers were drawn slowly into its vortex: they had to maximize gain, even if this gradually compromised their autonomy and social relationships, as well as the long-term welfare of their soil. In the end, farming as a way of life and the market system are simply not compatible.

The story of the small American farmer is that of modern man in a nutshell. Economic development means the end of the rich multiplex social structure of traditional society in which motives and ties of kinship, sociability, power, worship, and gain were all intermingled. In the market system, relationships are singular—for love or money, but not both, and increasingly for money rather than love (especially now that women too have been drawn into the market). If the "laws" of economics are permitted to rule, not just family farming but all social institutions and independent ways of life that cannot survive without "love" are bound for extinction.

This outcome would not have surprised Rousseau or Jefferson, both of whom argued strongly against economic development on the ground that commercial growth and technological progress would eventually lead to moral regress and political slavery. And modern thinkers not opposed to development in principle have also worried about its moral costs and political consequences—not only Marx but Durkheim, J. S. Mill, Nietzsche, Adam Smith, de Tocqueville, and Weber, among many others. And with ample justification. "The capitalist system['s] . . . very success," said Schumpeter, "undermines the social institutions which protect it, and 'inevitably' creates conditions in which it will not be able to live."

The worst of these conditions is a state of moral decay and social anomie that is politically dangerous. Modern totalitarianism, says Polanyi, is a violent attempt to restore organic community at the expense of freedom: "To comprehend German fascism, we must revert to Ricardian England," where the decision to liquidate organic community was first taken. Leaving this issue for later, let us begin to explore the fateful political consequences of economic development by seeing how it necessarily concentrates power, just as its critics feared.

Government Incorporated

As the story of American farming shows, the enrichment and empowerment of large private corporations and public bureaucracies follow naturally upon the destruction of small independent producers in a market economy and lead eventually to the emergence of a power complex uniting the private and public sectors. (State capitalism merely starts where private capitalism ends up.) As this is by and large a familiar story, we need only sketch the broad outlines of how economic wealth and power in America became concentrated at the expense of the common people.

Although it took the "conscious and often violent intervention" of the government to make economic development possible in Europe, the American government faced a much easier task, because Americans were, for the most part, ideologically committed to property rights and economic growth. Once basic laws and institutions favorable to economic activity were in place, the government had only to foster the physical infrastructure needed by commerce and industry and to supply public resources to individuals and entrepreneurs at little or no cost—in the form of concessions, leases, licenses, rights, homesteads, and the like. In this benign climate, small enterprise flourished.

Eventually, however, as competition became more stringent and the business cycle more painful, those who were stronger and better off tended to become even more so, just as farmers got bigger and better capitalized or went out of business. In this fashion, small enterprises gradually gave way to larger ones—and eventually to trusts and cartels, as only the largest and strongest economic entities could withstand market forces.

But money is the mother's milk of politics, and big enterprises have more of it than small ones. Hence the political power of successful corporations grew and grew. Naturally, this power was used to further entrench their economic position: why subject your enterprise to the vicissitudes of the market at all, when political influence and government programs will virtually guarantee profits year in and year out, almost without regard to competition and the business cycle? And the politicians were largely more than willing to cooperate. After all, the primary purpose of politics is to foster "prosperity" at all costs, since this is what "the people" want. Hence politicians have little choice but to make common cause with the corporate engines that generate it.

The upshot is that politicians and corporate managers are partners, however uneasy, in a joint enterprise—so much so that the government now routinely bails out any major player in danger of sinking. Although big government has indeed tried to restrain the worst manifestations of corporate greed and to maintain minimal standards of fairness, as well as to make prosperity as general as possible, its good intentions have been subverted at every turn by its tacit partnership with big business. It is therefore hardly surprising that government measures ostensibly designed to benefit the common people would, like farm programs, turn into welfare for the rich—or, at the very least, for the professional and managerial classes. Little wonder, too, that regulators have become the creatures of the regulated, as several generations of political scientists and social critics have complained to no avail whatsoever. The line separating business and government has thus become increasingly hazy: more than a partnership, it is now a condominium.

The global responsibilities assumed by the United States after World War II have made this condominium even more necessary and complete. Government is beholden to business not just for "prosperity" but for "national security," because military might in our age depends critically on the ingenuity and productivity of one's arsenal—on the "defense industry" or "military-industrial complex."

So it is an unequal alliance: big government cannot accomplish its aims without subsidizing big business, but subsidy does not mean control. On the contrary, even scholars basically friendly to the market paradigm of political economy, such as Robert Dahl and Charles Lindblom, see corporations as political rogues. The corporation, says Dahl, is a legal monstrosity born of an unwarranted extension of Lockean *private* property rights to *corporate* entities; this "extraordinary ideological sleight of hand" gave corporations so many political, legal, economic, and social advantages that they could no longer be effectively controlled by government. In fact, quite the reverse: public policy in key areas—resource allocation and depletion, technological innovation, the location of enterprise, work organization, products and prices, and so on—is made by nonelected corporate executives, while elected officials and public servants merely react as best they can. Hence the large "private" corporations outflank and outmaneuver the government at every turn, forcing the latter to do their bidding. In effect, says Lindblom, the corporations have become the contemporary equivalent of an entrenched social class—like the landed gentry of old, but with vastly more power, particularly the amplified power of the media as an instrument of ideological control. Moreover, the ruling values of the corporation—hierarchy, status, power, control, and discipline—are intrinsically antidemocratic. In the end, concludes Lindblom, the large private corporation is at almost complete odds with democratic theory and practice.

The free market is therefore an ideological fiction. Not only did the market system have to be created by the government in the first place, but it can continue to operate only with continuous government intervention and support thereafter. However, because of the disproportionate power of corporations, the economic tail wags the political dog. The upshot is the worst of both worlds: a top-heavy and heavy-handed state bureaucracy layered over a distorted and sometimes corrupt market economy. This "system" is operated by and for a class of financiers, managers, professionals, and technicians claiming power on the basis of their superior talent for making the system work. To use the epithets of various social critics, our lives are subject to the "radical monopoly" of a "technostructure" in the service of a "megatechnical" corporate state beholden to a "military-industrial complex." This is the reality of "government" in our day.

In the United States, this arrangement is shot through with hypocrisy, denial, bad faith, and multiple conflicts of interest: it is so contrary to our myth of yeoman democracy that we cannot openly acknowledge the truth to ourselves, much less behave rationally or consistently in accordance with it. (By contrast, thanks to Japan's Confucian tradition of centralized rule by elders, that country has no need to conceal the nature and extent of corporate-state condominium—it is manifestly "Japan, Inc.," which contributes mightily to its success.) But the truth is that, to a much greater extent than we would like to admit, the United States has become an undemocratic corporate state—an "America, Inc.," however disguised, conflicted, and inefficient.

This outcome was foreordained. As we have seen, the effect of adopting Hobbesian principles in politics is to create the conditions that make a political Leviathan necessary. Similarly with Hobbesian political economy: not only are all economic decisions—taxes, subsidies, transfer payments, interest rates, and so on—really political decisions in disguise, but to the extent that social atomization and economic competition destroy community and tend to create a state of nature in which individuals must ceaselessly pursue economic power lest they go under, the dynamic that calls for an increasingly powerful sovereign necessarily operates. The government must amass more and more power to prevent this struggle from exploding into a domestic war of all against all. And it must also preserve its wealth and power in a highly competitive and dangerous international arena. Economic development is therefore both pretext and cause for the emergence of a corporate-military Leviathan. In short, all other things being equal, modern economic development necessarily tends toward the attainment of absolute political power wielded by a small class of financiers, managers, professionals, and technicians who circulate between the public and private sectors and who make all the really important decisions.

With his usual prescience, de Tocqueville foresaw the danger. Warning that a "manufacturing aristocracy" could be "one of the harshest which ever existed in the world," he urged extreme vigilance, "for if ever a permanent inequality of conditions and aristocracy again penetrate into the world, it may be predicted that this is the gate by which they will enter." The foregoing analysis suggests that such a "manufacturing aristocracy" is an all but accomplished fact. In consequence, and in ways to be discussed in more detail later, we do indeed seem to be heading toward a new and more insidious kind of tyranny, potentially harsher than any "which ever existed in the world."

A Necessary Leviathan

To summarize, liberal political economy was predicated on an intensified invasion of biological capital—that is, on the systematic enslavement of nature—with grave long-term consequences we are just now beginning to acknowledge. It also fostered (or even required) the aggressive growth of military and imperial power, with equally grave implications for long-term human well-being and even survival. Worse yet, in the name of "progress," it deliberately and ruthlessly destroyed traditional ways of life by imposing economic development and the market system—sometimes legally, sometimes by main force. These in turn have produced major concentrations of economic wealth and political power—both within individual nations and, especially, within the international community of nations. From this perspective, the Enlightenment "solution" is a sham. It has intensified two of the classic ills of civilization, ecological destruction and military aggression, while adding a new ill perhaps more grievous than the rest: the grinding down of stable organic communities into incoherent crowds of social atoms, with long-term political consequences that, as we will see, appear to be just as grave as the destruction of the natural community of the biosphere.

Well, but surely all this was worth it? Economic development may have entailed terrible costs. It may have engendered political-economic Leviathans bristling with weapons of mass destruction. But nothing can be achieved without paying a price. And have we not in exchange found the answer to two of civilization's worst ills: old-style tyranny and socio-economic inequality? If not today, then certainly tomorrow or the day after? Or if not everywhere, then in at least a few favored countries? Leaving the issue of tyranny until later, let us in the next two chapters examine whether liberal political economy has really succeeded precisely where it claims to have done so: creating "affluence" and "abundance" in the supposedly advanced countries. Or is this a spurious success, a mere appearance that cannot withstand a closer scrutiny?

4

FALLACIOUS AFFLUENCE

It has often happened in history that a lofty idea has degenerated into crude materialism.

—*Boris Pasternak*

When goods increase, they are increased that eat them.

—*Ecclesiastes*

Men do not desire to be rich, but to be richer than other men.

—*John Stuart Mill*

Poverty is not the absence of goods, but rather the overabundance of desire.

—*Plato*

He who seeks equality should go to a cemetery.

—*Yiddish proverb*

THE ENLIGHTENMENT STRATEGY OF SEEKING TO CURE the ills of civilization by abolishing scarcity has consequences—ecological, military, social, political—that might cause a reasonable being to question its wisdom and efficacy. But the strategy has a still more damning defect: it does not work even in its own terms. The "affluence" created by mass prosperity does not in fact foster human happiness: it does not satisfy, it frustrates and addicts; it does not promote greater equality and social peace, it fuels the competition for wealth and status. Indeed, affluence does not even abolish scarcity, it paradoxically intensifies it. Reserving discussion of this latter point for the next chapter, let us explore the frustrating, addictive, and generally contradictory nature of affluence to show how the originally lofty idea of liberating humanity from penury has now degenerated into a crude materialism that enslaves rather than liberates.

The False Gospel of Growth

Although inspired by loftier ideals than crude materialism, the intellectual founders of the modern way of life all preached the gospel of salvation by economic growth, a gospel tirelessly repeated in cruder form by their latter-day epigones. Increase production to the point of abolishing natural scarcity, and you will solve the social problem: in a utopia of abundance, men and women will at last dare to be good and consent to be equal. The very pith and marrow of this gospel found classic expression in an essay by the most famous economist of our century, John Maynard Keynes. In "Economic Possibilities for Our Grandchildren," published in 1930, Lord Keynes says:

> Now it is true that the needs of human beings may seem to be insatiable. But they fall into two classes—those needs which are absolute in the sense that we feel them whatever the situation of our fellow human beings may be, and those which are relative in the sense that we feel them only if their satisfaction lifts us above, makes us feel superior to, our fellows. Needs of the second class . . . may indeed be insatiable; for the higher the general level, the higher still are they. But this is not so true of the absolute needs—a point may soon be reached . . . when these needs are satisfied in the sense that we prefer to devote our further energies to non-economic purposes.

Keynes then goes on to draw the conclusion that "assuming no important wars and no important increase in population, the *economic problem* may be solved, or at least within sight of solution, within a hundred years."

He therefore looks forward with relief to a future time when the human task will be to learn how "to live wisely and agreeably and well" on the social dividend of economic development. The necessity for capital accumulation has obliged us to adopt values and practices that are morally obnoxious, leading us to exalt "some of the most distasteful of human qualities into the position of the highest virtues." But once the economic problem is solved, and we are all rich, "we shall be able to afford to dare to assess the money-motive at its true value. The love of money . . . will be recognized for what it is, a somewhat disgusting morbidity, one of those semi-criminal, semi-pathological propensities which one hands over with a shudder to the specialists in mental disease."

Using biblical language—like many of the great economists, Keynes is a moralist at heart—he goes on to envision a utopian future:

I see us free, therefore, to return to some of the most sure and certain principles of religion and traditional virtue. . . . We shall once more . . . honour those who can teach us how to pluck the hour and the day virtuously and well, the delightful people who are capable of taking direct enjoyment of things, the lilies of the field who toil not, neither do they spin.

But he immediately qualifies his utopian vision by reiterating that it cannot come about unless we can control populations and avoid wars. We must also continue to give free rein to science and technology and to restrict consumption in favor of capital accumulation. And he warns against trying to grasp utopia prematurely:

But beware! The time for all this is not yet. For at least another hundred years or so we must pretend to ourselves and to everyone that fair is foul and foul is fair; for foul is useful and fair is not. Avarice and usury and precaution must be our gods for a little longer still. For only they can lead us out of the tunnel of economic necessity into daylight.

Alas, the genius of Lord Keynes notwithstanding, this is a false gospel in virtually every particular. In the first place, his key provisos are fantastic: populations have grown rapidly, and war has by no means been abolished; besides, arms races are nearly as expensive as wars. Moreover, the ecological and social impacts of technology are such that giving it a free rein is no longer possible. Although one might possibly forgive Keynes, writing in 1930, for not foreseeing World War II and the Cold War or the ecological problems of our day, his assumption that population growth would not threaten his rosy scenario is less understandable: as the epigraph from Ecclesiastes testifies, Malthus was by no means the first to suggest that more goods have always meant more mouths to eat them, leaving us no better off than before.

Second, current consumption cannot be restricted during the long march to utopia to the extent required by Keynes's vision. In the short run, as we have seen, achieving economic takeoff involves some degree of political repression. However, unless the repression is perpetual—so that, as Keynes himself warned, it is always "jam to-morrow and never jam to-day"—then regimes must at some point begin to satisfy rising consumer demand. (Witness the now-defunct Soviet Union: all guns and no butter is not a policy that can be sustained indefinitely, because eventually the people only pretend to work.) In the long run, therefore, the hedonistic values of "jam to-day" tend to prevail over the sacrificial values of "jam to-morrow," as production is increasingly devoted to current consumption instead of capital accumulation. (In fact, growth in popular consumption was precisely what saved capitalism from proletarian revolution.) In short, Keynes's millennium has been indefinitely postponed not only by more mouths but by more mouths demanding more goods.

Third, Keynes himself acknowledges that the desire for economic superiority may indeed be insatiable. Thus, over and above what will be needed to furnish more mouths with more goods, ever-increasing production will also be required to fuel a goods race based on conspicuous consumption and competitive display.

Fourth, Keynes's proposed solution is based on a false understanding of human physiology and psychology: to get more and more of what one "wants" is not necessarily advantageous in the long run, any more than rich food and drink constitute a healthy diet. Increased consumption may therefore lead toward debilitation rather than repletion. Or, as in the case of ancient Rome, toward debauchery, as individuals seek to gratify jaded appetites with increasingly outrageous pleasures.

Moreover, fifth, even if the increased consumption is not personally injurious, the overall social result may be harmful, as when higher private consumption causes environmental damage or other public harm. Yet Keynes virtually ignores the *costs* attached to production and consumption; he also seems not to understand that the gigantic quantitative changes he envisions would entail radical qualitative changes in society and polity at odds with his image of the future.

Sixth, Keynes is mistaken in thinking that there is some absolute threshold above which the economic urge is extinguished in favor of higher motives. In fact, he undercuts his own argument by admitting that "there will still be many people with intense, unsatisfied purposiveness who will blindly pursue wealth." He further concedes that the wealthy of his time, whom he called the "advanced guard" of his economic millennium, had for the most part "failed disastrously" to use their wealth and leisure "to live wisely and agreeably and well."

The Keynsian gospel of salvation by economic growth is therefore fallacious: universal affluence will neither solve the "economic problem" nor remedy the defects of human nature. To speak more generally, the assumption of the tradition of political economy in which Keynes was nurtured—that capitalism tends toward a state of maturity in which most of its worst ills will be alleviated—is mistaken. By its very nature, predatory development has no appointed end, no natural stopping place. Nor is the process of accumulation self-limiting. How could it be? Even if it were desirable to make everyone rich in worldly goods, as Keynes's utopian vision assumes, there seems to be no level of production that would succeed in doing so. And even if we were to succeed, universal riches would not in fact produce the outcome he desired. But let us probe more deeply into the flaws in Keynes's reasoning to see why mere affluence can neither satisfy the needs of individuals nor cure the ills of society. We have already given sufficient attention to the first point above in previous chapters, but the latter five, as well as other important issues not explicitly addressed by Keynes, deserve more extensive treatment.

Insatiability, Inflation, Frustration

Leaving aside for the moment the issue of "relative needs"—"those which satisfy the desire for superiority"—let us ask whether Keynes's "absolute needs" can actually be satiated. The answer is clearly no. The belief that there is some absolute level of economic well-being that, once attained, would bring genuine satisfaction, and thus a surcease of striving, does not reckon with the force of human desire—a force that Hobbes unleashed, but did not create. Modern psychological research has confirmed the Buddha's fundamental insight: craving is intrinsic to the human mind, so no sooner is one want satisfied than it is replaced by a new one. In fact, Keynes is somewhat exceptional within the economic tradition in asserting the possibility of human satiation. Economists ancient and modern have generally followed Aristotle in believing that "the avarice of mankind is insatiable." Lester Thurow, for instance, says flatly, "Man is an acquisitive animal whose wants cannot be satiated." And most political theorists have also followed Aristotle in believing that avarice is one of those deeply rooted human passions that must be checked by ethical codes and social norms—that is, by politics.

However, let us turn from human nature in general to the particular nature of modern men and women—to those who believe that they can consume their way to happiness. Unfortunately for them, insatiability is implicit in the very idea of "consumption." According to the dictionary, to "consume" means not only to "eat or drink up" but also to "expend," "waste," "squander," and "destroy." The satisfaction derived from consumption is therefore impermanent: a fleeting enjoyment of things that are soon used up or of pleasures that soon pall. The psychological essence of a way of life based on consumption was exquisitely captured in 1892 by Simon Patten, an early prophet of affluence: "The standard of life is determined, not so much by what a man has to enjoy, as by the rapidity with which he tires of the pleasure. To have a high standard means to enjoy a pleasure intensely and to tire of it quickly."

In other words, consumption is less about achieving satisfaction than escaping *dissatisfaction*: since ennui follows pleasure as night follows day, one has to reach for new pleasures as fast as possible. Having the wherewithal to do so continuously constitutes "a high standard of life." Consumption is a classic vicious circle: satisfaction is no sooner attained than it turns into dissatisfaction, which leads to grasping after more satisfaction, and so on, ad infinitum. Those who live as consumers are therefore insatiable.

Even without appealing to such a psychology, however, virtually no one in modern society ever has enough in the way of worldly goods to feel truly secure. One may have enough for today, but what about the future—especially when the price of desired goods, such as a suburban house or a college education or state-of-the-art medical care, is rising so rapidly? And what about the possibility of economic downturn or corporate downsizing? Besides, in a Hobbesian political economy, money is power, and who can ever have enough power? So one can never cease from acquisition. In brief, only prodigious and effortless abundance, truly utopian abundance, could alleviate the perceived insecurity of modern life enough to quench the acquisitive urge.

In addition, the decay of traditional religion has resulted in the transfer of aspirations for happiness and fulfillment from the next world to this one. The dangerous consequence is described by Irving Kristol: "Liberal civilization finds itself having spiritually expropriated the masses of its citizenry, whose demands for material compensation gradually become as infinite as the infinity they have lost." The citizen-consumer is therefore doomed to a double frustration: he can never engross enough goods to compensate for the loss of infinity; and the goods he does succeed in acquiring do not bring real spiritual happiness. (Spiritual expropriation also has other far-reaching psychological and political effects, as we will see in later chapters.)

But even if consumers were not vainly seeking spiritual satisfaction from worldly goods, the level of goods and services needed to feel merely well off just in material terms rises inexorably along with the general level of development. In fact, we do not really have a *standard* of living at all, because the luxuries of the previous generation are the necessities of this one, so we are always trying to hit an ever-receding target. A private automobile, for example, is now all but essential in most areas of the United States, because both our physical infrastructure and our economy are so completely predicated on the car that alternatives scarcely exist. And who would dare to suggest that a television set is not now an essential? (Speaking of television, advertising constantly urges its audience to aspire to ever higher levels of consumption, cleverly exploiting the spiritual hunger mentioned above as well as the longing for superiority and other factors to be discussed below.) The desire or even need for services also escalates constantly: modern medical care has become so expensive that medical insurance of some kind is indispensable; nor is a high school degree sufficient for more than menial employment, so college is now what high school used to be; and so forth. Moreover, for many interlocking reasons—the most prominent being advertising, media hype, political campaigns, and the feminist movement—the belief that one can and should "have it all" (and *now* rather than later) has become deeply rooted in the popular psyche in recent years. In short, increased output produces an escalation of demands: by its very nature, the development process causes perceived needs to rise along with, if not faster than, economic growth, making consumers perennially dissatisfied no matter how much they already have.

Another reason why more goods and services do not necessarily result in greater satisfaction is that development is always accompanied by disamenities that detract from or spoil the pleasures of consumption. As John Kenneth Galbraith pointed out long ago, the price of private affluence is public squalor. To use an ecological metaphor, as individuals strive to maximize their personal gain they cause a "tragedy of the commons"—a degradation of their milieu for which they have to pay, now or in the future. For example, those who drive must suffer not only the petty annoyances of traffic, tolls, parking problems, theft, high insurance rates, and so on, but they must also assume the risk of death or serious injury; in addition, they have to share in the social, economic, and ecological costs attached to automobile use. Indeed, an increasing proportion of private consumption is actually defensive spending necessary to alleviate or escape public squalor. Thus the satisfaction derived from increased consumption is never unalloyed, but is always vitiated or frustrated to some degree by the nuisances and costs attached to development.

This is why the usual statistical measures of well-being are fallacious: they do not account for the disamenities, much less for the long-term social effects of economic development. In this light, making the gross domestic product the measure of progress is exceptionally foolish. Hiring more police and prison guards to cope—ineffectively—with worse crime increases GDP, but this is hardly a sign of progress. Similarly, when individuals spend more on insurance and security or pay heavier taxes, their lives are not thereby improved but merely defended against the threat of something worse.

Moreover, the modern way of life must end in a generalized frustration, if only because its aspirations are so extraordinarily high. Witness Keynes's utopian vision: he aims to *solve* the economic problem once and for all. And the social perfection that is one of the goals of the Enlightenment is unattainable by even the richest nation. For example, the official aim of the World Health Organization is obviously to promote "health." But this is extravagantly defined in its constitution as "a state of complete physical, mental, and social well-being and not merely the absence of disease or infirmity." Not only have societies found it impossible—for obvious reasons!—to achieve the hopelessly inflated goal of total well-being, but they have not the slightest prospect of eliminating all disease and infirmity. In fact, they cannot even cure all *treatable* disease and infirmity, because although modern medicine is capable of quasi-miraculous feats, the cost of providing the very best of medical care to everyone would bankrupt any conceivable scheme for financing it. In general, then, consumer demand has outrun the capacity of societies, no matter how wealthy, to supply the goods. And the gap between aspiration and actuality cannot close, both because economic interests deliberately stir up wants and because politicians compete with one another in promising to fulfill the inflated desires of the masses. Hence popular expectations of fulfillment have been bid up beyond all possibility of satisfaction, creating frustration with a system that seems consistently to promise more than it delivers.

To speak of inflation is to penetrate the ultimate irony of a way of life based on the growth of consumption. As pointed out by historian John Lukacs,

> The principal characteristic of the modern age is inflation: inflation of money, of wealth, of production, of people, of society, of minds, of words, of communications. When there is more and more of everything, when things change hands more and more rapidly, they are worth less and less. It is as simple as that.

Paradoxically, then, surfeit is the enemy of satisfaction: even if it does not take more money to buy the same amount of goods, it now takes a much larger quantity of goods to obtain the same level of satisfaction. The statistics may say we are vastly better off, but this is to some degree a macroeconomic illusion that does not square with microeconomic reality—because the more consumers get, the less value it has, so they wind up chasing a will-o'-the-wisp. In effect, we have priced satisfaction out of the market.

More subtle kinds of frustration abound in advanced mass-consumption economies. Rising affluence and technical innovation radically transform the nature of the available goods and services. Automatic dishwashers and electric toasters are cheap and abundant; maids and cooks are not. Air travel to Kathmandu is a bargain (provided one consents to being treated like livestock), but regular passenger service by ocean liner across the Atlantic is no longer available. In similar fashion, many of the most basic goods and services have been industrially transformed, usually for the worse. Our produce has to be tough enough to survive machine picking; new houses are shoddily built of cheap and often toxic materials; the family doctor not only no longer makes house calls, but he has been replaced by a large, impersonal, and mercenary clinic; and so on. Thus the quality of many goods and services has declined—sometimes resulting in lower prices, but usually not. And there is little real choice: in a market society driven by technological innovation and competitive pressure, one takes what the system offers, not what one might like to have.

This used to be a problem mainly for the privileged few who found that they could not afford to duplicate the same level of "gracious living" enjoyed by their parents—and, even more so, by their grandparents—because the cost of gracious living has increased faster than real incomes. As more and more people become affluent and able to afford the so-called finer things in life, they bid up the marginal price of luxuries— meals in good restaurants, opera tickets, summer cottages, live-in help, private education, and custom-designed houses, to mention some of the most obvious. Conversely, when certain experiences are enjoyed by too many people, their worth declines, not just in terms of status but in actuality. For example, as more and more people attend university, the degree no longer means what it once did—and is valued accordingly. That is, when "everybody" has one, the degree declines not only in relative value but also in absolute value, both because the supply has increased relative to demand and because university education has to be watered down to make it accessible to "everybody." Similarly, mass tourism has degraded the experience of going on safari in Kenya or viewing Buddhist temples in Kyoto or seeing the artistic treasures of Florence. In consequence, the well off are not as affluent as they once were: the standard of living of the richest doctor or professor of today is in many respects not as high at that of the average doctor or professor of yesteryear—just in material terms, not to mention prestige and other intangibles—because his income buys less of these finer things. Those with pleasant memories of a bygone age of privilege are therefore likely to feel impoverished by comparison, no matter how high their income or how many technological toys they possess.

But why should we lament the fate of the privileged? After all, as Schumpeter noted, "the capitalist achievement does not typically consist in providing more silk stockings for queens but in bringing them within the reach of factory girls in return for steadily decreasing amounts of effort." In other words, the relative impoverishment of the few was a necessary and desirable trade-off for the increased purchasing power of the many. But the matter is not so simple, because the devaluation of things and experiences caused by inflation affects all within highly developed societies, not just the privileged—as many a recent university graduate can attest. Moreover, the trend toward increased purchasing power for the many has been checked or even reversed in recent decades. Indeed, the second part of the inflation paradox is that eventually all things, not just the finer things of life, become relatively more expensive at later stages in the development process (for reasons that will be explored in depth in the next chapter). Most consumers today therefore find themselves struggling to equal their parents' standard of living.

The higher expectations of the current generation, which cause its members to demand as a matter of right more and better goods than those enjoyed by their parents, are only part of the problem. The facts are clear: the cost of a middle-class lifestyle has risen steeply. Three statistical comparisons tell the tale: in 1990, median income in constant dollars was only $64 more than in 1980, but the median price of a house was up $16,170; the average price of a new car more than doubled in the same period; and college tuition also increased substantially—according to the American Council of Education, it was up 47 percent at private institutions and 60 percent at public. (As usual, such global figures conceal as much as they reveal: in general, higher-income groups are now relatively better off than they were in 1980, but the middle class has barely held its own, the lower-middle class has been badly squeezed, and the poor are much worse off.)

The prospect of downward mobility, or at least the threat thereof, is thus very real: whereas only thirty years ago we took it for granted that a middle-class man would earn enough to support a wife and two or three children in suburban comfort, it now takes two paychecks to keep the average family going. Hence most consumers are running harder to stay in the same place. To make matters worse, those with moderate incomes are less able to defend themselves against the declining quality of services and the increase in public squalor, which thus have a disproportionate impact on their real standard of living. For example, a computerized minority now enjoys ever greater access to information, while public libraries decline or even close. The effect of all this is to shrink the middle class: although the 1980s are notorious for having produced a large number of *nouveaux riches*, they also created an equal number of *nou-*

veaux pauvres, former members of the middle class who slid backward toward poverty.

External factors have exacerbated this dynamic. Three stand out: globalization, which puts pressure on domestic wages and causes many of the benefits of economic activity to "trickle out" rather than "trickle down"; the failure of the American educational system to provide students with the conceptual and vocational skills they need to be economically productive in this more competitive global economy; and shortsighted social and fiscal policies that have pushed the nation toward insolvency during the past two or three decades. However, the deeper cause of current economic unhappiness is the innate tendency of the development process to subvert and frustrate affluence in all the ways described above.

In sum, mere affluence is not the answer. Keynes to the contrary notwithstanding, "solving" the economic problem is not a simple matter of increasing output. Higher production does not necessarily lead to a higher standard of living, much less to greater human happiness. It all depends. And if human beings are indeed insatiable, no conceivable level of production can make them happy in any case. The result of higher production and more consumption may therefore be frustration, not satisfaction. As Tibor Scitovsky and others have pointed out, modern affluence does not and cannot confer joy or happiness. It produces comfort at best—or, more accurately, the absence of serious discomfort. But the mere absence of discomfort can hardly be expected to engender real satisfaction. Hence the deeper response to our alleged affluence may not be the repletion foreseen by Keynes but, rather, a profound dissatisfaction characterized by a half-conscious bewilderment, frustration, and anger.

A Bootless Chase of Felicity

This paradoxical result arises in large part because, as clearly implied above, consumption is an addictive process. That is, having failed to obtain genuine or lasting satisfaction from previous acquisitions, consumers must find something new, fresh, and exciting to acquire. Of course, the latter effort, too, will prove ultimately unsatisfactory, but they will try to assuage their disappointment with a renewed bout of consumption, and so on, ad infinitum. In this light, the rampant and undeniable reality of overt addiction in America today—to cigarettes, alcohol, and drugs, as well as to gambling and other compulsions—simply reflects our overall social addiction to "growth" and "progress."

Many will resist such a sweeping indictment of our way of life. It might seem to derive from the logical error of taking the superficial part for the deeper whole or from the mental trap of falling for a fashionable metaphor. But if we turn to the roots of modern political economy in Hobbes, we can see very clearly that our underlying social premises foster addiction. His definition of happiness, or "felicity," is extraordinarily revealing:

> Felicity is a continual progress of the desire, from one object to another; the attaining of the former, being still but the way to the latter. The cause whereof is, that the object of man's desire, is not to enjoy once only, and for one instant of time; but to assure for ever, the way of his future desire.

This is followed a few sentences later by his famous description of man's ceaseless drive for power (which he has earlier defined to include riches, honor, knowledge, and other goods): "I put for a general inclination of all mankind, a perpetual and restless desire of power after power, that ceaseth only in death." What is worse, Hobbes continues, a man "cannot be content with a moderate power . . . because he cannot assure the power and means to live well, which he hath present, without the acquisition of more."

A political economy based on such principles knows no bounds: no amount of "affluence" can slake its thirst or arrest its perpetual and restless pursuit of more. This is especially true in a money economy. Money, unlike such concrete goods as food or housing, is not physically limited, in either production or consumption. In addition, in advanced mass-consumption societies, money is used more and more to purchase not mere goods and services but stylish commodities conveying a fashionable image that is transitory by its very nature. Individual consumers thus pass their lives in an addictive and ultimately frustrating pursuit of a "felicity" that must forever elude them.

In fact, modern political economy does not *want* people to be satisfied with what they have: they would stop consuming and precipitate an economic collapse. So a huge cohort of the most talented and powerful individuals in the land devote their lives to exploiting the psychological vulnerabilities of consumers and devising ever more cunning means of tempting them into being as undiscriminating, impulsive, and insatiable as possible.

De Tocqueville well understood the propensity for a life spent pursuing "fresh gratifications" to frustrate rather than satisfy. Americans, he said, are a people "whose desires grow much faster than their fortunes." They "never stop thinking of the good things they have not got" and "are forever brooding over advantages they do not possess." Hence the American is tormented by a "vague dread":

> Besides the good things he possesses, he every instant fancies a thousand others, which death will prevent him from trying if he does not find them soon. This thought fills him with anxiety, fear, and regret, and keeps his mind in ceaseless trepidation.

For de Tocqueville, therefore, American life had a tragic quality: "Death at length overtakes him, but it is before he is weary of his bootless chase of that complete felicity which forever escapes him."

In this light, the current epidemic of drug addiction, which involves both legal and illegal substances, is no accident. Nor is it a mere "problem" that can be solved with more money and better social engineering, much less by a legal "war on drugs." It is instead the consequence of basing life on Hobbesian premises: drug abuse is but the most extreme and vicious manifestation of the pursuit of happiness via a direct and immediate pleasuring of the self. As such, it mirrors our grand social addiction to external material gratification, to the ceaseless quest for ever more wealth and power.

To sum up, a Hobbesian political economy based on material self-gratification preys on the terrible propensity for addiction within the nervous system that humans share with their mammalian ancestors. "Many people with intense, unsatisfied purposiveness who will blindly pursue wealth," as well as grosser and more self-destructive ends, are the inevitable product of such a system. No surer prescription for making human beings unhappy or reducing them to slavish dependence could be imagined. The Enlightenment myth to the contrary notwithstanding, mere affluence can never solve the problems of humankind, and a civilization hooked on having at the expense of being seems destined not for fulfillment but, instead, for the pitiable fate of Erysichthon.

A Relentless Pursuit of Superiority

The conclusion that mere affluence will not and cannot solve the economic problem is reinforced if we now turn to the second category of needs identified by Keynes—the "relative needs" that we feel "only if their satisfaction lifts us above, makes us feel superior to, our fellows." These, he acknowledges, "may indeed be insatiable." But if this is true, then his solution fails: no conceivable level of affluence can forestall the continual escalation of human wants if even a significant minority of men and women are bent on superiority rather than satisfaction.

Keynes's belief that the economic problem could be solved by a sufficiently high level of production is surprising if we consider that all of human history as well as anthropology testifies to the power and durability of the drive for superiority in men and women of every age and clime. And it is frankly astonishing if we then reflect on the central role that emulation and competition play in the modern tradition of political and economic thought. Even passing over such minor figures as Thorstein Veblen, who gave us the concept of "conspicuous consumption," we find that all the "sons" of Hobbes follow him in seeing human beings enmeshed in a continuous struggle for "power"—which Hobbes defines to include riches, honor, and knowledge, as well as dominion. And the point of this struggle is not to obtain "power" for its own sake but, instead, to raise oneself above others, as Locke made explicit: "Riches do not consist in having more gold and silver, but in having more in proportion than the rest of the world, or than our neighbours, whereby we are enabled to procure to ourselves a greater plenty of the conveniences of life." And what would Smith's thought be without market competition or Marx's without class struggle? Similarly, Rousseau's primary concern is the social inequality that results when beings who are impelled by nature to strive for superiority are not constrained to accept the radical equality of the general will. In brief, almost all of modern political and economic thought assumes as a matter of course that human beings will ever and always struggle to rise to the top of the social, cultural, economic, and political heap.

The long and short of it is this: although it is nice to be better off, it is ever so much nicer to be better off than others. As John Stuart Mill said, to be rich is always "to be richer than other men." This is why the relative price of the finer things in life has risen so steeply in our time. Thanks to affluence, "positional goods," like the Park Avenue apartments that make the owner feel "rich," have been bid up relative to mere "market goods," like the mobile homes that are cheap and serviceable but confer no status whatsoever. A great many people want to be rich in Mill's sense, and this means not merely to possess *but to possess what others do not*. In fact, as Christopher Jencks notes, the ultimate perquisite of wealth is to command the service of others:

> The rich are not rich because they eat filet mignon or own yachts. Millions of people can now afford these luxuries, but they are still not "rich" in the colloquial sense. The rich are rich because they can afford to buy other people's time. They can hire other people to make their beds, tend their gardens, and drive their cars.

Conversely, of course, nobody wants to be poor, much less commanded. And people will feel poor if they cannot enjoy what others have, even if their basic needs are well taken care of—indeed, even if they enjoy certain luxuries. In fact, many of those regarded as poverty-stricken today actually have a stock of goods that would have defined a solidly middle-class style of life not so very long ago, but they nonetheless feel poor because they remain at the bottom of American society. The low man on the totem pole does not care how high the pole is. In other words, position, not wealth, defines poverty: to be significantly worse off than others, no matter how much one possesses, is so painful that a "poor" American whose income and possessions would make him well off in Lima and wealthy in Ouagadougou will nonetheless feel acutely deprived in New York City.

Above a certain level of absolute deprivation, therefore, poverty is largely *a state of mind*, not a sociological datum. As Plato says, it is caused not by "the absence of goods," a physical condition, but by "the overabundance of desire," a mental condition. If this is true, however, then the solution to the economic problem envisioned by Keynes, and by modern civilization in general, is chimerical: if wealth and poverty alike are states of mind, then they are functions of social arrangements, not statistical measures. Again, only utopian abundance, a truly magical abundance that gave everyone a penthouse looking down on everyone else, could make the struggle for status via material possessions so utterly pointless that it would have to be abandoned. In the interim, a multitude of consumers will be trapped in a vicious circle that requires them to spend defensively to protect their relative status—or, at the very least, to avoid the squalor and crime that are the penalty for losing the economic race.

To summarize, growth economics is not a proper means to the laudable ends that Keynes desires. True, economic growth has lifted large numbers of people out of absolute poverty and made a middle-class way of life the norm in the developed nations—although whether this will continue to be the case is an open question. However, as we have seen, such affluence entails at least as much frustration, or even addiction, as satisfaction. Moreover, it has utterly failed to eliminate relative deprivation. Nor could it be expected to, for, when reduced to its essence, the Enlightenment program for fostering socioeconomic equality is an absurdity: there is no conceivable way to lift everyone above the average. One person's success in climbing above the mean necessarily implies another's failure to attain it. Even if the mean itself continually rises, about half the population must fall below it, at least statistically, and will therefore feel relatively deprived. Besides, given our utopian aspiration to provide to the common man the freedoms and pleasures formerly available only to the very rich—not to mention the total well-being called for by the World Health Organization—even those well above the average will still feel dissatisfied with their lot. What is worse, they will feel aggrieved: as Daniel Bell notes, "If consumption represents the psychological competition for status, then one can say that bourgeois society is the institutionalization of envy." In consequence, says Stuart Miller in *Painted in Blood*, "people are engaged in a daily, quiet, non-violent civil war. They have all the desires that democracy excites but never enough satisfactions, so they run after more and resent those others have managed to get."

The Manufacture of Inequality

What is worse, economic growth has the effect of increasing the extent and impact of relative deprivation by enlarging the scale along which deprivation is measured. Paradoxically, therefore, economic development manufactures inequality.

A quick historical comparison explains the paradox. Primal societies are characterized by the actual equality of natural unequals, both because the material basis of life cannot support significant differences of wealth and status between one individual and another and because the group will usually not allow one of its members to get too "big." An individual's reputation and influence thus depend almost entirely on personal qualities, not wealth or social rank. In medieval times, by contrast, wealth, power, and influence were all a function of social rank. However, although the political and social gap between high and low was extreme, the material gap between rich and poor was only moderate. That is, although kings were obviously much wealthier than peasants, the general level of material development was so low that rulers were not always that much better off in important respects than their subjects. In fact, in reasonably peaceful lands and prosperous times, the peasant may have been no less comfortable in his snug cottage than the king in his drafty castle, however luxuriously appointed. And if the king rode in a carriage, a rich peasant could keep pace on horseback, and even a poor one could sprint alongside.

But economic growth in modern times has amplified the scope of possible inequality. The extreme social gradation implicit in a monarchical system was overthrown—but only to be replaced by a new socioeconomic class system that was, although much more open, equally extreme and perhaps more pernicious in certain respects. For example, in transportation, the range now extends from shank's mare and the bicycle for the poor to the high-speed train and the Concorde for the rich. Similarly with medical care: we have gone from rough parity to the chasm that separates home remedies from organ transplants. And one part of humanity counts on its fingers or the abacus, while the other uses supercomputers.

In other words, thanks to energy slavery the amount of wealth and power that can be commanded by one man or one entity or one nation has grown explosively, so the gap between rich and poor has increased in proportion, by whole orders of magnitude. In this sense, inequality is greater than it has ever been, especially internationally: the poor of today are relatively far more disadvantaged economically and technologically than their medieval forebears. Modern society is therefore just the opposite of primal society: it is characterized by the actual and extreme inequality of supposed equals.

Apart from increasing the extent of deprivation, economic development manufactures inequality in other ways. To return to a matter discussed in the previous chapter, modern economies are structured to concentrate wealth and power, not to distribute it equitably. The small farmer was progressively impoverished by economic development, because the middleman, the banker, the manufacturer, and the bureaucrat appropriated more and more of the benefit of production. In effect, development creates a more elaborate food chain with more levels of predation, so the primary producer necessarily receives proportionately less of the total product. Indeed, without the profit that arises out of the unequally shared costs and differential rewards implied by this image, development would simply not occur. Economic growth is therefore not the correct formula for achieving socioeconomic equality. On the contrary, more growth can only make inequality greater, no matter how high it lifts the general level of prosperity.

Moreover, a society in which the avenues to success are few in number does not foster equality, because any one competitive arena offers real success and power only to the few. In other words, the smaller the number of arenas, the fewer the number of successful in proportion to the whole (and the more likely they are to dominate). By contrast, if there are many small tribes rather than one big one, then the ratio of chiefs to Indians rises (and each chief's power is relatively limited). Although he never fully articulated his reasoning, Edmund Burke clearly had this fact in mind when he decried the destruction of the "little platoons" of medieval society by an imperialistic market system: the more ladders to social status, financial reward, and political influence that exist, the more room at the top; the more room at the top, the more widely power and responsibility are spread.

The existence of many small and relatively independent institutions thus confers social dignity and personal worth on larger numbers of people, creating an autonomous social realm that forestalls tyranny. This was in fact the original liberal vision of society, especially in America: a multitude of small entrepreneurs, independent proprietors, and yeoman farmers who were free and equal by virtue of their private "estate." By contrast, a large, centralized, and monolithic industrial system is bound to be characterized by great and increasing inequality. In effect, a society made up of relatively independent little platoons has been replaced by a giant industrial army. And although the pay and perquisites may be nice and the titles impressive (if only through a kind of semantic promotion), it is, like all armies, hierarchically ordered into ranks.

The inequality of the industrial ranking system is rendered all the sharper because it is based on money. By its very nature, money is a coin that, however much we try to prevent it, tends to buy status, power, and advantage across the board. In a cash nexus, the almighty dollar reigns, so those who have the cash control the ranking system. Hence money, whose legitimate and proper sphere is the marketplace, begins to extend a tyrannical sway over all others. The industrial army is not only hierarchical, it is also ranked along a single, all-pervasive monetary dimension that both amplifies and advertises the vast difference between the big winners at the top and the big losers at the bottom. Those in the middle contend with one another in the daily civil war that determines if they will move up to join the former, slip back to share the fate of the latter, or merely hold their own.

It seems that we have been pursuing the goal of equality by means that are self-defeating. The melancholy conclusion of R. H. Tawney's classic *Equality*, first published in 1931, still stands: technological innovation and economic growth have done almost nothing to cure inequality. On the contrary, even if the whole level has been lifted, there has been no significant change for the better in the distribution of income. Worse, said Tawney, a manufacturing and financial aristocracy of the kind foreseen by de Tocqueville has emerged, and it runs an industrial army that treats human beings as cannon fodder in the war for profit and market share.

The Contradictions of Egalitarianism

That the logical outcome of economic development is inequality has naturally occasioned a major effort to remedy it, especially by Marx and his intellectual heirs. (Indeed, that was Tawney's aim: to make the case for democratic socialism.) Although the socialist remedy is now largely discredited, egalitarianism itself continues to be a powerful force, even in the most capitalist countries. However, all efforts to alleviate inequality encounter daunting and painful contradictions.

To obviate any possible misunderstanding, what follows is not an argument against equality: as will become clear below, I strongly support greater *social* equality. Nor is it intended to ridicule sincere efforts to solve the problems of poverty and racism in America. Still less is it a brief for reaction. My sole aim in this section and the one that follows is to show—without discussing particular social policies—that the pursuit of egalitarian goals as currently conceived is contradictory and, in the end, politically dangerous. If I question the means by which egalitarians hope to achieve greater equity and "fairness," it is because I believe them to be futile, not because I object to the end of equality *properly understood*.

One contradiction is peculiar to the United States: in their heart of hearts, Americans are deeply ambivalent about equality. J. R. Pole states the point bluntly: "Americans wanted a society run on egalitarian principles without wanting a society of equals." Why? Because although equality may be a highly cherished social ideal, it conflicts at almost every point with their most cherished political ideal—liberty. Hence would-be reformers are caught in a bind: the harder they push for egalitarian goals, the greater the political resistance they stir up, sometimes from the very people they would help. Hence the basic and apparently irreconcilable tension in American democracy between liberty and equality discussed by de Tocqueville continues to bedevil us. At some point, which is well short of even the minimal egalitarian goal, the claims of equality are forcefully checked by the countervailing claims of liberty.

The second contradiction is not peculiar to the United States, but it has proven to be particularly intractable here. It is that between quality and equality. On the one hand, like the citizens of any other advanced industrial nation, we desire greater national productivity and international competitiveness, for which a highly skilled and qualified elite is critical, so we support programs to train competent scientists, engineers, and managers. On the other hand, spurred by the desire to create an egalitarian rather than a hierarchical society, we also insist that schooling at all levels be as accessible and "democratic" as possible, so the educational system confers more and more degrees that mean less and less. At the extreme, which is now threatening to become the norm, it is entirely possible for an American youngster to emerge from twelve years of schooling without being either literate or numerate, much less equipped with the educational foundation for future study or work. But efforts to demand even minimal competence of the high school graduate draw charges of "elitism" or even "discrimination," so any serious program for quality education along European or Japanese lines is all but unthinkable. Except at the very highest levels (and not always even there), the American educational system is therefore frankly mediocre: it not only fails to transmit a cultural tradition, especially a common civic culture, but it has even ceased to teach basic skills. As Christopher Lasch noted sardonically, "Mass education, which began as a promising attempt to democratize the higher culture of the privileged classes, has ended by stupefying the privileged themselves."

There is no escape from this contradiction: by the very nature of things, the more equal, the more mediocre. In fact, a state of perfect equality would be a state of perfect entropy as well—marked not just by mediocrity but also by stagnation, exhaustion, even death. Unfortunately for the egalitarian, the very basis of life is "negentropy": the significant differences in potential or energy that make possible the flow and organized complexity of life. In this light, it is not surprising that a relentless nature has made people utterly diverse in character and ability. When we look at human populations, every trait and aptitude is implacably distributed in the classic (or should we say infamous) bell-shaped curve—a few very high or gifted at one extreme, a few very low or disadvantaged at the other, with the many who are more-or-less average clustered around the middle. Given reasonably equal opportunity, this brute fact of nature is bound to assert itself. It is therefore hardly surprising that the distribution of status and income within industrial societies follows this curve rather closely, with the great majority of the citizens near the median and the rest tailing off toward the two extremes of wealth or poverty. It could hardly be otherwise.

To make matters worse, unequal natural endowments are socially amplified. Although researchers are only just beginning to unravel the complex interaction between nature and nurture, two things are already abundantly clear: children react very individually and sensitively to the conditions under which they are raised; and too many children are being raised under conditions that seriously cripple their chances of fulfilling their genetic potential.

The implications of this finding are profound. Among other things, the family, the basic unit of society, is clearly a bastion of inequality. Men and women marry their peers and raise their children to be like themselves. Thus children of high-income, high-status families tend to have their natural endowments enhanced by their upbringing and to become high-income and high-status themselves—and, of course, vice versa. It is not poverty alone that is the problem, because parental neglect and incompetence are not—alas!—confined to the poor. (This is especially true now that both mother and father must labor to make a living wage: increasing numbers of children are, in effect, being raised by their television sets and their age-mates.) In short, natural potential is greatly affected for better or worse by the accident of birth into a particular family, guaranteeing that equality of opportunity will inexorably produce inequality of result.

Anyone who wants to bring about greater socioeconomic equity is thus faced with trying to legislate the bell-shaped curve out of existence and subverting or even negating family influence. This is probably impossible: the research referred to above casts grave doubt on our ability to overcome poor parenting with better schools or other social remedies. Although early social intervention can be beneficial, it is rarely decisive, because most of the damage is done well before school begins, sometimes even in the womb. And when massive social intervention is attempted, the price is likely to be horrendous. Trying to pummel the social order into conformity with some egalitarian ideal in which everyone is reduced to sameness produces a stifling result: all are equally impoverished or oppressed. China under Mao illustrates the human costs of such an approach when it is taken to the extreme. Modern welfare states that lack the political will or ability to impose such a stringent egalitarianism simply try to keep juggling the irreconcilable demands of equality of opportunity and equality of result. They end up crippling the former without achieving the latter, a compromise that satisfies no one. For the most part, therefore, egalitarian sentiments and programs have been thwarted at every step.

As a consequence of these contradictions, egalitarians have simply not been able to reconcile the end that they desire with the means by which they are pursuing it. Industrial civilization cannot operate at all, much less well, without a large cadre of qualified people possessing a trained technical intelligence and enjoying a substantial liberty to profit from it. The economic growth that is supposed to make it possible to abolish inequality at last cannot be generated without creating a meritocracy. Hence the egalitarians, most of whom are members of the meritocracy themselves, are compelled to fight the battle against inequality on the grounds of "fairness." Again, this cannot succeed. In fact, it only deepens the contradiction.

All social rules favor some at the expense of others and are thus "unfair." All meaningful tests rank some above others and are thus "unfair." Only a pure lottery is "fair" in that it is "impartial" and "free of favoritism." But it is precisely the consequences of the lottery of nature that the doctrinaire egalitarian cannot accept, because it produces the bell-shaped curve. In the end, trying to reconcile the end of equality with the means of growth by promoting greater fairness simply begs all the important questions.

For example, the problem with the intelligence and aptitude tests that now determine who wins access to the best schools and jobs is not so much that they are biased and inaccurate. True, one of the functions of any social screening device is "mystification"—that is, lending credibility and legitimacy to institutional decisions that support ruling political interests and ideas. But the particular screening devices used by modern industrial societies are exceptionally objective, open, and above board. Moreover, whatever their shortcomings, they are also reasonably accurate and effective in accomplishing their primary objective—*which is to grade individuals according to their ability to achieve meritocratic rank in the industrial army* (without regard to how they achieved that ability). In other words, the fundamental problem with these tests, including the infamous SATs, is not bias in the usual sense but something far more disturbing. It is the narrow way in which "intelligence" is defined that causes the problem: by excluding intuition, imagination, and creativity as well as other important attributes of human nature, the concept of IQ faithfully reflects the "rationality" of economic man—in other words, the very system of "modern" values espoused by the egalitarians themselves. In this light, tests that were absolutely accurate and completely unbiased would simply make matters much worse, further entrenching a social ranking system based on a narrow-minded rationalism.

As pointed out by the English sociologist Michael Young, who coined the term, a perfect meritocracy would be the most minutely and rigidly stratified society ever known—a modernized version of the old order of lords, vassals, and serfs, but based on allegedly "scientific" principles even less open to challenge than divine right. What is worse, says Young, in the long run a meritocracy founded on the narrow criterion of intelligence, however defined or measured, would tend to become a genetically based caste system—with all the brightest at the top and all the dimmest at the bottom, as in Huxley's Brave New World.

This problem would remain even if the criteria of selection were widened beyond IQ and academic achievement to include other criteria of merit. Pascal pointed out meritocracy's fatal flaw long ago: "Civil wars . . . are inevitable if we wish to reward desert; for all will say they are deserving." Or, to turn it around, all will fiercely resist the idea that they are somehow undeserving. In other words, as social selection is inescapable and always discriminates in favor of some and against others (and hence determines the fundamental nature of the ranking system), it is essential that the selection process seem to be based on justice, however defined, as opposed to merit alone, which gives people "no more than they deserve." It is even possible that the older concept of natural aristocracy, however "elitist," was actually preferable to today's meritocracy, because it did a better job of reconciling individual excellence for the few with personal dignity for the many and was therefore less demeaning to the losers in the competition for elite status.

Be this as it may, an idea of equality that cannot accommodate the full spectrum of natural human differences *and make a virtue out of it* is doomed to frustration. Refusing to acknowledge significant personal differences or the bell-shaped curve for fear of ratifying them as the basis for a class or caste system constitutes a denial of reality. And rejecting any type of social distinction as inherently unfair or discriminatory does nothing to solve the real problem of inequality. On the contrary, trying to impose equality of result, much less equality of sameness, on beings who are innately diverse and who seem to have a basic drive to distinguish themselves can never succeed—and if it were to succeed, it would be a kind of death. To revert to our thermodynamic metaphor, perfect equality is like perfect entropy, a state of undifferentiated sameness in which there is no potential for either work or life. The Yiddish proverb cited as an epigraph is exact: death alone makes us equal.

The Perversion of Equality

To be blunt, modern egalitarians have completely misconstrued the ideal of equality. Once again, a "lofty idea has degenerated into crude materialism," as the original goal of social equality has decayed into a demand for equal goods or equal roles within a competitive market system. But to pursue equality in this fashion is perverse and self-defeating: it ratifies and further entrenches the institutions that manufacture inequality in the first place; it also fosters hyperindividualism and moral entropy. The political direction taken by the feminist movement in recent years poignantly illustrates both of these tendencies. As Suzanne Gordon says in *Prisoners of Men's Dreams*, feminists have betrayed their original vision, which called for the transformation of society. Instead, they now promote a materialistic "equal opportunity" feminism that places "competition above caring, work above love, power above empowerment, and personal wealth above human worth." In short, pursuing their own personal equality within a system that institutionalizes a general inequality of condition makes women just as egotistical and selfish as men—and their success, although it creates more diversity within the winner's circle, leaves the losers no better off than before.

It seems that contemporary liberals do not understand what inequality really is, why it inflicts pain, nor how to get rid of it. No wonder our efforts to alleviate it only deepen the contradictions and foster the perverse form of aristocracy called meritocracy. Moreover, the psychological pain of deprivation is now paradoxically worse than ever: unlike medieval peasants, who did not aspire above their station, modern men and women are embittered by inequality, because they know that they should be "equal," even if they are not entirely sure what that means. What is worse, they also have an exaggerated idea of their "just deserts," for all the reasons we have explored previously. We therefore need to rediscover what equality really is, for only then can we expect to achieve it and thereby prevent egalitarianism from becoming a destructive force.

There could be no better guide to how and where the contemporary drive for equality has gone off the track than Rousseau, the father of modern egalitarianism. His famous *First Discourse* attacked the Enlightenment's belief in progress through development: he predicted that economic and technological growth would simply intensify social and political inequality, just as described above. Moreover, his goal as a political thinker was to discover a form of political association grounded on social equality, which he maintained was the indispensable prerequisite for political freedom. Yet he was not an egalitarian as we now understand the term. Rousseau accepted the natural range of human talents and had no objection to their display. On the contrary, in common with many other thinkers in the democratic tradition, such as Jefferson and de Tocqueville, he believed in natural aristocracy both as fact and as ideal. Thus, for Rousseau, equality was not a matter of overcoming or extinguishing the natural differences between one individual and another, even if they produced differential social rewards—indeed, even if they created a class structure. What then is inequality, and why is it so painful?

Rousseau's answer was that both inequality and the pain it causes result from *dependence on the will of another*. In *Emile*, Rousseau distinguished between dependence on things and dependence on men. The former, "which is from nature [and thus] has no morality, is in no way detrimental to freedom and engenders no vices." In other words, dependence on things does not demean or debase us. Dependence on men, however, does precisely that: it is socially imposed and therefore "engenders all the vices, and by it, master and slave are mutually corrupted." The fundamental aim of Rousseau's political thought was therefore to prevent the humiliation of forced subservience by creating a social order characterized by independence.

Rousseau's theory of equality was obviously revolutionary. Indeed, simply to utter it was to contradict the aristocratic order, root and branch. He was far more radical than liberal theorists, for whom equality was merely juridical. In Hobbes and Locke, the equality of man-in-the-state-of-nature is not a standard for judging the existing social order but, instead, a theoretical fiction, a mere premise for creating a political order to which all will give their consent. Once the commonwealth is created, the premise is largely forgotten, and the sovereign makes uniform rules for the public sphere that allow and even encourage the unequal private development of individuals. This unequal development, which is the consequence of individual initiative and talent, was the essential point of liberalism as a political and social doctrine: it aimed to replace an aristocracy of blood and land with one of character and ability. Liberalism, as opposed to democracy, is thus fundamentally meritocratic and hierarchical, which is precisely why Rousseau opposed it.

However, Rousseau's particular target was the *ancien régime* in France, because it so clearly exemplified what he detested about civilized hierarchy: by virtue of an inherited social position and without regard to character or ability, much less justice, the noble few lorded it over the plebian many. Exploited by and dependent on the nobility, commoners were stripped of all dignity and turned into cringing lackeys. It is precisely this psychological injury that constitutes the true pain of inequality, not the mere difference of property or status. (Indeed, the classic complaint of the bourgeois under the old regime was that both his wealth and his merit counted for nothing next to royal and noble privilege: the richest and most talented commoner was still a "nobody.") However, Rousseau also rejected the emerging bourgeois plutocracy as well, because he saw that it would simply create a new form of dependence.

Rousseau therefore called for a genuine equality of condition. By this he did not mean parity or sameness, as he made explicit in the *Social Contract*:

> With regard to equality, this word must not be understood to mean that degrees of power and wealth should be exactly the same, but rather that with regard to power, it should be incapable of all violence and never exerted except by virtue of status and the laws; and with regard to wealth, no citizen should be so opulent that he can buy another, and none so poor that he is constrained to sell himself.

By this standard, market economies are wicked not because the rich eat steak while the poor eat beans, to which the seemingly obvious solution is socialized steak, but rather because the poor man is forced to sell himself to the rich—or, in modern times, to the corporate-state complex.

This causes a psychological injury for which no amount of steak can compensate.

However, although parity may not be necessary to achieve the end of nondependence, the avoidance of extremes obviously is. That is, to prevent the poor from having to sell themselves, inequality of result must be contained within reasonable bounds. Rousseau therefore concluded the passage cited above by saying, "This presumes moderation in goods and influence on the part of the upper classes and moderation in avarice and covetousness on the part of the lower classes." To sharpen his point, he added a footnote:

> Do you then want to give stability to the State? Bring the extremes as close together as possible: tolerate neither opulent people nor beggars. These two conditions, naturally inseparable, are equally fatal to the common good. From the one come those who foment tyranny and from the other the tyrants. It is always between them that trafficking in the public freedom takes place. The one buys it and the other sells it.

Rousseau's vision of equality thus differs profoundly from that of classical liberals as well as latter-day egalitarians, whose idea of equality is universal steak within an affluent society. By contrast, Rousseau insists that genuine equality results only when no man or woman is beholden to another for his or her livelihood or well-being. It is this lack of dependence that confers a felt sense of equality and causes individuals to be mutually self-respecting. It is also the indispensable ground for political freedom. The essential political task is thus to construct a social order that checks all extremes of wealth, status, and power as inimical to the independence and self-respect of the citizen. In short, Rousseau maintains, as did Aristotle before him, that *equality is a function of justice*: citizens will feel equal in a political order they perceive to be fundamentally legitimate and well ordered, despite important differences of wealth, status, and power.

In this light, our current concepts of equality are revealed as seriously defective. We are trying to redistribute the spoils of an inherently unjust and unequal political economy after the fact, rather than seeking to create a just and equal one in the first place. In other words, the contemporary demand for equality in America is largely a sham, because it does not even begin to contemplate the kinds of radical measures that would be necessary to achieve it.

Nevertheless, the demand is very real and now threatens to overwhelm the polity. With his usual prescience, de Tocqueville understood the danger: he not only perceived egalitarianism to be a driving force of modern history, but he also foresaw that it could lead to pernicious ends. He warned that the "manly and lawful passion" for equality of condition then prevailing in America might one day be corrupted both by a growing materialism and by an upsurge of social envy. The latter was especially to be feared, because "there exists also in the human heart a depraved taste for equality, which impels the weak to attempt to lower the powerful to their own level, and reduces men to prefer equality in slavery to inequality with freedom." Indeed, de Tocqueville believed that the passion for equality would in the end become so "ardent, insatiable, incessant, [and] invincible" that it would lead men and women to choose despotism: "They will endure poverty, servitude, barbarism; but they will not endure aristocracy."

This comes close to describing the spirit of egalitarianism today: it will endure no aristocracy and seems not to care about the danger of "servitude." As legal scholar Richard Epstein notes,

> In the civil rights literature, there is scant reference to intellectual excellence, personal dedication, effort, entrepreneurial zeal. It is as though all benefits were the result of luck or impersonal forces and none the result of intelligence, initiative, creativity, or plain hard work.

In other words, the pervasive atmosphere of grievance and victimization noted in Chapter 2 reflects de Tocqueville's "depraved taste for equality," an equality of rancor and envy that targets all who stand out from the crowd. The demand for equality in our time has therefore become, says Epstein, a "new form of imperialism that threatens the political liberty and intellectual freedom of all."

What is worse, an equality of sameness that grinds individuals down into equal social atoms—all equally alike, equally alone, equally insignificant—simply produces a crowd, with all of its attendant political dangers. The worst of these dangers was succinctly articulated by Jung: "If all that is distinguished is leveled down, then all orientation is lost and the yearning to be led becomes inevitable."

In conclusion, we have learned that Keynes's utopian vision founders on the rock of his own admission that the human desire for superiority may be insatiable. Not only will this desire continue to be expressed almost without regard to the level of wealth attained, but the very process of achieving so-called affluence seems to create new and worse forms of inequality, even as it makes people better off. Indeed, liberal equality—merely juridical equality—permits vast inequalities of fortune worse in many ways than the preexisting inequalities of status, which at least implied mutuality and *noblesse oblige*. And all attempts to remedy this problem are either doomed to frustration or will lead us into political danger. Again, Keynes's purported solution to the economic problem is chimerical and self-defeating: like wealth and poverty, equality and inequality are a function not of numbers but of social and political arrangements. In the end, equality simply cannot be created by maximizing wealth as the Enlightenment program envisioned, for material goods are no substitute for justice, social dignity, and individual self-respect—not to mention spiritual fulfillment.

The Futility of Affluence

To sum up, more riches do not seem to have made us happier; nor better able "to live wisely and agreeably and well"; nor more equal. To the contrary: affluence enslaves men and women by addicting them to a continual pursuit of gratification. The consumptive way of life also throws them into conflict with others in "a daily, quiet, non-violent civil war." Like all wars, this one must have winners and losers, so it enriches and uplifts some as it impoverishes and degrades others. That our style of affluence can promote happiness or equality or social peace as Keynes believed is therefore a fallacy.

The Enlightenment scheme for improving human welfare was founded on a false understanding of what makes for human happiness. As usual, Rousseau put his finger on the problem. After arguing forcefully in his *First Discourse* that economic development was *not* the answer, in all the ways that we have already discussed, he then went on to provide a positive answer in *Emile*:

> In what, then, consists human wisdom or the road of true happiness? It is not precisely in diminishing our desires, for if they were beneath our power, a part of our faculties would remain idle, and we would not enjoy our whole being. Neither is it in extending our faculties, for if, proportionate to them, our desires were more extended, we would as a result only become unhappier. But it is in diminishing the excess of the desires over the faculties and putting power and will in perfect equality. It is only then that, with all the powers in action, the soul will nevertheless remain peaceful and that man will be well ordered.

In other words, when grasp and reach coincide, we are happy; but when reach exceeds grasp, we are not. It is as simple—and as profound—as that. To seek happiness by continually pursuing it is futile, because the goal "which at first appeared to be at hand flees more quickly than it can be pursued." Hence, says Rousseau, "one exhausts oneself without getting to the end, and the more one gains on enjoyment, the further happiness gets from us."

Paradoxically, then, concludes Rousseau, the savage is happiest of all,

> because the closer to his natural condition man has stayed, the smaller is the difference between his faculties and his desires, and consequently the less removed he is from being happy. He is never less unhappy than when he appears entirely destitute, for unhappiness consists not in the privation of things but in the need that is felt for them.

Yet Rousseau does not thereby suggest that happiness is to be found by returning to the forest to live with bears. On the contrary, he says explicitly that this is neither possible nor desirable: we can never again rejoin the "original affluent society," nor would we want to. He asks us instead to understand that morality, in the form of intelligent self-limitation on desire, is absolutely essential for both individual happiness and collective well-being.

In other words, we must learn the paradoxical lesson of savage life and then adapt it to the more complex and challenging conditions of civilized life. We must, that is, create a way of life that is no longer driven by desire—a post-Enlightenment culture that has learned how "to pluck the hour and the day virtuously and well" just as it comes, without *first* demanding to be rich and powerful. At the very least, we must abandon the amoral and futile pursuit of affluence, for it brings only increasing unhappiness and eventual servitude. This is especially true if we desire greater social equality, for the way to economic justice, said Aristotle, "is not so much to equalize property as to train the nobler sort of natures not to desire more."

To use more modern language, we have learned that Schumpeter's "perennial gale of creative destruction" will not blow itself out, leaving behind Keynes's utopia: capitalist development has no inherent limits, and human avarice is for all practical purposes insatiable. If capitalism is to reach a mature "steady state" in which the great majority are well and truly satisfied, it will only be because we decide to abandon acquisition as a way of life, having realized that affluence is not the way to human happiness or social justice.

In fact, we may have little choice but to forswear further acquisition, for, if this analysis is pushed one step further, we shall discover that what we celebrate as abundance is actually scarcity in disguise. In consequence, even if the pursuit of affluence did, contrary to everything said thus far, bring happiness and freedom and equality, it would still prove in the end to have been a "bootless chase of felicity" terminating in destitution.

5

FRAUDULENT ABUNDANCE

*The cost of a thing is the amount of what I will call life which is required
to be exchanged for it, immediately or in the long run.*

—Henry David Thoreau

*The market-industrial system institutes scarcity, in a manner completely
unparalleled and to a degree nowhere else approximated. . . .*
*We are inclined to think of hunters and gatherers as poor because they
don't have anything; perhaps better to think of them for that reason as free.*

—Marshall Sahlins

*There is, indeed, a most dangerous passage in the history of a democratic
people. When the taste for physical gratifications amongst them has
grown more rapidly than their education and their experience of free
institutions, the time will come when men are carried away, and lose all
self-restraint. . . . In their intense and exclusive anxiety to make a fortune
. . . they neglect their chief business, which is to remain their own masters.*

—Alexis de Tocqueville

THE LAST AND DEEPEST CONTRADICTION OF AFFLUENCE is that the "abundance" created by economic development is an ecological and thermodynamic illusion, for the net long-term effect of energy slavery is to turn natural abundance into artificial scarcity. Energy slavery is therefore a false means to the end of material well-being: the abundance that results is fraudulent. Worse yet, in pursuing a chimerical abundance, individual human beings and whole nations alike "neglect their chief business, which is to remain their own masters": the political price of energy slavery is a corresponding "energy despotism." Again, the Enlightenment program does not and cannot engender real progress.

The Paradox of Modern Abundance

Let us begin to explore the paradox of modern abundance—and also deepen our understanding of many issues raised in the last two chapters—by asking a question. Why can poor peasants in the Third World afford to have several children, whereas the cost of raising even one child in the United States today is so high, in terms of both money and time, that parents must plan and budget carefully before having one? In other words, what is it about the economic development process that transforms something that is a virtual "free good" in traditional societies into an expensive "commodity" in developed ones? If children, the most basic "commodity" of all, "produced" in vast quantities by the poorest of the poor, are less and less affordable by the so-called rich, what does this say about modern abundance? Could it be that it is not what it seems?

A quick look at the history of the American Dream over the years suggests that this might be the case. The nation has become more prosperous and powerful (or so we think), but in many ways individuals are actually worse off. In the early 1800s, for example, a moderately well-to-do couple could reasonably expect to have a large family and to raise it on a small estate—that is, to own a house and barn on substantial acreage, with orchards, gardens, and a stock of animals. The "estate" of a similar couple in the prosperous 1920s would have shriveled to a large house and garage on a half-acre lot, a car, a couple of dogs, and three or four children—still quite grand, perhaps, but hardly the same. In the 1990s, however, the dream has been "downsized": if a comparable couple can afford to own a home at all, it may be a condo in the city or a tract house in the suburbs, albeit one well appointed with various gadgets; their family, if they have one at all, will probably consist of one child in day care, two at the most; and both parents will have to work to afford such munificence. Paradoxically, then, although the standard of living has supposedly improved many times over, more has somehow become less.

Furthermore, thanks to the general decay in social conditions due to crime, drugs, pollution, and so on, the environment in which people now live is decidedly inferior. Indeed, although the statistics say that we are richer than ever, we seem to be less and less able to support public facilities of any kind—not just great cultural monuments, like the Parthenon or the Eiffel Tower, but ordinary schools, parks, and libraries. Even granting a high degree of fiscal and political mismanagement in recent years, as well as the previously noted propensity for private affluence to produce public squalor, this seems preposterous. How is it possible that communities could afford all of these things and more during the Great

Depression, but can no longer do so now that we are approximately four times "richer"?

This paradoxical situation is not simply an artifact of the fiscal heedlessness of the 1980s; nor is it merely the result of a temporary downturn in the business cycle or of the globalization of the economy. Although these and other factors are all part of the story, deeper forces are at work. For reasons that we shall spend most of the rest of the chapter exploring, the costs of economic growth, at first modest and negligible, increase inexorably and disproportionately during the life cycle of development. Beyond a certain point in the cycle, therefore, each further increment of growth brings more cost than benefit. Thus we must work harder just to keep what we already have, much less to get more. An economy in the later stages of the development cycle begins to resemble Lewis Carroll's Wonderland, where, as the Red Queen said to Alice, "it takes all the running *you* can do, to keep in the same place. If you want to get somewhere else, you must run at least twice as fast as that!"

Running is indeed the right word, for that is exactly how modern men and women spend their lives—running in the infamous rat race, a race nobody wins. Which brings us to the second part of the paradox of modern abundance: we have less time than ever before. In his pioneering work, *The Harried Leisure Class*, economist Staffan Lindner argued in 1970 that innumerable unpaid costs or "shadow prices" are inescapably attached to modern production and consumption. One of the greatest and least recognized of these is time. Lindner contrasted the superfluity of time in traditional cultures with our lack of it. The lowly medieval serf, for example, enjoyed approximately 115 holidays every year. We, on the other hand, possess what seems like vast wealth, but we must spend all our time making it and maintaining it, so we are too busy to enjoy our joyless affluence. Lindner could see no way out of this predicament and predicted the gradual emergence of a "time famine," whose arrival has now been duly acknowledged by the mainstream media and documented by scholars.

Lindner's heretical challenge to economic development on the ground that it destroys rather than creates leisure is supported by anthropology, which has utterly refuted the conventional view of primal life as "solitary, poor, nasty, brutish, and short." Compared to simpler societies, complex civilizations are hectic. In fact, hunter-gatherers are among the most leisured, unpressured, and economically secure peoples on Earth. The truth of this proposition can be heard in the words of a representative "savage." With the eloquence and wit for which Native American orators were renowned, an anonymous Gaspesian (now Micmac) chief responded as follows to the sneers of the "civilized" Frenchmen who had come to despoil Nova Scotia:

> I beg thee now to believe that, all miserable as we seem in thy eyes, we consider ourselves nevertheless much happier than thou, in this that we are very content with the little that we have. . . . Thou deceivest thyselves greatly if thou thinkest to persuade us that thy country is better than ours. For if France, as thou sayest, is a little terrestrial paradise, art thou sensible to leave it? . . . As to us, we find all our riches and all our conveniences among ourselves, without trouble, without exposing our lives to the dangers in which you find yourselves constantly through your long voyages. And whilst feeling compassion for you in the sweetness of our repose, we wonder at the anxieties and cares which you give yourselves, night and day, in order to load your ships. . . . Now tell me this one little thing, if thou has any sense, which of these two is the wisest and happiest: he who labors without ceasing and only obtains . . . with great trouble, enough to live on, or he who rests in comfort and finds all that he needs in the pleasure of hunting and fishing[?]

In other words, as anthropologist Marshall Sahlins argues after a careful comparison of "stone-age" and "civilized" economies, the traditional understanding that leisure is the product of civilization needs to be stood on its head, for in developed economies "the amount of work per capita increases, and the amount of leisure decreases."

Melvin Konner and others criticize Sahlins by pointing out that such comparisons are deceptive, at least in part. Although primal peoples need not toil to feed themselves (at least most of the time), they pay for their ease in other ways—for example, with high infant and child mortality and shorter life spans, as well as numerous lesser discomforts and privations. Moreover, the rest of their time is not totally free. They must manufacture and repair clothing, tools, weapons, and other implements. They must also spend many hours planning, politicking, and palavering, especially about interpersonal relations: life among the !Kung, says Konner pejoratively, is "one interminable marathon encounter group." (But is this a problem or a testimonial to psychological health? Stanley Diamond, for one, believes that primal society excels precisely in having developed highly effective customary methods for handling antisocial impulses and directing them to prosocial ends.) Nevertheless, Sahlins is essentially correct: we have only to read the complaints of old-time missionaries about the incurable "idleness" of the natives to see why the Gaspesians would have good cause, "in the sweetness of [their] repose," to pity the Frenchmen. Moreover, Konner's criticism misses a crucial point: primal peoples do not "work," they live. The profound difference between the "civilized" and "savage" modes of existence is epitomized in the chief's final sentence: primal man "finds all that he needs in the *pleasure* of hunting and fishing." Not only hunting and gathering, but all his activities, are part of a seamless way of life that is enjoyed for its own sake. Thus, for instance, a hunter making tools is more like a sculptor than a factory worker. To use Marxist language, the labor of the savage is not "alienated," so his "work" is really a kind of leisure.

The utilitarian bargain of civilization is therefore fraudulent. We think we exchange painful work for a pleasurable abundance of goods and leisure, but this is a delusion. The long-run effect of economic development is to provide more and more people with more and more goods that are paradoxically of less and less value (or are more and more expensive) and to turn life into a rat race that becomes more hectic and less leisured with each further increment of growth. In his autobiography, Jung said, "We refuse to recognize that everything better is purchased at the price of something worse." Hence our vaunted technological advances "by no means increase the contentment or happiness of people on the whole. Mostly, they are deceptive sweetenings of existence, like speedier communications which unpleasantly accelerate the tempo of life and leave us with less time than ever before."

Nature Ordains a General Scarcity

That "everything better is purchased at the price of something worse" reflects what Ralph Waldo Emerson called "the law of compensation"—that is, nature's tendency to keep its books in balance. Indeed, Jung's conclusion is the inescapable consequence of fundamental laws of nature: Newton's Third Law of Motion, and the First and Second Laws of Thermodynamics. These tell us that every action in the material realm will always produce an equal and opposite reaction; that matter and energy can neither be created nor destroyed, but only transformed from one form to another; and that every such transformation degrades or consumes matter and energy. Taken together, they explain why the overall shadow price of production must grow and grow, and why economic development must necessarily create artificial scarcity out of natural abundance.

The inescapable loss of matter-energy potential that is the consequence of the Second Law is an especially devastating blow to human hubris. In effect, nature levies a stiff turnover tax on every human conversion of matter and energy from one form to another. As we have seen, this turns all such transactions into losing propositions, for they engender greater entropy or disorder in the system as a whole. So the more transactions we make, the deeper into thermodynamic debt we go.

Few understand how high this "tax" is. In a typical food chain it takes about ten units of biomass at the primary production level to support just one unit at the grazing level. About 90 percent of the original energy is therefore taken by the thermodynamic taxman, so costs outweigh benefits by roughly ten to one! This seemingly exorbitant cost-benefit ratio is not a problem in natural systems, because nature has learned through evolution to accommodate to thermodynamic reality constructively by turning the costs of one energy transaction into benefits for the next—for example, by making one organism's wastes into food for others. In effect, nature practices thermodynamic tax avoidance by using energy with relatively great efficiency, thereby eliminating much of the shadow price from its transactions. (To be more precise, although nature is not particularly efficient in engineering terms, it achieves a relatively high degree of ecological efficiency by making the same quantum of energy serve multiple purposes.) The result is a rich and stable ecological structure in which the losses due to entropy are balanced by incoming solar energy in a "steady-state" biosphere.

By contrast, human matter-energy conversions are disruptive, if not destructive, because nothing mitigates or dampens their thermodynamic impact: man-made wastes are just that and nothing more, so the shadow price attached to human activities is very high. Moreover, as we have learned, this price can take many different forms—not only ecological but also aesthetic, hygienic, psychological, economic, social, and even political. For example, both the direct physical costs of the automobile, such as the expense of extracting and transporting petroleum from faraway lands, and the more immediate ecological costs, such as the associated oil spills, are very large. But they pale in comparison to the other costs: the replacement of natural landscapes by paved ugliness, the emission of smog- and cancer-causing chemicals, increased stress due to the fast pace of life, higher taxes to pay for freeways and higher insurance premiums to pay for trauma centers, more regulation and litigation, urban sprawl and inner-city decay, the rootlessness of mobility, the erosion of civic virtue due to the dissolution of community, and, last but not least, the necessity to maintain a large and expensive military establishment to protect our lines of supply. This list, which is by no means exhaustive, suggests the enormity of the shadow price attached to the private automobile—and more generally to our enslavement of fossil-fuel energy to support our way of life.

In this light, it should no longer seem paradoxical that greater apparent wealth in terms of dollars or even goods can indeed impoverish us—for our accounting system does not include most of the ecological costs in the price of commodities, much less any of the less quantifiable aesthetic, social, and moral costs. But the shadow price has to be paid somehow. If we do not pay in dollars, then we will pay in other ways— ways that may prove to be more painful and expensive in the long run.

Thoreau, a close friend and colleague of Emerson, expressed the essence of a thermodynamically informed economics when he said that the true cost of a thing "is the amount of . . . life which is required to be exchanged for it, immediately or in the long run." The paradox is thus explained: our vaunted abundance has actually impoverished us, because we have had to give up an inordinate amount of "life" in all its variety and splendor to get it.

Thoreau's acumen becomes even clearer if we distill the basic laws referred to above into a single axiom: contrary to the assertions of almost all economists and technologists, nature does indeed impose an inescapable *general* scarcity on all of life, including the human race. We humans, however, are uniquely equipped to control the impact of this scarcity by manipulating it physically and socially to create a preferred pattern of surplus and shortage. That is, although we cannot get a free lunch, we can use our technological command of matter and energy to decide who will get stuck with the tab, at least in the short run. Hence we can choose to have more for us, but less for them; more here, but less there; more of this, but less of that; and more now, but less later. So we can indeed alleviate scarcity in one area—but, thanks to the turnover tax imposed by the Second Law, *only by making it greater elsewhere.*

The effect of economic development is therefore to impoverish us over the long run. Development is not a matter of robbing Peter to pay Paul, which transfers money from one pocket to another while leaving the whole system no worse off. Instead, it takes ten dollars from Peter, but gives only one dollar to Paul, thereby inflicting a nine dollar loss on the system. Hence the surplus created by development is always overshadowed by the vast quantity of scarcity that it simultaneously produces—a scarcity that takes many different and sometimes paradoxical forms, as exemplified by the inverse relationship between leisure and development noted above. But the extent of the scarcity is not apparent, at least at first, because it is displaced in time or space—from one individual, group, class, territory, nation, generation, or species to another. In fact, the politics of development consists precisely in monopolizing as much of the surplus as possible for oneself (or one's group, class, territory, nation, generation, and species), while inflicting as much of the resulting scarcity as possible on others.

To use technical language, the profit in development comes from "externalizing" as many of the costs as possible, as opposed to "internalizing" them so that profit and loss appear on the same balance sheet. The degree to which our social accounting system is fraudulent is suggested by this passage from the report of the United Nations Commission on Environment and Development (the so-called Brundtland Commission Report published in 1987 as *Our Common Future*):

> We borrow environmental capital from future generations with no intention or prospect of repaying. They may damn us for our spendthrift ways, but they can never collect on our debt to them. . . . [T]hey do not vote; they have no political or financial power; they cannot challenge our decisions.

In essence, we simply do not count what we expropriate from nature or borrow from posterity. Our supposed abundance is an artifact of our dishonest bookkeeping.*

Writing in 1967, the eminent economist Paul Samuelson asserted that compound economic growth would continue for "as far ahead as the eye can see." He therefore boasted that "a growing nation is the greatest Ponzi game ever conceived." Unfortunately, we now know that Samuelson was both right and wrong: right that the game was a fraud, and wrong that it would continue forever. The universe is not constructed so that we can get something for nothing. By way of review, the inescapable costs of development can be placed into three categories. First, stolen goods—such as the rapine of nature and the exploitation of peoples, at times with main force and at others with technical or legal finesse. Second, deferred payments—such as the future cost of cleaning up toxic dumps or nuclear facilities, of feeding an expanded population, or of coping with gross changes in the Earth's climate. Third, hidden costs—such as the destruction of tranquility, amenity, and community. But this is much too abstract. In plain English, our abundance rests on theft, fraud, and delusion: we are like a ruthless king who massacres and enslaves others to aggrandize and enrich himself; a spendthrift heir who leaves his posterity penniless; and a glutton who wastes liver and

---

*We are just beginning to rethink how we account for economic activities. In the end, after a long struggle, we shall necessarily arrive at a theory of value based on thermodynamics—that is, one in which the flow of solar energy, which is the ultimate biophysical basis of life and thus the ultimate source of economic value, constitutes the ground of the accounting system.

longevity in riotous living. In sum, the proposition that we have in any way abolished scarcity or have the slightest prospect of doing so is one of the most ridiculous and mendacious ideas ever subscribed to by large numbers of people.

Limitation as a Creative Force

To approach the problem from a different direction, modern economic development is a drive to overcome existential limits by acquiring quasi-godlike powers and using them to create a terrestrial paradise of unlimited abundance. We have already seen that this drive for wealth and power reflects a kind of secular messianism: as Irving Kristol says, it cloaks an unconscious and vain attempt to compensate for the infinity lost when political economy vanquished dogmatic religion. But the futility of using worldly goods as a substitute for infinity aside, trying to overcome existential limits is a fundamentally mistaken strategy. Indeed, the hubris of the notion is astonishing. Not only are natural limits inescapable, but every attempt to defeat them in one area simply causes them to advance in another. In fact, if we are not careful, our very struggle against limitation will leave us worse off than before—that is, more, rather than less, limited. In brief, man cannot reasonably choose to be unlimited: he can only work with craft and care and art to create modes of existence that permit him to live "wisely and agreeably and well" within the limits imposed by nature, not in defiance of them.

A model for how to do this is provided by nature itself. The basic strategy that ecosystems use for coping with limitation is to become *qualitatively* better. This allows them to do more with the same limited amount of energy and to produce thereby a greater richness and diversity of life. In pioneer ecosystems, for example, the available energy produces a high yield—that is, rapid *quantitative* growth—but quality is low, and the energy is used inefficiently. By contrast, the yield is much less in climax ecosystems, but quality is far higher—because the available energy, which is the same in both cases, is used with greater efficiency to produce a richer and more complex ecosystem. Picture the difference between a field of weeds and a tropical rain forest: the former has a few species of plants and animals that grow rapidly and die off equally rapidly, leaving little behind to mark their passage; whereas the latter exhibits a rich organic tapestry of many diverse life forms mutually interacting with each other in complex ways. Depending on how it is organized, therefore, the same limited budget of solar energy can produce strikingly different outcomes: a brief and flashy display or a rich and enduring stock.

Although pioneer and climax ecosystems are both governed by natural limits, the role of limitation in the climax is much greater. In pioneer ecosystems, a few species are relatively free to use the available energy to produce large populations and colonize new territory. By contrast, because there are many more species in climax ecosystems, each is tightly constrained within a particular niche, which prevents it from growing freely. Rather than go into detail about predation rates and other forms of negative feedback that produce the climax, let me instead cut right to the heart of the matter: biologist Daniel McKinley calls the climax "a perennial feudal society." This political metaphor graphically suggests the extent and intensity of the mutuality (and thus the tightness of the constraints) within a climax ecosystem. And it is precisely these constraints that force the system to invest in quality rather than quantity. So biological wealth paradoxically results not from the freedom to grow but, instead, from the very lack of it.

One of the most critical limits to growth within ecosystems is increased maintenance costs. In fact, ecological succession is a direct response to the rise in such costs. Although a pioneer species such as a dandelion can use most of the available energy to grow taller, this is obviously not possible for a tree that is already twenty feet tall: to survive, much less grow, the tree must invest energy in a larger girth and a deeper root structure, as well as in self-protective measures like bark. In general, therefore, the inevitable concomitant of increased numbers or larger sizes is higher maintenance costs. To make a long story short, an exponential rise in such costs drives ecosystems toward the climax. In essence, as they are forced to divert more and more energy from growth to maintenance—that is, to accommodating the costs of past growth— they become steadily more complex or mature, until the forces of growth and maintenance come into long-term balance. Thereafter, in the steady state of the climax, there is replacement but no further growth.

Ecosystems thus obey the "law of form" so elegantly stated earlier in this century by biologist W. D'Arcy Thompson: nothing can grow forever, because whereas size increases geometrically, capacity grows only arithmetically. Every organism and thing therefore has an *absolute* size beyond which it simply cannot grow: a snail that added too many rings to its shell would not be able to move; a skyscraper that rose too high would require so much internal structure, including elevators and other facilities, that it could no longer contain any usable space. It follows, then, that every organism and thing also has an *optimal* size that represents the best compromise between size and capacity.* This optimum, which is always well short of the maximum, is the appointed end of organic development and the ideal toward which the human designer ought to strive. But ecosystems are subject to the same laws and constraints, albeit in a more complex fashion, so they too tend toward an optimum: the appointed end of ecological succession is the climax, the place where the forces of growth and maintenance reach optimal long-term balance.

We are now better placed to understand abundance and scarcity in the human ecosystem. The abundance of biological life owes its shape, if not its very existence, to the effects of scarcity—that is, to the constraints imposed by natural law that make organic growth tend toward the optimum, the state that best reconciles all the limiting factors. Indeed, if through accident or error growth continues beyond the optimal point, the result is deformity or disease. So natural limitations are a creative force: they do not restrict organic development, they make it possible; they are not enemies of natural abundance, they are its allies. Paradoxically, therefore, biological wealth is created by the *harmonious balance* of abundance and scarcity.

By contrast, economic development is a struggle to create abundance *in opposition to* scarcity by using technological power to extend or even abolish natural limits. Far from tending toward the optimum, growth in the human ecosystem is unbounded growth that tends toward disease and deformity. The essential problem of modern political economy is that it is limitless—it has no criterion of sufficiency, no appointed end, no climax toward which it aims. Since nothing limits it, economic growth must end in a grotesque hypertrophy that paradoxically intensifies scarcity over the long term.

Escalating Maintenance Costs in the Human Ecosystem

Having considered limitation in general and the ecological consequences of maintenance costs in particular, let us now focus more closely on what happens in human societies. The essence of the human ecological predicament is easily stated. In our avid pursuit of the high yields char-

---

*This principle was originally stated (albeit without Thompson's rigor and elegance) by Aristotle: "To the size of states there is a limit, as there is to other things, plants, animals, implements; for none of these retain their natural power when they are too large or too small, but they either wholly lose their nature, or are spoiled."

acteristic of the pioneer stage, we have over the years built up a very large stock of goods, as well as a growing population. But the larger the numbers, the higher the maintenance costs, and a dramatic rise in such costs now obliges us to devote more and more effort and energy to running "to keep in the same place."

However, we are addicted to the high yields that can be obtained only during the pioneer stage, so we resist the call to ecological maturity and refuse to accept limitation as a fact of life. Instead of seeing higher maintenance costs as signals warning us to abandon the pioneer quest for quantity and to embrace the climax ideal of quality, we cling to our outmoded growth mentality. We therefore do everything in our power to avoid, displace, postpone, or evade maintenance costs. Those that we cannot overcome with main force we banish with fraudulent accounting.

The apparent success of this deluded strategy is an illusion, for we now experience the worst of both worlds: most of the actual costs and complications, but little of the real integration, complexity, and richness of a climax system. And the strategy is now imperiled, because the bills from previous avoidance, displacement, postponement, and evasion are being presented: the shadow price of stolen goods, deferred maintenance, and hidden costs from the past has caught up with us.

In a magisterial work that merits more attention than it has received, the archeologist Joseph A. Tainter has examined all the theories that purport to explain the rise and fall of civilizations and proposes a new one that largely subsumes them all by revealing the essential similarity of the process of decline and fall across many different cultures. The essence of his argument is that increased investment in socioeconomic and political complexity offers high returns at first, but declining returns over time as "ever greater increments of investment yield ever smaller increments of gain." In fact, the process can reach a point where vastly increased investment does little more than maintain the status quo, as when previously constructed infrastructure—irrigation systems, highways, and the like—fall into disrepair and have to be reconstructed at great expense for no net gain in productivity. Worse yet, increased investment in complexity can even produce a negative return. Arms races are a classic example: one spends more to be less secure. In short, all other things being equal, what Tainter calls "the marginal product of increasing complexity" always declines over time, eventually becoming zero or even minus.

The primary reason, according to Tainter, is that

> more complex societies are more costly to maintain than simpler ones, requiring greater support levels per capita. As societies increase in complex-

ity, more networks are created among individuals, more hierarchical controls are created to regulate these networks, more information is processed, there is more centralization of information flow, there is increasing need to support specialists not directly involved in resource production, and the like. All of this complexity is dependent upon energy flow at a scale vastly greater than that characterizing small groups of self-sufficient foragers or agriculturalists. The result is that as a society evolves toward greater complexity, the support costs levied on each individual will also rise, so that the population as a whole must allocate increasing portions of its energy budget to maintaining organizational institutions. This is an immutable fact of societal evolution.

A secondary reason is that societies tend to take the line of least resistance, doing the easiest and cheapest things first. Hence any remaining problems are always harder and more expensive to solve. And costs inexorably increase relative to benefits as the cycle of development follows its predestined course.

Tainter documents the increase in allocations to the maintenance function across the board—in the growth of bureaucracy, regulation, and red tape; in higher taxes that require more effort and expense to collect; in rising expenditures for security and public order; in escalating insurance and litigation costs; in the emergence of what have been called "the diseases of science," which raise the cost of discovery and invention; in burgeoning military expenditures; in diminishing returns (in real terms) in resource production and extraction; and so on. Briefly stated, the higher the level of development, the higher still are the maintenance costs that must be paid just to preserve the status quo, much less to make further advances.

This is true even of education, usually considered to be an unmitigated good. Tainter points out that elementary education provides large social benefits at relatively low cost. But the same is not true of higher education, especially specialized education:

> While the performance of [specialized] tasks may be quite essential to the society's needs, it cannot be claimed that benefits for investment in education increase proportionate to costs. To the contrary, increasingly specialized training serves ever narrower segments of the system, at ever greater cost to the society as a whole. What is more, the benefits derived from specialized training are equally attributable to the generalized education which necessarily precedes it.

In sum, exactly as the theory of ecological succession predicts, human ecosystems experience the same inexorable rise in maintenance costs that drives the process of succession from pioneer to climax in natural systems. To use the language of economics, the net effect of increased maintenance costs is to subject human ecosystems to a "demultiplier effect" in which the financial capital and social effort needed for further progress is siphoned off for nonproductive ends, causing a progressive decline in both growth and yield. The outcome, as Tainter shows, is at best stagnation, at worst collapse. To reiterate, human systems are governed by exactly the same laws and principles as natural systems—but humans have a talent for manipulation that allows them to combat the operation of these laws and a capacity for self-deception that allows them to deny their existence. But only up to a point: as the deferred maintenance costs from the past catch up to us and the present costs of operating the system continue to escalate, it is becoming ever harder to engage in such denial.

Medicine as a Paradigm of Development

That the returns on our investment in complexity are bound to diminish over time is nowhere better exemplified than in the field of medicine. Most people regard improved health and longer life spans as among the greatest boons of modern life. Indeed, as noted in the previous chapter, in no other area of life are our aspirations so inflated: we want freedom from disease and infirmity, if not "a state of complete physical, mental, and social well-being." And we pin our hopes for such a utopia on the technological advances that will accompany further economic development. Modern medicine thus epitomizes the Enlightenment's dream of continual progress toward perfection via the conquest of nature. Alas, it is an impossible dream, because the price of medical progress has escalated dramatically over time, as a brief historical review will demonstrate.

Thanks to a general amelioration of social conditions during the nineteenth century (with better nutrition being especially important), public health improved significantly. To the extent that medicine also contributed to this achievement, it was due to better hygiene, not better treatment. That is, by 1915, well before physicians had effective treatments for most diseases, the death rate had dropped dramatically in response to relatively simple and inexpensive measures promoting greater cleanliness. Improved sanitation and antisepsis radically reduced not only infant and child mortality but also many other major causes of premature death, such as infectious disease and the complications of childbirth. In short, better food and better hygiene combined to cause a remarkable increase in average life spans, bringing them close to current levels by 1915. Most of the benefits we associate with modern scientific medicine therefore antedate by many years the striking improvements in medical treatment during the intervening years.*

Contrast these very large early gains at relatively low cost with the situation in the United States today. A gigantic medical establishment consumes about 14 percent of gross domestic product, but much of that expenditure is of little direct benefit to patients, because it is needed to pay for the escalating maintenance costs of the system itself: hospital administration, malpractice insurance, claims processing, excessive testing, unnecessary procedures, profits for all concerned, even outright fraud. Yet although the waste and profiteering peculiar to the American medical system often get most of the blame for the runaway growth of health-care costs, the real culprit is technology—new and improved means of saving or extending life cost more and more relative to the increased benefits received by patients. As economist Victor Fuchs points out, "We aren't doing more medical care, we are doing different medical care"—namely, using more expensive procedures, treatments, drugs, and devices. A secondary factor is what physician Willard Gaylin calls "our unbridled appetite for health care and our continuing expansion of the definition of what constitutes health." So a modest increase in life spans since 1915 has been purchased by a gargantuan rise in medical expenditures.

In other words, we are in precisely the predicament described by Tainter: rapidly diminishing returns on our social investment in medicine. Having already done the easiest and least expensive things to improve health and extend life, we must now spend very large sums to make relatively small gains, for "as each increasingly expensive disease is conquered, the increment to average life expectancy becomes smaller." In fact, epidemiological studies suggest that we may be approaching biological limits. For instance, eliminating all forms of heart disease, which is the leading cause of death in the United States, would improve life expectancy at age thirty-five by only a little more than three years. Similar studies of cancer are even less encouraging: total elimination of all forms of cancer would extend the average life by less than a mere two years. (These trifling gains from such major advances reflect what epidemiolo-

---

*Ironically, a reversal of this trend is now apparent: despite radically improved medical means, tuberculosis and other infectious diseases are making a comeback, with declining social conditions and public cleanliness being partly to blame. More important, however, is the rapid and alarming growth in bacterial resistance to antibiotics, which physicians and medical researchers describe in apocalyptic terms: "nothing short of a medical disaster," "a public-health nightmare," and so on. As Laurie Garrett points out, bacterial resistance is the product of human hubris: modern medicine has tried to overpower nature in defiance of evolutionary principles and ecological laws, thus guaranteeing that bacteria would eventually become immune to all the weapons in our chemical arsenal.

gists call the "theory of competing causes of death": as the average age of a population increases, the "years of life retrievable" by eliminating any particular cause of death necessarily become fewer.) Indeed, the emergence of new diseases like AIDS now obliges us to expend large sums merely to forestall a *drop* in life expectancy. Thus, although medical science continues to make real progress against these and other conditions, it is necessarily progress at the margin: we no longer take large bites out of mortality, only tiny nibbles—and each nibble, each further increment of progress toward the unattainable goal of perfect health, costs more and more.

Moreover, the costs of modern medicine are not simply financial: along with advances in medical science have come various "diseases of medicine," such as the iatrogenic (doctor-caused) illnesses that result from medical treatment itself. In fact, the statistics warn that one of the gravest health hazards is being admitted to a hospital. And the medical system now seems to inflict almost as much pain and suffering as it relieves, especially on the terminally ill.

The upshot is that medical resources are increasingly devoted to ends that bring little real gain to society and that are sometimes disadvantageous to the patients themselves. For example, more than half of our medical budget is dedicated to postponing the inevitable by a few months for the moribund old—which in too many cases means extending their agony, not their enjoyment of life. (To be specific, according to public health researcher Patrizia DiLucchio, "two-thirds of all Medicare expenditures . . . occur in the last year of life, and half of that amount occurs in the last month of life.") We also spend heavily to save the lives of a few premature or diseased infants who are likely to constitute a continuing financial and social burden, both to their families and to the general public. (DiLucchio again: "It is not unusual to end up spending $500,000 to 'save' a child who will turn out to be completely dysfunctional and end up surviving only a few years.")

So medical resources are largely consumed by heroic interventions at the two extremes of the life span, interventions that often do more harm than good. At the same time, the cost of treating the medical aftermath of social failure—crime, drugs, sexual promiscuity, and so on—is also very high and growing rapidly. This is not to deny or denigrate the blessings that many *individuals* in all the above categories have received from modern scientific medicine; but these vast expenditures do little to improve the overall health of the *population*. What is worse, no money is left over to pay for programs that bring great social and individual benefit at relatively low cost—for example, prenatal care and early-childhood immunization. In general, therefore, the comparatively small gains in public and personal health since 1915 have been achieved at costs that are utterly disproportionate to the benefits received.

Medicine therefore illustrates with stark clarity the nature of the developmental life cycle: exuberant growth and big gains at the beginning, diminishing returns and an inexorable rise in costs at the end. Hence, as medical science continues to make further strides, finding ever more high-tech and expensive ways of staving off death at both ends of the life span, the escalation of costs threatens us with bankruptcy.

Better management alone will not control medical costs. Because it is primarily technology that drives costs higher, it will take a social decision to forgo some of the miracles of medical science. But no one wants the job of belling the medical cat, for that would require us to make excruciating trade-offs between the end of saving individual human lives and the available social and financial means. Nevertheless, there is beginning to be widespread agreement that unless we make agonizing moral and political decisions about how to "ration" (for which the current euphemism is "manage") increasingly "scarce" medical care, the system will simply implode.

In any event, the futility of seeking to conquer natural limits with technology is pitilessly revealed. Not only have we no prospect whatsoever of completely eliminating both heart disease and cancer, but if we were to do so (at what price?) it would lengthen our days by no more than a few years (at what quality of life?). What is worse, given emergent diseases like AIDS and the phenomenon of bacterial resistance, we may be hard-pressed both technically and financially to preserve the status quo. The lesson of medicine is thus the lesson of development in general: because "everything better is purchased at the price of something worse," medicine's very success has generated problems and costs that now menace our financial and personal health.

The Vulnerability of Artificial Systems

A major part of the price that we have had to pay for our so-called abundance is that artificial human systems are now far more vulnerable to sclerosis, or to disruption from many causes, than are the natural systems they supplant. Economic development destroys organic communities that are largely self-regulating and self-maintaining and replaces them with man-made systems that are anything but. Our water is no longer supplied naturally by wells or streams, but artificially by gigantic hydraulic systems requiring a corresponding amount of money, effort, and energy to build and maintain. Similarly, the old and the ill are no longer cared for by family members, but by institutions—again, at a higher cost in money, effort, and energy. In brief, to replace the goods and services formerly supplied organically at little or no cost, we have had to erect an expensive, complicated, and unstable regime of artificial management.

In effect, we have replaced natural systems with bureaucratic ones. Unfortunately, bureaucracies are afflicted with various diseases, of which continuous Parkinsonian growth without regard to the quantity or quality of the services performed is only the most notorious. For all the reasons we have explored above, artificially managed systems therefore tend to become steadily less capable of performing the necessary functions or providing the desired benefits, while at the same time consuming more and more resources.

The growing resource appetite of the human ecosystem naturally raises the question of resource availability. And justifiably so, for we now consume in one year what it took the Earth many thousands or even millions of years to accumulate. Moreover, having exploited the richest and most convenient stocks first, we must now turn to resources that are poorer and less accessible—and thus more expensive.

Most troubling in this regard is that energy is slowly but inexorably becoming more expensive in terms of itself. That is, we are experiencing a gradual decline in "net energy yield," because more and more energy must be used to find, extract, transport, and process energy. Compare, for example, the first gusher of crude oil at fifty feet in Pennsylvania to the situation today: we now extract petroleum at great depths, in difficult environments, and in remote locations. Whatever the dollar price per barrel, petroleum is therefore more expensive in energy terms. (As we have recently learned, Persian Gulf oil is exceptionally expensive despite seemingly low production costs, because the diplomatic and military price of guaranteeing access is very high: in this sense, resource dependency has a very real price, in both cash and blood.) And the question is not whether net energy yield will continue to decline in the decades to come but only how rapidly and with what impact on prices.

A basic vulnerability of the human ecosystem stands revealed. Relatively cheap and abundant energy has enabled us to build an artificial human ecosystem as a dike to hold back the ocean of ecological scarcity created by our pursuit of abundance. A possible interruption in supply or even a major increase in costs is hence extremely threatening. Indeed, the human ecosystem is vulnerable not only to shortages of supply or rising costs but also to acts of God, terrorist attacks, breakdowns in public order, lapses in judgment, failures of will, operator blunders, and numerous other menaces. And the higher the level of development, the higher the level of vulnerability.

To put it another way, because the human ecosystem is not self-regulating and self-maintaining, a heavier management burden is thrust on us as the system grows in size and complexity. Unfortunately, the problems, but not always our ability to comprehend and deal with them, tend to grow exponentially. Indeed, as the example of bacterial resistance to antibiotics illustrates, some of these self-generated problems may have no technical solution. And as Tainter's analysis suggests, in the long run the problem of managing complexity is likely to become insuperable, so civilizations eventually decline.

To sum up, artificial management is not only more expensive and inefficient than organic self-management; it is also less safe, strong, and resilient. We have created a system that is enormously bigger and more powerful—yet also far more vulnerable. The problem is not size alone but the many dimensions of the problem—technical, administrative, intellectual, moral, social, political—all of which interact with each other to produce unanticipated and often unwelcome results, like the many vicious circles we have hitherto explored. As a people, we have crawled quite far out on the limb of civilized complexity, leaving us vulnerable to a long, hard fall if we should, for whatever reason, fail at the task of managing it effectively. And there are ominous signs, in at least some areas, of impending overload and collapse, as diminishing returns set in and running in place starts to consume most of our available resources.

Civilization and Scarcity: A Summary View

To conclude this discussion of abundance and scarcity in the human ecosystem, we can now see that our habitual equation of economic wealth with "abundance" is simple-minded at best, seriously flawed at worst. When we add together all the shadow prices, displaced costs, inefficiencies, and vulnerabilities of development, we find that not only has modern abundance impoverished us in many important ways, but it is really scarcity in disguise.

First, as pointed out in the Introduction, we are living on capital, not income. Modern economic development is based not on renewable or flow resources such as solar energy but, rather, on finite, nonrenewable stocks of thermodynamically scarce resources such as the concentrated energy in hydrocarbon deposits and the concentrated matter in mineral ores.

Second, we have used up the best of this capital first, providing a bonanza with which to fuel the developmental boom of the past five centuries. But such a one-time "energy subsidy" is not a basis for long-term sustainability. Moreover, the bonanza has now entered its final phase, both because the level of demand for resources has grown so enormous and because it takes more and more resources to get resources.

Third, we have used this energy subsidy to construct a complicated artificial regime that necessitates increasingly heroic efforts to bridge the gap between what is naturally available and what is humanly desired—and that shows a false profit on its ledger of accounts, inasmuch as we have temporarily "externalized" its actual costs of doing business.

We have therefore created a large and vulnerable human ecosystem characterized by acute scarcity. In effect, the higher we attempt to build the edifice of civilization above the ecological foundation that is biologically natural for the human animal, the greater the scarcity. As Sahlins says, "The market-industrial system institutes scarcity, in a manner completely unparalleled and to a degree nowhere else approximated." It presents the illusion of abundance only to those who have not examined the ecological books to see both the enormous debts already incurred and the burgeoning deficits that result from trying to maintain the illusion. Such an economy must eventually confront a day of reckoning when the Ponzi game of development finally collapses, as the previously overlooked costs reveal themselves and the thermodynamic bills for past malfeasance come due.

Up to now, we have found cleverer and more ruthless ways not to pay and to continue the slavery. But doing so may cost us more in the long run: postponing the day of reckoning increases the stakes, and therefore the risks, of the game. This has not previously bothered us, because we were sure that we could always come up with a technological fix to build the edifice yet higher. However, recent developments have shown us that constructing the next story of civilization will be much harder and riskier than all the previous ones. In fact, we may be hard-pressed to maintain what we have already achieved in some areas, even if we continue to make progress in others. Nor can we casually assume that future generations will be willing or able to pay the deferred costs of our spendthrift ways. Indeed, as the first generation to be saddled with major ecological clean-up costs, we ourselves are troubled by the dubious legacy of our industrial past. Finally, and most important of all, the more we succeed in postponing the day of reckoning physically, the higher the psychological, social, and political price we shall eventually have to pay.

From Energy Slavery to Energy Despotism

This latter point is crucial. One of the most insidious and ominous hidden costs of intensified economic development based on energy slavery is the inexorable growth of the technocratic structure of governance that anthropologist Marvin Harris calls "energy despotism." This is a necessary consequence of energy slavery: civilization is based on human concentration and control of matter and energy resources; and magnified power in the physical realm has always been accompanied by expanded power in the political realm. In short, and all other things being equal, intensified exploitation of matter and energy must lead to tighter social and political controls. (Naturally, circumstances alter cases: we have already seen how the exceptionally benign ecological conditions of early America helped to produce political democracy and social equality.) But modern economic development based explicitly on an intensified exploitation of nature greatly exacerbates this tendency: it wrecks both biological and social communities and thus throws an increasingly heavy management burden on society. Since the beginning of the Industrial Revolution, the forces fostering energy despotism have therefore grown much faster than the general rate of development. In effect, energy slavery has begun to enslave the putative masters.

This outcome was anticipated by a long and impressive list of thinkers, beginning with Rousseau, who challenged the Enlightenment assumption that economic development was the key to political progress. As we have seen, both Jefferson and de Tocqueville also feared the political and social consequences of economic development, and the latter warned specifically against the rise of a "manufacturing aristocracy."

What earlier thinkers saw as a future danger, Weber took to be an accomplished fact. Writing at a time when capitalist civilization seemed to be reaching its acme, Weber concluded his classic intellectual history of the Industrial Revolution by saying, "The tremendous cosmos of the modern economic order . . . determine[s] the lives of all the individuals who are born into this mechanism, not only those directly concerned with economic acquisition, with irresistible force." As a result, modern men and women were now imprisoned within an "iron cage," a state of "mechanized petrifaction" that was rapidly turning them into "specialists without spirit, sensualists without heart." Worst of all, Western civilization, blinded by pride, was not even aware of its cultural loss: "This nullity imagines that it has attained a level of civilization never before achieved."

Matters have not improved in the interim. In one of the best contemporary assessments of the sociopolitical impact of technology, Langdon Winner writes that technology has become "autonomous": "No matter which aims and purposes one decides to put in, a particular kind of product inevitably comes out." Thus it is *we* who must more and more adapt to *it*, a process he calls "reverse adaptation." The consequence is an all-encompassing "disenfranchisement" by a "megatechnical corporate-government alliance" that forces greater control, centralization, hierarchy, and inequality on us all.

In other words, technology has become the *essential* politics of our age: it literally determines our social and political destiny. Technological decisions, especially those that are about the first introduction of a new device or practice, are tantamount to legislative acts or even to political constitutions, because they establish an enduring framework of *public* order. And the public order that we have established through past technological "decisions" is utterly antithetical to our avowed social and political ideals. Ultimately, concludes Winner, the Enlightenment's utopian goal of combining high production with a benign politics is chimerical:

> One can seek the high levels of productivity that modern technological systems bring. One can also seek the founding of a communal life in which the division of labor, social hierarchy, and political domination are eradicated. But can one in any realistic terms have both? I am convinced that the answer to this is a firm "no."

Despite warnings by Rousseau, Marx, and Weber, among many others, that technological change is also social change—the Industrial Revolution was, after all, a total transformation of the sociopolitical order in all its dimensions—we have nevertheless given technology a free rein. The paradox is that polities which are otherwise quite conservative, such as our own, have allowed technology to become autonomous, thereby foisting radical sociopolitical changes on their peoples—changes that they did not always desire and certainly did not legislate. (Ironically, the supposed "conservatives" of American politics, who complain the loudest about many of these changes, especially moral decay, are the most laissez-faire with respect to the economic enterprise and technological innovation that produce them.) In return for technological freedom, we have indeed obtained higher levels of production, but we have had to pay the price in lost social cohesion and political autonomy, as the values of "efficiency" and "exchange" implicit in achieving greater productivity have invaded the sociopolitical realm. (The supposed "liberals" of American politics are just as deluded as the "conservatives": equally addicted to material progress, they also want to conquer nature with technology; but they foolishly believe that economic production is possible without economic power, that ordinary citizens can call the political and social tune when, in fact, it is economic and technological enterprise that pays the piper.) In short, with the collaboration of all parties, the technological servant has become the political master.

The reign of technology is rapidly becoming total. Even now, decisions of enormous import affecting every area of our lives—decisions about telecommunications, computing, international finance, electronic entertainment, medical treatment, genetic engineering, and the like—are being taken by small coteries of "experts" who incarnate Thorstein Veblen's "trained incapacity" to see beyond their professional or technical blinkers. What is worse, their decisions are motivated by profit, directly or indirectly. Yet what they decide will be tantamount to a constitution for the economic and social system of the twenty-first century. We have therefore effectively abdicated control over our political destiny to a vast and autonomous technological regime. We err profoundly in using the word *revolution* to refer to new and exciting technological developments: in fact, we are "governed" by a continuing technological *coup d'état*.

The technological *coup d'état* is a political *coup d'état* as well. Power is exercised by a class of lawyers, financiers, managers, and professionals who operate the technological system in accordance with legal, bureaucratic, technical, and financial criteria largely established by the class itself. Although power is not exercised by anyone in particular, the collective power of this class is awesome, greater than that of elected officials. In modern societies, it effectively decides what the problems are, what we should do about them, how to go about doing it, and whether the doing worked. This class therefore mostly determines the ends of the system and almost totally controls its means—organization, budget, personnel, technology.

This is an extraordinary grant of power to an extraconstitutional group. Even if it operates within an established constitutional framework, and glaring abuses are normally detected and punished, a class of persons without formal political status has now taken control of the affairs of the polity. (To his horror and outrage, President Clinton learned when he assumed office that the fiscal policies of the United States are set by Wall Street bond traders, not Washington officials.) So we have been effectively disenfranchised by technology. Yet those who wield this unauthorized and unconstitutional power are not thereby enfranchised, because in the end they too are just personnel—mere functionaries of the system and just as caught up in its ideological and bureaucratic toils as the average citizen, if not more so.

Yet the degree to which we have been effectively disenfranchised is little understood or acknowledged. One of the greatest ironies of an age that prides itself on knowing everything that happens as soon as it happens is that, to an even greater extent than suggested by Weber, few members of Western civilization understand their real conditions of existence. Discussing the impact of industrialization on the working class in England, Engels pointed out that

> the situation of the factory operative is less enviable than that of the medi-aeval serf. Slavery has been the lot of both the serf and the factory workers. While in mediaeval times serfdom was an honourable status, undisguised and openly admitted, the slavery of the working classes today is hypocriti-cally and cunningly disguised from themselves and the public. It is a far worse type of slavery than mediaeval serfdom.

Yet by today's standards, the slavery of the factory worker in Manchester was blatant. That of our own age is much more "hypocritically and cun-ningly disguised"—not only by the media circus and the fallacious afflu-ence already discussed, but also by the fraudulent myth of abundance and progress at the core of the Enlightenment ideology.

Both our profound disenfranchisement and the cloud of mystification that envelops it raise grave questions about our political future. In the long run, energy despotism and political despotism must go hand in hand. The situation has turned out precisely as de Tocqueville feared: "In their intense and exclusive anxiety to make a fortune," the American people have largely neglected "their chief business, which is to remain their own masters."

We have made this mistake through failing to understand that technol-ogy is *intrinsically political*. The struggle between Hamilton and Jeffer-son for the American soul was decided not philosophically nor ideologi-cally but technologically—that is, by economic growth, which created social conditions that rendered Jefferson's political ideas moot. As Win-ner emphasizes, *"Different ideas of social and political life entail different technologies for their realization."* Thus we shall not regain control over our destiny or remain our own masters thereafter until our political and social ideals are reflected in our technological means. Taking charge of our fate, instead of allowing it to be determined for us by autonomous technology, will require not only radical political reform but also a pro-found revisioning and reinventing of technology itself.

Civilized man prides himself on the great powers he commands. In fact, he commands nothing: his means decide his ends; his supposed slaves are in reality his masters; so it is his powers that control him. Hence modern civilization's tragic propensity for biocide and genocide: without control over the powers he supposedly commands, civilized man is compelled to destroy the last refuges of pristine nature along with the few remaining bands of natural men and women who live there. The irony is pointed out by Sahlins: our civilization "does not hesitate to destroy any other form of humanity whose difference from us consists in having discovered not merely other codes of existence but ways of achieving an end that still eludes us: the mastery by society of society's mastery over nature."

The Tragedy of Development

To recapitulate, the Enlightenment believed it had found a cure for the worst ills of traditional civilization: economic development via the technological conquest of nature. The resulting abundance would eliminate poverty, alleviate (or at least rationalize) inequality, and make possible the overthrow of tyranny. Reasonable in theory, the cure has failed in practice. First, economic development is predatory: it is a war on nature that also fuels the fires of human aggression. In addition, it attacks living communities of human beings, grinding them down into social atoms forced to fend for themselves within an impersonal market system. Worse, the affluence produced by development is fallacious: it fosters addiction instead of satisfaction. Moreover, far from moderating inequality, greater affluence only increases the extent of relative deprivation. And rationalizing inequality makes it paradoxically more odious, not less. An even greater paradox is that, in the end, when all the costs and benefits are fully and fairly accounted for, economic development magnifies scarcity instead of reducing it. The seeming abundance produced by energy slavery is fraudulent: it rests on a foundation of stolen goods, deferred payments, and hidden costs. It is also dangerous: the political concomitant of energy slavery is energy despotism, a technocratic regime that organizes and maintains the slavery and thereby enslaves the citizens. Hence we are no longer our own masters, politically or spiritually: our excessive devotion to self-enrichment has carried us away, and we now find ourselves in Weber's "iron cage."

We are enacting a great tragedy—a remorseless working of things that is bringing us exactly the opposite of what we intended—because the Enlightenment's purported cure for the ills of civilization is only a more virulent form of the disease. This tragedy cuts across every political and ideological boundary. It is common to advanced and backward, capitalist and socialist alike; all are caught in its fatal and ironic toils. "Conservatives" who thought that economic development would bring social stability and political peace are rewarded with moral entropy and factional war instead; "liberals" who believed it would eliminate poverty and inequality watch helplessly as these become more deeply entrenched despite every effort to combat them. But neither conservative nor liberal will abandon the true Enlightenment faith of salvation by economic development, and so we march ever deeper into a quagmire of scarcity that will swallow up the possibility of economic plenitude and political freedom.

The origin of the tragedy of civilization, says Sahlins, is that by abandoning the "original affluent society," man condemned himself to be forever thereafter "the prisoner at hard labor of a perpetual disparity between his unlimited wants and his insufficient means." The Enlightenment tried to cure the problems resulting from this original mistake with what amounted to more of the same. Inevitably, this has only compounded the error and deepened the tragedy: "the prisoner at hard labor" is now, as previously noted, confined in an "iron cage."

The fallacy of developmentalism, the ideological conviction that the solution to human problems and the path to human happiness lie in making humankind richer and more powerful, is that it tries to substitute having for being. The result is a moral and political debacle, whose tragic course was traced by Rousseau in his *Second Discourse*:

> Savage man, when he has eaten, is at peace with all nature, and the friend of all his fellow-men. . . . But for man in society . . . it is first of all a question of providing for the necessary, and then for the superfluous; next come delights, then immense wealth, and then subjects, and then slaves; he does not have a moment of respite. What is most singular is that the less natural and urgent the needs, the more the passions augment, and, what is worse, the power to satisfy them; so that after long prosperity, after having swallowed up many treasures and desolated many men, my hero will end by ruining everything until he is the sole master of the universe.

Marx and Keynes to the contrary notwithstanding, it is not that we shall one day be rich enough to afford morality but, rather, the reverse. The pursuit of riches without regard to moral purpose simply unleashes a self-devouring wolf of appetite within the human community: insatiable wants fuel a vicious circle of limitless Hobbesian power seeking, until man finds himself sole master of a ruined universe.

We therefore arrive at the same conclusion about liberal economics as about liberal politics: virtue is indispensable. The reason was succinctly stated by Rousseau: "For the impulse of appetite alone is slavery, and obedience to the law one has prescribed for oneself is freedom." From this perspective, trying to make ourselves rich enough to afford morality has matters the wrong way around and must lead to corruption, because enriching ourselves requires means that are "foul." It is instead morality—"obedience to the law one has prescribed for oneself"—that can give us the wisdom and the strength to step out of the tragedy and create a just social order characterized by real abundance, genuine equality, and authentic freedom. Virtue is therefore both the end and the means of true progress.

The economic solution parallels the political solution: both the political order and the economic order need to be guided by a moral purpose and a conception of the good life that subordinates having to being and that restores the proper relationship of economic means to political ends. Material well-being is by no means excluded from this notion of the good life—but it is radically deemphasized, because it asserts that the true wealth of human existence is to be found inside ourselves.

In this light, the proper aim of economics is an economy of sufficiency or plenitude that supports *social* abundance—that is, such a high level of cultural and spiritual wealth that the incentive to become inordinately rich in worldly goods is blunted. This ideal was expressed in its most utopian form by John Stuart Mill: "The best state for human nature is that in which, while no one is poor, no one desires to be any richer, nor has any reason to fear being thrust back by the efforts of others to push themselves forward." If this "best state" is perhaps too utopian for mere mortals, there is surely no need to go to the opposite extreme of exalting a money-grubbing preoccupation with the means of existence into the end of life—not even temporarily, for Keynes's proposal that we adopt "foul" and "semi-pathological" means to enrich ourselves, so that we can one day retire on our ill-gotten gains, is both morally obnoxious and practically unachievable.

A better guide to a virtuous economics is ecology, which tells us how to live simply and wisely on this Earth. Genuine ecological abundance is not a high yield obtained at the expense of the system's long-term health. It is instead a rich stock that is skillfully maintained with due regard for the relationship between ends and means and for the consequences of employing those means over the long term. In other words, ecological wisdom tells us to pursue policies of quality, not quantity; conservation, not consumption; being, not having. Ecology therefore offers us a vision of the good biological life, one in harmony with the deepest personal aspirations and highest political ideals of humanity.

How could it be that, with the very best of intentions, we went so far wrong, pursuing an economic strategy by which we systematically impoverish ourselves in the long run? The answer is that the political and economic problems and contradictions analyzed hitherto all have their origin in the flawed notion of reality bequeathed to us by the Enlightenment, so let us now critically examine the epistemology and ontology that underlie both liberal politics and economic development.

6

IRRATIONAL REASON

Mere purposive rationality unaided by such phenomena as art, religion, dream, and the like, is necessarily pathogenic and destructive of life.

—Gregory Bateson

The disease of reason is that reason was born from man's urge to dominate nature, and the "recovery" depends on insight into the nature of the original disease, not on a cure of the latest symptoms. . . . [T]he collective madness that ranges today . . . was already present in germ in primitive objectivization, in the first man's calculating contemplation of the world as prey.

—Max Horkheimer

The most dangerous stage in the growth of civilization may well be that in which man has come to regard all these beliefs as superstitions and refuses to accept or to submit to anything which he does not rationally understand. The rationalist whose reason is not sufficient to teach him those limitations of the power of conscious reason, and who despises all the institutions and customs which have not been consciously designed, would thus become the destroyer of the civilization built upon them.

—F. A. Hayek

A utilitarian civilization will always go on to its logical conclusion—forced labor camps.

—Romain Gary

It is possible, we now know, for a society to be the heir to the knowledge of all the ages, and to use it with the recklessness of a madman and the ferocity of a savage.

—R. H. Tawney

IT WOULD BE A MISTAKE TO MAKE IDEAS AND THEORIES of knowledge into *the* prime movers of history, for their impact depends on the people who embrace them and the situations in which they function. To achieve a full historical understanding, we must therefore take into account the sanity or madness of princes, the clash of competing classes and interests, the availability of ecological resources, and numerous other factors, along with all their interactions. Nevertheless, just as the wellsprings of individual human behavior are most clearly descried in a person's basic presumptions and attitudes, so too the behavior of societies and indeed whole civilizations faithfully mirrors their fundamental ideas about the nature of reality and the ends of life. In this sense, to know the root ideas or governing paradigms of a culture or civilization is to understand its behavior. History is thus a record of paradigms being played out through time: "The memorable events of history," said Le Bon, "are the visible effects of the invisible changes of human thought."

With this preamble, we come to the thesis for this chapter: the violence and self-destructiveness of modern civilization, as well as almost all the political and economic ills and contradictions explored hitherto, derive directly from a flawed epistemology. They result from a theory of knowledge that exalts reason in its narrowest and most unreasonable form—the merely instrumental, purposive rationality that, says Bateson, "is necessarily pathogenic and destructive of life." In other words, a small and calculating reason that does not include imagination, common sense, and a moral (or at least prudential) awareness of what is appropriate *in human terms*. Worse yet, this pathogenic epistemology makes a perfect instrument for the will to power underlying civilization in general and Western civilization in particular. Indeed, it is an expression of that will to power.

The fatal defects of Enlightenment epistemology have roots deep in human history, especially Western history. In fact, they originate in the rise of civilization itself. Civilization fostered not only the will to power but also an increased abstraction from the natural world that gave human beings a greater ability to understand and exploit their environment. At the same time, however, abstraction also detaches us from reality and leads our minds into many paths of delusion. Since we have not the space to explore this vast topic in any depth, one brief illustration of the costs of abstraction will have to suffice.

Literacy, a giant step on the long road from primal participation to abstract knowledge, exacted a high price: the constriction of human consciousness. As Walter Ong points out, "Writing . . . is a particularly preemptive and imperialist activity that tends to assimilate other things to itself . . . [and] tyrannically locks them into a visual field forever."* Moreover, since the visual field of literacy is narrow and artificial—the printed page, not the full panoply of nature—a literate culture tends to condemn its members to sensual impoverishment (to which television is not the antidote, for it merely floods the senses with artificial, manipulated media images).

In this light, just as modern ideas of political economy were not opposed to the basic thrust of all previous civilization, but instead constituted an intensification and amplification of it, the epistemology of the Enlightenment, for all its revolutionary aspects, is less a break with the civilized tradition than its logical continuation away from the natural and concrete toward the artificial and abstract—and hence toward the deformation of consciousness that this entails.

The New Inquisition

Enlightenment thought represents continuity rather than change in another key area as well: religion. Although it is famous for its hostility to organized religion, the Enlightenment was itself a quasi-religious movement that stole the sacred fire of the Judeo-Christian tradition and harnessed it to secular ends. Before turning to the epistemological revolution created by René Descartes and Francis Bacon, the principal authors of the new way of thinking, let us see how reason became a religion and Science a new Inquisition.

To this end, we must carefully distinguish between "science" in lower case and "Science" with a capital "S". The former is the normal, natural, and desirable human activity of investigating the world with the best intellectual and physical tools available to discover, insofar as possible, what is true. The latter is the historical and ideological phenomenon that ousted the church from its dominant position. The former activity, were it to be conducted in the right spirit, would bring primarily benefit to humanity. The latter phenomenon, despite the decency and goodwill of individual scientists and the many advantages it has brought us, has been a human and ecological debacle, due to the insanity of its motivations and

---

*Literacy is "imperialist" in another sense as well. Like any other technology, writing has an intrinsic politics: it makes administration (and therefore political oppression) possible. As Claude Lévi-Strauss put it, "The only phenomenon with which writing has always been concomitant is the creation of cities and empires, that is the integration of large numbers of individuals into a political system. . . . My hypothesis [is that] the primary function of written communication is to facilitate slavery."

the often simple-minded brutality of its methods (or so I will argue in the following pages). Thus my purpose in criticizing an imperial Science is to correct what I perceive to be a dangerous political situation, not to promote obscurantism and superstition, much less hinder scientific investigation of the former kind, for science can be conceived of and practiced in ways that support rather than destroy life. Nor am I trying to turn working scientists into scapegoats responsible for all modern ills. Blame is not appropriate: as creatures of the Enlightenment, we all share in its basic attitudes and are all equally implicated in its tragic flaws.

As noted in the Introduction, the Enlightenment arose as a reaction to—or, more accurately, a revulsion against—the perceived evils of organized religion as exemplified in the doctrines and deeds of the medieval church. Naturally, the church did its best to combat and nullify a threat to its monopoly of truth, its wealth, and its political power. But it lost the ideological war with Science for the heart and mind of an entire civilization: a new and quasi-established Church of Reason displaced the old Christian Church from the cultural hegemony and political sway it had maintained for over a millennium.

Ironically, the victory of this new Church of Reason was achieved by political, not rational, means. The Christian Church was overpowered, not converted; its worldview rejected, not refuted. Science simply asserted a new reality principle: a strict canon of "rationality" that guaranteed it would win all the debates. Alfred North Whitehead pointed out that the *philosophes*, for all their genius, were not real philosophers, but propagandists for a "one-eyed reason" who did not deign to debate: "Whatever did not fit into their scheme was ignored, derided, disbelieved." Hence, says philosopher Paul Feyerabend, an imperial Science prevails today "not because of its comparative merits, but because the show has been rigged in its favor." In practice, this means that Science cannot be challenged: it accepts only its own rules and sets itself problems only it can solve, rejecting all other approaches and questions as uninteresting, irrelevant, or nonsensical. It also means that the right to participate in public debate is limited to those who accept the rationalist rules of the game—just as in medieval times, when all argument had to begin and end with accepted Christian dogma. But it was only poetic justice that Christianity be overthrown politically, for it had defeated the so-called pagans in the same fashion: by seizing imperial power, rather than by effecting mass persuasion.

As the heir of the Christian Church, Science assumed not just its intellectual and political mantle but also many of its worst characteristics—above all, its intolerance. Pascal identified two equally pathological extremes—"to shut reason out, and to let nothing else in"—but it was precisely to these extremes that the two ideological opponents were driven. If the church claimed to be the sole proprietor of truth on the basis of a divine revelation that needed no verification, only belief in its absurdity, then almost willy-nilly Science had to adopt the opposite stance—namely, that religion in all its aspects was a pack of irrational superstitions and deceitful myths that exploited popular credulity for the benefit of a corrupt clergy and a decadent aristocracy. No middle ground was left. And because Science's political victory was not total—the church was vanquished, but not eliminated or even silenced—ideological militancy could never be relaxed. Science had to insist that, although individual scientists might well err on occasion, Science itself could not possibly err in the long run, for it alone possessed a certain path to truth. In short, any other road to knowledge but Science is delusion.

Imperial Science's claim to a monopoly on truth was not solely an outgrowth of this ideological struggle. It also reflected a fundamental characteristic of Western thought from ancient times: the demand for a single, omnipotent deity. In brief, the transition from so-called savagery to civilization made chiefs into kings, so monarchy emerged as a political principle—and monotheism, both as religious principle and as historical phenomenon, arose as a direct reflection of and companion to one-man rule. But the kings of antiquity were essentially warlords. To state the point baldly, monotheism is a warlord religion: like the quarrelsome kings of old, a bellicose deity watches jealously over his chosen place and people, vigorously repelling all would-be invaders and militantly seeking to extend his imperium. (Hence Voltaire's sardonic remark: "If God has made man in His image, we have certainly returned the compliment.") So monotheism is much more than a theology. It is also a political ideology justifying holy war: it is not *the* One but *our* One who must prevail. This is made explicit in biblical history, wherein the followers of Moses wage wars of extermination against those who do not believe in Yahweh, offering up whole cities and their inhabitants as literal hecatombs to this "jealous God." Little wonder, then, that the history of monotheism is rife with arrogance, rigidity, intolerance, militancy, cruelty, violence, and, indeed, genocide.

Besides incorporating this narrow-minded insistence on a single truth, Science inherited the Western religious tradition's eschatological drive toward progress and perfection. Christian doctrine may have been defeated, but its moral and redemptive passion poured over into the new

Church of Reason. Thus we are still bound for the Promised Land, but now by rational rather than religious means, and for profane rather than sacred ends. Science became, in effect, the new Messiah, come to save humankind from age-old ills. This identification of Science with salvation—both consciously and, more important, unconsciously—meant that to challenge the authority of the Church of Reason was to commit heresy: thou shalt have no other gods before Science.

At the same time, ironically, the replacement of religion with rationality, far from ending ideological strife, only intensified it. Because Science began by promoting a profound general skepticism and by debunking the alleged superstition of the Christian Church, it could not hope to confine critical reason to the laboratory. With no authority but rationality, demonstrating that everyone—oneself, of course, excepted—was the prisoner of "false consciousness" became only too easy. The upshot has been an ideological war of all against all, as intellectuals try to "deconstruct" the thought of their political enemies.

Moreover, despite its eschatological pretensions, Science could not hope to replace the church in meeting the emotional and spiritual needs of large populations. Indeed, it did not even pretend to do so: Science is physics, not metaphysics, and is thus "value free." Yet, as we shall see below, Science is fundamentally idolatrous: it is convinced that it describes reality, rather than merely representing it. Hence, despite its origins in skepticism, it has turned out to be even more dogmatic than scriptural religion in certain respects.

So the ground was prepared for a vast upsurge of ideology and ideological warfare, to such an extent that a common rubric for much of modern history is "The Age of Ideology." Paradoxically, therefore, the triumph of "reason" was accompanied by the luxuriant growth of numerous idolatrous secular religions, all seeking to restore lost meaning (a point to which we shall return later).

In sum, the revolutionary and liberating character of the Enlightenment has been overstated. From a larger political perspective, far from being a fundamental change of regime, the triumph of Science was more like a *coup d'état* that transformed the old politics without transmuting it. The relatively overt theological tyranny of the church was thus exchanged for the more subtle ideological tyranny of reason, as the old monotheistic and messianic spirit was poured into a new political bottle. The effect, said philosopher Miguel de Unamuno, was to create a "new Inquisition." In the end, Science's victory over the church left us with some of the worst ills of religion and none of its real consolations.

The Death of Nature

Having examined *how little* the overthrow of religion by rationality actually changed the essential spirit of Western civilization, we are now in a better position to appreciate the revolutionary impact of the new thought—to see *how much* it did, in fact, change its contents and hence alter its basic character. As always, our focus is on politics, not intellectual history for its own sake, so what follows is an epitome designed to lay bare the political consequences of the new thought.

Despite the continuities we have noted, the birth of the modern worldview was a tremendous intellectual discontinuity. Although humanity has moved gradually farther away from original participation in nature and toward greater abstraction of thought during the course of civilized existence, it is nonetheless true that the medieval mind was in many ways close to the mind of antiquity: medieval men and women still sought communion with an unseen supernatural reality. To this end, they relied on the faculties of revelation, intuition, insight, and imagination more than on logic. And however much they pursued power and other worldly things, their ultimate orientation was "not of this world." Moreover, all aspects of reality were spiritually united in a "Great Chain of Being." This was tantamount to a superorganism containing all of creation, from the angels above to the animals below, that was quickened by an *anima mundi* or world soul. Ancient and medieval worldviews therefore differed in degree, not in kind.

The modern era, by contrast, is dramatically different in kind. According to the new reality principle, men and women should no longer seek either participation in an unseen supernatural reality or salvation in an afterlife. Instead, they should pursue the things of this world "rationally," using empirical, logical, analytical, objective, and mechanical means. Life is no longer sacred, but thoroughly secular in end and means, for nature is sundered from the divine—or, rather, there is no longer any such thing as the divine. In place of the *anima mundi* there thus arose a *machina mundi*, a lifeless and soulless world machine.

The machine metaphor for the modern age is such a cliché that one is almost embarrassed to restate it. Cliché or not, however, it is our governing metaphor, and it has profound implications. It says that the stuff composing the world is dead matter in the form of discrete parts moved by discernible external forces, as when a rod moves a piston. It follows that the order of nature is fixed and stable and can be known by equally fixed and stable principles. It can therefore be described and analyzed logically, mathematically, and deterministically in ways that disregard the larger context, because a machine is no more than the sum of its fixed and stable parts. It follows, too, that the world as perceived is all of reality—in other words, there is nothing transcendent above or beyond it. And that the human mind is simply a kind of calculating machine standing apart from nature and operating on the raw sense data given to it by the organs of perception (assumed to be in direct contact with reality), rather than an instrument for seeing beyond appearances. Hobbes put this idea in its most extreme form by stating that "REASON . . . is nothing but *reckoning*, that is adding and subtracting."

The jargon used to characterize this attitude toward nature and life is revealing: objectivist, positivist, and reductionist. As an objectivist, one treats nature as a distant object to be observed and manipulated entirely separate and apart from one's own subjective feelings. As a positivist, one forswears all forms of intuition, appreciation, introspection, or speculation and takes the world as a phenomenological given, trusting only empirically observable and replicable sense data, so that anything which cannot be measured or metered (such as beauty) is regarded as unreal or epiphenomenal. As a reductionist, one deliberately deconstructs perceived reality, attempting to reduce it to ever smaller components, which, once understood, will explain the whole. The contrast with the previous worldview could hardly be greater, for now man is essentially unrelated to nature and pursues knowledge with a hardheaded rigor in which there is no room for human feelings or for data that cannot be quantified. Hence all those human qualities that we designate by the word *heart* and all those natural properties we assign to the word *alive* have no place in the new way of knowing. Truncated from organic life and from the full range of human experience, the mind has become a pure instrument of empirical observation and logical analysis.

As a result, the Scientific Revolution brought about what Weber called "the disenchantment of the world." In the new epistemology, he said, "there are no mysterious forces that come into play, but rather . . . one can, in principle, master all things by calculation"; and man is no longer at home in the world by right of birth, because the new rationalism expels him from the "enchanted garden" of nature. Marx clearly expressed the new view: "Nature [is] simply an object for mankind, purely a matter of utility." Thus the Scientific Revolution left nature dead and man an orphan.

The Violation of Nature

We now need to examine the psychological roots of the new epistemology, for underlying every system of knowing is a basic motivation or stance toward life that evokes it. When humans acquire knowledge, they always have a more or less conscious purpose, and this purpose shapes the epistemology. For example, those interested in living in intimate harmony with their natural environment perfect "the technologies of the sacred" practiced by the shamans of old; similarly, yogis aspiring to inner self-realization make a science of meditation, as in ancient India. What, then, is the underlying motivation of the new Science? The answer is clear and explicit: to dominate nature.

Of course, Western arrogance toward nature is nothing new. On the Christian side, it can be traced back to Genesis, which clearly asserts humanity's right to lord it over creation: man is to "subdue" nature and achieve "dominion . . . over every living thing." The Greek tradition delivers the same message: in his *Politics*, Aristotle said, "Nature . . . has made all animals for the sake of man." Nevertheless, these older traditions also made human dominion subject to ethical restraints: excessive greed and arrogance were explicitly believed to be morally wrong. The Enlightenment, however, cast off the moral chains on will and appetite and made man's dominion over nature absolute. The result was to intensify greatly the exploitation of nature and turn life into a naked pursuit of wealth and power.

That power was the fundamental motive behind the new Science was explicitly acknowledged by Descartes and Bacon. In his *Discourse on Method* (1637), Descartes said that he wanted to abolish profitless speculation and

> find a practical philosophy by means of which, knowing the force and the action of [natural phenomena], we can . . . employ them in all those uses to which they are adapted, and thus render ourselves the masters and possessors of nature.

Given this end, the means follow: the adoption of "geometric" or analytical reason. Practicing what he preached, Descartes made major mathematical contributions, especially in analytical geometry, that were the first steps toward the development of calculus and the other tools of modern mathematics. These tools then became the intellectual crowbars that allowed modern man to deconstruct the hitherto seamless unity of nature and to reveal, so it was thought, the ultimately mechanical and soulless character of physical reality postulated by Descartes.

Similarly, in *The New Atlantis* (1627), Bacon urged his contemporaries to take "command over natural things":

> The end of our foundation [for scientific research] is the knowledge of causes and secret motions of things and the enlarging of the bounds of human empire, to the effecting of all things possible.

In support of this clear aim, Bacon proposed a philosophy of investigation that, when allied to Cartesian mathematics and Galilean experimental techniques, became the basis of the modern scientific method. Bacon systematized the process of understanding nature in order to command her: he showed modern man how to use the crowbars to maximum advantage.

Because we have long since internalized the ethos of power seeking, putting nature under duress to extract as much as we possibly can from the Earth seems entirely normal and appropriate. But a fundamental irrationality resides at the heart of the modern paradigm, for behind the stated intentions of the Enlightenment epistemologists lurk unhealthy, even perverse, tendencies of mind. When all is said and done, Descartes, Bacon, Hobbes, and the other authors of the Enlightenment paradigm were megalomaniacs: their aim was not merely to dominate nature but to do so violently, brutally, absolutely.

For example, Bacon's attitude toward nature is cruel, even sadistic—like that of a medieval inquisitor confronting a witch, says historian Carolyn Merchant. His metaphors disclose the true motives lurking behind the seemingly rational aim of "effecting . . . all things possible." Calling nature a "common harlot," Bacon urges man to rip out the secrets hidden in her womb with the forceps of technology. And in pursuit of the knowledge necessary to this end, man must put aside all scruple: nature is to be vexed, hounded, driven, captured, imprisoned, interrogated, tortured, enslaved, and, last but not least, entered and penetrated in every hole and corner. Forced by this brutal treatment to yield up all her secrets, nature, hitherto niggardly with her favors, will now be "bound into service" and totally "possessed" by "man," whose conquering, penetrating intellect makes him her "master." In short, the governing metaphor of Baconian science is rape.

Nor is Bacon exceptional in wanting to violate nature. Newton too used similar imagery, saying that his aim was to "wrench the secrets of nature from her womb." And although Descartes's language was more discreet, his actions speak at least as loudly as Bacon's words. So secure was he in his belief that animals were but chemical machines that he dismissed the agonized howls of a dog being vivisected as but the squealing of an automaton. Descartes was therefore the founder of a tradition of appalling experimental cruelty that unfortunately persists even today, despite heightened consciousness and lessened callousness in recent times. And the larger implication is clear: nature is a mere biological machine to be dissected without compunction.

Little wonder, then, that the rise of Science coincides with what our histories call The Age of Discovery, but which might be more appropriately named The Age of the Conquistadors after the men who made discovery synonymous with the pillage and rape of whole continents. The new Science was a philosophy for producing conquistadors of nature who would further the expropriation of the ecological commons and the exploitation of the planet's resources for the benefit of the conquistadors themselves. In this light, is it really surprising that, despite everything positive one can say about Science's achievements, military destruction and ecological havoc are two of its principal fruits? It is fashionable to dismiss the Romantic reaction against Science as the merely poetic effusions of neurotic esthetes, but when, say, Tennyson likens the dissection of nature to murder, he is simply responding emotionally to what he sees—to the rapine and plunder of nature fostered by Science.

From Rational Epistemology to Power Politics

The new epistemology rapidly swept away the old worldview and the social order based upon it. Soon no other way of thinking and acting seemed possible, as society was reshaped in accordance with the principles of rationalism and mechanism. Above all, the new epistemological doctrines led directly and immediately to the new political thought.

Epistemology always undergirds politics, because implicit in any system of knowledge is a system of social relations. Although Marx and Nietzsche usually receive the credit for discovering that knowledge is power and that ideas are always a justification for rule, this understanding is actually far older: witness the critical importance of the image of the cave and the so-called noble lie in Plato's *Republic*. But even if epistemology were not inherently political, it would still have to affect politics. In the long run all aspects of a civilization—epistemology, ontology, ethics, economics, and politics—must be in accord, so the choice of a particular epistemology is bound to influence all else.

Indeed, the new way of thinking implied a basic value orientation that made modern civilization what it was to become. Although he excoriated values as but "the idols of the understanding," Bacon in fact put forward very clear values of his own: making "truth and utility . . . perfectly identical," he claimed superiority for the new epistemology precisely because it was useful. Useful for what? Why, for "the effecting of all things possible," of course. In this sense, the new Science was very far from being "value free": the domination of nature was both the end and the means of a rationalist epistemology.

The case of Hobbes, whose explicit aim was to reconstruct politics in the light of the new Scientific understanding, exemplifies, in even greater detail, the process of moving from epistemology to politics. As noted, he made building the commonwealth into a matter of engineering—that is, of applying mechanistic principles to social life. He therefore began *Leviathan* with an explanation of the basic principles of *mechanistic* philosophy precisely in order to establish the basis for an *individualistic* theory of politics. The other doctrines of liberalism then follow as a matter of course. Although the root metaphor of the chain of being is hostile to individualism, the machine metaphor not only permits it, it practically demands it: if nature is atomic, then surely society must be too. Hence individualism is a logical if not necessary sociopolitical outgrowth of the new epistemology. Similarly, although the chain metaphor implies hierarchy, and thus supports a politics based on social ranking, the machine metaphor implies equality, for the parts of a machine are in some important sense all equal—as was clearly articulated in Hobbes's political theory, which made the equality of man in the state of nature the basis of the social contract. Moreover, to the extent that there is still a political hierarchy, it is no longer moral: Hobbes's sovereign rules not in accordance with some standard of virtue, however derived, but prudentially, like a good mechanic taking care of a machine. In addition, because Science, the only valid way of reasoning, is concerned solely with utilitarian truth and cannot determine the relative merit of moral ideas or religious doctrines, human reason provides no ground for constructing anything more positive than the night-watchman state. Hence it is up to equal individuals to determine for themselves what is noble or base, constrained only by the prudential legal "hedges" established by the sovereign. In short, the basic features of liberal politics faithfully reflect the mechanistic epistemology adopted by Hobbes in nearly every particular.

Moreover, the fundamentally economic character of the new politics was also implicit within rationality itself. Rationality refers to

1. A certain way of thinking: logically, in accordance with clear and reasonable rules of procedure.
2. A certain way of acting: purposively, accommodating means to ends.
3. A certain way of organizing the world: efficiently, so that one gets "the biggest bang for the buck."

These are obviously what we would call "economic" values, so it is easy to understand why the rise of Science was accompanied by a "bourgeois" theory of politics based on a "social contract." And, more generally, why capitalism and industrialism were so intimately linked to Science. This is not to say that Science and the new epistemology "caused" these developments (or vice versa), for all these phenomena were part of a general transformation of consciousness and society. But the historical record shows that the new epistemology was rapidly and completely translated into the ontological, ethical, economic, and political doctrines of the new order, all of which conformed to the principles of mechanism and rationalism. Just as the previous era clearly evinced the values of the *anima mundi*, modern civilization in all its aspects became an expression of its own root metaphor, the *machina mundi*.

In this light, Science's appeal to "objective truth" determined by "rational" means was and is an attempt to pull the wool over our eyes, an intellectual trick intended to maintain its cultural hegemony. We do not see the ideological sleight of hand because utilitarian, rationalistic values dedicated to the conquest of nature are so integral to our current social and political arrangements that they seem to be not so much moral preferences as simple descriptions of the way things are. Witness the words of Keynes cited earlier: "Avarice and usury and precaution must be our gods for a little longer still." Such "gods"—revealing metaphor!—are the logical and necessary consequence of adopting a thoroughgoing rationality as one's epistemology.

To sum up, the Scientific revolution substituted one reality principle for another. Hence the polity had to undergo a revolution as well, renouncing its moral function and embracing Science's pursuit of earthly power. In the process, it had also to embrace the "gods" of expediency necessary to this end. But, said Virgil, "we make our destinies by our choice of gods," and so it is in our case. "All my means are sane; my motives and object mad," said Captain Ahab in a rare moment of sanity before his final, fatal encounter with Moby-Dick. Like Melville's tragic hero, a modern civilization that uses powerful means in pursuit of megalomaniacal ends is, for all its rationality, possessed by unreason.

Politics Overwhelmed by Science

It should now be apparent that Hobbes's preoccupation with power was by no means simply a personal quirk: it faithfully reflected the psychological wellsprings of the Enlightenment. Along with his friend and colleague Bacon, as well as Descartes and many others less well known, Hobbes was part of an intellectual and political movement that was intoxicated by power and that had as its explicit aim nothing less than the overthrow of "God," the personification of the divine principle. The transcendent power of the deity was now to be brought down to earth to reside, on the one hand, in Bacon's "foundation," which is quite explicitly a Scientific theocracy, and, on the other, in Hobbes's Leviathan. Thus the political order of the cosmos was overturned: the power formerly "not of this world" descended into it, there to be used by humanity to make itself rich by achieving power over nature, territory, trade, and peoples—in short, over "all things possible." But the idea that the human race as a whole could somehow exercise a common domination over nature is absurd, a mystifying abstraction. The concrete reality is different, for to achieve worldly power one must employ it—and, in concrete social situations, power is always exercised over other human beings. As C. S. Lewis said in *The Abolition of Man*, "What we call Man's power over Nature turns out to be a power exercised by some men over other men with Nature as its instrument." Inevitably, therefore, a Scientific revolution dedicated to achieving power engendered its political analog—a powerful and power-mad polity, along with new ruling classes and new forms of domination. So the victory of Science paved the way for the eventual triumph of Leviathan.

Hobbes himself clearly understood that the social power he was unleashing was unprecedented and badly needed taming. That is precisely the justification for an awe-inspiring Leviathan: it is the necessary political means to contain the unleashed passions of individuals who are no longer restrained by politically established religions. Unfortunately, as we have seen, the actual consequence of allowing politics to be governed by Hobbesian principles is almost always to amplify power and render it harder to control, in large part because Hobbes did not fully appreciate just how much power he was unleashing. Nor did he make provision for the emergence of economic and technological power, which would prove even less amenable to political control. Hence power in every sphere has simply outrun political authority.

Moreover, the ideologues of scientific and technological progress made essentially the same mistake as Locke: they relied on a strong civil society. They naively assumed, tacitly if not explicitly, that it was safe to overthrow the traditional canons of virtue and liberate the human power drive, because a new ethic based on firm knowledge of what is "natural" to man would sooner or later emerge to replace traditional morality. As we know, this has not happened: despite important moral improvements in some areas, such as human rights, ethical confusion is widespread, and moral entropy has caused a clear decline of mores.

In the end, our "command over natural things" has turned out to be a delusion. As Walter Lippmann pointed out, since reason is no longer the ruler of man's desires, but instead their instrument, "the power which science places in man's hands is ungoverned." Hence we see "that when modern man fights he is the most destructive animal ever known on this planet; that when he is acquisitive he is the most cunning and efficient; that when he dominates the weak he has engines of oppression and of calculated cruelty and deception no antique devil could have imagined."

In the end, the political order has been overwhelmed by Science. Even if, contrary to fact, the motives of those employing modern technology were quite sane, it is like a powerful engine that we do not really know how to control and that is therefore running away with us. To echo the words of Macauley, the ship of Science has turned out to be all sail and no anchor, and we know not to what dangerous shores it is carrying us.

The Destruction of the Cosmos

Indeed, not polity alone, but culture itself, has been overwhelmed by Science. The new mechanical philosophy, said historian of science Alexandre Koyré, caused a "scientific and philosophical revolution" that brought with it "the destruction of the Cosmos . . . and the utter devalorization of being." In other words, the work of destruction did not stop with nature: Science's crowbars were soon employed to deconstruct society and psyche as well. In 1611, well before Hobbes had published *Leviathan*, John Donne was already complaining that the new philosophy called all in doubt, and so,

> 'Tis all in pieces, all Cohaerance gone,
> All just supply, and all Relation: . . .

Donne's lament soon became general. For over three centuries, sensitive observers have complained of the incoherence—that is, the alienation, anxiety, and meaninglessness—of modern life. Indeed, in one way or another, this issue has preoccupied not just poets but most of the greatest thinkers about society and polity in the modern era. To cite only some of the most prominent, Burke, Marx, Nietzsche, Rousseau, de Tocqueville, and Weber have all attempted to come to terms with the "destruction of the Cosmos." In our day, art and literature seem to be concerned with little else, and one of the most famous and oft-cited poems of this century, "The Second Coming," completed in 1920 by William Butler Yeats, picks up precisely where Donne left off 309 years earlier:

> Things fall apart; the centre cannot hold;
> Mere anarchy is loosed upon the world, . . .
> The best lack all conviction, while the worst
> Are full of passionate intensity.

Of course, this argument is now hoary with age: "alienation," in particular, has become the ultimate cliché of modern culture criticism. Not unnaturally, we tend to turn a deaf ear to such an oft-repeated refrain. Yet the destruction of the cosmos, and its psychological aftermath, is the essence of the modern predicament. The issue must therefore be faced and seen for what it is: political dynamite.

Coherence has been destroyed at every level, with harmful consequences that are felt in all spheres of life. We have already seen, for instance, the political dangers attached to a lack of fundamental social agreement on morals and mores: with no agreed core of values, "the centre cannot hold." In the epigraph that begins this chapter, Hayek in effect recapitulates our earlier discussion of moral entropy and shows that a relentless questioning of all received ideals and values soon becomes destructive, shattering the moral consensus upon which society and ultimately civilization itself must be based. So we are already familiar with incoherence in its sociopolitical aspect and can move on to examine its psychological and intellectual dimensions.

As previously noted, the development of civilization involves a movement away from the immediacy of participatory perception within a largely natural environment and toward an increasingly abstract mode of perception within a predominantly artificial environment. The so-called savage participates in nature to such a degree that reality blazes with intrinsic meaning: life is directly perceived to be vital and sacred, as in Blake's vision of tigers burning brightly in the forests of the night. The myths of primal man are thus auxiliary, mere reminders of what his senses tell him directly, immediately, and continuously—namely, that he is connected to all of creation and that, like Blake, he holds

> Infinity in the palm of [his] hand
> And Eternity in an hour.

But as humankind moves away from primary participation and toward civilized abstraction, myth replaces direct perception: instead of seeing infinity and eternity for themselves, men and women learn about them through stories. This is the mythopoetic age, which is synonymous with the rise of civilization.

With further cultural evolution, literacy displaces orality, and stories give way to texts. Religion is now based on scripture. The mythopoetic or "pagan" ways, with all their emotional immediacy, are pushed to the margin. Truly civilized folk become "the People of the Book," and those who have mastered "the book"—be it called *Analects*, *Bible*, *Koran*, or *Torah*—are now in charge of the spiritual flock.

Yet, as noted above, until the beginning of the modern age the civilized worldview continued to be primarily oriented toward the supernatural and so remained fundamentally mythopoetic in spirit. Despite the attenuation of emotional immediacy, scripture-based religion still sufficed to provide a meaningful connection to the cosmic order. However, the rise of Science entailed the end of myth altogether, because Scientific rationality, whose primary aim is the construction of *knowledge*, is incompatible with the mythic mode of understanding, whose primary aim is the construction of *meaning*. This final abstraction from nature destroyed the cosmic connection formerly provided by myth.

The consequences are serious. Even if one does not believe in the metaphysical reality of myth—"Myth is the secret opening through which the inexhaustible energies of the cosmos pour into human cultural manifestation," said Joseph Campbell—one cannot deny its metaphysical function. That is, although Science has destroyed the meaning attached to myth and to the various religious traditions that emerged from the mythopoetic mode of understanding, it has neither abolished the need for human beings to make sense of their world—not merely intellectually but personally and morally as well—nor has it done away with their desire for satisfactory answers to the suffering attendant upon the vicissitudes and ultimate finitude of human life. As Ludwig Wittgenstein, the philosopher who pushed the hyperrationalistic doctrines of logical positivism to their bitter end, put it in his *Tractatus*, "We feel that even when all *possible* scientific questions have been answered, the problems of life remain completely untouched." Beyond rational explanation therefore lies a vast realm of "silence"—"whereof we cannot speak," said Wittgenstein—that contains all that is most important to us as human beings.

So the very epistemology that allowed Science to derive physical theory was hostile to the symbolic or psychic processes that have traditionally allowed human beings to construct emotional meaning. Scientific explanation was perhaps more satisfying to the human intellect than the myths it replaced, but the human heart suffered from having no way of understanding or communicating the mystery of being and nonbeing.

Hence, said Jung, modern "knowledge does not enrich us," but by "remov[ing] us more and more from the mythic world in which we were once at home by right of birth," it strips away our source of psychic wealth. The result of this impoverishment is rootlessness, disorientation, loneliness, anxiety, alienation, and a pervasive sense of loss—a feeling of being suspended over an abyss of metaphysical meaninglessness.

Spiritual Vertigo and Cultural Nihilism

This spiritual vertigo reaches deep into the lives of individuals and creates a paradoxical irrationality at the core of modern existence. By reducing reason to instrumental rationality and condemning everything outside this narrow field as unreal or irrational, we have pushed the major part of human life and experience outside the realm of reason. We have thereby expanded the realm of the so-called irrational and, by driving it underground, given it a hidden power. The irrational must then be countered with various rationalizations that attempt, with little success, to control it without giving it its just due. Thus new forms of superstition have arisen in the modern era—among them psychology and ideology, to be dealt with later.

Once rationality destroys the cosmos, there is no support for values outside the individual. Science takes a radically value-free position, and even its theoretical picture of the world is, especially in our day, so mathematically abstract that it seems unrecognizably remote from everyday experience. (As we shall see below, it is also so fragmented that it does not provide the foundation for a genuine philosophy of life.) Individuals are therefore left essentially alone to construct a worldview that gives their life intellectual coherence and emotional meaning.

This is a task beyond their powers. Discussing the role of religion in a democracy, de Tocqueville said that "men cannot do without dogmatical belief" and that "of all the kinds of dogmatical belief, the most desirable appears to me to be dogmatical belief in matters of religion . . . even from no higher consideration than the interests of this world." Why? Because it is impossible that everyman should act as his own philosopher and "settle his opinions by the sole force of his reason":

> None but minds singularly free from the ordinary cares of life—minds at once penetrating, subtle, and trained by thinking—can, even with much time and care, sound the depths of these so necessary truths. And, indeed, we see that philosophers are themselves almost always surrounded with uncertainties; that at every step the natural light which illuminates their

path grows dimmer and less secure; and that, in spite of all their efforts, they have as yet only discovered a few conflicting notions, on which the mind of man has been tossed about for thousands of years, without ever firmly grasping the truth, or finding novelty even in its errors. Studies of this nature are far above the average capacity of men; and, even if the majority of mankind were capable of such pursuits, it is evident that leisure to cultivate them would still be wanting.

In brief, few indeed possess the time, much less the intellect and temperament and education, to reconstruct the cosmos. Moreover, the slightest acquaintance with modern thought will show that even the philosophers and intellectuals—those presumed to be "far above the average capacity"—have failed utterly in the attempt. Those who were honest reached the same conclusion as Wittgenstein: rationality not only cannot provide meaning, it takes us to the edge of a vast "silence" that mocks the very idea of a rational explanation of life. Indeed, the mere experience of spiritual vertigo tends to induce a state of anxiety or even terror—a state in which, said Nietzsche, "man would sooner have the void for his purpose than be void of purpose."

Faced with the failure of rationality to provide human meaning and purpose, many contemporary thinkers have put forth a counsel of despair: root out the craving for these things from the human psyche; accept instead the utter solitude of life in a world of chance and necessity; and then enjoy the freedom that the cultural anarchy of the modern world affords. "Only on the firm foundation of unyielding despair," Bertrand Russell concluded, "can the soul's habitation henceforth be safely built." Although well meant, such counsel is bootless: none of these alternatives is realistically possible for ordinary men and women, who cannot easily bear to live either with psychological pain or without cultural orientation. And politics is hardly conceivable without some framework of "higher" values—what Lippmann, adapting the Chinese concept, called "the mandate of heaven." As Nietzsche made abundantly clear, living "beyond good and evil" is for supermen, not ordinary mortals. To leave each individual to invent his or her own meaning and morality thus portends not only the "unyielding despair" of the individual soul but also the demise of political community.

All talk of individuals determining their own morality is therefore nonsense. Masses of individuals do not and cannot generate values by and for themselves; they must get them from their culture. But modern culture, especially in the United States, is a shifting sea of transience and obsolescence in which the only constant is change. It is also a maelstrom of conflicting values: different races and nations with their differing economic and political systems, differing faiths, and differing ways of life collide in a colossal Nietzschean "transvaluation of all values" that subjects each culture and psyche to a continual buffeting. So the social order from which individuals are struggling to get their bearings is itself at a loss, reeling from the impact of impermanence and relativism. If we add to this profound outer disturbance the inner decay of moral entropy, as well as the increased complexity and fragmentation of thought to be discussed below, it becomes evident that contemporary culture is no longer a resource for the individual but, rather, a large part of the problem of disorientation that he must solve. What is worse, to the extent that individuals inevitably do receive their values from the ambient culture, the men and women of today cannot escape being imprinted with the confused or even toxic values of the decaying society in which they live.

In addition, because the arts have been pushed to the margin, where they splinter into subcultures populated by small coteries of specialists and aficionados, they no longer function as a school for human understanding as in the past. We have, for instance, nothing remotely comparable to the great dramatists of ancient Athens or Elizabethan England to help us come to grips with deep cultural questions. Popular art is mere entertainment—an appendix of commerce and advertising that is crass, trivial, sensational, and incoherent. Far from uplifting and orienting individuals, mass culture only further debases and bewilders them. Television is, of course, the worst offender: it has increasingly taken on a disorienting, dream-like, even nightmarish cast; its instantaneity, simultaneity, randomness, cynicism, sexuality, and violence reflect the logic of dreams and tend to activate the repressed negativity and irrationality that are part of the shadow side of even the healthiest psyche. (Artistic merit is not the issue, for the best work of the most talented popular artists is just as disorienting as the worst commercial trash—for example, the highly acclaimed but frankly nightmarish film *Blue Velvet* by the director David Lynch.) Hence the net effect of almost all forms of mass culture is to make our normal everyday world draw ever closer to the realm of the unconscious, a place in which even space and time no longer retain their usual solidity and in which "reality" becomes more and more surreal, if not perverse. As a consequence, if individuals learn anything from art cum entertainment, it is likely to be sadism and nihilism. So modern men and women are caught in a perfect vicious circle: lacking any "dogmatical belief" with which to orient themselves, they project their inner meaninglessness upon the world; and the world, more fragmented and chaotic with every passing day, returns the compliment.

To make matters worse, rational explanation is no longer what it once was. The sociology of knowledge and the history of science—as well as many basic scientific discoveries, especially in physics and the neurosciences—have begun to raise serious doubts about whether the world is constructed in the way that a rationalist theory of knowledge requires. Indeed, the cosmos seems to resemble Socrates' cave more than Descartes's automaton: "Modern physics," said Werner Heisenberg, "has definitively decided for Plato." Fellow physicist James Jeans made the point even more explicitly: "Imprisoned in our cave . . . we can only watch the shadows on the wall"; so our descriptions of reality are but "parables," and the universe is "more like a great thought than like a great machine." At best, therefore, rational explanation is only a part of the story, no matter how internally consistent and externally powerful the best scientific theories may be. At worst, it may be that all explanations are relative and depend on imagination and aesthetic choice to a far greater degree than rationalistic epistemologies would seem to allow.

To mention aesthetics is perhaps to come to the crux of the matter, for the loss of coherence is also the loss of beauty—and hence, as Keats would have it, of a certain kind of truth as well. Science's exclusion of the aesthetic was, said Whitehead, a "disastrous error" leading directly to dehumanization and hubris. Bateson used even stronger language: because "our loss of the sense of aesthetic unity" severed our direct connection to life, it was "an epistemological mistake . . . more serious than all the minor insanities that characterized those older epistemologies which agreed upon the fundamental unity." After all, the primary human response to phenomena is aesthetic: we are interested in and delighted by what looks and feels good to us. But the process of abstraction characteristic of civilization and carried to an extreme by Science veils the natural beauty of the cosmos behind progressively thicker layers of concept, language, theory, and ideology. This process has reached its nadir in our age: the death of nature tends to reduce reality to an ugly, soulless corpse. But the consequence of doubting and devaluing and destroying the sensual phenomenal world in which we have our animal existence and from which we derive our psychic grounding is to create a numbness, or even a kind of terror, in the human mind. Thus, says psychologist James Hillman, "beauty is an *ontological* necessity" without which we are almost literally dead to the world.

Not surprisingly, a ruling philosophy that makes beauty superfluous or unreal tends to turn the world into a wasteland: our environment is increasingly uniform, shoddy, nasty, brutish, and surreal, an aesthetic state of nature that faithfully mirrors back to us the ugly and deadly premises of our ruling philosophy. And it is yet another vicious circle: a dead and ugly external world further numbs the individual's psyche and pushes it toward nihilism—the state of not having, of not being able to have, any values or meaning whatsoever. In a desperate effort to escape nihilism, modern men and women—Weber's "sensualists without heart"—increasingly resort to diseased forms of beauty such as sensationalism and pornography. Ultimately, therefore, beauty is also a *political* necessity: "the denial of Aphrodite," says Hillman, surrounds us with a soulless and anti-aesthetic uniformity that is the natural soil of totalitarian politics.

Trying to Rationalize the Irrational

Ideological true believers of many different persuasions have tried to make the nihilistic welter of modern life cohere—but none have succeeded, which suggests that a new synthesis founded on purely rational principles is not attainable. Otto Rank, one of the founders of depth psychology, pointed out that the modern drive to rationalize existence is fundamentally deluded: "For the most part what we call 'irrational' is just the natural; but our 'rationale' has become so unnatural that we see everything natural as irrational." Hence our *fear* of the natural realm (clearly evident in Bacon's malevolence toward nature), and our consequent attempt to dominate it rationally as a way of overcoming this fear, is the core of the modern neurosis. (The neurosis was shared by Freud, who said in *Civilization and Its Discontents*, "Against the dreaded external world [we] can only defend [ourselves] by . . . going over to the attack against nature and subjecting her to the human will.") In choosing rationality as its prime principle, modern man has simply exchanged one horn of the dilemma for the other: he renounced a naive belief in the supernatural, which he formerly tried to control magically with shamanic techniques, only to fall into a neurotic dread of it, which he now tries to control intellectually by substituting a man-made rational order for the natural order. But, said Rank, such an attempt to "rationalize the irrational" cannot possibly succeed: the irrational is such precisely because it cannot be rationalized.

Rank included psychology itself in this condemnation: with but few exceptions, it is a failed "substitute for the cosmic unity which the man of Antiquity enjoyed in life and expressed in his religion, but which modern man has lost—a loss which accounts for the development of the neurotic type." Despite its real contributions to human understanding, psychology has therefore become the disease for which it purports to be the cure:

Not unlike the fool at the courts of medieval rulers, the neurotic of our time reflects our own foolishness under the guise of his symptoms. The only difference is that he really suffers from his foolishness, which is considered an illness, although it indicates just as much the cure for our own ills, namely, the need for legitimate foolishness, that is, creative expression of the natural self which we condemn as irrational. In this sense, psychoanalysis as the psychology of the neurotic type—but not the cure for it—is in itself a sign of a decadent civilization.

So the loss of "cosmic unity" predisposes modern men and women to neurosis, and neither the loss nor the illness can be cured by rational means. In fact, every attempt to do so only worsens the psychological disease and deepens the spiritual vertigo. As a power-mad culture pursues insane ends with supposedly sane means, individuals are mythically, morally, and psychologically adrift in what is tantamount to a permanent identity crisis. They are therefore reduced to scrabbling for values from a culture that is disintegrating around them, at the same time that it is being manipulated to serve powerful interests. But such incoherence, particularly when combined with resentment at being manipulated, leaves a gaping void that demands to be filled, as we shall see below.

From Information Overload to Cultural Idiocy

Meanwhile, however, let us continue to explore the theme of incoherence—but now within the sphere of knowledge itself, for the irony is that Science has not been able to achieve coherence even within its own bailiwick. As Milan Kundera complains, "Culture is perishing in overproduction, in an avalanche of words, in the madness of quantity," and Science is not exempt. A kind of Gresham's Law seems to operate within the economy of mind: we may have more apparent "knowledge," but it is at the same time simultaneously less, a trivialization or counterfeit of the real thing. Just as merely secular learning once replaced wisdom, so information has slowly overwhelmed knowledge, and now, in our day, data is threatening to inundate information. As is said of the modern specialist, we increasingly know more and more about less and less. Paradoxically, our vast increase in data and information has generated a kind of ignorance.

The paradox is partly explained if we carefully distinguish between genuine knowledge and mere data or information. Data are, by definition, raw facts. Information consists of facts in a context that gives them some kind of preliminary meaning. Knowledge is something more—facts fitted into a theory or otherwise arrayed in a useful or meaningful fashion. And wisdom is the ability to understand and use all of the above in an integrated, systematic, and beneficial fashion.

To illustrate, knowing that voter turnout in yesterday's elections was 22 percent is a bit of data that tells us very little. However, if we put it in context by saying that yesterday's turnout is less than half that in previous elections, we now have some real information, as well as a question that prompts us to inquire further. Once we learn why voter turnout declined so dramatically—a small but significant bit of knowledge—we can add it to an existing body of knowledge: namely, all that we have learned about electoral politics and the conditions fostering or frustrating civic participation at other times and places. This may in turn become the foundation for wise political action. In other words, raw data are meaningless: facts without context are mere factoids, like the trivial items that newspapers use to fill odd gaps in their pages. Because genuine understanding at every level is always *contextual*, more and more data combined with less and less context is a prescription for idiocy, not enlightenment.

But that is precisely our situation. Today, even the most dedicated specialists can scarcely keep up with the "literature" in their own fields. In addition, as we have seen, the ordinary citizen's mental world is made up of sound, image, or data "bites" that are never put into any kind of meaningful context. This flood of so-called knowledge cannot be digested, much less mastered or utilized, and therefore constitutes a kind of relative ignorance.

Thoreau's jibe that too much of modern knowledge consists in "counting the cats in Zanzibar" seems to have come true: we are swamped in data and information that have little or no meaning or personal relevance. Such a glut serves merely to titillate—or, what is worse, to stupefy and mystify—not enlighten. The alleged increase of knowledge has thus made society and its workings steadily more opaque. A reasonably well-educated citizen cannot, even in principle, comprehend the world in its totality, only his specialized portion of it, so he is essentially obliged to take the rest of the enterprise on faith. Above all, he must take Science on faith, accepting certain conclusions simply as dogmas, with little understanding of how they were reached or how scientific truth evolved and continues to evolve. In the end, far from being the perfectly rational being envisioned by the Enlightenment *philosophes*, the average man or woman is reduced to relating to the world as a kind of scientific mystery.

Nor are the knowledge specialists much better off. As noted, specialization today requires the sacrifice of breadth to depth, until learning becomes fragmented, or even segregated, into disciplines and then subdisciplines that tend more and more toward exclusivity and mutual incomprehensibility. One important consequence of this is that expert participants in public discussions of complicated issues tend to talk past one another, as each abstracts from a very large universe of data and information those bits that fit most comfortably within his disciplinary and professional formation or that reflect his particular cultural and political biases. It is the story of the blind men and the elephant writ large.

So Science itself seems incapable of integrating *scientific* knowledge, much less extricating us from general data glut and information overload; nor can it provide us with guidance on what to do with all this information and power. At best, therefore, our lives are beholden to narrow specialists lacking vision and wisdom. At worst, Ahabian experts use sane (or even insane) means to pursue megalomaniac ends.

Contrary to the assertion of many that we have entered a new and golden age of knowledge and learning, we are rather less knowledgeable—that is, more ignorant—than our ancestors in certain critical respects, especially when it comes time to convert knowledge into action. Ironically, premodern thinkers like Montaigne and early modern thinkers like Locke, with tiny personal libraries of a few hundred volumes, possessed a mastery of the best in the Western tradition since earliest times, as well as an integrated understanding of the workings of their respective societies. Whatever their own personal or intellectual shortcomings, they therefore commanded an overview of the human condition that was the best that their respective ages could achieve. But we have no such mastery or overview, and no prospect whatsoever of attaining it, despite our vastly greater and more accurate knowledge of many particulars. We collect, we measure, we analyze, we test—but we do not really understand, as our vast data bases are manipulated statistically in ways that largely reinforce our ingrained and unexamined assumptions, producing only a simulacrum of social knowledge. So we have an exact count of all the cats in Zanzibar, but meaning and coherence and vision utterly escape us.

Although hailed as a savior in the face of information overload, the computer is, upon closer examination, a false and potentially dangerous solution. The computer may be an essential tool for gaining systematic knowledge, which might allow us to construct a more holistic science, but it is not the cure for data glut. As with building freeways for automobiles, the result has been a bigger data jam than before. For all its undeniable success in making an excess of data go around faster, the computer is thus no answer to the fundamental problem represented by too much incoherent data to process in the first place.

In addition, the computer favors certain kinds of data over others—"hard," "objective," and, above all, "quantifiable." A computerized society represents the ultimate triumph of Weberian rationalization: vast armies of bureaucrats and technocrats crunching numbers with little or no regard for "soft" human factors. Indeed, the computer is primarily useful to those who have vast quantities of data needing to be rapidly processed and who can also most readily exploit the new electronic possibilities for greater efficiency, command, control, predictability, and profit—namely, governments, bureaucracies, financiers, and multinational corporations. In short, although the personal computer allied to powerful encryption techniques also has its subversive aspects—some foresee the eventual demise of the nation-state, as talent and wealth decamp into "cyberspace"—to the extent that the computer is a social solution, it seems to be one that favors large and impersonal organizations and enhanced social control for the vast majority.

Moreover, most of those who tout a new "information age" that will give us an increased command of nature and society have made a fundamental conceptual error. Speaking thermodynamically, "information" always implies *organization*—that is, meaningful coherence. Mere facts or raw data do not constitute information in this sense: when theorists speak of machines and organisms as possessing information, it is precisely their lawfulness and coherence that constitute the information. By contrast, a chaotic pile of parts or a random soup of cells would represent information's antithesis: entropy. The continued accumulation of mere data without the knowledge to integrate it into a coherent structure, much less the wisdom to use our knowledge in ways that preserve and enhance the whole, is therefore a movement away from genuine information and toward increasing entropy.

In fact, from the perspective of information theory, we have probably suffered a net loss of information in modern times. It seems very unlikely, for instance, that the increase in knowledge and order attributable to science and technology in the modern era outweighs the entropic losses that this increase has caused—namely, the sacrifice of genetic, biological, and cultural information due to plant and animal extinctions, the destruction of natural habitats, and the extirpation of indigenous and local ways of life during the same period. As in the economic sphere, the accountants of progress tend to cook the books, overvaluing what we have gained and overlooking what we have lost in the modern pursuit of knowledge.

To sum up, although the information provided by Science may well give us more *power*, we have paid the price in lost biological and cultural wealth. As Jung observed, "The world has sold its soul for a mass of disconnected facts." To put it another way, scientific information does little to help us to live the good life—on the contrary, our long-term well-being depends precisely on the kind of wealth we have destroyed. In this light, the current state of data glut and information overload is a symptom of regress, signaling a loss of genuine information and knowledge. Far from having achieved new heights of technical control or a new learning mode that will allow us to solve all our problems better than in the past, social learning—that is, the capacity to integrate and employ new knowledge intelligently for long-term social benefit—is probably the *weakest* point of our current system. Our inability to make sense of or employ wisely our plethora of data and information is pushing us to the brink of cultural idiocy.

Toward a Reign of Universal Ignorance

The danger of cultural idiocy is especially acute in the United States, where we seem to have made a clear social decision—partly deliberate, partly unconscious—to forestall genuine learning. As Christopher Lasch notes, "The whole problem of American education comes down to this: in American society, almost everyone identifies intellectual excellence with elitism. This attitude . . . threatens to bring about a reign of universal ignorance." The reaction identified by Lasch is understandable: because knowledge is a means to wealth and power, it is hardly surprising that the citizens of a democracy would instinctively react against its accumulation by an elite minority. Paradoxically, however, trying to prevent elitism in this fashion is not only politically dangerous (in ways we shall discuss in the next two chapters); it is also ultimately self-defeating. Leveling down educational standards does not prevent those seeking wealth and power from getting the specialized training that allows them to compete effectively for these prizes, but it decreases the likelihood that they will know how to use them well, either for themselves or for the community, because their education has not taught them wisdom or self-restraint. They will be mere technocrats or meritocrats, not natural aristocrats or statesmen; they will know cost-benefit analysis but not the lessons of history, and marketing psychology but not Shakespeare or Freud. So the product of our educational system is a pseudo-elite of highly skilled barbarians who are out for plunder and a large mass of know-nothings who are just as greedy, but who lack the talent or training to aggrandize themselves.

Although it is little wonder that elitism has a bad name today—or that, in a truly vicious circle, the curriculum has become increasingly debased and anti-intellectual in the name of democracy—a willed reign of universal ignorance is not the solution. In this area, as in so many others, the attempted cure turns out to be the disease itself. Genuine knowledge depends on coherence; coherence in turn requires learning a tradition; and real learning is always an excellence attained by the gifted and dedicated few—by a genuine elite, whose absence creates an intellectual and moral void at the heart of a culture. When all is said and done, substituting universal ignorance for elite learning works to the paradoxical disadvantage of the nonelite, because it threatens to turn society into an arena for competing barbarians in which common folk get trampled.

That the American educational system produces a paradoxical ignorance is a logical consequence of the basic epistemological premises we have been examining. If character and values have no rational standing, then it is hardly to be expected that they will be taught to students. On the contrary, if power is the end, then the educational system must inculcate the means of rational efficiency. As we have seen, the industrial system needs well-trained and obedient bureaucrats and technicians the way armies need cannon fodder. And one of the most important qualifications of the good organizational soldier is the unwillingness—or, better yet, the Orwellian incapacity—to think for oneself. It follows that education must be narrowly economic and technical in its content and methodology, lest the soldiers begin to entertain subversive ideas.

A Forced Reconstruction of Meaning

Having examined the incoherence, vertigo, and fragmentation produced by a rationalist epistemology, we are now ready to discuss the human consequences. We saw in an earlier chapter that formerly "settled folk" were forcibly turned into "shiftless migrants," literally uprooted from their ancestral homes and figuratively uprooted from family, custom, tradition, and, in general, a community and culture that supported and nourished them. Now we see that the uprooting has been mental, emotional, and spiritual as well: the modern mind is a migrant mind, having no metaphysical or psychological roots in myth, nor even a clear and satisfying mental picture of the world. In essence, modern man is at a loss, both literally and figuratively: he has destroyed the old cosmos and forfeited the traditional answers, but in their place he has created a mere anarchy that offers no answers at all. Homeless within a cosmos that appears to be a meaningless play of chance and necessity, and adrift without clear philosophical or practical answers to the basic problems of life, he is disconnected from history, nature, place, phenomena, bodily existence—and from self above all, which inevitably means from others as well. In plain language, nobody knows who he is, why he is living, or what kind of world he is living in.

This is a staggering loss, and it has left a gaping void that modern men and women have tried to fill by making a fierce effort to reconstruct the lost coherence—but ideologically, rather than mythologically. Because it tries to do what Rank declared to be impossible—to "rationalize the irrational"—this strategy is doomed to defeat from the outset. Moreover, it must also result in an unhealthy and dangerous "return of the repressed," as irrational forces masquerading as rational doctrines are unleashed on the social order.

Outbreaks of irrationality are, of course, nothing new in the history of civilization, but the modern ideologies that are the fruit of the Enlightenment are especially dangerous in this regard. As we have already seen, the Enlightenment did not so much overthrow religion as secularize it, directing the spiritual drive of the Judeo-Christian religious tradition toward worldly ends. Moreover, by comparison with other spiritual traditions, the Western religions (including Islam) are fundamentally ideological: belief in a creed, in a particular set of religious ideas and ideals derived from holy writ, is the basis of faith; and adherents are expected to uphold this creed at all costs. By secularizing the religious impulse, the Enlightenment therefore poured gasoline on an already raging fire: it created new temporal religions that were purely ideological, causing modern men and women to die for their supposedly rational ideas just as premodern men and women had perished for their religious beliefs.

Moreover, rational ideologies are worse than religious creeds in one key respect. As noted above, in exalting the rational one paradoxically strengthens the irrational. To paraphrase G. K. Chesterton, the consequence of ceasing to believe in God is not that one will thereupon believe in nothing; it is rather that one will thereafter believe in anything—anything at all, provided it seems to give coherence to experience. The destruction of authentic religion thus gave rise, says Irving Kristol, to "millions of spiritually sick people . . . shopping around for a patent medicine of the soul"; so cults and ideologies have flourished in exact proportion to the rationalization of society.

Hence the unremitting effort to create a rational society has failed: despite the Enlightenment, said Jung, "the world has not grown poorer by a single superstition since the days of antiquity." But our superstitions now take the seemingly rational form of ideologies, the doctrines that constitute modern man's attempt to reconstruct with brute intellectual force the mythological meaning lost when reason conquered faith. And because these ideologies descend from ancient monotheism, they inherit the latter's propensity for wars to end all wars, crusades, inquisitions, genocides, and final solutions—but to a heightened degree, precisely because they are more "rational."

Idolatry and Ideology

This dangerous tendency is reinforced by the ideological pretensions of Science itself. It is, of course, the hubris of every civilization to think that it has achieved a final description of reality and to believe that other cultures' descriptions are either quaint or deluded. Science, however, carries this attitude to an extreme: it asserts that its methods, and its methods alone, give a final description of reality and a kind of absolute truth never before attainable. Such an attitude is fundamentally religious in the pejorative sense and would have astonished the great scientists of antiquity, for until modern times scientific hypotheses only "saved the appearances"—that is, they accounted for natural phenomena, but they were not taken to be essentially true. As Owen Barfield points out, this was the genuinely revolutionary aspect of the Copernican Revolution: hypothesizing that the Earth revolves around the sun (a proposition well known to antiquity) was hardly new, but asserting that this hypothesis represented the sole and absolute truth—in short, Reality—was a radical change.

Now it may well be that heliocentrism is ultimately true, but mistaking one's hypotheses for the final truth is a treacherous mental habit that can readily lead one into deifying one's intellectual constructions. Indeed, although sophisticated practitioners and philosophers of science are well aware that the outcomes of the scientific method are useful *models* of reality, which are not to be confused with reality itself, the ideology of Science fosters this way of thinking. Thus the tendency in modern culture to lapse into the intellectual equivalent of erecting graven images, as scientific descriptions are taken for absolute truth. For instance, those who explain some aspects of nature mechanically with relative success then go on to assert that nature is a machine, a proposition that does not follow logically and that ignores the organic aspects of nature. Thus also the tendency toward Whitehead's "fallacy of misplaced concreteness" in which obvious artifacts of human thought such as "utility," "the market," and "rights" are set in intellectual concrete and treated as ultimately real. And this is the essence of idolatry: it casts reality in a particular form, whether a particular image of the deity or a particular set of ideas, and then adores it.

In effect, the so-called Age of Reason did not replace faith with reason: one set of beliefs supplanted another. And the new set of beliefs was not necessarily more reasonable than the one it replaced in one critical respect: self-awareness. In all the Western religious traditions, it is obvious that the ground of "faith" is a creed that needs to be planted deeply in the tender and unformed minds of children by means of a catechism, lest they grow up as unbelievers. The new Scientific catechism, however, is more insidious: it inculcates not a creed—or so it is claimed—but instead a description of Reality. Hence no real possibility of disbelief remains. Modern man therefore adores idols of his own intellectual making with the same fervor as the religious traditionalist of old worshiped the icons of his faith, but with less awareness of what he is professing (or even *that* he is professing). In the end, the vast majority are credulous believers in a secular monotheism that deifies Science, the mighty god that will lead us to the promised land of progress.

The Roots of Passionate Intensity

The combination of secularized monotheism and idolatrous faith has proven to be a heady and dangerous mixture, especially when it is yoked to the peculiar arrogance or hubris of the modern ethos. Yet we still do not understand fully why it is that in our time "the worst are full of passionate intensity" while "the best lack all conviction." The answer is to be found in the dynamics of the human psyche, which foster the growth of ideological passion.

First and foremost, human beings necessarily impose concreteness and consistency on their world. As numerous psychological experiments have shown, humans are virtually compelled by their nervous systems to construct their world coherently. In addition, the evidence from depth psychology of a basic hunger for the kind of coherence traditionally offered by myth would seem to be overwhelming.

Having already cited Jung and Rank, I now turn to Julian Jaynes, whose investigation of the origins of consciousness virtually ignores depth psychology. He nevertheless concludes that human beings are ever and always seeking what he calls "archaic authorization":

> The overwhelming importance of religion both in general world history and in the history of the average world individual is of course very clear from any objective standpoint, even though a scientific view of man often seems embarrassed at acknowledging this most obvious fact. For in spite of all that rationalist materialist science has implied since the Scientific Revolu-

tion, mankind as a whole has not, does not, and perhaps cannot relinquish his fascination with some human type of relationship to a greater and wholly other, some *mysterium tremendum* with powers and intelligences beyond all [rational] categories, something necessarily indefinite and unclear, to be approached and felt in awe and wonder and almost speechless worship.

No code of ethics or secular ideology can meet this intense demand of the human psyche for a direct relationship to the mystery of life. As Carl Kerényi, a close colleague of Jung, expressed it, "Mythology, like the severed head of Orpheus, goes on singing even in death and from afar." To the extent that this quasi-instinctual drive for mythological meaning is thwarted, it will necessarily evoke an urgent response from the psyche. In our time, because our whole way of life is pervaded by incoherence, the response has been extravagant—either to lack all conviction and fall back into nihilism at one extreme or to become a passionate true believer at the other.

· In addition, as noted above, insisting on rationality at the conscious level paradoxically fosters precisely the opposite at the unconscious level. This is due to a basic law of the human psyche, articulated by Jung:

> If anything of importance is devalued in our conscious life, and perishes
> . . . there arises a compensation in the unconscious. We may see in this an
> analogy to the conservation of energy in the physical world. . . . No psychic
> value can disappear without being replaced by another of equivalent intensity.

This is the reason for the return of the repressed: the devalued psychic energy always seeks for some way to return to consciousness. To be specific, in a highly rational society that emphasizes and exalts only one very narrow aspect of the total human experience, *an obsessive unconscious demand for exactly the opposite* will arise within the psyche and eventually break out again into consciousness, usually in an unhealthy or even dangerous form. Moreover, the more complete the repression or the longer the expression is delayed, the greater the fury with which it will erupt and the more likely the eruption will be dangerous and perverse. Václav Havel captures the danger in graphic language:

> When traditional myth was laid to rest, a kind of "order" in the dark region
> of our being was buried along with it. And what modern reason has attempted to substitute for this order . . . has consistently proved erroneous,
> false, and disastrous, because it is always in some way deceitful, artificial,

rootless, lacking in both ontology and morality. . . . [W]ith the burial of myth, the barn in which the mysterious animals of the human unconscious were housed over thousand[s] of years has been abandoned and the animals turned loose—on the tragically mistaken assumption that they were phantoms—and . . . now they are devastating the countryside.

It should now be clear why ideological thinking tends toward the paranoid, virtually guaranteeing that "millions of spiritually sick people" will cast about for scapegoats and enemies. Most individuals are poor psychologists and bad philosophers, only partially self-aware and marginally rational. Hence few are capable of discerning, much less acknowledging or articulating, their existential concerns; and even fewer, of responding to them in reasonable ways once they have been discovered. People strongly impelled by an inner void to restore the coherence lost when they were stripped of all supporting myths and folkways are therefore very likely to look outside themselves for a devil to whom all their ills can be attributed. And even if they avoid demonizing particular groups, they will almost certainly latch on to facile explanations or grasp at simplistic solutions that are, to reiterate, but another manifestation of the disease—precisely because neither the explanations nor the solutions are rooted in historical, psychological, or philosophical self-reflection. In short, rather than confront the complexity of the real world, the ideologue finds someone or something else to blame.

The ideologue is therefore virtually compelled to manufacture enemies, as a way both of satisfying the intense demand for ideological purity and of providing a scapegoat against whom the repressed energy can be directed. Naturally, as is true of the paranoid, the ideologue must always resolutely deny that his beliefs are ideological: he has an exclusive franchise on truth, while all others are lost in the folly and delusion of false consciousness and self-serving beliefs. Hence the worst ideologues of all are those who insist that they are not themselves ideological.

All of the above factors are amplified in large populations—that is, in crowds. Both depth psychology and modern social psychology support Le Bon's basic insight: individuals are strongly influenced by group pressures, to such an extent that it is entirely proper to speak of psychic contagion and shared delusions. "Madness is rare in individuals," said Nietzsche, "but in groups, parties, and nations, it is the rule." This is especially true when the process of rationalization fostered by the Enlightenment has destroyed the balance between conscious and unconscious in the human mind—a condition that must necessarily lead, says psychologist Erich Neumann, "to an activation of the deeper-lying layers which, now grown destructive, devastate the autocratic world of the ego with transpersonal invasions, collective epidemics, and mass psychoses." Thus hidden drives within millions of individual psyches become collectivized, justified ideologically, and then acted out historically.

In essence, ideology is tantamount to a shared mental disease. This disease originates in the individual human psyche as an epistemological neurosis in which the fearful mind grasps desperately for certainty and coherence, for "truth." But men and women are social beings and take their cues from their fellows. Indeed, if they do not, they risk being judged "insane." The truth that is grasped will therefore be the ideology of a particular culture, group, or movement. Once grasped, the individual then defends this tenuous truth to the death—not only psychologically but, all too often, literally as well. Naturally, some forms of this mental illness are more virulent or extreme than others, but all involve the lapse into a one-sided truth, all contain projections of the darker side of the human psyche, all involve intense social pressure to conform, and all are false and dangerous religions—superstitions at best, Molochs demanding human sacrifice at worst.

Modern Molochs may well be the worst of all. True, all of human history is replete with psychic epidemics in which masses of individuals were swept away by irrational forces spawning violent inquisitions, crusades, revolutions, pogroms, and purges—in brief, most of what we know as man's inhumanity to man. But the rational ideologies of the modern age have been especially heartless. Precisely to the extent that our own era has insisted not just on *the* truth, as in the past, but on a peculiarly narrow and specific *kind* of truth, it has produced ideologues notorious for their cold-blooded ruthlessness. Dostoyevsky's Grand Inquisitor is an executioner of innocents, but he is nevertheless a tragic figure: he murders out of misguided love, truly believing that he is saving souls. His modern counterpart is more like an impersonal killing machine, an Eichmann preoccupied with keeping the trains to the death camps running on time. In a similar vein, speaking of the Khmer Rouge in Cambodia, Paul Johnson says, "Like Lenin, they were pure intellectuals. They epitomized the great destructive force of the twentieth century: the religious fanatic reincarnated as professional politician. What they did illustrated the ultimate heartlessness of ideas."

One of the most characteristic features of modern times is thus what Kundera calls "the totalitarian poesy that leads to the gulag by way of paradise." In other words, to "forced labor camps"—Gary's "logical conclusion" to "a utilitarian civilization"—whose cruel spirit was exposed by Lenin's terrifying slogan for the Solovky camps, the cancerous seed from which the Gulag Archipelago eventually grew: "With an iron hand, mankind will be driven to happiness!"

From Despotic Rationalism to Despotic Politics

To conclude, exalting the particular mode of reasoning known as rationality has produced a paradoxical, contradictory, and ultimately dangerous outcome. Whatever its theorctical merits, rationality has in practice destroyed the human cosmos, producing a world of incoherence in which individuals find it all but impossible to orient themselves metaphysically or practically. In effect, modern men and women have simultaneously lost their bearings and demolished the means by which they might take them. They therefore fall into spiritual vertigo and cultural nihilism, into a life stripped of meaning and beauty that leads directly to a state of existential despair, which in turn fuels the secularized monotheisms we call ideology. In the end, the Enlightenment's "one-eyed reason" has not liberated humankind from the evils of religion, it has only driven the religious impulse underground, where it grows in passionate intensity. Far from being the intellectual and social panacea touted by Enlightenment propagandists, the single-minded pursuit of "mere purposive rationality" at the expense of "art, religion, dream, and the like" is thus, as Bateson says, "necessarily pathogenic and destructive of life." Indeed, in the final analysis, rationality turns out to be but another name for hubris: in Tawney's biting words, it has become the means for appropriating "the knowledge of all the ages" and using it "with the recklessness of a madman and the ferocity of a savage" in the service of our collective megalomania.

That the lives of modern men and women are ruled by quasi-religious ideologies that are dangerous and irrational precisely to the degree that they aim to be completely rational is bad enough. What is worse is that such ideologies also foster political despotism. Totalitarian poesy is implicit within rationality itself: a reality principle that is intellectually coercive and socially destructive is also politically tyrannical as well. As de Tocqueville warned,

> When there is no longer any principle of authority in religion, any more than in politics, men are speedily frightened at the aspect of this unbounded independence. The constant agitation of all surrounding things alarms and exhausts them. As everything is at sea in the sphere of the mind, they determine at least that the mechanism of society shall be firm and fixed; and, as they cannot resume their ancient belief, they assume a master.

Instrumental rationality and moral entropy are two sides of the same coin: together they pave the way for Leviathan. This tendency is strongly reinforced by the failure of rationality to provide the kind of intellectual understanding and practical control of society envisioned by the *philosophes*. Much of modern knowledge is either ignorance in disguise or irrelevant for solving pressing social problems. Our frenetic pursuit of knowledge seems to have brought about a paradoxical state of social idiocy that mocks the original Enlightenment goal of perfect social understanding. In actuality, we are less and less capable of comprehending our problems or of acting wisely and effectively to solve them. So the end of all our striving for power and domination has been to create exactly what we most feared and did not want: a world that is increasingly out of control.

Hence we have created the preconditions, if not yet the actuality, of a thoroughgoing despotism: in a vain effort to stay in control, we have allowed the power and rights of individuals to be eclipsed by the magnified power of gigantic administrative systems, especially those of the state. So let us now analyze the way in which individual liberty, the precious jewel of liberal theory, has been largely vitiated by the sociopolitical conditions created by liberalism in practice.

7

INTRINSIC TOTALITARIANISM

That it is to be a dictatorship of test tubes rather than hobnailed boots will not make it any less a dictatorship.

—Jacques Ellul

The destructive capacity of the individual, however vicious, is small; of the state, however well-intentioned, almost limitless. Expand the state and that destructive capacity necessarily expands too, pari passu.

—Paul Johnson

What prepares men for totalitarian domination . . . is the fact that loneliness, once a borderline experience usually suffered in certain marginal social conditions like old age, has become an everyday experience of the evergrowing masses of our century.

—Hannah Arendt

When the old gods withdraw, the empty thrones cry out for a successor.

—E. R. Dodds

WE COME NOW TO THE DENOUEMENT of the Enlightenment tragedy. We have learned that Hobbes's basic political doctrines are ultimately self-destructive: embedded in them is a remorseless logic that brings into existence the very state of affairs he was most concerned to prevent—a ceaseless and all-consuming struggle for power. We have seen in earlier chapters how moral entropy and social breakdown lead to hyperpluralistic factionalism and electronic barbarism; how addictive frustration and covert domination are inherent in liberal political economy; and how a narrow and imperialistic rationality destroys meaning and cosmic connection, a loss that mere ideologies cannot restore. In this chapter, I shall tie together all of these themes to argue that Hobbesian politics is intrinsically totalitarian. That is, it tends toward a "monolithic unity upheld by authoritarian means." Then, in the following chapter, I shall describe the particular form that this totalitarianism will take (indeed, has already taken): an administrative despotism that reduces ordinary men and women to "a state of permanent humiliation."

This tragic denouement was foreshadowed in the two great dystopias of the twentieth century. George Orwell's *Nineteen Eighty-Four* depicts the ultimate Hobbesian nightmare: *both* authoritarian rule *and* perpetual war. Aldous Huxley's *Brave New World* is more peaceful and benign—but a benevolent despotism of chemical and psychological conditioning, accompanied by the last word in bread and circuses, is despotism nonetheless. And underneath its round of sensual pleasure and drug-induced nirvana lies profound loneliness and despair, not real felicity. None would, I think, willingly choose either of these destinations. Yet it is toward one or both that we are bound (to the extent that we have not already arrived), and to reach some other terminus will require a heroic reorientation of our civilization and a moral regeneration of our politics. But let us now examine the various factors abetting totalitarianism, beginning with the trend toward technocratic absolutism.

A Dictatorship of Test Tubes

As we have repeatedly seen in previous chapters, the modern paradigm is explicitly aimed at power and control—in politics, in economics, and in science. A primary vehicle through which this power drive is expressed is technology, which seems to contain an intrinsic logic that leads toward technocracy—or, in Ellul's arresting phrase, "a dictatorship of test tubes."

When the Hobbesian desire for "commodious living" is wedded to a Baconian science dedicated to "the effecting of all things possible," the result is bound to be a restless and perpetual quest to extend man's technological dominion over nature. The language we habitually use to describe many of our most cherished projects is profoundly revealing—not only "domination" and "control" but "war," "conquest," "crusade," and the like. Our clearly expressed intent is to use technology to *overpower* everything that stands in the way of human supremacy—be it natural barriers, bodily diseases, social problems, or mental limitations—so that we can fulfill the Cartesian dream of making ourselves "the masters and possessors of nature."

As many myths and stories remind us, however, the possession and exercise of power has a dangerous shadow side—and the greater the power, the bigger the shadow. Lord Acton's famous dictum—"Power tends to corrupt and absolute power corrupts absolutely"—is but one such warning. Hence the tendency toward megalomania so characteristic of modern civilization. To be more specific, as even some of its foremost advocates admit, technology's shadow side is that the devil exacts a price for all that power: our "technological fixes" involve a "Faustian bargain."

First, because the exercise of control in any system creates so-called side effects that soon require a further extension of control, power seeking is addictive, and the terms of the bargain keep escalating. Thus, for example, computerization is not a luxury but a necessity to stay on top of growing complexity; and the aim of the impending biotechnical revolution is control of the life process itself.

Second, by its very nature, and notwithstanding the claim of too many of its propagandists, technology is never neutral—a mere "tool" without a morality or politics of its own. Even if, contrary to fact, the context of technological choice were not a political and economic order mad for power, technology's very rationality constitutes an intrinsic bias toward efficiency and the "one best way" defined in narrowly technical terms— that is, in favor of rational, bureaucratic, centralized control. For example, because nuclear power generation is so exacting and dangerous, it imposes a certain kind of political order: among other things, the civilian use of nuclear energy cannot be divorced from military applications, and the industry must therefore be stringently regulated, either by international organizations or by central governments. Even technology that seems entirely benign at first glance may have profound political implications. Broadcasting, for example, expresses a fundamentally antidemocratic idea—the idea of a mass society in which the few talk, the many listen. And the current rush to computerization, in which algorithms (problem-solving rules) are substituted for human judgment, has already unleashed one of Schumpeter's gales of "creative destruction" with political implications that loom very large. To reiterate, one's choice of a technological system is always a *political* act, because such decisions determine our social future. In the end, therefore, politically unconscious technological development all but guarantees that we will be ruled by Ellul's "dictatorship of test tubes."

Third, as Langdon Winner's apt phrase "reverse adaptation" makes explicit, it is human beings who must conform, both politically and in every other way, to the impersonal but exigent requirements of technological systems, not vice versa. This is especially true now that technology has become less mechanical and more social or intellectual, so that what Ellul calls "technique" intrudes ever more deeply into human lives: for example, "health systems" that process people according to standard rules that in turn decide who they shall see and how they shall be treated, forcing doctors to be bureaucrats instead of healers and turning patients into supplicants instead of customers. In short, technocracy—Marvin Harris's "energy despotism"—is implicit in the technological means we have chosen to embrace.

Fourth, for the foregoing reasons, the system tends inexorably toward the rule of a "priesthood of responsible technologists" who monopolize the know-how needed to keep the system running and who mask their power by appealing to the gods of efficiency. Thus political and social domination is an intrinsic part of the Faustian bargain: to reprise the observation of C. S. Lewis, technological power is always exercised "by some men over other men."

The third point above warrants expansion. Modern men and women believe that they are freer than their ancestors, but this may be a delusion. Ancient monarchs and tyrants were certainly powerful: the simple words "Off with his head!" dispensed with a man. Yet their power, although absolute as far as it went, did not always extend very far. As the epigraph by Johnson suggests, the damage that can be done by one individual, no matter how vicious, is limited; whereas the destructive capacity of the modern state, however well intentioned, is "almost limitless." Only in modern times is something like Stalin's Gulag Archipelago or Hitler's Final Solution possible. Fortunately, although too many in the developing nations still suffer torture and death at the hands of brutal tyrants, state power in the developed world is rarely turned to such horrendous ends (and even the Gulag Archipelago has now been washed by freedom's tide). In most modern states, therefore, direct and arbitrary political oppression is the exception, not the rule.

In exchange, however, modern men and women are subjected to large and impersonal forces beyond any individual's ken, much less control—indeed, beyond any legislature's or executive's ken or control. In this light, much of our vaunted freedom is illusory, because these forces determine core policy in all modern states—and human beings, including the supposed "leaders," adjust as best they can. For example, especially in a borderless world increasingly devoted to accumulation and governed by the logic of "winner-take-all capitalism," the invisible hand of the market imperceptibly but implacably determines who will be rich and who poor—as well as the basic shape of the society inhabited by everyone, rich or poor. The same with technological change: the clock, for instance, has stealthily but radically restructured human life in the last several centuries, yoking us to mechanical time. Similarly, as noted in

Chapter 2, the political and social power of the automobile has been all but absolute until very recently (now, at least, it is being questioned). Along the same lines, we have seen how television has, in a few short decades, utterly transformed our lives and politics. But the worst is yet to come, for impending technological developments, such as the biotechnical revolution, portend even more radical changes—changes that may transform the very meaning of human nature.

The lives of individuals are therefore subject to vast, impersonal, and virtually uncontrollable forces. At the same time, as the growth of "energy despotism" illustrates, technological development constitutes the pretext for further extensions of centralized power, especially state power. Having overthrown the tyranny of kings, we find ourselves ruled by Ellul's "technique," by technologically driven forces that both create and undergird a political Leviathan. But the resulting "dictatorship of test tubes" is not perceived for what it is, so the illusion of freedom persists.

In effect, we are slouching toward some form of technocratic absolutism. The late Buckminster Fuller, a fervent apostle of technology, did not mince words: our choice is between "utopia or oblivion." Unfortunately, the word *utopia* in this context has politically sinister implications. Human beings, the remaining uncontrolled element in the engineering equation, must be brought into line. As the explosion of the space shuttle *Challenger* and the meltdown of the nuclear reactor at Chernobyl demonstrated, the weak link in all engineered systems is not usually the technology itself but the human beings who design and operate them—because, unlike mechanical devices, human beings can be complacent, bored, inattentive, mistaken, intimidated, pressured, and panicked. Lest they compromise the efficiency and safety of technological systems, or so Fuller's logic implies, they must be either eliminated from the system or made more like machines.

It is yet another Hobbesian vicious circle: the application of power and the extension of control lead to disturbances and perturbations, whether in societies or in ecosystems, that necessarily invoke greater applications of power and further extensions of control. So Hobbesian man is obliged by an addictive process to move toward the total control of a "utopia"—a technocratic regime in which law and morality are largely replaced by force, however veiled or rationalized, and in which human behavior is governed by technological imperatives.

To put it another way, an organic way of life is for the most part self-regulating and thus requires only a minimum of external governance. But when human actions vitiate self-regulation, the resulting chaos must be countered either by restoring the preexisting organic balance or by escalating power and control. Civilization has almost always chosen the latter path, especially since the Enlightenment, so it now confronts the inescapable consequence: the necessity to achieve "utopia," lest it fall into "oblivion." Hence we are headed for a monolithic, authoritarian regime in which all the so-called externalities, especially the unpredictable and troublesome human element, have been internalized—creating a society that, however "rich" or even "happy," will be totalitarian to a degree that we can scarcely imagine.

The National-Security State

Military power, which grows directly out of technological power, also pushes liberal polities toward totalitarianism. This dangerous trend is clearly visible in the United States, where a national-security state characterized by a military-industrial complex and an imperial presidency has grown up during the last fifty years. The Cold War is usually blamed for this development. However, this is only one part of the story: as we saw earlier, militarism, if not imperialism, is intrinsic to liberalism. Because economic development is essentially predatory, it requires resources, markets, and spheres of influence or even control that rest on the ability and willingness of the so-called haves to back up the market system and their position in it with force whenever necessary. Economic growth, technological development, and military power are therefore inescapably intertwined. Indeed, since modern political economy is driven by the will to power, we should not be surprised when development serves martial rather than humane ends. Or, to put it the other way around, if war is politics by other means, and if in modern times economics has also become politics by other means, then economics is now (or soon will be) a kind of war by other means. Hence, as virtually all of modern history attests, a struggle for resources, market shares, and influence is endemic to the modern way of life.

So the Cold War's end will not usher in automatic peace. On the contrary, far from having come to an end, history has reawakened from nearly a half-century of hibernation: we have exchanged a kind of world order, however peculiar and perverse, for a new world disorder that will present us with far more complex and dangerous problems. Long-frozen political, ethnic, and religious passions have thawed, and the old basis for international cooperation is simultaneously melting away, as countries focus on their own problems and needs instead of on the common threat. We are therefore entering a period of turbulence in which political borders and identities and the international rules of the game will be challenged across the board. Even the possibility of a classic "hegemonic war" cannot be excluded. To use Hobbesian language, we are lapsing into an anarchic state of nature, with all the political and military consequences that follow from that fact. Hence international politics will be more than ever governed by *raison d'état*, and statesmen will have to follow the principles enunciated by Lord Palmerston in 1848: no eternal allies and no perpetual enemies, only vital interests that must be asserted with vigor and, when necessary, defended with force.

But our world is more dangerous and less manageable than the one inhabited by Palmerston: the rapid proliferation of ballistic missiles and other weapons of mass destruction; the even greater spread of a military technology that, paradoxically, facilitates terrorism, insurrection, and guerrilla warfare despite the existence of these weapons; the concentration of the most critical global resource, petroleum, in one of the most volatile global regions, the Middle East; exploding populations and increasing economic inequities fueling a seemingly inexorable trend toward mass migration; the impact of instantaneous communications and global media, especially on crowded masses in colossal "hypercities"— these and a host of other complications have made the "game" of international politics much more difficult and deadly. In such a risky and competitive environment, there will certainly be a concerted effort to construct a stable world order based on transnational institutions—indeed, this is the only conceivable solution to the new world disorder— but there will also be continual diplomatic and military maneuvering, albeit of a kind different from that of the last five decades, as the various nation-states (including many emerging regional powers in the Third World) struggle to advance their interests and to control their destinies within an unstable neo-Palmerstonian world system.

The point of this brief excursion into international politics is twofold: to remind the reader of the intrinsic imperialism of liberal political economy and to correct any possible misapprehension of our actual historical situation. The end of the Cold War will not mean the withering away of the national-security state or the end of the *realpolitik* that provided its rationale. To be sure, many things are now better. The ideological clash between capitalism and communism, for example, is no longer a factor, thus removing a major source of irrationality and danger. Moreover, the profound *embourgeoisement* of Western Europe, as well as the progress toward economic and political integration already achieved, makes a repetition or continuation of World Wars I and II unlikely. On the other hand, some things are worse, and the stakes, both economic and military, are now much higher. The recent Gulf War, for example, was fought by the United States and its European allies not only to maintain control of the petroleum vital to their economies but also to prevent a regime avowedly hostile to their interests from amassing more military power, especially in the form of nuclear weapons. But more and more nations (as well as terrorist groups) are slowly but surely acquiring the means of mass destruction, and we may reasonably surmise that they will want to employ these means to ends that threaten our interests. It is therefore utopian to believe that the national-security state will be dismantled in our lifetime.

This is very bad news indeed—especially for American democracy. The so-called leader of the free world has been on a war footing for more than half a century and has therefore acquired the antidemocratic attitudes and habits that accompany the prosecution of a war. As a consequence, the amoral ethos of the Hobbesian state of nature has not merely contaminated domestic political life, it has done so in the worst possible way—stealthily and covertly, as a protracted and morally dubious war has been waged as much as possible away from the glare of publicity and the vagaries of democratic debate. The result has been government by subterfuge, as the mentality of ends justifying means and the mind-set of a garrison state have infected American politics, particularly at the highest levels. Although the corruption and scandal produced by this infection require no elaboration or documentation, they do cry out for a better understanding of what has produced them: the Iran-Contra affair, for instance, was not so much an aberration to be blamed on particular individuals, however easy or attractive that might seem to be, as it was the logical consequence of living in a national-security state.

In effect, making all due allowance for the differing degree of evil, America too has become an "evil empire" that tends to place state interests above other considerations. Although the United States is by no means alone among its former allies in pursuing *raison d'état* to extreme ends, we are unfortunately one of the worst offenders, displaying a distressing tendency to betray our own principles for the sake of *realpolitik* by cozying up to dictators, subverting governments distasteful to us, and even invading nations that refuse to knuckle under. Thus, as in the old story of the pot calling the kettle black, we who denounce "terrorism" also carry it out; we who purport to be for "the rule of law" also flout it; we who condemn "merchants of death" also sell arms to dictators; and we who complain of "disinformation" also practice systematic mendacity. This is more than garden-variety hypocrisy. It represents the triumph of a national-security Leviathan utterly incompatible with democratic principles and practices.

That a garrison state is the enemy of an orderly democracy has been understood since ancient times. A major part of the tragedy of Athenian politics was that the imperialism made necessary by commercial expansion could not in the end be reconciled with a stable democratic polis. The dilemma of national defense policy in our age is the same: too little, said Eisenhower, and you have no security; too much, and you risk "destroying from within what you are trying to defend from without." And if the aim is hegemony rather than mere self-defense, then the danger is obviously much greater. All this was well understood by the Founders, who warned strongly against military ventures that would concentrate power and thus encroach upon the liberty of the people. De Tocqueville summed up the lesson in one sentence: "All those who seek to destroy the liberties of a democratic nation ought to know that war is the surest and shortest means to accomplish it." Alas, fifty-plus years of life in a national-security state have already done much to destroy our liberties, and there is no relief in sight.

The Solitude of the Lonely Crowd

That technocracy and the garrison state are noxious to the health of a democratic polity is publicly recognized and debated. These outward threats are therefore the lesser part of the problem: although insidious, they are at least visible and acknowledged. By contrast, the inner longing for totalitarianism, to which subject we now turn, is much more dangerous, because it is the unconscious shadow side of our cherished way of life and the principles we espouse. Hence we do not understand how our very "liberation" could paradoxically be forging totalitarian chains.

Modern politics is a politics of solitude. The assertion that man is a solitary being was one of Hobbes's great departures from the political tradition that he inherited. Unfortunately, such a premise is self-fulfilling. Just as a social order characterized by dog-eat-dog competition follows logically from the postulate of a war of all against all in the state of nature, so too does a society peopled by lonely and isolated individuals follow naturally from the assumption of solitariness. The situation is most acute in the United States, because our form of democracy is and always has been radically individualistic: "Democracy," said de Tocqueville, "throws [every man] back forever upon himself alone, and threatens in the end to confine him entirely within the solitude of his own heart." But the social isolation foreshadowed in these memorable words has gradually become the universal condition of existence in all modern societies. This is the point of Arendt's epigraph: loneliness has been transformed from a "borderline experience" suffered by those at the social margin to the "everyday experience" of the average man or woman, who is thus prepared for "totalitarian domination."

We have already seen that the liberal tradition virtually ignores the social damage it causes. Indeed, the destruction of organic community and its replacement by mass society is normally represented as a triumph of liberation—and so it was in one sense, for the stable and binding roles of traditional society were indeed constraining. Yet the same roles also provided social support and a clear sense of belonging, so the benefit of liberation was obtained at the cost of security and identity. Free-floating anxiety and perpetual identity crisis are therefore the lot of liberated modern man.

As a result, says political scientist Sheldon Wolin, liberal polity must be judged a "masochistic failure," for it does not promote human felicity. In *The Good Marriage*, Judith Wallerstein, a psychologist who has devoted her life to studying the American family in good times and bad, is even more scathing: "The prevailing value system is a recipe for misery."

In fact, when one reads between the lines of liberal thought it becomes apparent that the so-called pursuit of happiness is more like a flight from the misery of existing in the insecurity and loneliness of modern society. This is, again, especially true in the United States. As pointed out by sociologist Philip Slater in his aptly titled *The Pursuit of Loneliness*, the quest for individual happiness has now become a self-defeating attempt to escape from the consequences of the pursuit itself: "The longing for privacy is created by the drastic conditions that the longing for privacy produces." We see here again, but on a larger scale, the addictive and intrinsically frustrating nature of the liberal order. Modern men and women are driven creatures—ever pursuing, and therefore knowing no rest from toil and no relief from insecurity. The inescapable price of "liberation" is the pain of "solitude."

Ironically, liberation, which is supposed to empower the individual, in fact leads to a progressive loss of control over one's life and hence to a sense of powerlessness. After all, the whole point of liberal freedom is that nobody shall control me—but the corollary is that *I shall have no control over others*. Perhaps this would be a fair bargain if I were actually free—that is, if I escaped every form of social control save the bare minimum of police power—but this is not so. As we have seen, individuals may no longer be constrained by family ties and other social roles as in the past, but they are in return subjected to vast impersonal forces beyond any kind of social, much less personal, control—so they are not so free after all.

At the same time, the individual's general level of skill, competence, and autonomy has been degraded in mass society. The people who inhabit organic communities can by and large grow their own food, make their own clothes, and even construct their own dwellings—all of which gives them a sense of self-sufficiency and independence not enjoyed by modern men and women, who must depend on the "system" to provide every requisite of life as an "output." Summarizing the vast sociological literature, Krishan Kumar says,

> The triumphs of industrialism . . . involved a progressive decline in the skills, competence, autonomy, and responsibility of the bulk of the population in the industrial societies. Knowledge and skills have gone into machines and the professionalized service institutions; authority and autonomy into the hierarchical and bureaucratic structures of large-scale organization. . . . As Marx put it . . . "the more the worker produces, the more he diminishes himself."

In other words, the common people have been reduced to a dependent proletariat at the mercy of the corporate state. All in all, therefore, modern men and women suffer from a pervasive sense of vulnerability and powerlessness, because they have no more control over their physical and social environment than a savage—in fact, rather less.

Even in the political sphere more narrowly defined, although it may be true that they are no longer under the direct control of feudal lords or village elders, citizens are subject to the overwhelming power of the modern nation-state to tax, conscript, and generally compel. And, as Paul Johnson points out, it is not certain that the latter is necessarily to be preferred to the former—not when the state numbers in the hundred millions, the bureaucracies that administer it answer largely to themselves or to their special-interest allies, and the elections that supposedly make the citizens the master of the state seem increasingly manipulated and meaningless. What Edmund Burke called the "little platoons"—family, neighborhood, parish, guild, county, and all the other local structures of cooperation, integration, and authority within an organic community—may have constrained men and women, often severely at times, but they also served as bulwarks against a more impersonal tyranny. These bulwarks are now gone. In fact, the old liberal distinction between "society" and "state" has been virtually obliterated: the state is now the primary focus of allegiance and identity and almost the only remaining source of social authority. Thus nothing but the unreliable goodwill of those who control the state defends the individual from the "monolithic unity" of totalitarianism.

The Flight from Freedom

Given the sense of vulnerability and powerlessness that pervades modern existence, it is hardly surprising that many observers have perceived a widespread fear of freedom in mass society. If "solitude" engenders personal loneliness compounded by feelings of rootlessness, anxiety, frustration, and powerlessness—in short, existential despair—the desire to escape from the burden of this pain would have to become compelling, consciously or unconsciously. A characteristic feature of modern or modernizing societies is therefore the flight from freedom. This takes two principal forms: fundamentalism, or the effort to restore a lost sense of certainty and belonging by clinging to the old verities, and anesthesia, or the effort to block out pain and abdicate responsibility.

The fundamentalist resembles the ideologue, but rather than adopt a secular religion as an antidote to the meaninglessness of a mythless existence, he chooses to reject modern values in favor of traditional ones. By cleaving faithfully or fanatically to the old ways and old certainties—whether these are religious, cultural, or nationalistic—the fundamentalist tries to negate the modern world and assuage his existential pain with true belief. And like the rabid ideologue, the fundamentalist is paranoid: he not only rejects modern values more or less categorically for himself, but he demonizes those who espouse them, seeing the devil's hand behind their every intention and act. Although the degree of paranoia obviously varies, this is as true of the extreme religious right in the United States as it is of the Iranian ayatollahs and the Irish Republican Army: the enemy is Satan, the personification of evil, against whom a no-holds-barred war is obligatory. Fundamentalism is thus responsible for many of the pathologies that afflict modern polities—civil war, terrorism, organized racism, extreme political activism, religious and quasi-religious cults, and so on. Fundamentalism and secular ideology are two sides of the same coin: they are both ways of fleeing the psychological burden of individual freedom by embracing true belief, whether in a social utopia, a political struggle, a racial cause, a cultural tradition, or a religious creed.

The dangers of fundamentalism are comparatively well understood, if only because extremist groups habitually commit violent acts that outrage public sensibilities. Unfortunately, despite the increasing salience of the street-drug problem, the society-wide extent of the flight from freedom into anesthesia is little acknowledged, or even denied. To the extent that we do take the "drug problem" seriously, we tend to define it as a matter for the police rather than the polity. Yet it is probably our most basic, most ominous, and least tractable social ill.

As we have seen, Hobbesian political economy is fundamentally addictive in character, and addiction of all kinds is hence the norm in liberal society: most citizens are hooked on one or more means of denying or drowning out existential pain, with the officially proscribed drugs being only the tip of an enormous iceberg. That is, addiction is by no means confined to heroin, cocaine, marijuana, or other illegal drugs—as extensive and damaging, both personally and socially, as the use of such substances is. Nor does it stop with the abuse of such legal drugs as alcohol and nicotine, as well as numerous prescription and even nonprescription drugs, although we have finally begun to grasp how pervasive and harmful such abuse is. Rather, the addictive search for anesthesia extends to virtually the whole of our way of life—eating, shopping, sex, music, work, sports, and television, to cite only the most obvious. The point is not to condemn all amusing activities and pleasurable substances per se: the problem is that these tend to be used as opiates by very large numbers of people. Although we do not ordinarily classify, say, work or the media as "narcotics," they are nevertheless used as such, as we tacitly acknowledge when we call someone "a workaholic" or "a media junkie." Addiction to television is especially pervasive: even leaving aside the insidious way in which it pushes commodities, purveys cheap thrills, and numbs minds with trivial pursuits, it seems literally to entrance viewers physiologically. It has therefore become the almost universal narcotic of mass-consumption societies.

Fundamentalist fanaticism and narcotic escape are thus basic features of our social order: most people are addicted to opium, either the opium of true belief or the opium of anesthesia. But these very same things are the basis of social control in the dystopian visions of Orwell and Huxley. In *Nineteen Eighty-Four*, fanatical religious adoration of Big Brother and equally passionate hatred of the current "enemy," supplemented by cheap gin, are the primary means of keeping the populace in line. In *Brave New World*, similar means are employed with more finesse: obligatory sexuality, artificial religious ecstasy, and, when all else fails, the anodyne of "soma" are used to keep the populace "happy." The ways that people today try to alleviate or escape their existential pain are precisely those that Orwell and Huxley identify as constituting the basis of their totalitarian orders.

That the desire to escape reality with some form of opium is so strong in liberal society suggests that the latter is indeed fundamentally inhuman. As Freud pointed out, all forms of civilization are shadowed by the "discontents" that arise out of the "repression" that is seemingly required by life in complex societies. But only liberal society—Wolin's "masochistic failure" and Wallerstein's "recipe for misery"—seems to drive the great mass of men and women toward existential despair.

The political danger represented by this situation was apparent to Le Bon when he wrote nearly a century ago that crowds are driven by unconscious forces to behave in accordance with instinct, not reason. In psychological terms, members of a crowd "regress" emotionally toward the primitive and the infantile. In consequence, said Le Bon, they are subject to "emotional contagion"; they are dominated by religious fervor; and they thirst for leaders who will rule them on the basis of conviction and charisma. The lonely crowd thus longs for a political solution: mass man secretly desires the tutelary state, because it seems the only antidote to the inhumanity of liberal society. As Spanish philosopher José Ortega y Gasset said earlier in the century,

> Before long there will be heard throughout the planet a formidable cry, rising like the howling of innumerable dogs to the stars, asking for someone or something to take command, to impose an occupation, a duty. . . . to give people something to do, to fit them into their destiny, to prevent their wandering aimlessly about in an empty, desolate existence.

In sum, we should not be surprised if modern men and women secretly long to embrace either Big Brother or Sister Morphine. Liberal society is not a community but a lonely crowd of merely solitary individuals lost in an uncaring mass. Traditional community may involve the constraints implicit in tight social bonds, but liberal freedom entails the isolation, frustration, anxiety, and, ultimately, despair of "solitude." Lonely, anxious, frustrated, powerless, and despairing individuals thrown back upon themselves alone are wide open to ideological or fundamentalist persuasion and defenseless against state power; fearful and lacking a firm sense of identity, they hunger for security and a sense of belonging; and to the extent that they do not get them, they long for escape. Hence the necessary and sufficient conditions for totalitarian politics exist to a greater or lesser extent in all modern polities; and since all the bulwarks against monolithic power are gone, there must sooner or later be a totalitarian outcome.

False Gods Usurp the Empty Throne

But the real roots of totalitarianism lie deeper still: ultimately, the fear that freedom evokes is spiritual, rather than social-psychological, in origin. Modern man is not the first to be afflicted by such dread. As E. R. Dodds pointed out, the "open" society of Greece in the third century

B.C. was much too open for most of its members, for the loss of tradition occasioned terrible anxiety rather than joy. Thus, said Dodds, the Greeks "refused the jump": instead of embracing intellectual freedom, they "turned tail and bolted from the horrid prospect," relapsing into mere irrationality.

Although there are many lessons to be learned from this cautionary tale (see Box 7.1), the pertinent point for now is that modern men and women are in the same predicament. As a consequence of "wandering aimlessly about in an empty, desolate existence," they suffer from an intense spiritual vertigo that constitutes a potent source of unconscious longing for certainty and domination. Dodds's epigraph reinforces the conclusion of Ortega y Gasset: "When the old gods withdraw, the empty thrones cry out for a successor." The famous "death of God" has therefore opened the way for false prophets preaching false religions, for the great helmsmen and maximum leaders of modern times and their political opium.

Nietzsche, the philosopher who formally proclaimed "the death of God," made the potential horror of the deity's demise utterly clear: without divine sanction for moral behavior, "the will to power" must necessarily reign. The consequence is a brutal world resembling that described by Thucydides, one in which "the strong do what they can and the weak suffer what they must." In these conditions, the rule of a "superman" who is "beyond good and evil" and who dominates the "slave class" made up of those too timid to give up the inherited "herd morality" becomes an attractive way out. Nietzsche thus foresaw (although he certainly did not endorse) the prophetic irrationalism of our times—all the political religions and personality cults that have blighted the history of the twentieth century. The abyss of existence without spiritual meaning is directly responsible for the gangster statesmen and totalitarian hells of the modern era.

In this light, spiritual vertigo is not just a problem for theologians and psychologists. It is *the* core political issue of our time. To recall the words of Walter Lippmann, one cannot create a "spiritual proletariat" consisting of "masses without roots [and] crowds without convictions" without also creating "the chaos in which the new Caesars are born." The greatest fallacy of contemporary political thought is the belief that a benign and effective authority can exist apart from a civil society that is grounded on moral tradition. As Locke himself made explicit, without such a foundation a liberal political order must either collapse or decay into tyranny, which is by definition the exercise of power that is not morally justified.

Box 7.1
The Greeks Destroy Themselves

The Greek case strongly suggests that rationalism, commercialism, and individualism are dangerous in and of themselves, and positively lethal in combination.

Ancient Greek civilization was destroyed largely by a rationalist revolution resembling our own so-called Enlightenment. Like the eighteenth-century *philosophes*, the sophists championed reason: they exposed superstition, questioned custom, exalted the individual, fostered ambition, and generally undermined the traditional order. William McNeill describes the impact on the polis:

> If law was a conspiracy of the weak against the strong, and if morality was no more than a man-made convention, as some of the sophists held, then clearly the sentiments of self-dedication and sacrifice for the good of the polis—so strenuously inculcated by former generations—were the merest self-delusion. A real man would see through such fictions and conduct himself in such a way as to indulge his own "natural" impulses so far as it was safe to do so, without regard for common goals or public good.

In effect, the sophists created an early version of Hobbesian man. They thus subverted the moral basis of Greek politics and fueled the political fratricide, both within and between the city-states of Hellas, that left the Greeks defenseless against Macedonian aggression.

Manufacturers and merchants finished the job begun by the sophists, especially in Athens. The original basis of Athenian democracy was the independent yeoman and artisan. By the time of Solon, however, production for export had replaced mixed farming and craftsmanship. So the city grew wealthy from manufacture and trade, but at the expense of the social order: the yeoman and the artisan were driven to near-extinction by a money economy based on specialization, technological innovation, and, above all, slave labor; the citizens became a minority within a polis increasingly populated by the rootless, the parasitic, and the enslaved; and extremes of wealth and poverty divided the citizens themselves into classes whose interests were fundamentally opposed. Moreover, a commercial empire had no choice but to become a military and political empire as well. In addition, ecological degradation accompanied economic growth.

The so-called light of Athens was therefore cast by the bonfire that consumed it: materially as well as intellectually, ancient Athens traveled a path leading to self-destruction much like our own—and for essentially the same reasons. "The greatness of the Greeks in individual achievement," said Bertrand Russell, was the cause of the "political incompetence" that led to political and military downfall. Even thinking Greeks understood as much: both Aristotle and Plato pointed out that the pure democracy of the Athenian polis tended inexorably toward chaos and self-destruction, because it failed to contain individual passion and folly. Hence, said Will Durant in *The Life of Greece*, Greece's glory was also its tragedy: "Individualism in the end destroys the group, but in the interim it stimulates personality, mental exploration, and artistic creation. Greek democracy was corrupt and incompetent, and had to die." Change but a single word, and Durant's summary dismissal of Greek democracy becomes, if not yet an epitaph, then at least a portent of our own fate.

In other words, to reiterate, a good politics depends in the end on good values. And good values do not emerge out of thin air, only out of a moral tradition concretely expressed in social institutions. Indeed, good political values are always concrete and particular: a diffuse liking for humanity or a vague attachment to the concept of democracy may show one's good intentions, but neither is politically meaningful. (After all, Hitler believed himself to be a great benefactor not just of the German people but of the human race; and Lenin regarded himself as a true democrat.) The moral foundation provided by a working civil society is therefore absolutely indispensable to a benign politics.

It is for this reason that political thinkers otherwise as different as Aristotle, Burke, Machiavelli, Montesquieu, Rousseau, and de Tocqueville all made mores, including manners, more important than laws. Aristotle, for example, pointed out that "there is no profit in the best of laws, even when they are sanctioned by general civil consent, if the citizens themselves have not been attuned, by the force of habit and the influence of teaching, to the right constitutional temper."

In other words, good mores support both good laws and the propensity to obey them, whereas bad mores undermine and eventually destroy even the best of laws along with the willingness to be law-abiding. Why? Because mores are *the concrete and politically relevant expression of moral values* in relationship to particular persons and situations. But, again, mores do not arise in a vacuum: they are based on and justified by "self-evident" moral truths believed to have spiritual sanction—that is, by a religious tradition of some kind, however defined. In the end, therefore, the Enlightenment's willful demolition of tradition and religion turns out to have been an act of political self-destruction as well.

To be more specific, making morality a question of individual choice has the eventual consequence of negating all forms of public principle in favor of private "values." But *private* values have no moral foundation: they are little more than prejudices or, especially in a competitive environment, rationalizations of self-interest. So moral relativism leads to a kind of nihilism, to the replacement of moral coherence with the moral chaos of "value freedom"—and therefore to the collapse of social authority. Indeed, the whole tenor of modern life is "against authority." In the arts and in philosophy, from Dada to Derrida, the history of the twentieth century is the record of a self-conscious attempt to destroy any semblance of a pretension to authority.

The consequences are devastating. With no agreed principles for deciding difficult issues, how can governments make genuinely authoritative decisions? If citizens are supposed to decide by and for themselves what is true and right, what obligates them to obey any decision with which they do not agree, even if it is made with due process and is clearly desired by a majority? In a word, nothing—as the abortion war clearly shows. In short, authority is *authoritative* only within the context of a moral tradition that lends weight to some choices rather than others and thereby imparts genuine force to political decisions: no morality, no authority.

What is worse, if men and women are mere bundles of will and appetite and there is no higher goal than the satisfaction of same, then what limitations are there on their conduct? And why do they have rights or a personal dignity that we must respect? In other words, without some sense of morality, some feeling that human beings are more than Sadean animals, there are no limits either on individual conduct or on what can be done to the individual: no morality, no rights—only the unlimited right of Caesar over the things that are Caesar's, namely everything.

This, then, is the core political predicament of modern man: the demise of the deity not only destroyed moral and spiritual meaning, but it also removed the possibility of genuine authority. The resulting chaos or radical openness, in both society and psyche, constitutes a moral and political vacuum that is soon filled by secular "authorities" trying to fulfill not just the mundane needs of the people but their ultimate needs as well. This is both impossible and dangerous. Not only are ultimate ends beyond the capacity of mortal men to achieve by earthly means, but political authorities made up of fallible and corruptible human beings are exceedingly ill-suited to achieve them. More important, politics rests ultimately on coercion, so it can never be a perfect realm of love and justice. To prevent it from straying too far, it must continually be checked by moral criticism. If there is no spiritual principle with which to criticize the political realm—or, worse, if this realm arrogates to itself the mantle of divinity—then the state will in practice stray increasingly far from love and justice; and the more spiritually arrogant the state, the farther it will ultimately stray.

Political evil has, of course, always existed. But modern political evil is fundamentally different. As the frightened masses of our age refuse the jump to freedom and bolt for the security of the closed mind, they make mass evil possible. Until the purges and pogroms unleashed by Stalin and Hitler, there had never before been a total effort to purify and perfect society by systematically and completely exterminating entire classes of people using assembly-line methods. The tragedy of modern politics is that the famous death of God tends to engender a kind of mass madness that can become the impetus for a radical (and yet utterly banal) evil beyond the imagination or capacity of the worst tyrants of the past.

The obvious solution might seem to be to resurrect the spiritual principle and reinstitute a politics that strikes an appropriate balance between the realms of worldly power and sacred truth. Unfortunately, we have been so traumatized by the totalitarian hells of our time that although we long for moral principle we are also mortally afraid of it. The idea that there could be some vision of the good life, if only as an ideal to strive for, is greeted by ridicule or worse. And any attempt to uphold, much less impose, standards or to suggest that there is indeed a public interest to which private interests must at times be subservient is fiercely resisted: such ideas are "elitist" at best, "totalitarian" at worst. *But it is precisely the lack of genuine moral standards* that creates the Nietzschean abyss and therefore lays the liberal order wide open to totalitarian rule. We see again the ironic and ultimately tragic nature of Hobbesian politics: the more it insists that there are no spiritual principles for guiding politics, the worse the political values it gets. In the absence of genuine moral visions, the Nietzschean supermen who are now the sole pretenders to the empty throne will impose their horrific ones.

The Dialectic of Authority and Tyranny

To reiterate, Hobbesian politics creates what it fears: power politics in the most sinister sense of that phrase. This is the logical consequence of its basic principles. How could one simultaneously unleash the human passions and destroy the social and moral basis of politics without also creating a lonely and frightened crowd that begs for Leviathan? To put this another way, such a politics contravenes basic laws of nature, so it is bound to fail in the long run. To see what this means in practice, let us turn to a political axiom articulated by Burke:

> Men are qualified for civil liberty in exact proportion to their disposition to put moral chains upon their own appetites. . . . Society cannot exist unless a controlling power upon will and appetite be placed somewhere, and the less of it there is within, the more there must be without. It is ordained in the eternal constitution of things, that men of intemperate minds cannot be free. Their passions forge their fetters.

Hence virtue and coercion are not separate phenomena; they are dialectically linked. Any lessening of internal control must lead to a proportionate increase in external compulsion. Similarly, all the other elements of a political system stand in a dialectical relationship to each other—so less virtue also means more vice, less authority means more tyranny, and so on. In short, the choice is not *whether* to have chains on will and appetite but *what kind* of chains they should be.

This is not just one philosopher's conservative interpretation of history but a political law rooted in the nature of reality. The world is fundamentally ecological: everything is mutually interrelated, so nothing can be done in isolation or without consequences. Moreover, everything in it, from the hardest of physical objects to the softest of mental phenomena, exists within a system and therefore obeys the fundamental natural laws that govern systems behavior. One such law is Newton's Third Law of Motion: "For every action there is an equal and opposite reaction." This applies universally, affecting not only billiard balls and spacecraft but also complex psychological and social systems. Although the actions and reactions of the latter are often subtle and therefore hard for us to track, especially in the short term, they are nevertheless governed by Emerson's "law of compensation": as Jung warned, "Everything better is purchased at the price of something worse," and whatever is repressed "returns." In other words, Burke's axiom expresses a fundamental truth about human affairs: every change in a political or social system must be compensated—directly or indirectly, positively or negatively. But since the human system is no longer organic, it has lost the capacity to respond in spontaneous or healthy ways, so the compensations have become increasingly diseased and destructive. Having destroyed authority and virtue, we are now being compensated with tyranny and vice, their dialectical opposites.

The laws of thermodynamics teach the same lesson. We saw in Chapter 1 that any system requires a measured and structured input of energy to maintain itself in a state of balance against entropy, the natural tendency toward disorder and decay; and if this input of energy is insufficient or inappropriate, the system unravels. In political systems, civic virtue allied to legitimate authority performs the same essential maintenance function: without them, there is a fall into moral entropy, causing a social breakdown that is the forerunner of absolute power. In this respect, Hobbes was both more astute and more honest than most of his followers, who largely overlooked the dialectical shadow side of the ideas they borrowed from him. Although Hobbes obviously could not foresee (nor would he have approved of) the modern police state, he did understand clearly that abandoning virtue and condoning vice—that is, allowing the free play of individual passions—would *necessarily* have to be compensated for by the *absolute* power of the sovereign.

The operation of this dialectic is implacable. All attempts to diminish authority and virtue will simply produce an equivalent increase in their opposites. Will and appetite are constants in human life: the failure to constrain them in an appropriate fashion by political morality, manifested inwardly as virtue and outwardly as authority, simply leaves a vacuum soon filled by mere power. Although this power may be exercised with restraint and according to law at first, all history teaches that it tends to decay into tyranny, as moral and legal principle are increasingly sacrificed to expediency. *Thus it is the very effort to liberate himself from morality and authority that is causing Hobbesian man to become enslaved.*

In sum, the most fundamental dialectical choice that confronts the political animal is never between authority and freedom but, instead, between authority and tyranny. Rousseau's shocking conclusion is correct: unless man contrives to "force" himself to be free—by being virtuously obedient to a self-imposed authority—he must be a slave. The freedom and felicity for which the human spirit longs are always the consequence of a sane and organic way of life rooted in a moral community that creates social harmony by authoritatively upholding certain canons of virtuous behavior. In the end, true democracy is *self*-rule, not the pursuit of a merely sensual and purely selfish happiness. In a dialectical universe, striving for liberty and happiness at the expense of moral community, instead of contriving to find them within it, can result in nothing but license and misery—in a chaos that makes Leviathan inevitable.

The Psychopathic State

Because the quest for power in the Hobbesian system is never ending, the power of the state must grow and grow, destroying everything that tries to stand in its way. In consequence, says Wolin, "the evolution of the modern state is a story of an internal form of imperialism that we call centralization of power and of the steady destruction of local power and traditional authorities that we call modernization." The upshot is "democracy without the citizen": an administrative Leviathan that is only nominally under democratic control.

Although the administrative state is a serious danger in its own right (as we shall see in the next chapter), our present concern is with the way in which Hobbesian politics creates the preconditions not just for authoritarianism but for totalitarianism. The essence of totalitarianism in the usual sense is that it seeks total, dictatorial control of the polity: with malice aforethought, rulers use police-state methods to destroy Burke's little platoons and Locke's civil society. The resulting atomization of society fosters the monolithic unity that is one of the defining characteristics of a totalitarian order. Yet precisely the same outcome is achieved by the liberal order "inadvertently," as a by-product of technologically driven economic development and its political aftermath. And although such an end is supposedly achieved "noncoercively"—unlike, say, Stalin's forced collectivization of the peasants—this simply means that the liquidation and expropriation necessary for economic development took longer to accomplish and were for the most part enforced by legal writs instead of bayonets. But the end result is the same: the destruction of civil society.

The social and psychic consequences of this destruction are frankly horrendous. A society ground down into atoms is a lonely crowd. It consists of solitary and powerless individuals who suffer from a spiritual vertigo that few have the intellectual or moral resources to withstand, so they resort to pathological means of coping. Although men and women in this desperate situation hunger for meaning and authority, all sources of legitimate meaning and authority have perished along with civil society, which leaves only illegitimate meaning and authority in the form of propaganda and power. The long-term effect of Hobbesian polity, then, is to reduce the people to a proletariat, to a political vacuum that can only be filled by power: the logical, if not inevitable, response to "electronic barbarism" is Michael Sandel's "electronic Bonapartism."

What is worse, the clear danger is that such a polity will follow Nietzsche's lead in taking the void for a purpose rather than being void of purpose. Leaders and people alike will embrace political madness: a megalomaniac regime ruling over an increasingly psychopathic populace will forcibly reconstruct meaning and authority with ideology and terror. This might seem far-fetched were it not the clearly established trend— particularly in the United States, the quintessential liberal society. Writing in the late 1950s, Norman Mailer predicted that the psychopath might well become the dominant personality type by the end of the century. Seemingly preposterous at the time, Mailer's prediction is becoming true: in recent years, every kind of social pathology has grown faster than the gross domestic product, especially among the younger generation.

This is most evident in the explosive growth of crime. The number of murders and rapes in America has reached record levels, and criminal violence has become ever more random; worse, it increasingly involves children, both as victims and as perpetrators. It could hardly be otherwise. Discussing the "ironies" of American law enforcement, which microcosmically reproduces the overall irony of Hobbesian politics, David Bayley says, "The American criminal justice system is failing . . . not because it is perversely constructed but because it is trying to do an impossible job, namely, making up for the looseness of the weave of American society." The reason we have a serious and growing crime problem—and, conversely, why Japan does not (at least not like ours)—is our "assertive independence" and "rampant individualism." In sum, says Bayley (emphasizing his conclusions), "*our problems of criminality, as well as our difficulties in meeting them, are products of our very virtues—specifically, the extent to which we believe in and insist on unprecedented individual freedom*"; our "tragic" situation is that "*the form of freedom Americans prize not only undermines the informal discipline that is important for a moral social order; it leaves the state as the only effective instrument for social reconstruction.*"

Our "crime problem" is therefore the direct and immediate consequence of living by liberal principles. Neither the hard-hearted reactionaries who call for more punishment nor the soft-headed reformers who seek rehabilitation seem to understand that it cannot be solved in its own terms. Both punishment and rehabilitation have proven to be equally futile, because they address the symptoms instead of the disease—which is the social breakdown that has cast a whole population morally adrift and destroyed informal controls on behavior. So the American justice system is swamped beyond any possibility of reform or redemption by a demoralization that begets criminals as a matter of course.

Indeed, what else could one expect in the Nietzschean abyss of modern times? In foreseeing the emergence of mass psychopathology, Mailer did no more than echo Nietzsche, whose basic point was precisely that the so-called death of God destroys all possibility of a moral order—that is, of a psychologically and socially healthy way of being—and hence creates the preconditions for a criminal order. Nietzsche's state is "beyond good and evil": without regard to decency or morality, individuals motivated by the will to power pursue purely selfish ends. So "the strong do what they can and the weak suffer what they must" in a society that is for all intents and purposes a Hobbesian state of nature—for which the only cure is a superman sovereign.

Liberal polity is therefore its own worst enemy: in the end, it creates demoralized masses thirsting for authoritarian leadership. But the most dangerous and insidious form of totalitarianism may not be Nietzschean. Instead, the more proximate danger, especially in the United States, is the gradual and stealthy eclipse of liberty and democracy by an almost invisible despotism of total administrative control. In other words, as Wolin's "democracy without the citizen" proceeds to its logical terminus, the most probable outcome of current trends, at least for the foreseeable future, is not a sudden and dramatic fall into an Orwellian nightmare but, rather, a more gradual descent, already well advanced, into a monolithic regime of media manipulation and bureaucratic centralism resembling Huxley's Brave New World. Let us therefore examine this menace in greater depth.

8

DEMOCRATIC DESPOTISM

After having thus successively taken each member of the community in its powerful grasp, and fashioned him at will, the supreme power then extends its arm over the whole community. It covers the surface of society with a network of small complicated rules, minute and uniform, through which the most original minds and the most energetic characters cannot penetrate, to rise above the crowd. The will of man is not shattered, but softened, bent, and guided; men are seldom forced by it to act, but they are constantly restrained from acting: such a power does not destroy, but it prevents existence; it does not tyrannize, but it compresses, enervates, extinguishes, and stupefies a people, till each nation is reduced to be nothing better than a flock of timid and industrious animals, of which the government is the shepherd.

—Alexis de Tocqueville

The true danger is when liberty is nibbled away, for expedience and by parts.

—Edmund Burke

Government can do something for the people only in proportion as it can do something to the people.

—Thomas Jefferson

This culture . . . represents . . . the fulfillment of an old managerial ideal: to exact universal assent, not through outright force, but by creating an environment that would make dissent impossible.

—Mark Crispin Miller

ALTHOUGH MEN AND WOMEN OPPRESSED by loneliness may yet rush to embrace an Orwellian Big Brother or an electronic Bonaparte, this is probably not the immediate threat to a nation whose attachment to the democratic ethos remains strong, at least in principle. However, a more gradual erosion of liberty and democratic control is indeed a serious danger, because the stealthy advance of a Huxleyan regime is both much less visible and far harder to defend against. Any fool can spot a putsch, but the glacial creep of an administrative despotism is barely noticeable. Or, if noticed, not perceived as fundamentally dangerous, because a welfare state dedicated to solving the people's "problems" and making them "happy" seems on the surface to augur nothing but good. What harm in increased state power if it becomes the benevolent provider of cradle-to-grave benefits? Surely none, unless what later becomes apparent is that the people have become the creatures of the state—"nothing better than a flock of timid and industrious animals, of which the government is the shepherd." Nor does the danger end there, for as pointed out by Bertrand de Jouvenel, "A society of sheep must in time beget a government of wolves." So let us conclude our discussion of liberalism's totalitarian propensities by examining the administrative despotism that has already begun to subvert American democracy.

An Immense and Tutelary Power

Tracing the process by which democracy might terminate in despotism, de Tocqueville accurately envisioned the emergence of a mass-consumption society: "an innumerable multitude of men, all equal and alike, incessantly endeavoring to procure the petty and paltry pleasures with which they glut their lives." And of the lonely crowd: confined "within the solitude of his own heart," each is separate and alone, "a stranger to the fate of all the rest." Such social conditions would make a powerful administrative state all but inevitable:

> Above this race of men stands an immense and tutelary power, which takes upon itself alone to secure their gratifications, and to watch over their fate. That power is absolute, minute, regular, provident, and mild. It would be like the authority of a parent, if, like that authority, its object was to prepare men for manhood; but it seeks, on the contrary, to keep them in perpetual childhood: it is well content that the people should rejoice, provided they think of nothing but rejoicing. For their happiness such a government willingly labors, but it chooses to be the sole agent and the only arbiter of that happiness; it provides for their security, foresees and supplies their necessities, facilitates their pleasures, manages their principal concerns, directs their industry, regulates the descent of property, and subdivides their inheritances: what remains, but to spare them all the care of thinking and all the trouble of living?

De Tocqueville thus foresaw that men and women addicted to self-gratification would willingly sell their political souls to a government that promised them comfort and security. In addition, he argued, such a decayed public, lacking any basis for intellectual independence in tradition or religion, could neither avoid conformity to majority will and opinion nor resist government manipulation and propaganda. What is worse, as an avalanche of social and economic change swept away not only tradition and religion but all the other "barriers which formerly arrested tyranny," the hapless individual would be left with only "his personal impotence to oppose to the organized force of the government." In such conditions, elections would become essentially meaningless: "The people shake off their state of dependence just long enough to select their master" before lapsing again into political stupor. "Democratic despotism" under the aegis of "an immense and tutelary power" was thus the likely terminus of American democracy.

De Tocqueville noted that this "administrative despotism," a term he used interchangeably with "democratic despotism," might well be worse than previous forms of tyranny. Unlike the autocracy of kings, which was "extremely onerous to the few, but . . . did not reach the many," the despotism of an administrative state would be all-pervasive. Moreover, although administrative despotism is neither cruel nor arbitrary, it is nonetheless degrading, because it "enslaves men in the minor details of life." Even though the new administrative despots would be not old-style autocrats but, rather, guardians and schoolmasters acting for the public good, their supposedly beneficent rule would demean the citizens, robbing them of their will and autonomy and bringing about a new and exceptionally oppressive form of "servitude." In the end, it would constitute "a more insufferable despotism . . . than in any of the absolute monarchies of Europe."

De Tocqueville saw but one avenue of escape from the threat of "perpetual childhood." To preserve their political autonomy from encroachment by the state, Americans would have to continue to participate vigorously in voluntary local associations of all kinds—civic above all, but also social, commercial, intellectual, technical, and cultural. The spirit of liberty, he said, is ineradicably local: its roots must therefore be nourished at the local level. Only an imposing structure of autonomous "partial" institutions could counterbalance a centralized administration seeking constantly to extend "its arm over the whole community." In addition, the leadership appropriate to a democracy could be forged and tempered only in the crucible of local association. A cadre of strong and independent local leaders would not only defend popular sovereignty against the machinations of the government, but it would also, or so he believed, guide the crowd to better ends than the worship of mammon. In short, de Tocqueville made vigorous participation in local associations the sine qua non for preserving a living democratic ethos.

Although the partisans of democracy (both within the academy and on the hustings) have continued to cling to this participatory vision, we have already seen that modernization has mostly destroyed the kinds of partial associations that de Tocqueville relied upon, especially those directly concerned with politics. Civic associations either have been co-opted by the administrative state or they have decayed into mere interest groups agitating for particular rights and entitlements: political activism today involves minorities pursuing minority agendas, not broader-based groups seeking more general goals, as in de Tocqueville's time. And both the hyperpluralism and the factionalism that result feed the growth of administrative despotism—because they are directed to the end not of *checking* bureaucratic power but of *capturing* it. Moreover, local leadership of the kind desired by de Tocqueville no longer exists to any significant degree: for the most part, local leaders have sold out either to the administrative state or to the interest groups whose livelihood depends on extracting concessions from that state. Hence the political activism of today is part of the problem of liberal decay, not the solution to it.

Similarly, the electoral process has become largely meaningless: not only do the so-called citizens emerge briefly from their political stupor simply to exchange one set of masters for another, but the elected masters no longer represent them in any meaningful sense. The decline of political parties and the rise of television have made politicians into independent careerists. Moreover, Congress is largely immune to popular will in the usual sense: incumbents possess so many political advantages that they are rarely defeated. Thus, although they must obviously stay on top of the mood swings of the electronic mob to remain in office, politicians can safely focus on advancing their own careers rather than on representing the fundamental interests of constituents. What this increasingly means in practice is that they instead represent the interests of those who supply the money they need to get reelected.

In other words, despite being an elective body, Congress has become part and parcel of the "permanent government" that endures regardless of election results. This permanent government consists not only of vast administrative bureaucracies in all three branches of government, as well as the military, but also of its allies and counterparts in the rest of society—above all, in the media and in the legal and lobbying establishment, both local and national. Once elected, politicians soon shift their focus and allegiance to the permanent government to which they now belong. In any event, even if they wished to bring about major changes, they do not have the power: the inertia of the permanent government and the influence of the interest groups are simply too great. Paradoxically, therefore, in one respect the shepherds are little better off than the flock. They may enjoy more perquisites and power, but they too are fellow creatures of a political Leviathan that has come to dwarf and overawe even its nominal masters.

De Tocqueville's concern for the American future did not reflect an aristocratic bias against democracy (as some critics have alleged). His remarkably even-handed and generous work contains little evidence of any longing for the vanished world of the old regime. In fact, he stated explicitly that aristocracy was no longer workable, much less desirable, as a political principle: "The question is not how to reconstruct aristocratic society, but how to make liberty proceed out of that democratic state of society in which God has placed us."

In any event, de Tocqueville's fears for the future of democracy were shared by both Jefferson and Rousseau, two of its greatest theorists and proponents. Although Jefferson eventually made his peace with the Constitution, he never regarded the political system established by the Federalists as truly democratic: it was, he said, little more than an "elective despotism." And Rousseau condemned any form of representative democracy as intrinsically fraudulent: "The English people thinks it is free. It greatly deceives itself; it is free only during the election of the members of Parliament. As soon as they are elected, it is a slave, it is nothing."

Rousseau also argued that a fatal tendency to administrative despotism is inherent in democracies:

> Just as the private will acts incessantly against the general will, so the government makes a continual effort against [popular] sovereignty. . . . [S]ooner or later the prince [government] must finally oppress the sovereign [people] and break the social treaty. That is the inherent and inevitable vice which, from the emergence of the body politic, tends without respite to destroy it, just as old age and death destroy the body of a man.

In sum, if de Tocqueville was concerned about the future of American democracy, he was in excellent company. Indeed, most of those who have grappled with the problem of creating a genuine and lasting democratic polity have expressed similar concerns—including many of the Founders, not to mention the Anti-Federalists. De Tocqueville's essential point stands: American democracy contains within itself the seeds of an administrative despotism that was bound to flower once economic development vitiated the social conditions necessary for genuine democracy.

The Democratic Leviathan

In a literature so vast that surveying it fully would take a lifetime, contemporary social scientists have documented precisely the outcome foreseen by de Tocqueville. For example, Robert Dahl, one of the most respected democratic theorists of our time, traces the decline of American democracy very much along the lines adumbrated by de Tocqueville. According to Dahl, a thriving democracy emerged out of the original liberal-republican polity established by the Founders. However, industrial capitalism, which involved an unwarranted extension of the Lockean concept of private property to corporate entities, foisted a process of radical technological innovation and rapid social change upon the polity that soon destroyed the agrarian context of democracy. (Moreover, the internal government of corporations is antidemocratic: hierarchical at best, despotic at worst.) Responding to this threat, progressives tried to preserve the spirit and restore the practice of democracy—but the chief effect of their reforms, especially during the "imperial presidency" of Franklin Delano Roosevelt, was to create a huge structure of powerful government agencies that are, like corporations, governed hierarchically. When the United States then became an active great power following World War II, all these antidemocratic tendencies were exacerbated by the government's fixation on national security. In this fashion, says Dahl, we have muddled our way into a welfare-warfare state—resulting in the near total bureaucratization of American life and an enormous magnification of the power of the government, especially that of the imperial president.

As a consequence, representative democracy has decayed into "polyarchy": a system of hyperpluralist electoral politics operating within a political context that is totally bureaucratized and partially militarized. Dahl nevertheless defends polyarchy, which can be more or less benign and democratic, as better than any of the alternatives realistically available to us. Yet it is a grudging defense, for he concedes that although human beings have become collectively powerful in polyarchic states, because they can now mobilize vast resources and accomplish great deeds, individual men and women have become largely powerless. In the end, says Dahl, "even polyarchy is a democratic Leviathan, more often than not benign and decent, but like Kafka's Castle vast, remote, inaccessible."

Dahl's position is entirely representative of serious political analysis today. The adjectives used by other critics and scholars to describe contemporary American democracy are revealing: *weak, thin, token, ritualistic, symbolic,* and the like—all synonyms, to one degree or another, of *bogus.* In effect, according to these critics and scholars, democracy no longer exists in any meaningful sense: we are but the subjects of the multiple, overlapping bureaucracies of an administrative cum national-security Leviathan that operates according to the principles of formal or legal rationality elucidated by Weber. Even criminal justice is now thoroughly rationalized, because almost all cases are disposed of before trial by "plea bargaining"—that is, administratively by judicial bureaucrats, not substantively by judges and juries (a point to be expanded below).

Indeed, it is not so much that we are all Marxists today as that we are all Leninists: we believe that it is the task of government to use rational means to remake society for secular ends. Although Weber worried about the kind of civilization that bureaucratic rationalism seemed likely to produce—a "nullity" without spirit or heart—Lenin entertained no such doubts. He both preached and practiced what Trotsky later condemned as "bureaucratic collectivism"—that is, the single-minded, top-down political organization of society for rational economic ends with little regard for cultural or personal consequences. Although most now reject the political excesses of Leninism, both Lenin's secular ends as well as his administrative means have become well-nigh universal.

In this light, it is hardly surprising that some observers would see "apple-pie authoritarianism" or "friendly fascism" lurking in the American future. Even less apocalyptic commentators acknowledge serious political problems and suggest major reforms. For the most part, however, these are hair-of-the-dog proposals that would, to the extent that they are feasible, actually reinforce the hyperindividualistic behavior and the overreliance on administrative solutions that have produced the democratic Leviathan in the first place. One of the most common proposals, for example, is to encourage greater participation. However, as we have already seen, more participation by itself, without other fundamental changes, would only fuel hyperpluralism and factional struggle. More radical proposals are occasionally aired, but they are swiftly brushed aside as utopian. In effect, when push comes to shove, the critics prefer the polyarchic devil they know to any of the "feasible" alternatives: like Dahl, they therefore defend the democratic Leviathan not by lauding its virtues but by invoking the specter of something worse.

The Politics of Stealth

Space does not permit a complete description, much less analysis, of the democratic Leviathan. I shall therefore focus here on four of its most ominous features: the stealthiness of its advance, the dependency it produces, its oligarchic character, and the humiliation that results. This will complete the task I set myself of exposing the fatal ironies and contradictions of Hobbesian politics.

The real danger posed by the administrative state resides not so much in its legal and institutional text, which purports to be democratic, as in its subtext, which is all too often despotic. To illustrate how the process works in general, let us begin with three nongovernmental examples.

The first example is already quite familiar. Although the text of television is entertainment and information, the subtext is consumerism and propaganda. In other words, the underlying thrust, if not the explicit aim, of television is the ideological control of mass society, including its politics, via "the engineering of consent."

Similarly, the ostensible curriculum of our schools, colleges, and universities is "education," including career preparation. But the system also has a "hidden curriculum" that is not about education in the classic sense; nor even about preparing students for a genuine career or profession (in the sense of calling or life's work); rather, it is about schooling (as one "schools" a horse). In other words, the American educational system's subtext is inculcating the right aptitudes for life in a bureaucratic and technocratic mass society and the right attitudes for service in the postindustrial army. This is well understood (albeit not always consciously) by those doing the schooling. John Taylor Gatto, the New York State Teacher of the Year for 1991, celebrated his award by biting the hand that gave it to him: "School is like starting life with a 12-year jail sentence in which bad habits [such as passivity and obedience] are the only curriculum truly learned."

Along the same lines, medical care is now being rationed behind the patient's back by the so-called health management organizations that are gobbling up independent practitioners and small clinics. Unfortunately, the driving force behind these medical bureaucracies is not better care but cost containment. So patients are routinely given the cheapest treatment or medication rather than the best, are sometimes kept away from specialists even when they might benefit from seeing one, and are not even informed of possibly superior, but more expensive, alternatives. So, we are "managing" medical care, but stealthily rather than openly—and, it need hardly be said, to the detriment of patients.

As these examples show, the personal autonomy of the American people is being eroded not by an explicit grab for power on the part of some would-be tyrant or group of tyrants but, instead, by hidden agendas and covert consequences—that is, by the subtext rather than the text of our basic institutions.

The same is true in the political arena. The government does not set out to attack the liberty of the people as a matter of policy, but its legal and administrative response to our problems nevertheless accomplishes this end indirectly, if not always inadvertently. Hence, as Burke warned, our liberty is being "nibbled away, for expedience and by parts," by a politics of stealth in which policies are neither openly debated nor formally decided, but instead are smuggled in via the administrative backdoor. Several additional examples will show why the danger to liberty resides primarily in the subtext.

To cut down on tax evasion and fraud, Congress allowed the Internal Revenue Service to mandate the use of social security numbers (SSNs) to identify taxpayers. To make a long story short, not only has the use of SSNs within the tax and financial system steadily increased over the years, but they have become de facto national ID numbers. That is, both public agencies and many private bureaucracies—universities, utility companies, medical offices, and the like—routinely demand them, *whether or not they have the legal right to do so*. In effect, with no debate whatsoever, much less a formal vote on the question of whether to have a national system of identification based on the SSN, we now have one—as a "spillover effect" from a measure intended to catch tax chiselers. And there is no prospect whatsoever of reversing this *fait accompli*, which is simply too useful to those who control the electronic databases that are the command levers of the information age. Hence the despotic subtext of the administrative state subverts the democratic text, with the SSN providing an almost paradigmatic case of how our liberty is being "nibbled away."

A second and even more worrisome example is the increasing resort to administrative justice mentioned above. The problem with plea bargaining in particular is that, as pointed out by John Langbein, it operates on the same basis as medieval justice, which depended on the threat of torture to extract confessions. The dilemma of the modern defendant is, to be sure, less extreme than that of his medieval counterpart, but it is similar in principle. If he is cooperative, the prosecutors will go easy on him—but if not, then they will "throw the book at him," and he can also expect a harsher sentence if convicted. Not surprisingly, defendants in such circumstances, just like those formerly confronted by the inquisitor's rack, hasten to "cop a plea" that will entail only minor punishment.

But when plea bargaining becomes the norm, the presumption of innocence that is a fundamental tenet of our jurisprudence is effectively nullified (even though this is not the intent of prosecutors): anyone inside the Kafkaesque castle of administrative justice is for all intents and purposes guilty until proven otherwise; indeed, the castle's minions are primarily concerned not with guilt or innocence but, rather, with keeping an overburdened system from foundering by clearing as many cases as possible as quickly as possible.

The Racketeering-Influenced and Corrupt Organizations Act (RICO) also illustrates how we are allowing justice to become increasingly arbitrary and expedient as we struggle against a rising tide of malfeasance. As the name clearly states, RICO's avowed target is organized crime, whose clandestine structure and great wealth have frustrated law-enforcement officials for generations. So prosecutors asked for and got sweeping new powers from Congress. However, they quickly turned these new weapons to ends that RICO's framers did not intend, such as prosecuting white-collar crime as well as obscenity and even abortion-protest cases. Moreover, prosecutors have sometimes proceeded so ruthlessly under RICO as to create the perception of unfairness or even, especially in obscenity cases, of flouting the constitutional rights of the accused.

However, even when RICO is fairly used on appropriate targets, it still raises disturbing questions. First, making "conspiracy" the essence of the crime means that the burden of proof on prosecutors is significantly less than if they had to prove each in a series of separate crimes "beyond a reasonable doubt." Second, "conspiracy" is a concept so vague and all-encompassing that some legal critics have compared RICO to the infamous Soviet law against "hooliganism," which meant whatever the KGB wanted it to mean. Third, RICO is a legal blunderbuss that gives prosecutors overwhelming firepower: the pretrial sanctions are so severe—they include the seizure of allegedly ill-gotten gains *prior* to conviction—that they can seriously impede the ability of those charged to mount an adequate defense. In other words, those indicted, or even threatened with indictment, are in effect convicted and punished before they have been judged: even Wall Street giant Drexel Burnham Lambert found the act's legal presumptions and sanctions impossible to overcome, leaving no alternative but to plead guilty. Again, as with plea bargaining, a fundamental principle of American jurisprudence has been undermined, if not explicitly overturned. In short, the subtext of RICO is vastly more important than the text: because the act significantly enhances the general power of police and prosecutors and diminishes the specific rights of citizens, its ultimate target is the people at large.

Such examples could be multiplied. As civil society continues to fall apart, administrative control steadily escalates. Because of the challenges with which it is confronted—urban rot, ethnic tensions, illegal migration, drugs, crimes of every variety, and so on through the whole range of domestic problems, plus a multitude of difficult international problems—the government faces a chronic low-grade emergency. Hence it is almost forced to respond with policies and actions that contain a dangerous subtext. To be specific, the drug war not only provided a large part of the impetus for RICO, but it has also led to military involvement in civilian law enforcement—not only in a "splendid little war" against Panama but also in numerous other ways (some acknowledged, but mostly not). In addition, this war has spawned an oppressive network of banking regulations: ostensibly designed to trap money launderers (the text), they also eliminate financial privacy for everyone else (the subtext).

In other words, the government increasingly resorts to measures that may be justifiable under the circumstances, but that are dangerous to the liberties and privacies we have traditionally enjoyed. They lead us toward a bureaucratic centralism that is more and more arbitrary, expedient, and, to use de Tocqueville's word, *minute*. So the subtext of the measures found necessary by the state to cope with our problems is administrative despotism. However, we shall arrive at this terminus not by way of public policies openly decided by democratic means but, instead, by stealth—as our liberties are "nibbled away, for expedience and by parts," by the ever-encroaching democratic Leviathan.

Cradle-to-Grave Clients

But could it be that the administrative state is the price we must pay for social welfare, which brings us personal advantages that outweigh any political disadvantages? The answer is no: the text of the welfare state may be equality and compassion for the less fortunate, but its subtext is dependency, which is the antithesis of equality—or even victimization, which inflicts worse suffering than all but the most extreme forms of material deprivation. Let us see how such a perverse and ironic outcome is created.

A significant minority has always opposed the welfare state as contrary to the laissez-faire principles that produce the "wealth of nations." In latter days, however, opposition to it in practice has also grown among some former supporters of it in principle. These so-called neoconservatives have come to believe that the great lesson of twentieth-century history is that politics is not the answer and that the state is not the solution but rather a potential monster—even when, or especially when, it sets out to do good.

To be specific, they have pointed out that most of the benefits of the welfare state go to the wrong people—large agricultural corporations rather than small family farmers, middle-class administrators of poverty programs rather than the poor themselves, and so on. In other words, we have created a welfare state for the well-off, the inescapable result of abandoning the Jeffersonian principle of special privileges for none and replacing it with special privileges for all. These critics also note the economic inefficiency and general mediocrity that seem to characterize its activities: without the discipline of the market, and despite the best efforts of many dedicated public servants, inexorable bureaucratic growth and chronic organizational constipation all but guarantee high cost, poor quality, and indifferent service. As Richard Cornuelle mordantly asks,

> If it is true that the state is bound by its nature to bungle the business of making steel or shoes, what makes us think it is any better at the vastly more complex responsibilities of the modern full-service state: educating the children, providing pensions and health care, eliminating unemployment, protecting depositors from the imprudence of their bankers and providing hundreds of other services, presumably necessary but beyond the reach of the market, not just for the few who have been left behind, but for practically everyone?

Moreover, the welfare state's activities are distorted by external political pressures from a diversity of interest groups; and by the internal imperatives of bureaucratic self-perpetuation and self-aggrandizement. What is worse, this unmanageable administrative behemoth causes the private sector to become mired in a morass of taxes, regulations, and paperwork that stifles, enervates, and frustrates its activities, leading to inefficiency and a decline in productivity. And ultimately the constitutional system is undermined when not only states, counties, and cities but also universities, clinics, and even individuals are forced to dance to the tune of the federal pipers. Hence state compassion leads inexorably to state compulsion, because there is no escape from Jefferson's axiom: "Government can do something for the people only in proportion as it can do something to the people." In the end, say the neoconservatives, the effort to do good using the resources of the state has had mostly bad, or even dangerous, effects; we must therefore rethink our entire strategy for helping those in need within postindustrial society.

As the neoconservative critique is by now comparatively well known and well articulated, I propose to say no more about it here. Instead, let me examine the basic premise of the welfare state—namely, that it is necessary and good to provide benefits to those in need. In other words, supposing that it were possible to solve all of the above problems—supposing that a lean, competent, dedicated cadre of caring professional civil servants were to deliver vast benefits with great efficiency at low cost to all who were genuinely in need (and *only* to those in need)— could we then count the welfare state a success? In fact, no. For the persons who ultimately lose in the welfare state are the beneficiaries themselves. Ironically, the better and more efficient the welfare state, the worse off the citizen.

The paradoxical position of the African-American minority within the American political system illustrates the problem at its most extreme. Bluntly put, although the black community is by no means homogeneous, the community as a whole has a secret investment in victimization and poverty, because the grievances carried over from the enslaved past to the disadvantaged present constitute its main claim to political power. This unconscious attachment to their own victimization and poverty is one reason why large numbers of blacks are worse off now than they were three decades ago—despite diminished institutional racism, increased civil rights, and significantly improved opportunities to "better" themselves. However, for blacks to give up their status as victims of white oppression would not only abandon their primary source of political entitlement, it would also hand a kind of moral victory to those who have all along dismissed white racism as *the* explanation for black backwardness. African-Americans thus continue to cherish their victimization, says Shelby Steele, even though to do so is "odd and self-defeating," because "taking responsibility for bettering ourselves feels like a surrender to white power."

The same paradoxical psychology of victimization prevails in the welfare state as a whole, albeit in a less extreme and debilitating form. If I define myself as having personal problems that I cannot solve by myself, but only with the help of the administrative state and its bureaucratic minions, then I have to that extent abdicated my own power and proclaimed myself a victim. In other words, there is a fundamental psychological difference between government programs that help us to do collectively what we cannot do individually—keeping the peace and managing the currency—and those that constitute a kind of subsidy or dole, no matter how well conceived or justified. The issue is not so much one of receiving money from the government: a one-time disaster-relief check has radically different consequences and implications than a year-in-year-out subsidy. And the principle is the same whether the recipient of the check is a poor mother on perpetual welfare or a rich farmer whose profitability depends on perennial federal aid. In either case, the effect of dependence on a paternalistic state is to turn citizens into clients, perpetual sufferers of deficiencies that require the patronage of the government.

Hence not only the truly impoverished and disadvantaged but the great mass of the population now find themselves reliant to one degree or another on "welfare" in one of its many guises—from food stamps to research grants, from tax breaks to corporate subsidies, from Medicaid to Social Security. The core problem with all forms of dependency, as Irving Kristol points out, is that Lord Acton's dictum applies in reverse: "Dependency tends to corrupt and absolute dependency corrupts absolutely." Obviously, the problem is worst where the dependency is most blatant. The welfare state fosters irresponsibility and vice, not self-respect and civic virtue, among those who receive the dole, so a demoralized urban underclass is the inescapable result. But this is only the most egregious instance of the corruption caused by dependence on the welfare-warfare state, which affects all races and classes and which pervades American society from the ghettos of major cities to the boardrooms of defense contractors, from the hollows of Appalachia to the quadrangles of the Ivy League. The upshot is that the citizen has lost his autonomy and independence: he has become a subject-client of an administrative despotism, of a democratic Leviathan that undertakes to provide all things to all men.

Moreover, it is not the state alone that strips the citizen of his autonomy. As we saw in the last chapter, modern political economy systematically disempowers individuals: they no longer fend for themselves but, instead, depend on the outputs of large impersonal systems and therefore on the ministrations of others. Simply put, we have managed to create a postmodern culture so thin that it provides almost no support for the individual, especially in hard times. In such an impoverished culture, individuals develop psyches so lacking in inner resources that they can no longer surmount the ordinary and typical vicissitudes of life, much less live autonomously, because all the old social and psychological support systems have collapsed. The upshot is a "service economy" that creates clients in just the same way as the welfare state has done. The emergence of "bereavement counseling" as a new specialization within the social-work profession is symbolic of the general trend: what was once provided by family, friends, and neighbors must now be provided professionally, because the personal and social resources that used to get people through life's trials no longer exist, and few have the strength to cope alone and unaided. The recent growth of so-called self-help groups organized around various problems or afflictions is a reassuring sign that American voluntarism still lives, but it has not altered the fundamental situation: weak personalities within a thin culture must turn to professional providers of personal services at every stage of life.

Of course, at a deeper level, people are really seeking to escape from the Nietzschean abyss, which leaves them feeling naked and alone: like the lust for worldly goods, the quest for ever greater rights and entitlements and for more and more services is a literalization of a demand that is ultimately spiritual. Not understanding this, however, individuals try to assuage their loneliness and alienation concretely by consuming social services provided either by the state or by corporations and professionals. But concrete solutions of this type, no matter how skillful, only alleviate the symptoms while leaving the underlying disease untouched. In fact, an enfeebling dependence on external support leaves individuals feeling even *less* autonomous and powerful than before, so the demand for services continues to escalate in a vicious circle that produces frustration rather than satisfaction—the story of liberal society in general.

In addition, not only is the demand for services growing constantly, but there is also an abundance or even overabundance of supply in the form of a large professional-managerial class whose social power and economic livelihood depend on others being dependent on them. As Ivan Illich points out, "knowledge capitalism" has largely replaced finance capitalism as the preferred means to elite status; and the professional-managerial class that "owns" this "capital" guarantees its hegemony by establishing a "radical monopoly" over all important areas of life. Accountants, architects, doctors, educators, and lawyers have joined with the state to make it difficult, if not impossible, for us to dispense with their services, practically or legally. The tax laws are so complex that no ordinary person can understand them; buildings must be constructed according to strict codes that severely discourage amateurs; medicine and law cannot be practiced without a license, and even relatively simple medical and legal procedures have been made to seem so mysterious and forbidding that individuals are prevented from acting on their own behalf; and so on. And once inside one of these service bureaucracies, one plays by its rules. In other words, this class claims to know, better than the citizens themselves, what it is that they need—for their own good, of course—and then also arrogates to itself the exclusive right to provide the needed services (as well as to set the fees for doing so in most cases). The result is a populace made up of obligate clients supporting those who "service" them.

We have therefore created a service economy that needs people in need just to keep going, much less growing. In effect, we have a vested interest in bad teeth, marital strife, problem children, drug addiction, and the like: reduced levels of deficiency and dependency would be an economic disaster, throwing a whole class of people out of work. Hence the economic health of the so-called service economy paradoxically depends to a considerable extent on a self-destructive society.

Again, we have created a vicious circle. By converting former community functions into services that are marketed to us, such as bereavement counseling, or administratively supplied, such as social security, we now have to pay for things that used to be "free," either directly over the counter or indirectly through taxes. This does not constitute genuine progress. As we saw in Chapter 5, where the social significance of maintenance costs was discussed, ecological functions such as recycling and pollution control are quasi-automatic and cheap if we let nature do most of the work, but complicated and expensive if we have to organize them artificially. Similarly in the human sphere: when social support happens as a matter of course within functioning communities, it costs relatively little; but once the community has broken down, and complicated bureaucratic and economic arrangements have to be substituted, then the cost in every sense of the word is far greater, because we receive a diminishing return on our ever-increasing investment in complexity. Above all, such arrangements are less effective and far less humane than the traditional ones. Socioeconomic "progress" defined in terms of "welfare benefits" and "consumer choice" turns out to be ultimately self-defeating, obliging us not only to pay for what we used to receive free but also to accept the artificial caring of administrative entities and the artificial services of commercial interests as inferior substitutes for the real thing.

Despite what may have been implied above, the reduction of citizens to clients is not primarily due to a deliberate power grab by a conniving elite. Rather, we have set up a spiral of increasing dependency that can only produce a despotic outcome: liberal polity is self-destructive and so requires services that are either state-provided or state-sanctioned to remedy the deficiencies that result from moral entropy; but each further increment of service reduces the capacity of the individual to be autonomous and further entangles him in the toils of state and corporate bureaucracies dedicated to cradle-to-grave schooling and servicing. As usual, de Tocqueville foresaw the outcome: "The manufacturing aristocracy of our age first impoverishes and debases the men who serve it, and then abandons them to be supported by the charity of the government."

Day care provides a final, poignant illustration of the vicious circle in operation. Because most mothers now work outside the home, caring for the children they leave behind becomes a "problem." Although neither the government nor the corporations want the responsibility of raising young children, they nevertheless find themselves compelled to provide day care as the "solution." On the surface, this seems unexceptionable. After all, this is what other welfare states, alleged to be more advanced on social issues, do as a matter of course. But the implications are profound. When all the women are in corporate uniforms and all the children in state-run or state-sanctioned crèches, everybody within mass society will be literally incorporated from cradle to grave; and dependence on administrative and corporate bureaucracies for every requisite of life will be total. The basic institutions of Brave New World will then be in place, needing only gradual improvement and further refinement to take us the rest of the way.

In sum, we do not need to solve our problems, we need to reexamine our premises. We have set in motion powerful forces that foster dependency—and therefore administrative despotism. On one side, we have the state and its corporate and professional allies seeking to extend their hegemony and to make it more total and invisible; on the other, a crowd that finds itself desperately in need of succor and so demands more of the services that will only reinforce its deficiency and dependency in the long run. So we go willingly to our servitude, not because "they" have set out to enslave us or because we really want to be enslaved (at least consciously), but because we have based our politics on premises that ultimately require this outcome. If the good life is the superficial happiness of a comfortable and painless existence, then we must grant the welfare state the power it needs to provide it, even if this costs us our liberty. In pursuing self-gratification as the highest good, liberals therefore doom themselves to be consumers, clients, and subjects instead of citizens. The final irony is that the welfare state does not even achieve its original goal of equality. As we learned earlier, the essence of inequality is dependence upon the will of another, so pursuing equality by means that produce mass dependency is utterly contradictory. Those kept in "perpetual childhood" by an "immense and tutelary power" are neither equal nor free: they are instead "a flock of timid and industrious animals" awaiting an oligarchy of wolves.

The Democratic *Nomenklatura*

Indeed, such an oligarchy is already taking shape. Moreover, it begins to bear an uncomfortable resemblance to the infamous *nomenklatura* that governed the former Soviet Union—a relatively small and privileged class that makes all the important decisions, receives the best that the system has to offer, and then passes on its social advantages and political status to the next generation.

Political scientists put it more tactfully. The polyarchy of today, says Dahl, grafts "the symbols of democracy to the de facto guardianship of the policy elites." This is the logical consequence of all the developments hitherto explored—the proliferation of interest groups, the ascendancy of a "manufacturing aristocracy," the tendency toward technocracy, and the existence of a permanent government that justifies its permanency by a complexity that only "experienced professionals" can comprehend and control. In general, then, political questions have been converted into technical and administrative ones, making politics dependent on expertise. The result is an oligarchy made up not only of officials, elected and appointed, but also of all the quasi-officials that swarm around them—experts, lobbyists, lawyers, and, last but not least, the journalists who proclaim and thereby validate the activities of all the rest.

What is worse, the permanent government operates partly in the shadows, because many organs and activities of the administrative state are covert or even clandestine, with the CIA being only the most obvious and notorious. Just how much is in the shadows is indicated by the so-called black budget of the Defense Department, which pays for many of these programs: in 1989, according to Tim Weiner, it amounted to $36 billion—that is, more than the military budget of any other nation in the world except for the former Soviet Union. In addition, there has been an enormous proliferation of law enforcement agencies of all kinds in recent years. And even agencies having no connection to national security or the more dangerous kinds of police work cloak themselves in secrecy and foster an institutional culture more appropriate to a police state than a democracy. For example, as amply documented by David Burnham's *A Law Unto Itself*, in classic totalitarian fashion the Internal Revenue Service tends to regard those who impede or even criticize its activities as enemies subject to official reprisal. Thus the democratic *nomenklatura* that governs us is both high-handed and corrupt, albeit to nowhere the same degree as its namesake. To amend one of Adam Smith's most famous sayings, today it is not only "people of the same trade" but members of the permanent government who "seldom meet together, even for merriment and diversion, but the conversation ends in a conspiracy against the public."

That the democratic Leviathan will be governed oligarchically and even covertly is a consequence not only of democratic despotism itself but also of American political culture, which is strongly and explicitly anti-elitist. This seems paradoxical: Why would such a society in fact foster rule by a small coterie or faction of the people—that is, "elitism" in the pejorative sense? The answer is that the prejudice against elites flouts political reality, which exacts its revenge by creating a hidden oligarchy.

The dictionary defines *elite* in a contradictory fashion that reflects popular ambivalence: it is both "the best or most skilled members of a given social group" and "a narrow and powerful clique" (presumably acting in its own interest). The existence and even rule of an elite in the first sense is inescapable: whatever the situation, the few who are the best or most skilled are likely to wind up in control of any field of activity. And, says Barbara Tuchman, "What is government but an arrangement by which the many accept the authority of the few?" So the question is not whether we will be ruled by a political elite but which kind it will be: aristocratic or oligarchic? That is, one that at least aspires to rule in accordance with some broad ideal or one that rules only in accordance with its own narrow interests? Unfortunately, in a political culture that strongly distrusts elites as narrow and powerful cliques, the aristocratic option is largely foreclosed, so we are governed by an oligarchy of manipulators, demagogues, and dissemblers. In other words, because Americans shirk the political task of elevating a genuine elite, they get precisely the kind that is dangerous—an in-group that rules covertly by deprecating its role, concealing its activities, and obfuscating its purposes.

Indeed, our technocratic guardians have been so successful in making oligarchy seem natural, simply part of the way things are, that they have become almost invisible. When most people worry about leaders escaping democratic control, it is not the unseen hegemony of the policy elites but individual malfeasance that comes to mind—as in the case of Watergate, the paradigmatic political scandal of our time. The more sophisticated may also worry about legislative legerdemain and chicanery in the House, the decline of the Senate from deliberative body to millionaires' club, the imperial pretensions of successive presidents, the unwarranted meddling of activist courts, the secret machinations of the spies, the capture of the regulators by the regulated, the nefarious activities of the military-industrial complex, and the like—that is, the multiple conspiracies against the public by the various organs of the permanent government. But it is rare that the extent and all-encompassing character of policy-elite guardianship over a formerly democratic polity is fully acknowledged. In effect, oligarchy has become routine within the American polyarchy.

Moreover, the periodic revelation of political scandal actually helps to conceal this fact. The media uses the exposure of wrongdoing to make it appear that it takes the people's side against corrupt officials. This mystifies not only the ideological reality of mass society, which is largely controlled by the mass media, but also the political reality of the democratic

Leviathan, which is managed by the policy elites. In other words, when the media exposes political scandal and then draws the conclusion for us that "the system worked," it validates not just its own watchdog role but also the oligarchic system of which the media is a crucial and increasingly dominant part. Hence the reality of covert governance and media hegemony within an administrative despotism goes mostly unremarked.

We therefore confront another dialectical law of politics: rule by an elite of some kind is inescapable, so the question is not whether to have one but which persons exemplifying which principles and possessing which qualifications for rule will constitute it. To the extent that this is not acknowledged—so that the appropriate persons can be recruited, elevated, and then held accountable—the political elite will be inferior in ability and character, but superior in dissembling and manipulation. Moreover, in the social order more generally, since people seem to have an innate need to look up to something, which manifests itself as a fascination with the doings of the "elite," the void left by the absence of an authentic elite will be filled by a false one: in our case, by a meretricious media elite made up of the stars and celebrities that constitute the pop royalty worshiped by the common man. Or, what is far worse, instead of taking its cues from above, the populace begins to take them from below. Hence the surly attitudes and uncivil behavior of the underclass, white and black, increasingly permeate American society and now threaten to become the norm. In short, just as the choice is between authority and tyranny, the alternative to an elite in the best sense is a hidden or bogus elite, whose natural concomitant is a feral populace.

It is important to remember that until comparatively recently the United States was governed by a tacitly acknowledged elite, an "establishment" made up of "the best and brightest." Horribly "elitist" by contemporary standards—in that they were for the most part recruited from a narrow social, cultural, and educational stratum—the members of this group nevertheless believed strongly in the ideal of public service and usually behaved accordingly. Although they were certainly not oblivious to personal and class interests, they took a broad view of those interests and so pursued policies tending to foster the general welfare. Unfortunately, after its postwar heyday, the American establishment fell victim to inner decay, to the social changes of the 1960s, and, above all, to the aftermath of the war in Vietnam, which turned an entire generation against authority. But its eclipse left a void filled more and more by a mere meritocracy—that is, by a technocratic elite defined in terms of its cognitive ability to deal with the increasingly complicated administrative problems of the democratic Leviathan.

Unfortunately, although meritocracy is well suited for creating a "de facto guardianship of the policy elites," it cannot produce a genuine political elite. Statesmanship is a question not of merit narrowly defined but of a certain kind of excellence broadly defined (even though modern conditions do indeed demand technical skill as well). As Václav Havel says, it requires "good taste." In addition, we have seen that the long-term political implications of meritocracy are very dangerous. It tends to produce a talent-based caste system along the lines of Brave New World—all the brains at the top, all the brawn at the bottom. And there are signs that precisely such a stratified social order has begun to emerge: a new upper class of talented, educated, and well-rewarded meritocrats; a middle class whose numbers, opportunities, influence, and wages are declining; and a growing underclass forced to choose among the minimum wage, welfare, or crime.

What is worse, the meritocratic class, whose influence and wealth have increased significantly in recent years, shows every sign of becoming an oligarchy in the worst possible sense: an anti-establishment interested primarily in its own welfare that uses its influence to pursue class interests and its wealth to opt out of a decaying social order (e.g., by abandoning the public schools to those who can afford nothing better). Such an internal secession from the commonwealth by the meritocrats would lead to an even greater contrast between private affluence and public squalor than exists today; and eventually to a political and economic system of, by, and for the oligarchs, a kind of information-age banana republic in which the majority of the population has become irrelevant, impoverished, and oppressed.

To sum up, the democratic *nomenklatura* that now governs us threatens to become both more corrupt and more deeply entrenched. Again, a nonelitist politics is a contradiction in terms: the alternative to a genuine political elite is rule by an oligarchy, by "a narrow and powerful clique." We therefore shirk the political task of creating, maintaining, and controlling a true elite at our peril. The Founding Fathers have become the targets of intense criticism in latter days—for being slaveholders, for being men of property, for being "fathers," for being, in short, "elitist" in some allegedly very bad ways. Yet whatever their individual and collective failings, they were also an undeniable elite in the best sense. How many of those who now rule us, directly and indirectly, are their equal in character, intellect, and public spirit? We have no such elite today in large part because we do not want one. But by making it impossible for what Jefferson called "a natural aristocracy of talents and virtue"—or, at the very least, an establishment dedicated to public service—to guide our affairs, we all but guarantee the almost invisible mastery of manipulators and meritocrats. Our very anti-elitism thus fuels the vicious circle that is tending to produce a democratic *nomenklatura*, a kind of public mafia that runs the administrative state in its own interest. Ultimately, as was well understood by Shakespeare, the alternative to "degree," or an acknowledged and respected hierarchy, is a chaos in which the wolf of will and appetite runs free:

> Take but degree away, untune that string,
> And hark what discord follows. . . .
> Then everything includes itself in power,
> Power into will, will into appetite;
> And appetite, an universal wolf,
> So doubly seconded with will and power,
> Must make perforce an universal prey,
> And last eat up himself.

A State of Permanent Humiliation

Those on the other side of the former Iron Curtain have been quicker to see that Hobbesian polity is a vicious circle that tends toward Leviathan—a state that may be more or less democratic, benign, and prosperous, but that is fundamentally despotic. Speaking as a still-oppressed dissident, before the Velvet Revolution that elevated him to the presidency of Czechoslovakia, Havel analyzed the Kafkaesque character of contemporary totalitarianism: his own experience of imprisonment to the contrary notwithstanding, it rarely involves

> direct violence, brutality, or terrorism from the regime. What one does encounter, however, is something that George Orwell saw, and that is more dangerous in certain respects. From morning to night, everything every ordinary citizen does is in some way interfered with by the system. The regime leaves its mark on everything.

From the outside, such a system might not seem particularly harsh. But if outsiders were magically transformed into insiders, they would soon experience the psychological wounds inflicted on men and women who are completely

> at the mercy of the all-powerful bureaucracy, so that for every little thing they have to approach some official or other. They would observe the gradual destruction of the human spirit, of basic human dignity. They would see how, from the nursery to the old people's home, people live their lives in a state of permanent humiliation.

Why do people tolerate permanent humiliation as a way of life? Because they have internalized the basic norms and values of the system. The paradox of modern totalitarianism is that its subjects are simultaneously innocent victims and cynical accomplices:

> The domination of a large group of powerless people by a small powerful group has long since ceased being totalitarianism's most typical feature. Nowadays, what is typical is the domination of one part of ourselves by another part of ourselves. It's as if the regime had an outpost inside every single citizen. . . . Everyone supports it and helps create it—by mutely acquiescing in its version of reality, by voting in formal elections, and by observing its various rituals and ceremonies. . . .

For all their vaunted freedom, openness, and democracy, the Western nations are not fundamentally better off. Even Soviet totalitarianism was only the most extreme manifestation of a development common to all modern societies—namely, "a trend toward impersonal power and rule by megamachines or colossi that escape human control." Hence

> the totalitarian systems warn of something far more serious than Western rationalism is willing to admit. They are . . . a grotesquely magnified image of its own deep tendencies, an extremist offshoot of its own development and an ominous product of its own expansion.

Indeed, concludes Havel, the reason why we are all in the same totalitarian boat today is that "we live in the first atheist civilization in human history." Having ceased to hold or respect "any higher metaphysical values"—not necessarily a personal god, but "whatever is absolute, transcendental, suprahuman"—men and women have lost their essential grounding and orientation in the world. Worse, modern civilization has begun to run amok, for when "humanity declared itself to be the supreme ruler of the universe—at that moment, the world began to lose its human dimension." An inhuman state of permanent humiliation is therefore the ultimate, bitter reward for the hubris of modern civilization.

Beneath the ideological labels, the basic nature of modern governance is increasingly the same: we are all ruled by administrative states that are more or less observant of due process and the rituals of democracy, but that pursue the standard aims of economic development, national security, and popular welfare by rationalist means. Civil liberties may be more or less respected in one place rather than another, and worldly goods may be in greater or lesser supply, but the basic character of life within the differing administrative despotisms East or West is roughly the same, because both foster a vicious circle of deepening dependency and domination. Moreover, there is the same spiritual void at their core. It is not just communism that is "Godless": *all* Hobbesian polity is predicated on social, if not personal, atheism; and this lack of the absolute or transcendent dimension leads directly to demoralization and humiliation. In brief, says Havel, they are "no more than two diverse ways of moving toward the same global totalitarianism."

This is not to deny the vast differences between the two alternatives. Democratic despotism tends toward Brave New World, a relatively benevolent police state, whereas proletarian dictatorship tended to duplicate the malevolence of Nineteen Eighty-Four. And one might well prefer a despotism in which there were shorter lines, in which the *petits fonctionnaires* we must approach "for every little thing" were reasonably polite, and in which certain basic rights were on the whole respected. But all of these are perfectly compatible with the "permanent humiliation" of an utter and complete dependence on an all-powerful system.

Others who have been able to compare the two alternatives at firsthand echo Havel: they see the Western and Eastern versions of modern politics not as fundamentally different but, rather, as variations on the same political theme. For example, Aleksandr Solzhenitsyn, the most famous of all Soviet émigrés until his recent return to Russia, has sharply criticized the West: we Westerners possess rights but lack inner freedom; we are rich in goods but poor in spirit; in short, we have lost our soul. The stir caused by Solzhenitsyn's critique was due not to the content of his ideas, which were quickly dismissed as reactionary, but to his perceived effrontery and ingratitude: How dare he bite the hand that rescued him from the gulag? However, the extremity of his position notwithstanding, Solzhenitsyn's views are shared by other émigrés. The exiled film director Andrei Tarkovsky, who rejected Solzhenitsyn's ultraconservative politics, nevertheless expressed similar sentiments: "The longer I stay in the West, the more I find that man has lost his inner freedom. In the West everybody has their rights, but in an internal, spiritual sense, there is no doubt more freedom in the Soviet Union." In other words, however grateful for asylum or critical of the gulag, Soviet émigrés have not found a democratic paradise in the West. On the contrary, they have discovered Western societies and regimes to be mirror images of those in the formerly Soviet East. We may have more riches and rights, and they a greater depth of culture as well as more spiritual or inner freedom, but both forms of Hobbesian polity subject human beings to amplified and all-encompassing power, to a Leviathan that reduces persons to things.

In this light, the undeniable and important differences between the two alternatives do not have the absolute character we customarily give them. Witness the more recent assessment by philosopher Erazim Kohak:

> Half of each year I now live and work in Prague, but for forty-two years I have lived and worked in America. I am struck much more by their similarities than by any difference. The social disintegration in the lands of the former Soviet empire seems to me simply to bring out in stark relief what in the West has been masked by affluence but is no less present—the weakness of a civilization that has lost its legitimating vision, its sense of reality and of personal responsibility.

What a colossal irony if, as the Cold War recedes into the past, we come to see with the eyes of a future historian that World War II was in many ways a Pyrrhic victory of devastating proportions for the West, especially the United States. Why? Because it led its peoples to misconstrue the totalitarian threat as external rather than internal; and because it deluded them into believing that they were free simply because the lines at the butcher shop were shorter and the authorities mostly respected their rights. It would be an even bigger irony—or, rather, tragedy—if the West were now to believe that it "won" the Cold War. The real significance of *glasnost* and *peristroika* was that Gorbachev and his fellow reformers came to a conscious awareness of what Western leaders have practiced unconsciously all along. The best totalitarian regime is one that is invisible and therefore, as Mark Miller says, fulfills "an old managerial ideal: to exact universal assent, not through outright force, but by creating an environment that would make dissent impossible." Why run a Gulag Archipelago when, according to an old Russian proverb, the best way to kill a cat is to drown it in cream?

Governance Versus Administration

Although an administrative despotism managed by a more or less democratic *nomenklatura* seems to be the foreordained outcome of a politics based on the rationalist premises of Hobbes, the growth of Leviathan in our time has been enormously abetted by the intellectual muddle of modern liberalism. We have seen, for example, that the dialectical relationship between equality and quality or reason and rationality or authority and tyranny or aristocracy and oligarchy have been largely forgotten, causing absurd and even dangerous political ideas to flourish. Another egregious example of contemporary confusion is the jumbling together of two very different aspects of the political process: governance and administration.

No human group can exist without governance—that is, without a fundamental agreement among its members on how their communal life is to be conducted, both in general and with regard to particular issues. On the other hand, human beings who live in relatively small and homogeneous groups can survive quite well without administration. Indeed, so-called primitive tribes dispense with it entirely—leading some early observers to conclude, erroneously, that they had no politics. Conversely, it is possible for governance to be almost completely overshadowed by administration. Such was the case in the former Soviet Union, where the state came to be little more than an administrative *apparat* existing virtually for its own sake—especially in its latter days, when the political spirit that once gave it life and meaning was all but extinguished. In short, even though they are always intimately interrelated in the real world, governance and administration are not one and the same thing but, rather, two separate political functions, and to lump them together leads to theoretical confusion and practical danger.

To see why, let us take the ecological problematique as a real-world example. Dealing with the predicament outlined in the Introduction will obviously require more governance—that is, stronger checks on competitive overexploitation of the ecological commons and therefore on human self-aggrandizement. But it does not necessarily follow that we need more administration. On the contrary, given the preceding discussion plus the appalling record of the administrative state in this century, the better answer is not to erect an ecological Leviathan that will protect the environment by closely and minutely supervising our every act, but instead to establish basic laws and institutions that oblige us to live within our ecological means. In other words, unless we want to be tyrannized by ecological despots, the "solution" is not more agencies and regulations but stronger governance.

For example, taxing energy use would be a prudent and appropriate act of ecological governance. Not only would such a tax be an important first step toward a thermodynamic economics, but it would also be more effective in curbing waste and pollution and in fostering conservation and innovation than any form of administered energy policy. It would have important fiscal and foreign-policy benefits as well, increasing government revenue and decreasing dependence on foreign supplies. And it would accomplish these ends with a minimum of administrative meddling and interference in the lives of citizens, who would be constrained by higher costs but who would be otherwise free to live as they pleased. That we do not adopt a policy that would kill four birds with one stone reflects a brute political fact: we do not want energy use to be effectively governed, because the profligate use of resources is part of the current American definition of freedom. Equally important, however, we are so addicted to administrative solutions to our problems that we do not even see the possibility, much less the eventual inevitability, of a governmental solution to the ecological problematique. So we have, by reflex as it were, set up large bureaucracies to administer an almost nonexistent energy policy and a haphazard, inconsistent, and ineffective environmental policy.

To put it another way, we need basic laws and institutions to contain the wolf of will and appetite *in the first instance*, because trying to catch him in bureaucratic traps once he has already begun to ravage the countryside is futile. Measures taken after the fact will always be too little and too late: for example, trying to deal with social breakdown and crime in the inner city with mentoring programs for fatherless boys in the mostly vain hope that they will somehow make it against appalling odds—and then building prison cells for them when they don't. The fundamental delusion of the democratic Leviathan is to think that social problems can be solved by administrative or technological means rather than basic political decisions. But there are no technical solutions to social and political problems, only governmental policies that are more or less judicious and effective. Trying to handle such problems administratively is therefore either an evasion of responsibility or a prescription for failure. There is but one place for the wolf: inside the cage of governance.

The distinction between governance and administration thus has profound implications. The folly of creating a powerful administrative state is obvious: a moment's reflection will show that merging the two political functions must beget a total institution hostile to liberty. Concerned lest the young nation betray its republican principles, de Tocqueville warned that "if, after having established the general principles of government, [the polity] descended to the details of their application . . . freedom would soon be banished from the New World." Until we learn to govern rather than merely administer, we will continue to grease the skids for democratic despotism, automatically resorting to administrative "solutions" without seeing where they lead.

To sum up, one major reason why we have become the subjects and clients of a democratic Leviathan is that we have neglected to uphold the most basic principle of republican government: "In a free society," said Walter Lippmann, "the state does not administer the affairs of men. It administers justice among men who conduct their own affairs." And, as Wendell Berry points out, to administer justice means to protect "the small and weak from the great and powerful," *not* to make the government into "the profligate ineffectual parent of the small and weak after it has permitted the great and powerful to make them helpless."

The Tragedy of Liberalism

The tragedy of liberalism as a political doctrine is that it contains within itself a remorseless working of things that produces an illiberal outcome. In theory, liberalism is dedicated above all to the preservation of the autonomous power of the individual from the potentially arbitrary power of the state. But the actual effect of liberal principles in practice, especially in their current confused and debased form, is to create precisely the opposite outcome: not an independent people but a dependent proletariat incapable of resisting the advance of tyranny. The result, said Lippmann, is "a new form of absolute state, a self-perpetuating oligarchy and an uncontrollable bureaucracy which governs by courting, cajoling, corrupting, and coercing the sovereign but incompetent people."

Only the outward form of democracy remains. We are ruled bureaucratically and oligarchically, by an administrative state and a democratic *nomenklatura* that, to borrow Madison's words, abridge our freedom "by gradual and silent encroachments." This creeping tyranny is checked not by popular consent and democratic control but, rather, by the passions of the increasingly unruly electronic mob—a mere crowd thirsting for meaning and charisma, which it projects onto the state, as well as for security and comfort, which it demands from the state.

The process that has created this tragic outcome is actively abetted by virtually all elements of the American polity—by the so-called liberals who insist that we need a more powerful state to uphold equality and rights; and by the so-called conservatives who demand a more powerful state to achieve growth, grandeur, and morality. It therefore matters not at all whom we elect or what they profess. The end of every duly-elected administration leaves the ordinary citizen more deeply subject to the increasingly arbitrary and expedient power of the state.

To pile irony upon tragedy, the democratic Leviathan is incapable of governing in any meaningful sense. True, by the deliberate intent of the Founders, the American government has never governed very effectively, at least by the standards prevailing elsewhere. But the growing strength of the administrative state has paradoxically weakened governance still further. As de Tocqueville warned, an administrative despotism may have great powers to oppress and enervate, but it cannot achieve positive ends: it is so lacking in vision that it cannot exercise leadership; it is so beholden to special interests that it cannot legislate effectively; and it is so wary of provoking the electronic mob that it cannot say no to the plethora of popular demands. All such a Leviathan can do is administer—and this it does, in ever more minute and oppressive detail.

In practice, therefore, this megamachine is on automatic pilot: although it gives lip service to the shibboleths of contemporary liberal democracy, it is not a government striving for and achieving positive ends; it is a mere *apparat* serving primarily its own needs. The clear danger is that the United States will slowly become a police state without the usual consolations thereof: laws against smoking and the like will be rigorously enforced, but the trains will not run on time, and people will continue to be gunned down in the streets.

What an ignoble end to the liberal dream. One could possibly accept Brave New World as the seemingly inevitable terminus of modern politics, provided that it were the product of a shared political vision skillfully executed by a competent and incorruptible government—so that every man, woman, and child would soon be made "happy" in this sensualist's Eden. But democratic despotism offers no such utopian prospect, not even one as dubious as Brave New World. The democratic Leviathan is a mere Leviathan—"vast, remote, inaccessible." True, it is also relatively "benign and decent," at least so far, but it does not and cannot use its great powers competently and effectively to achieve even its own professed aims, much less any nobler ends. In fact, it can neither preserve public order nor build prisons fast enough to confine the criminals. Hence not only is the Leviathan a megamachine on automatic pilot, but its direction has become erratic and its functioning ineffectual.

This raises a terrible specter: What if it goes on the rocks? What if the administrative despotisms of our time run out of ecological living space, implode under their own bureaucratic weight, encounter progressive technological failure, partially annihilate themselves with weapons of mass destruction, or find themselves unable to cope with declining morale and increasing madness among their subjects? Will they then abandon Huxley for Orwell? When they no longer deliver benefits, but mostly exact sacrifice and obedience, it will be too late to reverse the process that turned their peoples into flocks of sheep tended by wolves. And, at that point, our inherited political institutions will be of no avail—for, said Learned Hand, when liberty dies in "the hearts of men and women . . . no constitution, no law, no court can save it."

The aim of liberalism—to preserve the dignity and autonomy of individuals—was good. But its basic values and, above all, its means were bad, because the latter conspire to destroy the former. In particular, thinking that the administrative state could possibly be the means of achieving the end of preserving and enhancing personal autonomy and individual freedom is sheer folly—defying not only all the lessons of political history, as well as the caveats of the Founders, but also the clearly expressed warnings of the liberal tradition itself. What has been forgotten in recent years is that accepting the burdens and responsibilities of self-government is essential to attaining the end of freedom from arbitrary rule. If the muscles of personal autonomy and self-reliance are not regularly exercised by the citizens, then they will atrophy, leaving the body politic too weak to resist the advance of tyranny. As John Stuart Mill said in concluding *On Liberty*,

> A government cannot have too much of the kind of activity which does not impede, but aids and stimulates, individual exertion and development. The mischief begins when, instead of calling forth the activity and powers of individuals and bodies, it substitutes its own activity for theirs.

Alas, by tolerating and even encouraging this "mischief," we have already traveled far down the path that leads toward the "perpetual childhood" of existence within "an immense and tutelary state."

CONCLUSIONS

The Political Tragedy
of the Enlightenment

*The free peoples of the Western world have lived upon a great inheritance
which they have squandered recklessly. . . . [T]hey took the blessings of
this inheritance so totally for granted that they no longer knew, and their
schools had almost ceased to teach them, and their leaders were afraid to
remind them, how the laws and the institutions and the great controlling
customs of our civilization were made. . . .*

*What is left of our civilization will not be maintained, what has been
wrecked will not be restored, by imagining that some new political gadget
can be invented, some new political formula improvised that will save it.
Our civilization can be maintained and restored only by remembering and
rediscovering the truths, and by re-establishing the virtuous habits on
which it was founded.*

—*Walter Lippmann*

THE DREAM OF THE FOUNDERS OF THE AMERICAN POLITY was to establish
a political order in the New World permanently free from the corruption
and tyranny of the Old. That dream now lies shattered: a virtuous republic has decayed into a democratic despotism. Why? Because Americans
embraced with especial fervor the political principles of the Enlightenment—principles that were once thought to be the highest achievement
of the human mind and the royal road to perpetual social progress, but
that now stand revealed as the path to ecological and political ruin.

The tragedy of Enlightenment politics is that they devour the capital
upon which civilization is founded. This is most obvious in the area of
ecology, where we destroy in decades what it took the life force eons to

create. But modern civilization eats up cultural capital as well, consuming all the landscapes, monuments, arts, skills, folkways, myths, and moral codes created by human communities over many centuries. Above all, modern politics unshackles will and appetite from the chains with which traditional civilizations had sought to bind them, thereby unleashing moral entropy and destroying the civic virtue that undergirds both society and polity. And in the process of consuming our inheritance from the past, we also despoil the future: unlike the men and women of past generations, who struggled to leave posterity better off, we rob our children. The motto of modern civilization is thus, as Marx said, that of the Old Regime: *Après nous le déluge*.

The root cause of this tragedy is that the Enlightenment tried to cure the ills of civilization by means that only aggravated its essential psychopathology. That is, by aiming to become "the masters and possessors of nature," the Enlightenment *philosophes* necessarily fostered greed and fomented the will to power. In effect, they licensed the predatory behavior of the modern conquistador, who has used the superior technological means provided by Science to dominate both nature and the "lesser breeds without the law."

In addition, more generally, when politics is amoral, power is free to grow without limit—not the personal power of the premodern autocrat (although some of that unfortunately survives and is now much amplified by modern techniques) but, rather, the impersonal power of vast systems dedicated to economic and bureaucratic control. Thus it is now we who are dominated and controlled by a Hobbesian system, as the power we have loosed upon the world has been turned back upon ourselves. In short, just as Hobbes said, living by his principles means living under a Leviathan.

In the end, therefore, not only did the Enlightenment paradigm of politics fail to achieve many of its avowed goals—for example, equality (at least to the extent hoped)—but it also inflicted a wanton destruction on the world, becoming thereby both its own worst enemy and the author of new forms and possibilities of tyranny undreamt of by ancient despots. Everything that does not work, all that we hate and fear about the modern way of life, is the logical or even foreordained consequence of the basic principles we have chosen to embrace. Explosive population growth, widespread habitat destruction, disastrous pollution, and every other aspect of ecological devastation; increasing crime and violence, runaway addictions of every kind, the neglect or abuse of children, and every other form of social breakdown; antinomianism, nihilism, millenarianism, and every other variety of ideological madness; hyperpluralism, factionalism, administrative despotism, and every other manifestation of democratic decay; weapons of mass destruction, terrorism, the structural poverty of underdevelopment, and many other global pathologies—all are deeply rooted in Hobbesian politics, whose basic principles set up a vicious circle of power seeking and self-destruction. In other words, *the most intractable problems of our age are due not to human nature itself but, instead, to the way in which the Enlightenment in general and Hobbesian politics in particular have encouraged the worst tendencies of human nature to flourish in the modern era.*

We are therefore in a genuine crisis—that is, in an extremity or impasse that calls into question not the skill of our leaders or the effectiveness of our means but our essential worldview, our basic philosophy, and, above all, our political paradigm. We do not have "problems" we can reasonably expect to "solve," because these problems result from contradictions in our ruling ideas. "Solutions" that simply rearrange the contents within the old structure will produce no effective change: exactly the same conditions will recreate themselves. Hence no "new political gadget" can have the slightest effect, because we need a new vision of the good life and a new philosophy of politics, not yet another social, economic, or technological fix.

Thus it is not simply a question, as Lippmann's epigraph seems to imply, of "remembering and rediscovering the truths" and "re-establishing the virtuous habits" of original liberalism: what liberalism has destroyed it cannot hope to restore. It is the liberal conception of politics *itself* that is defective. Human greed, rapacity, ambition, and arrogance are held in check only by civic and personal virtue—by "habits of the heart" rooted ultimately in a code of morality, if not in a sense of the sacred. By denying the latter and trying to base politics on the merely rational pursuit of individual desire, the Enlightenment undercut the moral community that orients, controls, and sanctions human behavior.

Liberal doctrine to the contrary notwithstanding, no political order can survive as what Aristotle called "a mere alliance" of self-interested individuals; it must instead be based on "a rule of life" that fosters a shared morality and a sense of common destiny. Why? Because, to borrow the famous words of Burke, the state is "a partnership between those who are living, those who are dead, and those who are to be born." Without such a partnership, without a genuine political community based on moral principle that unites the generations in the joint enterprise of civilization, no society or state can long endure—and it is precisely this partnership that liberal politics first erodes, then corrodes, and finally dissolves, despite the banner of "progress" under which it marches.

The essential lesson of this political tragedy is that taught by the ancient philosophers: liberty is not freedom, and happiness is not felicity, because mere liberty and the heedless pursuit of individual happiness are ultimately self-defeating. Paradoxically, genuine freedom and felicity require self-rule: inner control of the self by the self to avert outer coercion and the cancerous growth of the state. Not only is such inner control impossible within the social vacuum created by Hobbesian amorality and Cartesian rationality, but the latter also systematically destroy the outer context of civic virtue and moral authority needed to sustain and support individual self-rule. Nor can the throne left empty by the death of God be filled with some merely secular ideal of heaven on Earth: the path of social perfectionism and political utopia leads only toward totalitarian hells.

The fatal flaw in Hobbes's political philosophy was identified centuries ago by Aristotle:

> For as man is the best of the animals when perfected, so he is the worst of all when sundered from law and justice . . . [because he] is born possessing weapons for the use of wisdom and virtue, which it is possible to employ entirely for the opposite ends. Hence, when devoid of virtue man is the most unholy and savage of animals.

By renouncing the aim of perfecting the political animal—that is, of teaching him to use his "weapons" for wise and virtuous ends, instead of for contrary ones—the liberal polities founded on Hobbesian principles effectively abandoned the vocation of politics, which is precisely to foster an Aristotelean "rule of life" among the citizens. It was thus inevitable that "the best of the animals when perfected" would be progressively "sundered from law and justice" and turned into "the worst of all"—into an amoral or even immoral creature of will and appetite who must be ruled by force, if he can be ruled at all. In the end, *mere liberty is not and can never be the basis for a workable philosophy of politics over the long term.* Man's "weapons for . . . wisdom and virtue" must be directed to positive ends, or the resulting social order is bound to be both "unholy and savage."

It comes down to this: modern civilization has no future. It confronts the same lethal combination of ecological collapse and inner decay that has extinguished previous civilizations. Liberalism has no future. Its basic principles are contradictory and ultimately self-destructive; and its mostly laudable ends are subverted by its largely pernicious means. A fortiori, the American polity in its present form has no future. It epitomizes the modern, liberal way of life and hence exhibits all of its contradictions and problems in their most extreme and dangerous form. The political animal must therefore reinvent politics: only radically new forms of governance can cope with the aftermath of liberalism and meet the challenges of the coming century; only a new and radically different philosophy of governance can foster the wisdom and virtue that are indispensable both for the felicity of the individual and for the peace, welfare, and justice of the community. We seem to be in the precise situation described in the Prologue: modernity is moribund, so we need a major advance in civilization, yet bringing it about will all but wreck the society in which it occurs. The question is, Will we cling fanatically to our decaying way of life and outmoded ideas or help the phoenix rise from the ashes?

The Political Challenge of the Twenty-first Century

The medieval theology, or the Roman corruption of morals, poisoned only their own people, a small part of mankind; today, electricity, railways, and telegraphs spoil the whole world. Everyone makes these things his own. He simply cannot help making them his own. Everyone suffers in the same way, is forced to the same extent to change his way of life. All are under the necessity of betraying what is most important for their lives, the understanding of life itself, religion. Machines—to produce what? The telegraph—to despatch what? Books, papers—to spread what kind of news? Railways—to go to whom and to what place? Millions of people herded together and subject to a supreme power—to accomplish what? Hospitals, physicians, dispensaries in order to prolong life—for what? How easily do individuals as well as whole nations take their own so-called civilization as the true civilization: finishing one's studies, keeping one's nails clean, using the tailor's and the barber's services, travelling abroad, and the most civilized man is complete. And with regard to nations: as many railways as possible, academies, industrial works, battleships, forts, newspapers, books, parties, parliaments. Thus the most civilized nation is complete. Enough individuals, therefore, as well as nations can be interested in civilization but not in true enlightenment. The former is easy and meets with approval; the latter requires rigorous efforts and therefore, from the great majority, always meets with nothing but contempt and hatred, for it exposes the lie of civilization.

—Leo Tolstoy

So much for the diagnosis. What is the cure? It is implicit within the diagnosis, and its essence is simply stated. Because negative freedom has been tried and found wanting, we must choose positive freedom. That is, since the "freedom from" of liberalism—the liberty to do what we want, provided only that our acts do not directly injure others—is no longer a viable basis for politics, we need instead a "freedom for" in which we obey a "natural law" or fulfill our "higher nature," however defined.

The case made by Isaiah Berlin and other defenders of negative freedom is beguiling. Liberty is undeniably attractive as a fundamental political principle: Who would not wish to be free of all constraints except the need to keep the peace? And since individuals differ fundamentally in their psychological makeup, why should they not be allowed to pursue their own self-defined ends free of interference by others or the state? Moreover, *laissez-faire* and *laissez-innover* have made us economically wealthy and technologically advanced; ergo, liberty is the royal road to "progress." Most important, however, since tyranny can be (and has been) justified in the name of freedom, let us for God's sake cleave to liberty at all costs, abandoning forever any hope of fulfilling our so-called higher nature by political means.

Alas, beguiling or not, the force of the liberal case is vitiated first of all by the practical outcome it produces: moral entropy and all the other problems explored hitherto. But even the theoretical cogency of liberalism is not what it once was. First, to reiterate, economic development has demolished the original ground of liberalism: in high mass-consumption societies dominated by gigantic corporate enterprises, both public and private, it is no longer possible for most individuals to acquire Lockean "estate" (as opposed to mere possessions), because they are dependent wage earners rather than independent proprietors. Even doctors are now employees. This is precisely why Berlin and other latter-day liberal thinkers have tried to shift the ground from economics to psychology, from social independence to individual difference. As we have seen, however, this attempt to save liberalism from intellectual incoherence and practical obsolescence fails: psychological liberation is not a viable basis for polity over the long term. Thus the end of independent proprietorship probably means the end of genuine liberalism as well. Second, again thanks to economic development, the classical liberal position on injury—my fist's freedom stops just short of your nose—is no longer tenable. In large, crowded, complex, interconnected societies such as our own, we can scarcely breathe without harming, hindering, or constraining others. We therefore require a moral code that judges our acts according to their effects on society *as a whole and over the long term*—in other words, a morality that is fundamentally ecological in spirit (as will become clearer below). Third, the axiomatic linkage between liberty and "progress" has been called into question by rapid economic growth in East Asia, which charts its course by Confucius, not Locke or Smith. In fact, some East Asian leaders openly disdain the Anglo-American libertarian tradition as practically unworkable and morally obnoxious.

In brief, liberalism has failed both practically and theoretically. Hence, despite legitimate concerns about the dangers of tyranny, a more positive notion of freedom—some vision of the good life, some moral ideal that transcends mere liberty—has now become indispensable, and the central task of twenty-first century politics will be to discover and establish this new ground of governance.

But we cannot now describe, much less prescribe, a "rule of life" for this future polity. The future contains not only many possibilities but many that we cannot now imagine, in large part because posterity will almost certainly think and act on premises radically different from our own. Indeed, it is all but impossible to stand in one paradigm and see into another. Thus we are bound to understand the future anachronistically. In other words, we never see a society on the verge of radical change in terms of what it will be in the future but, rather, primarily or even exclusively in terms of what it is now ceasing to be. Our very language betrays us: to talk in terms of "postmodern" or "postliberal" or "post" anything is necessarily to remain beholden to the intellectual constructs of the present. In addition, the crisis of modern civilization has no simple or straightforward solution; nor do we yet understand the problem well enough to think in terms of a solution. And the rationalist model of problem solving does not apply: "Cultural solutions," says Wendell Berry, "are organisms, not machines, and they cannot be invented deliberately or imposed by prescription."

All of this having been said, we can nevertheless talk in a general way about the politics of the future: if we assume that there will indeed be polity rather than anarchy, at least in the longer term, then the task of any future polity will necessarily be to overcome the tragic flaws of the present one. Approaching the problem in this fashion, we can identify four prime requisites for a humane and viable politics for the twenty-first century and beyond.

The first is ecological maturity. In the Introduction, the model of ecological succession was used both to illuminate the character of the environmental problematique and to delineate its solution. We learned that the human species now has no choice but to transform its relationship to the biosphere, abandoning the role of parasitic despoiler and learning to be a mutualistic symbiont (i.e., an organism that gives as much as it takes, as when the bee pollinates in return for the flower's nectar, thereby enhancing, rather than diminishing, the beauty and integrity of nature). In other words, humanity must grow up ecologically, exchanging pioneer values for the more mature values of the climax.

This will involve a human relationship to the natural world that is rooted ultimately in a love for creation, rather than a selfish calculation of costs and benefits. Although "stewardship" is the metaphor often used to characterize such a relationship, to the extent that this word implies that humanity should take charge of nature, it is seriously and even dangerously misleading. As James Lovelock notes, "I would sooner expect a goat to succeed as a gardener than expect humans to become responsible for the Earth." It is instead man who must adapt his attitudes and behavior to nature's needs: the point is not to manage the Earth but to manage *ourselves*. Marriage is thus a far better metaphor, suggesting both the extent of mutuality and the depth of accommodation that will be required to achieve a mutually beneficial, synergistic alliance of man and nature in place of the current one-sided, destructive exploitation of the latter by the former. This does not mean, says Berry, that we can live harmlessly:

> To live, we must daily break the body and shed the blood of Creation. When we do this knowingly, lovingly, skillfully, reverently, it is a sacrament. When we do it ignorantly, greedily, clumsily, destructively, it is a desecration. In such desecration we condemn ourselves to spiritual and moral loneliness, and others to want.

In the end, to achieve ecological maturity means to undergo a spiritual transformation. If precivilized man was a dependent child of nature, and civilized man an adolescent destroyer of nature, then postcivilized man must become an adult partner of nature—joining with her in a harmonious, fruitful, and enduring union of the machine and the garden that is no mere marriage of convenience but, instead, a deep commitment to live on and with the Earth in a sacramental way.

It follows both logically and practically that ecological maturity cannot be separated from political, social, and moral maturity. Ecological heedlessness is but one aspect of the general failure of civilization thus far to restrain human will and appetite, a failure that is exacerbated in a modern civilization based on Hobbesian principles. All of civilization hitherto has therefore been a juvenile phase, exemplifying to a greater or lesser degree the predatory ethos of the conquistador and the foolish narcissism of the adolescent. Attaining ecological maturity will force us to deal with this larger problem, not just to devise harmless technologies. In fact, ecology virtually entails a radically different kind of politics: implicit within the metaphors above, for example, are a set of social values—reverence, respect, caring, mutuality, reciprocity, interdependence, and the like—largely opposed to our own.* Achieving ecological maturity will therefore require a formidable leap to a new level of moral awareness and social integration—a major advance in civilization, rather than a mere paradigm shift.

Second, we need a politics of consciousness. The story of modern civilization has been one of increasing "command" or "mastery" of the material environment, so that more and more matter and energy have been appropriated for human ends, either to live higher on the ecological hog or to support greater numbers. We have called this "progress," but it now stands revealed as a self-destructive strategy for meeting basic human needs, both material and cultural. Not only is such a way of life intrinsically unsustainable, but it may fail even to promote genuine happiness and well-being. Tolstoy is but one of many to maintain the contrary: a merely material civilization is a "lie," for it can never foster "true enlightenment." Gandhi put the same point more positively: "The essence of civilization consists not in the multiplication of wants but in their deliberate and voluntary renunciation."

It seems that we have nearly exhausted the possibilities of material development—not just ecologically but, to a very large extent, humanly as well. At this point in our history, greater material development will not meet the deeper needs or fulfill the higher aspirations of humankind. We are therefore left with little choice but to foster spiritual development instead. That is, we critically need some concept of a "higher nature" that we wish to fulfill and some positive notion of an authentic freedom that would result from its fulfillment, for in no other way will we be able to check the greed, ambition, and selfishness that are destroying both the planet and civil society. (Paradoxically, embracing such an antimaterialist social vision would help us solve our most intractable material problem: the poverty of the "underdeveloped." As long as our primary cultural goal is accumulating wealth—and the power that goes along with it—the tendency for the rich to get richer and the poor poorer is well-nigh unavoidable.) In short, we need a new vision that makes growing in wisdom, not gratifying our appetites, the central purpose of human life.

Third, we need a recovery of morality. The story of modern civilization has been one of progressive demoralization in all three senses of the

---

*One metaphor in particular—the union of the machine and the garden—also points to the path not taken in American history. It points, that is, to Jefferson, who envisioned just such a man-nature alliance as the essential basis for a genuinely free and democratic way of life balanced between the extremes of savage primitivism and urban decadence.

word: the corruption of morals, the undermining of morale, and the spreading of confusion. We can now see clearly the problems such demoralization has already caused and the ominous terminus toward which it tends. It is apparent that virtue, like wisdom, must also be cultivated and indeed inculcated by the social and political order, or these "weapons" will be turned to perverse ends and destroy both the society and the polity. Our political future therefore depends on finding a new moral basis for civil society—for the "habits of the heart" that are the bedrock of politics.

Nor is morality the insoluble problem that hard-core rationalists pretend it is: we do know in a general way what personal and political virtue are. For example, Lao Tsu, Socrates, and Thoreau, to pick just three sages from very different eras and traditions, agree fundamentally on the nature and meaning of human life and also, in a more general way, on the political implications that follow from this understanding. In other words, with all due respect for the difficulty of the task, there would appear to be plenty of room for a reasoned middle ground between a fundamentalist dogmatism that wants to inflict a narrow-minded moral code and a laissez-faire relativism that denies both the necessity and the possibility of constructing one.

Moreover, to approach the problem in a way that may be more congenial to the modern scientific temperament, it seems that we have at least the beginnings of a new theory of natural law. That is, we now know enough anthropology, biology, ecology, psychology, and history to make some educated guesses about what would constitute a just, workable, healthy, and sustainable society. And what we know goes well beyond mere rules of prudence that must be obeyed lest we destroy ourselves.

For example, whatever their sectarian differences, all schools of depth psychology agree on one thing: both individuals and cultures must deal skillfully with unconscious forces or suffer the consequences. If repressed, these forces "return" to cause the kinds of personal illness and mass psychosis that have blighted the history of the twentieth century; if acted out or "desublimated," they create a Sadean chaos, like the moral wasteland that is the poisoned legacy of liberalism. One of the goals of a genuinely enlightened polity would therefore be to foster a constructive engagement with the unconscious through myth, rite, ritual, and self-exploration—in other words, a way of life conducive to psychological balance and health.

Similarly, the clearest lesson of ecology is limitation. Natural systems work on the basis of feedback mechanisms: these constrain organisms in ways that foster orderly communities and, ultimately, a harmonious biosphere. Restated in positive moral terms, this comes close to being a scientific justification for the Golden Mean—for "moderation in all things" and the control of appetite by the higher human faculties. Or for a neo-Confucian politics that encourages individuals to relate sanely and constructively to the natural and social orders by balancing their legitimate desire for independence against the inescapable fact of interdependence.

In sum, a moral politics founded on naturalistic principles discovered by human reason would seem to be possible. (Indeed, paradoxically, discovery of the moral order implicit within the natural order was one of the original goals of the Enlightenment, before rationalism vanquished reason.) Moreover, unless we go back to revelation, no other ground is available for erecting a political theory of the ecologically mature civilization—a theory that would permit us, despite all the shortcomings of human nature, to live harmoniously with our fellow creatures and virtuously with our fellow human beings.

This leads naturally to the fourth and final requisite of a future politics: the restoration of governance. The story of modern civilization in its political aspect is one of emancipating the human passions and maximizing individual liberty. Although the effects were indeed liberating at first—not only with respect to civil and human rights but in many other ways as well—in latter days the destructive side of liberalism has come to predominate. In other words, just as with material development, we have almost exhausted the possibilities of selfish individualism as a ground of governance, so we shall have to find a new one.

The fundamental problem with liberal polities is that they do not actually govern, except in the most minimal sense. According to the dictionary, to govern means to control, guide, direct, and restrain. This is precisely what liberal polities are *not* supposed to do in theory and what they try not to do in practice. (Nowadays, of course, they are more and more obliged to do so by force of circumstance—but largely to remedy the problems caused by liberalism itself, rather than to achieve positive ends, so the result is administrative despotism at best and futility at worst.) To govern in the true sense, however, is always to control, guide, direct, and restrain in accordance with some political and moral ideal. Otherwise it is not governance but adhocracy or tyranny. And that is precisely our situation today: because we shirk this task, a tyrannical future is being created for us by all the interlocking vicious circles described above. To escape such a remorseless working of things, we must learn once again to govern—controlling, guiding, directing, and restraining individuals who would otherwise behave selfishly and destructively, so that they respect the interests and needs of the larger human and natural community of which they are a part.

It seems that Rousseau was right. As he predicted, the unbridled individualism and unrestrained hedonism of liberal polity have proven to be morally and socially destructive. A politics based on mere liberty is unsustainable: to achieve real freedom, we must govern our appetites. Whether we like it or not, therefore, we need to be politically encouraged to higher ends than self-gratification and self-aggrandizement. We must, in other words, be "forced to be free." But this does *not* mean to be tyrannized, only to be *governed by our own consent* in accordance with some notion of morality and some vision of the good life. And Rousseau was convinced, as am I, that to be so governed leads ultimately to a greater happiness than can be found in gratifying ego's desires—to the genuine felicity that arises only when we give ourselves to some higher purpose, some larger enterprise, than mere appetite.

This, then, is the political challenge of the twenty-first century: to invent a new form of politics that manifests this higher purpose and promotes this larger enterprise—but that also preserves, as far as possible, the basic civil and human rights which are the precious legacy of liberalism. That this challenge will be far from easy or free of risk goes without saying. The ruling ideas and governing paradigms of any society are in effect civil religions to which people are strongly or even fanatically attached. In this light, although it is relatively easy to envision the general principles of a viable and humane politics for the future, it is much harder to imagine that we would readily embrace such a radically different philosophy—in this country above all. Or that it could be adopted without causing enormous turmoil across the board. Alas, Whitehead is correct: "The major advances in civilization . . . all but wreck the societies in which they occur." But we would seem to have little choice. Given the tragic failure of liberalism, the inescapable and appalling alternative to reinventing politics is moral and social collapse followed by anarchy or a regime of iron. Once again, the question is, Will we cling to our moribund principles at all costs or help the phoenix rise from the ashes?

I cannot conclude without reiterating that the challenge far transcends politics narrowly conceived: we need to discover a new way to be civilized. Modern civilization, the peculiar way of life based on the ideas of the Enlightenment, represents not a break with all past civilization, as is usually thought, but rather an intensification and amplification of most of its worst tendencies. Modern civilization did not invent war, poverty, oppression, and exploitation, even though it has made these more devastating and widespread than ever before. Reinventing politics as an arena of wisdom and virtue that sustains authentic human freedom will therefore be only one part, however crucial and difficult, of the much larger task, which is to transform civilization along the lines envisioned by Rousseau—as well as by Thoreau, who maintained that the ultimate goal of civilization is to produce "a more experienced and wiser savage."

The human race has reached a critical time in its social evolution when it has no choice but to make peace with its biological origins and to learn how to live once again as a member and partner of the natural community rather than as its dominator and destroyer. In other words, we must rediscover how to live as our savage ancestors once lived—*in* nature, rather than apart from it, much less above it. We must, that is, invent the civilized analogue of the hunter-gatherer way of life, the only sustainable mode of human existence the planet has ever known. Suggesting that we live in a much simpler and more natural way does not imply a return to the Stone Age or anything like it: we have many possibilities open to us that were not available to our forebears, for we have been enormously enriched and enlightened by the long experience of civilization (or at least so one hopes). Nevertheless, how such a profound transformation of civilization toward a more experienced and wiser savagery can be achieved is obviously an immensely difficult question, because it will clearly entail radical changes in every aspect of our way of life.

Just how radical is suggested by one of the most poignant and pointed critiques of modern civilization ever uttered. Breaking into a filmed interview on the destruction of the Amazon rain forest, an anonymous Kayapo Indian woman shouted, "We don't want your dams. Your mothers did not hold you enough. You are all orphans." It is perhaps too simple to say that the good society is one in which your mother—and by extension your father, your community, and indeed your entire way of life—holds you enough, so that you grow up feeling that the world is a good place and that life is intrinsically satisfying just as it is and that there is thus no need to make it more satisfying by accumulating endless wealth and power at others' expense. But this at least points in the right direction: to become more experienced and wiser savages, to meet the real political challenge of the twenty-first century, we shall have to create cultures so rich and nurturing that we would have no need to pursue happiness; we could simply enjoy it.

Epilogue

Since the advent of civilization, the outgrowth of property has been so immense, its forms so diversified, its uses so expanding, and its management so intelligent in the interests of its owners, that it has become, on the part of the people, an unmanageable power. The human mind stands bewildered in the presence of its own creation. The time will come, nevertheless, when human intelligence will rise to the mastery over property. . . . A mere property career is not the final destiny of Mankind, if progress is to be the law of the future, as it has been of the past. The time that has passed away since civilization began is but a fragment of the past duration of Man's existence, and but a fragment of the ages yet to come. The dissolution of Society bids fair to become the termination of a career of which property is the end and aim—because such a career contains the elements of self-destruction. Democracy in Government, brotherhood in society, equality in rights and privileges, and universal education foreshadow the next higher plane of society to which experience, intelligence, and knowledge are steadily tending. It will be a revival, in a higher form, of the liberty, equality, and fraternity of the ancient Gentes.

—Lewis Henry Morgan

THE ENLIGHTENMENT PROJECT HAS FAILED—and failed badly, exposing humanity to an unprecedented planet-wide catastrophe-in-the-making that is the ironic product of its highest ideals. The Enlightenment aspired to overthrow the tyranny of kings and oligarchs, which subjected peoples to arbitrary power; the tyranny of nature, which enslaved the mass of humankind to scarcity and want; and the tyranny of religion, which bound the minds of men and women to superstition and subservience. This was a worthy aspiration—but it was pursued with hubris and without balance or wisdom, producing all the perverse and self-de-

structive consequences explored in the present work. The political failure of the Enlightenment is especially grievous: far from taming power as
it was intended to do, Hobbesian polity in all its forms and aspects simply leads to its universalization, to the triumph of Leviathan. A new
worldview and a new political theory are therefore imperative.

The direction of the required change is clear. It is simply not possible
over the long run to have liberty without authority, exploitation without
husbandry, equality without excellence, individualism without fraternity,
self-seeking without morality, or rationality without reason. Above all, it
is not possible to have the world without the spirit, for it is as true today
as it was two millennia ago that man does not live by bread alone. Instead of exploiting matter ever more viciously, we must therefore turn to
exploring and bringing into play the most underdeveloped resource on
the planet: the human psyche.

This, then, is the phoenix stirring in the ashes of the funeral pyre consuming liberal polity. A politics based on dead matter must have a deadly
outcome, but a spiritual politics rooted in the mythic depths of the
human psyche and the organic wealth of the natural order can make possible a very different kind of future—one in which all of life, human and
nonhuman alike, can continue to flourish. Only a renewed connection to
the transcendent realm will permit a humanity grown too numerous and
too powerful for its own good not just to survive but to achieve the good
life in the centuries to come. The exploration of consciousness and the
pursuit of self-knowledge can no longer be the work of isolated individuals and groups, as in the past. Rather, society must be reorganized and
politics reinvented to make the Aristotelian quest for wisdom and virtue,
and the Platonic search for truth and beauty, into the *raison d'être* of the
planetary civilization now struggling to be born.

The essential politics of such a civilization are foreshadowed in the final
paragraph of Lewis Henry Morgan's *Ancient Society*. The human mind
will achieve a genuine mastery over matter only when it has risen above "a
mere property career"—that is, when it has finally tamed the self-destructive material dynamic unleashed by the Neolithic Transition and intensified by the Enlightenment. In so doing, humankind will ascend to "the
next higher plane of society"— "a revival, in a higher form, of the liberty,
equality, and fraternity of the ancient Gentes." Thus the problematique of
modern civilization has a genuine "solution." It is by becoming Thoreau's
more experienced and wiser savages that we can fulfill our true destiny as
civilized beings, guarantee the continuity of civilization itself, and preserve the real political achievements of the Enlightenment from the
forces of endarkenment now threatening to engulf them.

BIBLIOGRAPHIC NOTE

All of Western philosophy, said Whitehead, is but a footnote to Plato's *Republic*. Hyperbole or not, this statement is true of my own work, because it is inspired by the Platonic desire that politics be based on truth and beauty rather than on accident and force. My primary debt is therefore to Socrates, the guiding daimon of political philosophy, as well as to the great tradition of discourse that he founded.

More proximately, however, I owe this work to Rousseau, the standard-bearer of Socratic politics in the modern era; to Jefferson, the so-called American Rousseau; to de Tocqueville, still the most prescient critic of American democracy; to Thoreau, the American Socrates; to Le Bon, the original and best analyst of mass society; and to Jung, the preeminent twentieth-century exponent of the examined life. In other words, with all due respect to the many others from whom I have learned and whose contributions have enriched my analysis, I am principally indebted to a comparative handful of "classics" drawn from the Western "canon." (But since this canon has no monopoly on political wisdom, I have also listed Iyer's discussion of Gandhi as well as works by the Taoist sages Chuang Tsu and Lao Tsu.)

My work therefore owes relatively little to contemporary social science. This has distressed some readers of the work in manuscript, because they believe that I have slighted the contributions of living scholars. But I did not get my ideas from these scholars. For example, to the extent that "moral entropy" is not due to my reading of Plato and Rousseau, I owe it to Ortega and Unamuno. (Besides, too much of contemporary social science and political criticism consists in reinventing the wheel already discovered by these and other "classical" authors—so if anybody is being slighted, it is the latter. Why, for instance, does the vast literature on "public goods" virtually ignore Rousseau's *Social Contract*, which diagnoses the problem and proposes a solution?) In any event, to reiterate what I said in the Preface, this is an essay, not a monograph or a review of the literature. Yet at the same time I have done my utmost to give credit where credit is due, if not in the body of the text, then in this Bibliographic Note or the annotated List of Sources that follows.

For Rousseau, de Tocqueville, Thoreau, and Le Bon, the reader can proceed directly to the works cited in the List of Sources. However, Jefferson and Jung are less easily approached. Jefferson never wrote systematic philosophy, in part because he was caught up in practical politics for most of his life and in part because his mind did not run in that direction. In addition, the myth of Jefferson-the-mainstream-democrat has so overshadowed the reality of Jefferson-the-radical-political-thinker that rediscovering the latter is by no means easy. I have therefore listed Padover's anthology of representative (but mostly mainstream) quotations, along with the interpretations of Agar, Koch, Matthews, and Wills. Although Koch is the most useful overall, Matthews is especially illuminating, because he highlights Jefferson's palpable radicalism. Finally, Leo Marx's classic discussion of the basic tension in American life—that between Hamilton and Jefferson, or between the machine and the garden—supplies the indispensable context of Jefferson's thought.

By contrast, Jung's oeuvre is systematic, but so vast and abstruse that an unguided reader can easily go astray. His autobiographical *Memories, Dreams, Reflections* is certainly the clearest and best starting point. The other works cited, two of them written for non-Jungians, would logically come next. Of the many fine interpretations of Jung, I have listed only Stevens, because he not only explains Jungian psychology in understandable terms but also goes on to explicate and amplify Jung's core ideas in terms of contemporary anthropology, ethology, and neuroscience, thus grounding them in the later scientific developments that Jung largely anticipated. Finally, the two essays by Czuczka and Odajnyk not only summarize Jung's social and political ideas but also show where they can be pursued in greater depth. Because Jung does not stand alone, I have also included works by Campbell, Eliade, Hillman, Neumann, and Santillana and Durchend, all of whom support or amplify Jung; by Freud and Rank, who both support and contradict Jung; and by Raschke, who opposes Jung's "gnosticism" as being dangerously antinomian.

Although Socrates is the original source of my belief that politics needs to be understood in terms of basic ideas and deep structures, I have borrowed the now widely accepted term *paradigm* from Kuhn as a main element of my own analysis. But Braudel, whose histories wonderfully exemplify the explanatory power of deep structures, and the works of Boorstin, Boulding, Harman, and Polak, who explore the powerful or even determining influence of basic images, are also recommended.

Despite springing primarily from the classical tradition and the handful of works mentioned above, my analysis has many precursors. Of these, I have cited only a few, because my purpose is, again, not to review the literature, only to acknowledge those to whom I owe the most while at the same time guiding the reader to works most likely to prove interesting for further investigation. Foremost among these are Arendt, Ellul, Lippmann, and Mumford, so I have included several books by each (or, in the case of Lippmann, the comprehensive anthology by Rossiter and Lare). With no intention of slighting the others, who demand a greater effort from the reader (especially Ellul), I recommend Lippmann's *The Public Philosophy* above all. This succinct summary of a lifetime spent reflecting on the contradictions of modern politics is still as fresh and pertinent as when it was written (1955) and has the virtue of exposing the pretensions and contradictions of liberal democracy from within the perspective of liberal democracy itself. In addition, the two works by Bellah et al., which have de Tocqueville and Lippmann as their guiding spirits, are worthy not just in their own right but also because they review the history of democratic criticism in America (ground covered in a different way by Hofstadter as well), something I have not tried to do. Moreover, the final section of *The Great Society* is devoted to a program for reconstructing American democracy, so readers unhappy with my lack of same have somewhere to turn. (However, I believe a clearer *vision* of how liberal democracies and market economies can save themselves from themselves can be found in Havel's *Summer Meditations*.)

Others who share to some degree my belief that political philosophy is the best lens through which to understand contemporary problems are Connolly, Dahl, Jacobson, MacIntyre, Macpherson, Walzer, Will, and Wolin, who is a particularly acute critic of the modern political order. (I shall have more to say about Dahl later.) Concerning the vocation of political philosophy, the three articles by Glass restate the Socratic position in a way that I find particularly congenial: his thesis is that the political philosopher is a kind of shaman whose task is to drive corruption out of the body politic with Eros-restoring visions.

I have also included a representative selection of contemporary social scientists critical of American democracy's failings. The works by Barber, Bell, De Leon, Edelman, Galston, Kariel, Lowi, Mansbridge, Margolis, McWilliams, Olson, Pangle, Putnam, Sennett, and Dennis Thompson cover the gamut. Bell's *Cultural Contradictions* is particularly trenchant (and pertinent to my own analysis). With the exception of Bell, Kariel, and Pangle, none propose or foresee radical changes; most urge greater participation as the antidote to current democratic ills.

For coverage of the same territory by leading journalists, see Phillips, the premier analyst of American electoral politics; Dionne, who explains how and why the political process came to be characterized by ideological deadlock and legislative gridlock; Rauch, who provides the gory details on hyperpluralism; and Grieder, who describes in convincing detail the vast chasm between our democratic pretensions and the actuality of corporate and policy-elite machination. Haynes Johnson and Barlett and Steele also offer useful facts and insights, while Frum rakes American conservatives over the coals for having sold out to the politics of hyperpluralism and factionalism. Lazare goes deeper than all of the above: he impugns the Constitution itself. Toffler and Toffler also make a case for fundamental constitutional reform to meet the changed conditions of the information age. Meanwhile, Thurow (in all the cited works) and Samuelson examine the current political struggle from an economic perspective. The failures and contradictions of "money equality" are ably described by Kaus, but for a deeper and more serious discussion of equality see Tawney and Walzer. More radical political perspectives are offered by Bookchin, Kohr, Charles Reich, Robertson, Sale, Schmookler, Taylor, and Toynbee: to the extent that they all share a common solution, it is devolution to small-scale, local, ecologically viable democracy; to the extent that they all share a common failing, it is begging most of the hard political questions.

Concerning particular issues or themes, see Schlesinger, whose "liberal" credentials are impeccable, for a vigorous defense of the orthodox American position on multiculturalism (in *Disuniting*). But Brimelow, Ravitch, and Steele (especially the latter's trenchant article) also confront this issue squarely. Feminist politics are incisively criticized by Gordon and Sommers. The nature and consequences of modern alienation are covered from many different perspectives by Berger, Marshall Berman, Buber, Samuel Edgerton, Fromm, Gardels (in "Last Modern Century"), Geertz, Lasch, Marcuse, May, Nisbet (in *Quest*), Ogilvy, Saul, Slater, Spragens, and Steiner. The impact of technology on politics is discussed obliquely by many, but directly by Anderson, Ferkiss, Pool, Postman (in *Technopoly*), Rosalind Williams, and, above all, Winner, who I highly recommend. Media, popular culture, and politics are well covered by Ewen, Fallows, Gardels and Connors, Hertsgaard, Marshall McLuhan, Meyrowitz, Miller, Postman (in *Amusing*), Anthony Smith, and Twitchell.

Turning to the more economic aspect of political economy, in addition to Karl Marx himself (both in the work cited and in the Tucker reader) I have listed only Galbraith, Hayek, Heilbroner, Lane, Lindblom, Schumpeter, Tawney, and Wallerstein because together they seem to cover the spectrum. However, that spectrum is changing rapidly as contemporary thinkers have begun to widen their perspective (primarily by taking ecology into account) and to propose radically different alternatives: those cited are Burns, Daly, Daly and Cobb, Jonathan Harris, Hawken, Henderson, Hirsch, Leiss (in *Limits*), Lutz and Lux, Schumacher, Schwartz, and Scitovsky. Schumacher, especially, manages to capture the essential spirit of an economics "as if people mattered" that traces its roots back to Aristotle.

The new economics, as is made explicit by Daly and Henderson, grows out of a new epistemology and worldview. This is necessary because, as explained in the main text, a flawed epistemology is at the root of almost all our problems and dilemmas. Appleyard, Barfield, Morris Berman, Ehrenfeld, Feyerabend, Horkheimer, Leiss (in *Domination*), Merchant, Richter, Rubenstein, Toulmin, Turner, Watts, and Weber all argue that Science has fostered estrangement, ideology, and domination. (As Evernden brilliantly demonstrates, even most so-called environmentalists are prisoners of the fundamentally anti-ecological mindset of modern life.) On the other hand, we need to understand that the dominant notion of Science no longer conforms to the best scientific understanding. The general outline of the new epistemology is presaged in the works of Bateson and Jantsch, who describe an intelligent and "self-organizing" universe. The emerging ecological synthesis is summarized by Lovelock, whose book is an excellent (and delightful) primer of basic biological, chemical, and physical principles and their implications (and see also Calder for a complementary perspective). Colinvaux (in *Why*), Leakey and Lewin, McHarg, Myers,

Pimm, and Edward Wilson also state basic ecological principles; whereas Barney, Harrison Brown, Lester Brown, Catton, Davis, Garrett, Hardin, Higgins, Kassiola, Ophuls and Boyan, and Orr make the ecological case against industrial civilization. The critical importance of energy and entropy for understanding both nature and culture is discussed by Cottrell, Lovins, Odum and Odum, Ophuls and Boyan, Rifkin (in *Entropy*), and Ryan (whose two outstanding articles are unfortunately hard to come by). These works (and the literature to which they lead) provide the background for the discussion of thermodynamic accounting in Chapters 3–5. Tainter complements and completes the analysis of these chapters, arguing that the rise and fall of civilizations is a function of waxing and waning returns on energy investment. Finally, the two works by Meadows describe the systems paradigm and demonstrate both its explanatory power and its practical utility.

The domestic decay of the United States is occurring in an international context to which the text refers only obliquely. Perhaps the best short overview is Kaplan's article, but there is now a burgeoning literature on America's economic decline, actual or impending, as well as on the troubled aftermath of the Cold War. Kennedy marshals a powerful case for American decline that has been too quickly dismissed by some: it is not "imperial overstretch" alone but overstretch in lethal combination with strategic folly, political failure, and fiscal bankruptcy that threaten to do us in with unprecedented speed and severity. Luttwak, Malabre, Pfaff, Michael Porter, Robert Reich, Schlossstein, and Thurow (in *Head to Head*) amplify Kennedy's argument (with Pfaff being especially recommended); Nye disputes it; and Attali, Brzezinski, Gardels (in "Soul"), Lacqueur, Moynihan, William Irwin Thompson, and Thurow (in *Future*) provide additional perspectives on the new world disorder. However, I believe the most perceptive overview of the current state of the world and the direction in which it is tending is offered by Guéhenno.

All of the above needs to be understood in historical perspective. McNeill's one-volume history of the world from the Western point of view is first-rate; and his discussion of polyethnicity is, I believe, more relevant to our current situation than Schlesinger's restatement of American orthodoxy. As the twentieth century is only sketched by McNeill, I have included more detailed accounts by Hobsbawm and Paul Johnson. Keegan describes how the "advance" of civilization has been accompanied by "advances" in weaponry that have made warfare more cruel and destructive than ever. And Hopkirk's account of last century's "Great Game" may prove prescient with regard to the next century. But perhaps the past is not a good guide: Barraclough, Lukacs, Toynbee, and Tuchman (in *Distant Mirror*) suggest that the telltale signs of epochal historical change are now visible and that the modern age is therefore coming to an end, with consequences that we cannot predict. (Tuchman's other work, *March of Folly*, warns that clinging to outmoded ideas—as we seem bound and determined to do—is the principal cause of historical disasters.) A few honorable exceptions aside, until very recently historians virtually ignored one of its main protagonists: nature. Fortunately, this error is now being rectified—as shown by Braudel (again), Colinvaux (in *Fates*), Crosby, Flannery, Hobhouse, Donald Hughes, Martin, Ponting, Webb, Wilkinson, and Worster. Thus we are at long last beginning to comprehend the story of humankind in its true context.

Indeed, the story has been extended ever farther into prehistory to illuminate our biological and social past: we now understand better than ever before who we humans are as a species, how we evolved to become civilized, and how our natural origins continue to influence our behavior. (Unfortunately, this knowl- edge has not yet had much of an impact on political or social thought: as a cul- ture, we are just beginning to digest Darwin, we are only now swallowing ecol- ogy, and we have yet to ingest recent findings in anthropology, ethology, and evolutionary biology and psychology.) The evolutionary story is well told in Jared Diamond, Fisher, Konner, Ornstein, and Wright, while Reader provides an en- gaging overview of human ecology. Though it may cause much gnashing of teeth among diehard moderns, for whom the conquest of natural limits is an article of faith, nature is indomitable. Thus anatomy is indeed destiny in a very profound sense. One of the great scientific discoveries of the late twentieth century is just how irredeemably "natural" we humans still are, and it is precisely our failure to take our creaturely nature into account that makes us into sick and self-destruc- tive animals. Hence the absolute necessity to reevaluate biological man, also known as the "savage." In addition to those above, works that will assist in this effort are Clarke and Hindley, Clastres, Cohen, Stanley Diamond, Eiseley, Farb, Fox, Marvin Harris (in *Cannibals*), Highwater, Hyde, Lee, Lévi-Strauss, T. C. McLuhan, Maybury-Lewis, Sahlins, and Shepard. They tell us that the savage is already quite wise—so we must become wiser still (but see also the cautionary notes of Robert Edgerton, Sagan, and Torgovnick).

As this work is offered in a dialectical spirit, I urge the reader to examine two works that contradict my own: Fukuyama's defense of liberalism on Hegelian grounds and Dahl's defense of democracy along standard liberal lines. Although curiously half-hearted and based on a partial reading of Hegel, Fukuyama's argu- ment is interesting and illuminating nevertheless. If the truth is, as Woolf says, "only to be had by laying together many varieties of error," then the reader would find it instructive to lay Fukuyama's error alongside my own. (However, Steven Smith is a more reliable guide to Hegel's thought: he not only expounds it with authority and lucidity, but he also demonstrates its continuing relevance; as Smith aptly puts it, today's critics of liberal democracy are usually reinventing the wheel of Hegel.) By comparison, Dahl's *Democracy and Its Critics* is a magis- terial work, the crowning achievement of the leading democratic theorist of our times. For all its brilliance, however, what stands out is the utter dependence of his case on the standard Enlightenment epistemology, which rules out any pos- sibility of natural, moral, or historical law. Take away this assurance, and many of his most ingenious and subtle arguments lose much of their force; in addi- tion, the essential ground of Plato's and Rousseau's theories of politics can no longer be so cavalierly dismissed. Nevertheless, Dahl's closely reasoned argument is the highest and best statement of the conventional liberal-democratic wisdom at century's end, and to lay his error alongside my own would substantially enhance the reader's understanding of the difficult and fateful choices that lie before us.

Finally, because fiction often conveys certain essential truths better than nonfiction, I recommend several novels. Melville's *Moby-Dick* captures perfectly the hubris and peril of modern man's insane quarrel with the cosmos. Quinn's *Ishmael* tells the story of how Adam became Ahab. Dostoyevsky's *Brothers Karamazov*, especially the Grand Inquisitor scene therein, exposes the spiritual cataclysm of modern times (more recently exemplified both by the content of Rushdie's *Satanic Verses* and by the murderous response to its publication). And the fate of Macondo in García Márquez's *One Hundred Years of Solitude* warns of the ephemeral character of "economic development": as the jungle of ecological scarcity closes over modern civilization, will we be left, like the last of the Buendías, to rut in the ruins of our vanished prosperity?

LIST OF SOURCES

The following annotated list of sources is selective and includes mainly works that substantially support or extend my own argument, especially ones that would be useful to a reader wishing to pursue certain topics in greater depth. It is therefore not a review of the literature or of my background reading, much less a record of every work consulted. Nor have I cited every source from which quotations are drawn, for that would have lengthened the list considerably without substantially increasing its usefulness. In addition, I have included only a handful of articles. Finally, no note is appended if the title or previous discussion makes the nature and importance of the work sufficiently clear.

Agar, Herbert. *Land of the Free* (Boston: Houghton Mifflin, 1935). [revisits the argument between Hamilton and Jefferson; tries to find realistic ways of preserving the spirit of the latter within megalopolis]

Anderson, Walter Truett. *To Govern Evolution: Further Adventures of the Political Animal* (Boston: Harcourt Brace Jovanovich, 1987). [on the challenge of biotechnology]

Appleyard, Bryan. *Understanding the Present: Science and the Soul of Modern Man* (New York: Doubleday, 1993).

Arendt, Hannah. *The Origins of Totalitarianism* (Cleveland: Meridian, 1958).

———. *Between Past and Future* (Cleveland: Meridian, 1963).

———. *On Revolution* (New York: Viking, 1963).

Aristotle. *The Politics*, trans. H. Rackham (New York: G. P. Putnam's Sons, 1932). [but some quotations are from the Barker translation]

Attali, Jacques. *Millennium: Winners and Losers in the Coming World Order*, trans. Leila Connors and Nathan Gardels (New York: Random House, 1991). [a useful European perspective on the new world disorder]

Aveni, Anthony F. *Empires of Time: Calendars, Clocks, and Cultures* (New York: Basic, 1989). [examines the cultural construction of time, with special emphasis on the Western obsession with time and its measurement]

Barber, Benjamin R. *Strong Democracy: Participatory Politics for a New Age* (Berkeley: University of California Press, 1984).

Barfield, Owen. *Saving the Appearances: A Study in Idolatry* (New York: Harcourt, Brace & World, 1965). [a critique of Enlightenment epistemology]

Barlett, Donald L., and James B. Steele. *America: What Went Wrong?* (Kansas City: Andrews & McMeel, 1992).

Barnet, Richard J. *The Lean Years: Politics in the Age of Scarcity* (New York: Simon & Schuster, 1980).

Barney, Gerald O., et al. *The Global 2000 Report to the President: Entering the Twenty-First Century* (Washington, D.C.: Government Printing Office, 1980). [contains detailed information on environmental threats]

Barraclough, Geoffrey. *History in a Changing World* (Norman: University of Oklahoma Press, 1955).

Bateson, Gregory. *Steps to an Ecology of Mind* (New York: Ballantine, 1972).

_____. *Mind and Nature: A Necessary Unity* (New York: Dutton, 1979).

Bayley, David H. "Ironies of American Law Enforcement," *Public Interest* 59:45–56 (Spring 1980).

Bell, Daniel. *The Coming of Post-Industrial Society* (New York: Basic, 1976). [a now-classic analysis of the changing capitalist order; should be read along with Kumar]

_____. *The Cultural Contradictions of Capitalism* (New York: Basic, 1976).

Bellah, Robert N., et al. *Habits of the Heart: Individualism and Commitment in American Life* (Berkeley: University of California Press, 1985).

_____. *The Good Society* (New York: Knopf, 1991).

Berger, Peter L., et al. *The Homeless Mind: Modernization and Consciousness* (New York: Random House, 1973).

Berlin, Isaiah. *Four Essays on Liberty* (New York: Oxford University Press, 1969). [the great champion of negative freedom]

_____. *The Hedgehog and the Fox: An Essay on Tolstoy's View of History* (New York: Mentor, 1957). [on the other hand, a defender of reason against mere rationalism]

Berman, Marshall. *All That Is Solid Melts into Air: The Experience of Modernity* (New York: Simon & Schuster, 1982). [on the essentially Faustian character of modern civilization]

Berman, Morris. *The Reenchantment of the World* (Ithaca: Cornell University Press, 1981).

_____. *Coming to Our Senses: Body and Spirit in the Hidden History of the West* (New York: Simon & Schuster, 1989).

Berry, Wendell. *The Unsettling of America: Culture and Agriculture* (San Francisco: Sierra Club, 1977). [a farmer-poet's neo-Jeffersonian/ecological jeremiad]

Bookchin, Murray. *The Ecology of Freedom: The Emergence and Dissolution of Hierarchy* (Palo Alto: Cheshire, 1982).

Boorstin, Daniel J. *The Image: A Guide to Pseudo-Events in America* (New York: Atheneum, 1975). [still an outstanding guide to the "thicket of unreality" generated by media]

Booth, William James. *Households: On the Moral Architecture of the Economy* (Ithaca: Cornell University Press, 1993). [analyzes the tension between the household and the market, from Aristotle to Marx: Do we want security without freedom, or freedom without security?]

Boulding, Kenneth E. *The Image* (Ann Arbor: University of Michigan Press, 1961).

Bramwell, Anna. *Ecology in the 20th Century: A History* (New Haven: Yale University Press, 1989). [an attack on the alleged atavism and primitivism of the ecological movement]

Braudel, Fernand. *The Mediterranean and the Mediterranean World in the Age of Philip II*, trans. Sian Reynolds (New York: Harper & Row, 1972). [a pioneering work of ecological history; explains how natural constraints shaped a crucial epoch]

Brilliant, Larry. "The Health of Humanity," *Whole Earth Review*, Fall 1993, pp. 58–67 [on the epidemiology of death in our age]

Brimelow, Peter. *Alien Nation: Common Sense About Immigration and the American Future* (New York: Random House, 1995). [on the problems and dangers of multiculturalism]

Brown, Harrison. *The Challenge of Man's Future* (New York: Viking, 1954). [a seminal book: one of the first to point out that "progress" has a price—at first physical, but ultimately political]

Brown, Lester R., et al. *State of the World* (Washington: Worldwatch Institute, 1984–). [an authoritative annual report on environmental trends]

Brzezinski, Zbigniew. *Out of Control: Global Turmoil on the Eve of the Twenty-First Century* (New York: Scribner's, 1993).

Buber, Martin. *Paths in Utopia*, trans. R.F.C. Hull (Boston: Beacon, 1958). [examines family and community as the essential basis for polity]

Bunzel, John H. *Anti-Politics in America: Reflections on the Anti-Political Temper and Its Distortions of the Democratic Process* (New York: Vintage, 1970).

Burke, Edmund. *Reflections on the Revolution in France* (London: Dent Everyman, 1971).

Burnham, David. *The Rise of the Computer State* (New York: Random House, 1983).

————. *A Law Unto Itself: Power, Politics and the IRS* (New York: Random House, 1989).

Burns, Scott. *The Household Economy: Its Shape, Origins, and Future* (Boston: Beacon, 1977).

Calder, Nigel. *Timescale: An Atlas of the Fourth Dimension* (New York: Viking, 1983). [outstanding overview of the history of the planet from cosmological, geological, and biological perspectives]

Campbell, Joseph. *The Inner Reaches of Outer Space: Metaphor as Myth and as Religion* (New York: Alfred van der Marck, 1986).

Catton, William R., Jr. *Overshoot: The Ecological Basis of Revolutionary Change* (Urbana: University of Illinois Press, 1980).

Caulfield, Catherine. *In the Rainforests* (New York: Knopf, 1985). [an appalling report from the front lines of the war against the world's forests]

Chuang Tsu. *Inner Chapters*, trans. Gia-Fu Feng and Jane English (New York: Vintage, 1974).

Clarke, Robin, and Geoffrey Hindley. *The Challenge of the Primitives* (New York: McGraw-Hill, 1975).

Clastres, Pierre. *Society Against the State: The Leader as Servant and the Humane Uses of Power Among the Indians of the Americas*, trans. Robert Hurley (New York: Urizen Books, 1977). [on liberty, equality, and fraternity among the savages]

Cohen, Mark Nathan. *The Food Crisis in Prehistory: Overpopulation and the Origins of Agriculture* (New Haven: Yale University Press, 1977).

_____. *Health and the Rise of Civilization* (New Haven: Yale University Press, 1989).

Colinvaux, Paul. *Why Big Fierce Animals Are Rare* (Princeton: Princeton University Press, 1978). [delineates the basic principles of ecology in narrative form]

_____. *The Fates of Nations: A Biological Theory of History* (New York: Simon & Schuster, 1980).

Connolly, William E. *Political Theory and Modernity* (New York: Basil Blackwell, 1988).

Coontz, Stephanie. *The Way We Never Were: American Families and the Nostalgia Trap* (New York: Basic, 1992). [a salutary reminder that the good old days were not always so good; and that curing today's very real family problems will therefore involve transforming society, not merely restoring "traditional" family units or values]

Cornuelle, Richard. "The Power and Poverty of Libertarian Thought," *PEGS Newsletter* 5(1):34–38 (Spring 1995).

Cottrell, Fred. *Energy and Society: The Relation Between Energy, Social Change, and Economic Development* (New York: McGraw-Hill, 1955).

Cox, Richard H. *Locke on War and Peace* (Oxford: Oxford University Press, 1960).

Crosby, Alfred W. *Ecological Imperialism: The Biological Expansion of Europe, 900–1900* (New York: Cambridge University Press, 1986). [the fundamental role of ecological factors in New World history]

Czuczka, George. *Imprints of the Future: Politics and Individuation in Our Time* (Washington, D.C.: Daimon, 1987).

Dahl, Robert A. *After the Revolution?: Authority in a Good Society* (New Haven: Yale University Press, 1970).

_____. "On Removing Certain Impediments to Democracy in the United States," in Horwitz, pp. 234–256. [a capsule history of U.S. political development]

_____. *Democracy and Its Critics* (New Haven: Yale University Press, 1989).

Daly, Herman E. *Steady-State Economics* (San Francisco: W. H. Freeman, 1977). [an outstanding discussion of ecological economics]

Daly, Herman E., and John B. Cobb, Jr. *For the Common Good: Redirecting the Economy Toward Community, the Environment, and a Sustainable Future* (Boston: Beacon, 1989). [a diagnosis and treatment based explicitly on the Christian prophetic tradition; relative to my own approach, expresses similar concerns, and even draws some similar conclusions, but very different in spirit]

Davis, W. Jackson. *The Seventh Year: Industrial Civilization in Transition* (New York: Norton, 1979).

Dawkins, Richard. *The Blind Watchmaker* (New York: Norton, 1986). [describes how the operation of simple and basic natural laws can over time produce complex organic systems]

De Leon, David. *The American as Anarchist: Reflections on an Indigenous Radicalism* (Baltimore: Johns Hopkins University Press, 1978). [describes how equality is eclipsing freedom, exactly as feared by de Tocqueville]

Devall, Bill, and George Sessions. *Deep Ecology: Living As If Nature Mattered* (Salt Lake City: Peregrine Smith, 1985). [an excellent review of the literature]

Diamond, Jared. *The Third Chimpanzee: The Evolution and Future of the Human Animal* (New York: HarperCollins, 1992). [an outstanding discussion of human biology and ecology]

Diamond, Stanley. *In Search of the Primitive: A Critique of Civilization* (New Brunswick: Transaction Books, 1974). [from an anthropological and Marxist perspective]

DiLucchio, Patrizia. "The Trouble with Health Care," *Whole Earth Review*, Fall 1993, pp. 88–89 [examines the ever higher expenditures being made for ever diminishing increments of life]

Dionne, E. J., Jr. *Why Americans Hate Politics* (New York: Simon & Schuster, 1991).

Dodds, E. R. *The Greeks and the Irrational* (Berkeley: University of California Press, 1964).

Dostoyevsky, Fyodor. *The Brothers Karamazov*, trans. Constance Garnett (New York: Signet, 1957).

Drexler, K. Eric, et al. *Unbounding the Future: The Nanotechnology Revolution* (New York: Wm. Morrow, 1991).

Dumont, Louis. *Homo Hierarchicus: An Essay on the Caste System*, trans. Mark Sainsbury (Chicago: University of Chicago Press, 1970). [examines hierarchy as an inherent and necessary tendency of human association that cannot be suppressed without harm]

Edelman, Murray. *Constructing the Political Spectacle* (Chicago: University of Chicago Press, 1988).

Edgerton, Robert B. *Sick Societies: Challenging the Myth of Primitive Harmony* (New York: Free Press, 1992). [argues that socially maladaptive beliefs and practices are well-nigh universal, because human nature is refractory and human reason limited; so far, so good, but by confounding primal society and primitive agricultural society, Edgerton makes a fundamental category error, inasmuch as the two ways of life have entirely different social and psychological consequences]

Edgerton, Samuel Y., Jr. *The Renaissance Rediscovery of Linear Perspective* (New York: Basic, 1975). [a major milepost in the process of increasing abstraction]

Ehrenfeld, David. *The Arrogance of Humanism* (New York: Oxford University Press, 1981). [on the necessity of accepting natural limits]

Eiseley, Loren. *The Invisible Pyramid: A Naturalist Analyzes the Rocket Century* (New York: Scribner's, 1970). [see especially "The Last Magician," which argues for a wiser savagery]

Eliade, Mircea. *The Myth of the Eternal Return: Cosmos and History*, trans. Willard R. Trask (Princeton: Princeton University Press, 1971). [history in the light of myth]

Ellul, Jacques. *The Technological Society*, trans. John Wilkinson (New York: Vintage, 1964).

_____. *Propaganda: The Formation of Men's Attitudes*, trans. Konrad Kellen and Jean Lerner (New York: Knopf, 1969).

_____. *The Political Illusion*, trans. Konrad Kellen (New York: Vintage, 1972).

_____. *The Betrayal of the West*, trans. Matthew J. O'Connell (New York: Seabury, 1978).

_____. *The Technological Bluff*, trans. Geoffrey W. Bromiley (Grand Rapids: William B. Eerdmans, 1990). [the best way into Ellul's oeuvre: summarizes and extends his critique of modern technomania]

Engels, Frederick. *The Origin of the Family, Private Property and the State* (New York: International Publications, 1972). [a Marxist recension/adaptation of Morgan]

Epstein, Richard A. *Forbidden Grounds: The Case Against Employment Discrimination Laws* (Cambridge: Harvard University Press, 1992). [argues that using the law to enforce social policy is immoral, counterproductive, unconstitutional, and dangerous]

Etzioni, Amitai. *The Spirit of Community: Rights, Responsibilities, and the Communitarian Agenda* (New York: Crown, 1993). [manifesto for the restoration of morality and community—but with no explanation of how or why they decayed in the first place]

Evernden, Neil. *The Natural Alien: Humankind and Environment* (Toronto: University of Toronto Press, 1985).

Ewen, Stuart. *All Consuming Images: The Politics of Style in Contemporary Culture* (New York: Basic, 1988).

Fairfield, Roy P., ed. *The Federalist Papers* (Garden City: Anchor, 1966).

Fallows, James. *Breaking the Press* (New York: Pantheon, 1996). [argues that media expropriation of the political process exacerbates conflict and fosters cynicism]

Farb, Peter. *Man's Rise to Civilization as Shown by the Indians of North America from Primeval Times to the Coming of the Industrial State* (New York: Dutton, 1968).

Ferkiss, Victor. *The Future of Technological Civilization* (New York: George Braziller, 1974).

Feyerabend, Paul. *Science in a Free Society* (London: NLB, 1978).

_____. *Farewell to Reason* (London: Verso, 1987). [two representative works by a philosopher of science who has made a career out of exposing Science's ideological pretensions—ruthlessly and, at times, intemperately]

Fisher, Helen. *The Anatomy of Love: The Mysteries of Mating, Marriage, and Why We Stray* (New York: Ballantine, 1992). [delivers much more than the title promises—specifically, by explaining how the life of our savage ancestors fostered balance and equality, and how evolutionary logic continues to shape our psychology and behavior, especially with respect to sex and mating]

Flannery, Timothy Fridtjof. *The Future Eaters: An Ecological History of the Australasian Lands and People* (New York: Wm. Braziller, 1995). [an important book: the essential nature of the postmodern future—cultural involution that conforms to ecological and evolutionary principles—can be descried in its sobering account of the past]

Fox, Robin. *The Search for Society: Quest for a Biosocial Science and Morality* (New Brunswick: Rutgers University Press, 1989).

Freud, Sigmund. *Civilization and Its Discontents*, trans. James Strachey (New York: Norton, 1961).

Fromm, Erich. *To Have or to Be?* (New York: Harper & Row, 1976). [a distinguished psychologist's analysis of the essential question confronting modern civilization]

Frum, David. *Dead Right* (New York: Basic, 1994). [a sharp analysis of the hyperpluralist follies, and a droll critique of conservative cowardice]

Fukuyama, Francis. *The End of History and the Last Man* (New York: Free Press, 1992).

Fuller, R. Buckminster. *Utopia or Oblivion: The Prospects for Humanity* (New York: Bantam, 1969).

Galbraith, John K. *The Affluent Society* (Boston: Houghton Mifflin, 1958).

_____. *The New Industrial State* (Boston: Houghton Mifflin, 1967).

Galston, William A. *Liberal Purposes: Goods, Virtues, and Diversity in the Liberal State* (New York: Cambridge University Press, 1991). [asserts (correctly) that liberalism does indeed imply an idea of the good life, but then (reluctantly) concedes that this idea is being dissolved in the acids of modernity]

García Márquez, Gabriel. *One Hundred Years of Solitude*, trans. Gregory Rabassa (New York: Harper & Row, 1970).

Gardels, Nathan, ed. "The Last Modern Century," *New Perspectives Quarterly* 8:2 (Spring 1991). [a series of articles on spiritual vertigo and other portents of modernity's imminent demise]

_____. "Soul of the World Order," *New Perspectives Quarterly* 10:3 (Summer 1993). [argues that with the end of the Cold War, Islam and other non-Western traditions have begun to dispute the assumed universality of Western liberalism; a struggle for the soul of the new world order therefore impends]

Gardels, Nathan, and Leila Connors, eds. "Republic of the Image," *New Perspectives Quarterly* 11:3 (Summer 1994). [elucidates the media's impact on politics, culture, and mass psychology]

Garrett, Laurie. *The Coming Plague: Newly Emerging Diseases in a World Out of Balance* (New York: Farrar, Straus & Giroux, 1994). [argues that as technological medicine collides with ecological limits and evolutionary forces, new diseases emerge, old diseases reemerge, resistance to antibiotics grows, and public health decays]

Gaylin, Willard. "Faulty Diagnosis," *Harper's Magazine*, October 1993, pp. 57–64 [an incisive analysis of what ails the American health nonsystem]

Geertz, Clifford. *Local Knowledge: Further Essays in Interpretive Anthropology* (New York: Basic, 1983).

Glass, James M. "The Philosopher and the Shaman: The Political Vision as Incantation," *Political Theory* 2:181–196 (May 1974).

_____. "Political Theory as Therapy: Rousseau and the Presocial Origins of Consciousness," *Political Theory* 4:163–184 (May 1976).

_____. "Machiavelli's *Prince* and Alchemical Transformation," *Polity* 8:503–528 (Summer 1976).

Gordon, Suzanne. *Prisoners of Men's Dreams: Striking Out For a New Feminine Future* (Boston: Little, Brown, 1991).

Greeley, Andrew M. *No Bigger Than Necessary: An Alternative to Socialism, Capitalism, and Anarchy* (New York: Meridian, 1977). [a Catholic perspective on the modern problematique]

Grieder, William. *Who Will Tell the People: The Betrayal of American Democracy* (New York: Simon & Schuster, 1992).

Gross, Bertram. *Friendly Fascism: The New Face of Power in America* (New York: M. Evans, 1980).

Guéhenno, Jean-Marie. *The End of the Nation-State,* trans. Victoria Elliot (Minneapolis: University of Minnesota Press, 1995).

Gurr, Ted Robert. "On the Political Consequences of Scarcity and Decline," *International Studies Quarterly* 29:51–75 (1985).

Hacker, Andrew. *Two Nations: Black and White, Separate, Hostile, Unequal* (New York: Scribner's, 1992 [on the enduring character and terrible consequences of American racism]

Hardin, Garrett. *Living Within Limits: Ecology, Economics, and Population Taboos* (New York: Oxford University Press, 1993). [a trenchant statement of the neo-Malthusian case]

Hardison, O. B., Jr. *Entering the Maze: Identity and Change in Modern Culture* (New York: Oxford University Press, 1981). [a lively and wide-ranging discussion of the roots and future of American culture]

Harman, Willis W. *An Incomplete Guide to the Future* (San Francisco: San Francisco Book Co., 1976).

Harris, Jonathan M. "Ecological Economics: A New Perspective," *The Good Society* 5(3):18–21 (Fall 1995). [an excellent short review of the literature]

Harris, Marvin. *Cannibals and Kings: The Origins of Cultures* (New York: Random House, 1977). [describes how a vicious circle of population growth, intensified production, and environmental depletion has driven human history and created institutionalized violence, drudgery, exploitation, and oppression]

———. *Why Nothing Works: The Anthropology of Daily Life* (New York: Touchstone, 1987). [argues that as maintenance costs escalate, efficiency declines and energy despotism becomes inevitable]

Hartz, Louis. *The Liberal Tradition in America: An Interpretation of American Political Thought Since the Revolution* (New York: Harcourt Brace, 1955). [classic intellectual history]

Havel, Václav. *Living in Truth*, ed. Jan Vladislav (London: Faber & Faber, 1987).

———. *Summer Meditations*, trans. Paul Wilson (New York: Knopf, 1992). [a manifesto for a humane, postcommunist, postcapitalist political economy that is fundamentally Jeffersonian in spirit]

Hawken, Paul. *The Ecology of Commerce: A Declaration of Sustainability* (New York: HarperCollins, 1993). [explains how to make business more ecological, primarily by making market prices reflect the true costs of commercial transactions]

Hayek, F. A. *The Road to Serfdom* (Chicago: University of Chicago Press, 1944).

———. *The Constitution of Liberty* (Chicago: University of Chicago Press, 1960).

Heilbroner, Robert. *21st Century Capitalism* (New York: Norton, 1993). [argues that if capitalism survives at all, it is not likely to be the American version]

Henderson, Hazel. *Paradigms in Progress: Life Beyond Economics* (Indianapolis: Knowledge Systems, 1991). [calls for a neo-Aristotelian *oikonomia* based on solar energy; contains many references to the burgeoning literature]

Herrnstein, Richard J., and Charles Murray. *The Bell Curve* (New York: Free Press, 1994). [what has unfortunately been lost sight of in the furor caused by this work's alleged racism is that it clearly documents the emergence of a meritocracy along the lines foreshadowed by Young: a society stratified by socially selected "intelligence" that threatens in the end to become a genetically based caste system]

Hertsgaard, Mark. *On Bended Knee: The Press and the Reagan Presidency* (New York: Farrar, Straus & Giroux, 1988). [a chilling account of how media politics works: you *can* fool most of the people most of the time]

Hewlett, Sylvia Ann. *When the Bough Breaks: The Cost of Neglecting Our Children* (New York: Basic, 1991).

Higgins, Ronald. *The Seventh Enemy: The Human Factor in the Global Crisis* (New York: McGraw-Hill, 1978). [examines the management problem as the most intractable part of the environmental problematique]

Highwater, Jamake. *The Primal Mind: Vision and Reality in Indian America* (New York: Meridian, 1982). [delineates what the primal vision of life has to offer to an overcivilized humanity]

Hillman, James. *The Thought of the Heart*, Eranos Lectures No. 2 (Dallas: Spring Publications, 1984).

Himmelfarb, Gertrude. *The De-Moralization of Society: From Victorian Virtues to Modern Values* (New York: Vintage, 1996). [describes how far we have fallen in one hundred years]

Hirsch, Fred. *Social Limits to Growth* (Cambridge: Harvard University Press, 1976).

Hobbes, Thomas. *Leviathan, or the Matter, Forme and Power of a Commonwealth Ecclesiastical and Civil*, ed. Michael Oakeshott (New York: Collier, 1962).

Hobhouse, Henry. *Forces of Change: An Unorthodox View of History* (New York: Arcade, 1989).

Hobsbawm, Eric. *The Age of Extremes: A History of the World, 1914–1991* (New York: Pantheon, 1994).

Hofstadter, Richard. *The American Political Tradition and the Men Who Made It*, rev. ed. (New York: Knopf, 1979).

Hopkirk, Peter. *The Great Game* (New York: Kodansha International, 1992).

Horkheimer, Max. *Eclipse of Reason* (New York: Oxford University Press, 1947).

Horwitz, Robert H. *The Moral Foundations of the American Republic*, 2nd ed. (Charlottesville: University of Virginia Press, 1979).

Hughes, J. Donald. *Ecology in Ancient Civilizations* (Albuquerque: University of New Mexico, 1975).

Hughes, Robert. *Culture of Complaint: The Fraying of America* (New York: Oxford University Press, 1993). [an essential guide for the culturally perplexed: wittily demolishes both the would-be deconstructors and the hide-bound defenders of Western culture; modestly proposes a return to mutual tolerance, high standards, and genuine learning]

Hunter, James David. *Culture Wars: The Struggle to Define America* (New York: Basic, 1991). [an excellent analysis of contemporary factionalism in historical context]

Huntington, Samuel P. "The Clash of Civilizations?" *Foreign Affairs* 72(3):22–49 (Summer 1993). [argues that cultural differences will replace ideology and economics as the primary source of international conflict]

Huxley, Aldous. *Brave New World* (New York: Perennial, 1969).

———. *Island* (New York: Perennial, 1972). [Huxley's utopian answer to his own dystopia depicts a life of more experienced and wiser savagery]

Hyde, Lewis. *The Gift: Imagination and the Erotic Life of Property* (New York: Vintage, 1983). [argues that humans need to exchange gifts as well as buy and sell property]

Illich, Ivan. *Tools for Conviviality* (New York: Harper & Row, 1973).

———. *Toward a History of Needs* (Berkeley: Heyday Books, 1978).

Iyer, Raghavan. *The Moral and Political Thought of Mahatma Gandhi* (New York: Oxford University Press, 1973).

Jacobson, Norman. *Pride and Solace: The Function and Limits of Political Theory* (Berkeley: University of California Press, 1978). [a despairing account of political philosophy's decline in modern times]

Jantsch, Erich. *The Self-Organizing Universe: Scientific and Human Implications of the Emerging Paradigm of Evolution* (Elmsford: Pergamon, 1980).

Jaynes, Julian. *The Origin of Consciousness in the Breakdown of the Bicameral Mind* (Boston: Houghton Mifflin, 1982).

Jencks, Christopher, et al. *Inequality: A Reassessment of the Effect of Family and Schooling in America* (New York: Basic, 1972).

Johnson, Haynes. *Divided We Fall: Gambling with History in the Nineties* (New York: Norton, 1994).

Johnson, Paul. *Modern Times: The World from the Twenties to the Eighties* (New York: Perennial, 1985).

Jouvenel, Bertrand de. *On Power, Its Nature and the History of Its Growth*, trans. J. F. Huntingdon (New York: Viking, 1949).

Jung, Carl G. *Modern Man in Search of a Soul*, trans. W. S. Dell and Cary F. Baynes (New York: Harcourt, Brace & World, 1933).

_____. "The Spiritual Problem of Modern Man," in Jung's *Civilization in Transition*, trans. R.F.C. Hull (New York: Pantheon, 1964).

_____. *Memories, Dreams, Reflections*, ed. Aniela Jaffe, and trans. Richard and Clara Winston (New York: Vintage, 1965).

Jung, Carl G., et al. *Man and His Symbols* (Garden City: Doubleday, 1964).

Kahn, Herman, et al. *The Next 200 Years: A Scenario for America and the World* (New York: Wm. Morrow, 1976). [the ever-onward-and-upward scenario]

Kaplan, Robert D. "The Coming Anarchy," *Atlantic Monthly*, February 1994, pp. 44–76 [a short and sobering look at "how scarcity, crime, overpopulation, tribalism, and disease are rapidly destroying the social fabric of our planet"]

Kariel, Henry S. *Beyond Liberalism* (Novato: Chandler & Sharp, 1977).

Kassiola, Joel Jay. *The Death of Industrial Civilization: The Limits to Economic Growth and the Repoliticization of Advanced Industrial Society* (Albany: SUNY Press, 1990).

Kaus, Mickey. *The End of Equality* (New York: Basic, 1992). [a harsh critique of "money liberals" and "money equality" that is trenchant and illuminating in part, but that largely reinvents the wheel: astonishingly, for a work dedicated to the goal of "civic equality," it contains not a single reference to Rousseau or Jefferson, and only one insignificant reference to de Tocqueville!]

Keegan, John. *A History of Warfare* (New York: Knopf, 1993). [describes how we have moved from limited war to Clausewitzian total war that cannot be politically controlled]

Kennedy, Paul. *The Rise and Fall of the Great Powers* (New York: Vintage, 1989).

_____. *Preparing for the Twenty-First Century* (New York: Random House, 1993). [analyzes the sweeping commercial, demographic, environmental, and technological factors that will transform world politics in the next century; an important complement to the previous work]

Keynes, John Maynard. "Economic Possibilities for Our Grandchildren," in Keynes's *Essays in Persuasion* (New York: Norton, 1963).

Kitto, H.D.F. *The Greeks* (Harmondsworth: Penguin, 1957). [the glory that was Greece in a nutshell]

Koch, Adrienne. *The Philosophy of Thomas Jefferson* (Chicago: Quadrangle, 1964).

Kohr, Leopold. *The Breakdown of Nations* (New York: Dutton, 1978). [a size theory of history and politics: argues (without reference to Rousseau or Jefferson!) that the solution to nearly all forms of "social misery," including war, is the dismemberment of large social units, from the city to the modern centralized state]

Konner, Melvin. *The Tangled Wing: Biological Constraints on the Human Spirit* (New York: Perennial, 1983). [an outstanding examination of human nature in the light of current biological and anthropological knowledge; more technical than Jared Diamond]

Koyré, Alexandre. *From the Closed World to the Infinite Universe* (Baltimore: Johns Hopkins University Press, 1957).

Kristol, Irving. *Two Cheers for Capitalism* (New York: Basic, 1978). [the neoconservative case in a nutshell]

Kuhn, Thomas S. *The Structure of Scientific Revolutions,* 2nd ed. (Chicago: Phoenix, 1970).

Kumar, Krishan. *Prophecy and Progress: A Sociology of Industrial and Post-Industrial Society* (Harmondsworth: Penguin, 1978). [an important critical analysis of the "postindustrial" thesis; picks up the story where Polanyi leaves off]

Lacqueur, Walter. *A Continent Astray: Europe 1970–78* (New York: Oxford University Press, 1979). [a "reassertion of authority" impends there too]

Lane, Robert E. *The Market Experience* (Cambridge: Cambridge University Press, 1991). [argues that a market economy does not foster human happiness or self-development]

Langbein, John H. "Torture and Plea Bargaining," *Public Interest* 58:43–61 (Winter 1980).

Lao Tsu. *Tao Te Ching,* trans. Gia-Fu Feng and Jane English (New York: Vintage, 1972).

Lasch, Christopher. *The Culture of Narcissism: American Life in an Age of Diminishing Expectations* (New York: Norton, 1978).

Lazare, Daniel. *The Frozen Republic: How the Constitution Is Paralyzing Democracy* (New York: Harcourt Brace, 1996). [an excellent diagnosis, but offers dangerous and already obsolete solutions (for an ecological, electronic age)]

Leakey, Richard, and Roger Lewin. *The Sixth Extinction: Patterns of Life and the Future of Humankind* (New York: Doubleday, 1995). [this cutting-edge ecological-evolutionary theory supports a forecast of vast extinctions]

Le Bon, Gustave. *The Crowd: A Study of the Popular Mind* (New York: Viking, 1960).

Lee, Dorothy. *Freedom and Culture* (Englewood Cliffs: Spectrum, 1959). [very good on equality in primal culture]

Leiss, William. *The Domination of Nature* (New York: George Braziller, 1972).

_____. *The Limits to Satisfaction: An Essay on the Problem of Needs and Commodities* (Toronto: University of Toronto Press, 1976).

Leonard, George B. *The Transformation: A Guide to the Inevitable Changes in Humankind* (New York: Delta, 1972). [the crisis of civilization from a "New Age" perspective]

Lévi-Strauss, Claude. *The Savage Mind* (Chicago: University of Chicago Press, 1966).

_____. *Tristes Tropiques*, trans. John and Doreen Weightman (New York: Atheneum, 1974). [a subtle and profound meditation on savagery and civilization, contrasting the vitality of the former with the entropy of the latter]

Lindblom, Charles E. *Politics and Markets: The World's Political-Economic System* (New York: Basic, 1977).

Lindner, Staffan B. *The Harried Leisure Class* (New York: Columbia University Press, 1970).

Lippmann, Walter. *The Public Philosophy* (Boston: Little, Brown, 1955).

Locke, John. *Two Treatises of Government*, ed. Peter Laslett (New York: Mentor, 1965).

Lovelock, James. *The Ages of Gaia: A Biography of Our Living Earth* (New York: Norton, 1988).

_____. *Healing Gaia: Practical Medicine for the Planet* (New York: Harmony Books, 1991).

Lovins, Amory B. *Soft Energy Paths: Toward a Durable Peace* (New York: Harper & Row, 1977). [on the relationship of energy to politics, economics, etc.]

Lowi, Theodore. *The End of Liberalism: The Second Republic of the United States,* 2nd ed. (New York: Norton, 1979). [on the rise of the administrative state]

Lukacs, John A. *The Passing of the Modern Age* (New York: Harper & Row, 1970).

Luttwak, Edward N. *The Endangered American Dream: How to Stop the United States from Becoming a Third World Country and How to Win the Geo-Economic Struggle for Industrial Supremacy* (New York: Simon & Schuster, 1993).

Lutz, Mark, and Kenneth Lux. *Humanistic Economics: The New Challenge* (New York: Bootstrap Press, 1988).

Lux, Kenneth. *Adam Smith's Mistake: How a Moral Philosopher Invented Economics and Ended Morality* (Boston: Shambhala, 1990). [heaps too much blame on Smith]

Machiavelli, Niccolò. *The Prince and Other Works*, trans. Allen H. Gilbert (New York: Hendricks House, 1964).

MacIntyre, Alasdair. *After Virtue: A Study in Moral Theory,* 2nd ed. (Notre Dame: Notre Dame University Press, 1984). [the problem of moral entropy from an Aristotelian viewpoint]

Macpherson, C. B. *The Political Theory of Possessive Individualism: Hobbes to Locke* (New York: Oxford University Press, 1962).

_____. *Democratic Theory: Essays in Retrieval* (New York: Oxford University Press, 1973).

Malabre, Alfred L., Jr. *Beyond Our Means: How Reckless Borrowing Now Threatens to Overwhelm Us* (New York: Vintage, 1988).

Mansbridge, Jane J. *Beyond Adversary Democracy* (New York: Basic, 1980).

Manuel, Frank E., and Fritzie P. Manuel. *Utopian Thought in the Western World* (Cambridge: Belknap, 1979). [on the "utopian propensity" of Western thought]

Marcuse, Herbert. *One-Dimensional Man* (Boston: Beacon, 1964). [a flawed but nevertheless interesting critique of modern civilization from a Marxist-Freudian perspective]

Margolis, Michael. *Viable Democracy* (New York: St. Martin's, 1979).

Martin, Calvin Luther. *In the Spirit of the Earth: Rethinking History and Time* (Baltimore: Johns Hopkins University Press, 1992). [on the arrogance of civilization]

Marx, Karl. *The Economic and Philosophic Manuscripts of 1844,* ed. Dirk J. Struik (New York: International, 1964). [although the Marxist solution has been utterly discredited, Marx is still essential reading (especially these early essays): due to economic globalization, his analysis of capitalism's contradictions may be more pertinent than ever]

Marx, Leo. *The Machine in the Garden: Technology and the Pastoral Ideal in America* (New York: Oxford University Press, 1964).

Matthews, Richard K. *The Radical Politics of Thomas Jefferson: A Revisionist View* (Lawrence: University of Kansas Press, 1984).

May, Rollo. *Love and Will* (New York: Norton, 1969). [on the importance of Eros]

Maybury-Lewis, David. *Millennium: Tribal Wisdom and the Modern World* (New York: Viking Penguin, 1992).

McGlashan, Alan. *The Savage and Beautiful Country* (Boston: Houghton Mifflin, 1967). [a poetic manifesto for consciousness revolution: let us explore the savage and beautiful country of the human psyche]

McHarg, Ian. *Design with Nature* (Garden City: Natural History Press, 1969). [the science, poetry, and practice of ecology in a nutshell]

McKeown, Thomas. *The Role of Medicine: Dream, Mirage, or Nemesis?* (Princeton: Princeton University Press, 1979). [describes how improved health and increased longevity resulted from nutritional, behavioral, and environmental changes, not medical treatment]

McLuhan, Marshall. *Understanding Media: The Extensions of Man* (New York: McGraw-Hill, 1964).

McLuhan, T. C., ed. *Touch the Earth: A Self-Portrait of Indian Existence* (New York: Touchstone, 1971). [the savages speak for themselves with wit and humanity]

McNeill, William H. *The Rise of the West: A History of the Human Community* (Chicago: University of Chicago Press, 1963).

_____. *Polyethnicity and National Unity in World History* (Toronto: University of Toronto Press, 1986).

McWilliams, Wilson Carey. *The Idea of Fraternity in America* (Berkeley: University of California Press, 1973).

Meadows, Donella H. "Whole Earth Models & Systems," *The CoEvolution Quarterly*, Summer 1982, pp. 98–108 [a brief but comprehensive explanation of the systems paradigm]

Meadows, Donella H., et al. *Beyond the Limits: Confronting Global Collapse, Envisioning a Sustainable Future* (Post Mills: Chelsea Green, 1992). [a revision of the classic *Limits to Growth* that reaffirms not only its methods and conclusions but also its call to action]

Melville, Herman. *Moby-Dick or, the Whale* (Berkeley: University of California Press, 1981).

Merchant, Carolyn. *The Death of Nature: Women, Ecology, and the Scientific Revolution* (New York: Harper & Row, 1980). [a first-rate intellectual history from a feminist perspective that illuminates the intrinsic violence of modern thought]

Meyrowitz, Joshua. *No Sense of Place: The Impact of Electronic Media on Social Behavior* (New York: Oxford University Press, 1985).

Mill, John Stuart. *On Liberty*, ed. Alburey Castell (New York: Appleton-Century-Crofts, 1947).

Miller, Mark Crispin. *Boxed In: The Culture of TV* (Evanston: Northwestern University Press, 1988).

Minogue, Kenneth R. *The Liberal Mind* (New York: Vintage, 1968). [examines the many confusions, ambiguities, and contradictions in liberal thought]

Montaigne, Michel de. *Essays*, trans. J. M. Cohen (Harmondsworth: Penguin, 1958). [to read Montaigne is to understand the difference between rationalism and reason]

Morgan, Lewis Henry. *Ancient Society*, ed. Eleanor Burke Leacock (New York: World, 1963 [1877]). [a classic treatment of the transition from primal to civilized life that is still valuable despite being overtaken in many details by more recent scholarship]

Moynihan, Daniel Patrick. *Pandaemonium: Ethnicity in International Politics* (New York: Oxford University Press, 1993).

Mumford, Lewis. *The Transformations of Man* (London: George Allen & Unwin, 1957).

_____. *Technics and Human Development* (New York: Harvest, 1967).

_____. *The Pentagon of Power* (New York: Harvest, 1970).

Myers, Norman, ed. *GAIA: An Atlas of Planetary Management* (Garden City: Anchor, 1984). [an excellent primer of human ecology, albeit one flawed by the delusion that we can "manage" the biosphere]

Neumann, Erich. *The Origins and History of Consciousness*, trans. R. F. C. Hull (Princeton: Princeton University Press, 1970).

_____. *Depth Psychology and a New Ethic*, trans. Eugene Rolfe (New York: Harper & Row, 1973).

Newman, Katherine S. *Declining Fortunes: The Withering of the American Dream* (New York: Basic, 1993). [on the breakdown of the American social contract]

Nietzsche, Friedrich. *The Birth of Tragedy and the Genealogy of Morals*, trans. Francis Golffing (Garden City: Anchor, 1956).

Nisbet, Robert A. *The Quest for Community* (New York: Oxford University Press, 1953). [on the destruction of the "little platoons" and its aftermath]

_____. *History of the Idea of Progress* (New York: Basic, 1980).

Nye, Joseph S., Jr. *Bound to Lead: The Changing Nature of American Power* (New York: Basic, 1990).

Odajnyk, Volodymyr Walter. *Jung and Politics: The Political and Social Ideas of C. G. Jung* (New York: NYU Press, 1976).

Odum, Howard T., and Elisabeth C. Odum. *Energy Basis for Man and Nature* (New York: McGraw-Hill, 1976).

Ogilvy, James A. *Many Dimensional Man: Decentralizing Self, Society, and the Sacred* (New York: Oxford University Press, 1977). [a manifesto for greater personal and social self-consciousness as the antidote to secular monotheism]

Oldenburg, Ray. *The Great Good Place* (New York: Paragon House, 1989). [argues that the physical isolation of American life reflects our social isolation: there is no longer any place where community can happen]

Olson, Mancur. *The Rise and Decline of Nations: Economic Growth, Stagflation, and Social Rigidities* (New Haven: Yale University Press, 1982). [an excellent analysis of how and why the public good and the private good are at war, and why the latter wins out; but the failure to acknowledge and profit from Rousseau's discussion of the general will as opposed to the will of all is unfortunately symbolic of the way contemporary social science slights the tradition from which it emerged]

Ong, Walter J. *Orality and Literacy: The Technologizing of the Word* (New York: Methuen, 1982).

Ophuls, William. *Ecology and the Politics of Scarcity: Prologue to a Political Theory of the Steady State* (San Francisco: W. H. Freeman, 1977).

Ophuls, William, and A. Stephen Boyan, Jr. *Ecology and the Politics of Scarcity Revisited: The Unraveling of the American Dream* (New York: W. H. Freeman, 1992). [revision of the above, with an Afterword that responds to my critics]

Ornstein, Robert. *The Evolution of Consciousness* (New York: Simon & Schuster, 1991). [argues that, because it evolved in an ad hoc way to cope with primal conditions, the human mind is poorly adapted for life in complex civilizations]

Orr, David W. *Ecological Literacy: Education and the Transition to a Postmodern World* (Albany: SUNY Press, 1992). [what we need to know about living in the age of ecology]

Ortega y Gasset, José. *The Revolt of the Masses* (New York: Norton, 1957).

Orwell, George. *Nineteen Eighty-Four* (New York: Signet, 1961).

_____. *Animal Farm* (San Diego: Harcourt Brace Jovanovich, 1990). [the definitive critique of the revolutionary delusion]

Padover, Saul K., ed. *Thomas Jefferson on Democracy* (New York: Appleton-Century-Crofts, 1939).

Paglia, Camille. *Sexual Personae: Art and Decadence from Nefertiti to Emily Dickinson* (New Haven: Yale University Press, 1990). [invaluable despite its flaws and outrages: insists on the autonomous power of sex and nature and the consequent necessity to deal realistically, rather than ideologically or idealistically, with them]

Pangle, Thomas L. *The Ennobling of Democracy: The Challenge of the Postmodern Era* (Baltimore: Johns Hopkins University Press, 1992).

Peterson, Wallace C. *Silent Depression: The Fate of the American Dream* (New York: Norton, 1994). [amply documents middle-class decline]

Pfaff, William. *Barbarian Sentiments: How the American Century Ends* (New York: Hill & Wang, 1990). [argues that America's loss of power and influence is largely due to the nation's long-established preference for fantasy over reality in foreign policy]

Phillips, Kevin P. *Post-Conservative America: People, Politics, and Ideology in a Time of Crisis* (New York: Random House, 1982). [on the prospect of "apple-pie authoritarianism"]

_____. *The Politics of Rich and Poor: Wealth and the American Electorate in the Reagan Aftermath* (New York: Random House, 1990). [on the decline of the middle class and its implications]

_____. *Boiling Point: Democrats, Republicans, and the Decline of Middle-Class Prosperity* (New York: Random House, 1993). [argues that a crisis of legitimacy impends as the era of American exceptionalism ends]

_____. *Arrogant Capital: Washington, Wall Street, and the Frustration of American Politics* (Boston: Little, Brown, 1994). [calls for a Jeffersonian revolution to sweep out the entrenched antidemocratic interests that support a permanent government]

Pimm, Stuart L. *The Balance of Nature: Ecological Issues in the Conservation of Species and Communities* (Chicago: University of Chicago Press, 1991). [on extinction as a biological chain reaction]

Plato. *The Republic of Plato*, trans. Allan Bloom (New York: Basic, 1968).

Polak, Frederik L. *The Image of the Future* (New York: Oceana, 1961).

Polanyi, Karl. *The Great Transformation* (Boston: Beacon, 1957).

Pole, J. R. *The Pursuit of Equality in American History* (Berkeley: University of California Press, 1993).

Ponting, Clive. *A Green History of the World: The Environment and the Collapse of Great Civilizations* (New York: St. Martin's, 1993).

Pool, Ithiel de Sola. *Technologies Without Boundaries: On Communications in a Global Age* (Cambridge: Harvard University Press, 1990).

Porter, Bruce D. "Parkinson's Law Revisited: War and the Growth of American Government," *Public Interest* 60:50–68 (Summer 1980).

Porter, Michael E. *The Competitive Advantage of Nations* (New York: Free Press, 1990). [Porter's exhaustive analysis of the factors underlying economic competitiveness in today's global economy lends weight to the fears of the so-called declinists]

Postman, Neil. *Amusing Ourselves to Death: Public Discourse in the Age of Show Business* (New York: Viking, 1985).

_____. *Technopoly: The Surrender of Culture to Technology* (New York: Knopf, 1992). [very good on the ideological content and implications of technology; also contains an interesting proposal for curriculum reform that would foster better understanding and management of it]

Putnam, Robert D. "Bowling Alone: America's Declining Social Capital," *Journal of Democracy* 6(1):65–78 (January 1995) [on the precipitous decline of participation in civic associations of every kind, especially political]

Quinn, Daniel. *Ishmael* (New York: Bantam, 1992).

Rank, Otto. *Beyond Psychology* (New York: Dover, 1941).

Raschke, Carl A. *The Interruption of Eternity: Modern Gnosticism and the Origins of the New Religious Consciousness* (Chicago: Nelson-Hall, 1980).

Rauch, Jonathan. *Demosclerosis: The Silent Killer of American Government* (New York: Times Books, 1995).

Ravitch, Diane. "Multiculturalism: E Pluribus Plures," *American Scholar* 59:337–354 (Summer 1990).

Reader, John. *Man on Earth: A Celebration of Mankind* (New York: Perennial, 1990). [a first-rate overview of human ecology; focuses on the exquisite balance between culture and nature, and on what it takes to maintain it]

Reich, Charles A. *Opposing the System* (New York: Crown, 1995). [analyzes the political and social tyranny of an out-of-control economic machine and explains what to do about it]

Reich, Robert B. *The Work of Nations: Preparing Ourselves for 21st-Century Capitalism* (New York: Knopf, 1991).

Richter, Horst-Eberhard. *All Mighty: A Study of the God Complex in Western Man*, trans. Jan van Heurck (Claremont: Hunter House, 1984). [on the megalomania of modern culture]

Riesman, David, Nathan Glazer, and Reuel Denney. *The Lonely Crowd: A Study of the Changing American Character* (New Haven: Yale University Press, 1961). [the sociological classic that gave the phrase to the language]

Rifkin, Jeremy. *Entropy: A New World View* (New York: Viking, 1980).

_____. *Biosphere Politics: A Cultural Odyssey from the Middle Ages to the New Age* (San Francisco: HarperCollins, 1991). [a useful and detailed but often sketchy narrative of the growth of the modern power complex that unfortunately ends by begging almost all the hard political questions]

Robertson, James. *The Sane Alternative: A Choice of Futures* (St. Paul: River Basin, 1979). [on the transition to an ecological future]

Rosenberg, Nathan, and L. E. Birdzell, Jr. *How the West Grew Rich: The Economic Transformation of the Industrial World* (New York: Basic, 1986).

Rossiter, Clinton L. *Constitutional Dictatorship: Crisis Government in the Modern Democracies* (Princeton: Princeton University Press, 1948). [on the function and necessity of constitutional dictatorship even in democracies]

Rossiter, Clinton L., and James Lare. *The Essential Lippman: A Political Philosophy for Liberal Democracy* (New York: Random House, 1963).

Rothfeder, Jeffrey. *Privacy for Sale: How Computerization Has Made Everyone's Private Life an Open Secret* (New York: Simon & Schuster, 1992).

Rousseau, Jean-Jacques. *The First and Second Discourses*, trans. Roger D. and Judith R. Masters (New York: St. Martin's, 1964).

_____. *On the Social Contract*, trans. Judith R. Masters, and ed. Roger D. Masters (New York: St. Martin's, 1978).

_____. *Emile, or On Education*, trans. Allan Bloom (New York: Basic, 1979).

Rubenstein, Richard L. *The Cunning of History: The Holocaust and the American Future* (New York: Harper Colophon, 1978). [examines the Holocaust as a logical consequence of the marriage of Judeo-Christian domination to the rationalism and secularism of the Enlightenment]

Rushdie, Salman. *The Satanic Verses* (Dover: The Consortium, 1992).

Ryan, Charles J. "The Overdeveloped Society," *The Stanford Magazine*, Fall/Winter 1979, pp. 58–65

_____. "The Choices in the Next Energy and Social Revolution," *Technological Forecasting and Social Change* 16:191–208 (1980).

Sagan, Eli. *At the Dawn of Tyranny: The Origins of Individualism, Political Oppression, and the State* (New York: Knopf, 1985). [a psychoanalysis of the complex societies (petty kingdoms) that were the intermediate stage between the primal and the civilized state]

Sahlins, Marshall. *Stone-Age Economics* (Chicago: Aldine-Atherton, 1970).

_____. *Culture and Practical Reason* (Chicago: University of Chicago Press, 1976).

Sale, Kirkpatrick. *Human Scale* (New York: Coward, McCann & Geoghegan, 1980). [argues that bigger is *not* better]

_____. *Dwellers in the Land: A Bioregional Vision* (San Francisco: Sierra Club, 1985).

Samuelson, Robert J. *The Good Life and Its Discontents: The American Dream in the Age of Entitlement, 1945–1995* (New York: Times Books, 1995). [as the dream collides with reality, the hubris of postwar America is pitilessly revealed]

Sandel, Michael. "Post-National Democracy vs. Electronic Bonapartism," *New Perspectives Quarterly* 9(4):4–8 (Fall 1992).

_____. *Democracy's Discontent: America in Search of a Public Philosophy* (Cambridge: Belknap Press, 1996). [an outstanding discussion of the tension between the democratic and republican conceptions of freedom: explains why a merely procedural, value-neutral polity must fail, even in its own terms; and why we therefore need a genuine public philosophy to orient us and guide us toward the good life]

Santillana, Giorgio de, and Hertha von Durchend. *Hamlet's Mill: An Essay on Myth and the Frame of Time* (Boston: Gambit, 1969).

Saul, John Ralston. *Voltaire's Bastards: The Dictatorship of Reason in the West* (New York: Free Press, 1992).

Schlesinger, Arthur M., Jr. *The Cycles of American History* (Boston: Houghton Mifflin, 1986).

_____. *The Disuniting of America: Reflections on a Multicultural Society* (New York: Norton, 1992).

Schlossstein, Steven. *The End of the American Century* (New York: Congdon & Weed, 1989).

Schmookler, Andrew Bard. *The Parable of the Tribes: The Problem of Power in Social Evolution* (Boston: Houghton Mifflin, 1984). [a neo-Hobbesian analysis of human civilization]

Schor, Juliet B. *The Overworked American: The Unexpected Decline of Leisure* (New York: Basic, 1992).

Schumacher, E. F. *Small Is Beautiful: Economics as if People Mattered* (New York: Harper & Row, 1973). [delineates basic economic principles for a materially frugal but spiritually rich steady-state society]

Schumpeter, Joseph A. *Capitalism, Socialism and Democracy* (New York: Harper & Row, 1975). [still one of the best analyses of capitalism's dilemmas and contradictions]

Schwartz, Barry. *The Costs of Living: How Market Freedom Erodes the Best Things in Life* (New York: Norton, 1944).

Scitovsky, Tibor. *The Joyless Economy: An Inquiry into Human Satisfaction and Consumer Dissatisfaction* (New York: Oxford University Press, 1976).

Sennett, Richard. *The Fall of Public Man* (New York: Knopf, 1977).

Shepard, Paul. *The Tender Carnivore and the Sacred Game* (New York: Scribner's, 1973).

_____. *Nature and Madness* (San Francisco: Sierra Club, 1982).

Slater, Philip. *The Pursuit of Loneliness: American Culture at the Breaking Point* (Boston: Beacon, 1970).

_____. *Earthwalk* (Garden City: Anchor, 1974). [together with the above, one of the best critiques of the fundamental inhumanity of modern American life]

Smith, Adam. *An Inquiry into the Nature and Causes of the Wealth of Nations*, ed. Edwin Cannan (New York: Modern Library, 1937).

Smith, Anthony. *The Geopolitics of Information: How Western Culture Dominates the World* (New York: Oxford University Press, 1980).

Smith, Steven B. *Hegel's Critique of Liberalism: Rights in Context* (Chicago: University of Chicago Press, 1989). [illuminates many problems and contradictions in the liberal tradition to which I only allude; particularly good in showing how liberalism justifies itself by a conceptual sleight of hand, asserting that a life of possessive individualism is somehow "natural"]

Sommers, Christina Hoff. *Who Stole Feminism? How Women Have Betrayed Women* (New York: Simon & Schuster, 1994). [a devastating deconstruction of "gender feminism"]

Sowell, Thomas. *A Conflict of Visions: Ideological Origins of Political Struggles* (New York: Wm. Morrow, 1987). [analyzes the fundamental cleavage within American politics between the liberal and democratic tendencies]

Spragens, Thomas A., Jr. *The Irony of Liberal Reason* (Chicago: University of Chicago Press, 1981). [argues that the "impoverished philosophy" of "positivistic rationalism" is the direct cause of the "irrationalist" barbarism of our times]

Steele, Shelby. *The Content of Our Character: A New Vision of Race in America* (New York: St. Martin's, 1990).

_____. "The New Sovereignty: Grievance Groups Have Become Nations unto Themselves," *Harper's Magazine*, July 1992, pp. 47–54 [describes how factionalism has become politically entrenched in the universities]

Steiner, George. *In Bluebeard's Castle: Some Notes Toward the Redefinition of Culture* (New Haven: Yale University Press, 1971). [argues that modern civilization is disintegrating not because it hasn't achieved its goals but precisely because it has]

Stevens, Anthony. *Archetypes: A Natural History of the Self* (New York: Wm. Morrow, 1982).

Storing, Herbert J., ed. *The Complete Anti-Federalist*, Vol. I: *What the Anti-Federalists Were* For (Chicago: University of Chicago Press, 1981).

Tainter, Joseph A. *The Collapse of Complex Societies* (New York: Cambridge University Press, 1988). [a masterwork that provides deep insight into the civilizational process]

Tarnas, Richard. *The Passion of the Western Mind: Understanding the Ideas That Have Shaped Our World View* (New York: Harmony Books, 1991). [describes how the Western intellectual tradition has gradually and completely deconstructed itself; Tarnas's solution, similar in spirit to mine, is the recovery of the deep feminine]

Tawney, R. H. *The Acquisitive Society* (New York: Harcourt, Brace & World, 1920).

_____. *Equality* (New York: Capricorn, 1961).

Taylor, Gordon Rattray. *Rethink: A Paraprimitive Solution* (New York: Dutton, 1973). [more critique than solution, but seeks to combine the material advantages of technological society with the social advantages of premodern society]

Templeton, Kenneth S., Jr., ed. *The Politicization of Society* (Indianapolis: Liberty Press, 1979). [various authors on creeping despotism]

Thompson, Dennis F. *The Democratic Citizen: Social Science and Democratic Theory in the Twentieth Century* (London: Cambridge University Press, 1970).

Thompson, W. D'Arcy. *On Growth and Form* (Cambridge: Cambridge University Press, 1942).

Thompson, William Irwin. *Pacific Shift* (San Francisco: Sierra Club, 1985). [a provocative speculation on the shape of the emerging global culture]

Thoreau, Henry David. *Walden and Other Writings*, ed. Joseph Wood Krutch (New York: Bantam, 1962).

Thucydides. *The Complete Writings of Thucydides: The Peloponnesian War*, trans. Richard Crawley (New York: Modern Library, 1951). [describes how Athens went from Periclean glory to Hobbesian anarchy in little more than a generation]

Thurow, Lester C. *The Zero-Sum Society: Distribution and the Possibilities for Economic Change* (Harmondsworth: Penguin, 1981).

_____. *Head to Head: The Coming Economic Battle Among Japan, Europe, and America* (New York: Wm. Morrow, 1992). [sets forth the current economic facts of life, both domestic and international, with clarity and force, describing the enormous difficulty of economic development in our time and the radical reforms necessary to forestall continued American decline]

_____. *The Future of Capitalism: How Today's Economic Forces Shape Tomorrow's World* (New York: Wm. Morrow, 1996). [describes the "tectonic" movements that are undermining the economic and social basis for liberal democracy]

Tocqueville, Alexis de. *Democracy in America*, ed. Richard D. Heffner (New York: Mentor, 1956). [an abridgement of the classic Reeves-Bowen translation that contains the essential de Tocqueville; however, I have taken an occasional quote from other translations]

Toffler, Alvin, and Heidi Toffler. *Creating a New Civilization: The Politics of the Third Wave* (Atlanta: Turner Publishing, 1995). [briefly sketches the impact of the information age on politics; insightful, at least in part, but better on the nature of the wave than on the political implications]

Torgovnick, Marianna. *Gone Primitive: Savage Intellects, Modern Lives* (Chicago: University of Chicago Press, 1990). [examines the tangled thicket of colonial pretensions, ideological attitudes, and unconscious projections that contaminate the West's uneasy relationship to the primitive]

Toulmin, Stephen. *Cosmopolis: The Hidden Agenda of Modernity* (Chicago: University of Chicago Press, 1990). [a revisionist intellectual history of the modern age; attempts to rescue reason from the current morass of hyperrationality by resurrecting the balanced, skeptical, humane spirit of the sixteenth century]

Toynbee, Arnold. *Mankind and Mother Earth: A Narrative History of the World* (New York: Oxford University Press, 1976).

Tuchman, Barbara W. *A Distant Mirror: The Calamitous 14th Century* (New York: Ballantine, 1979).

_____. *The March of Folly: From Troy to Vietnam* (New York: Knopf, 1984).

Tucker, Robert C. *The Marx-Engels Reader,* 2nd ed. (New York: Norton, 1978).

Turner, Frederick. *Beyond Geography: The Western Spirit Against the Wilderness* (New York: Viking, 1980). [argues that estrangement and domination are characteristic of the West's relation to nature]

Twitchell, James B. *Carnival Culture: The Trashing of Taste in America* (New York: Columbia University Press, 1992). [argues that mass-mediated idiocy and vulgarity have triumphed so completely that the latter category has effectively ceased to exist]

Unamuno, Miguel de. *Tragic Sense of Life*, trans. J. E. Crawford Flitch (New York: Dover, 1954).

Veblen, Thorstein. *The Theory of the Leisure Class* (New York: New American Press, 1963). [the definitive treatment of human insatiability due to the drive for superiority]

Vickers, Geoffrey. *Freedom in a Rocking Boat: Changing Values in an Unstable Society* (Harmondsworth: Penguin, 1972). [examines modern politics from a systems perspective; finds numerous social traps, vicious circles, and positive feedback loops causing unprecedented instability]

Wachtel, Paul L. *The Poverty of Affluence: A Psychological Portrait of the American Way of Life* (Philadelphia: New Society, 1989).

Wagar, W. Warren. *A Short History of the Future* (Chicago: University of Chicago Press, 1989). [an interesting speculation that explores three possible futures: capitalist, socialist, and ecological]

Wallerstein, Immanuel. *The Capitalist World-Economy* (Cambridge: Cambridge University Press, 1979).

Walzer, Michael. *Spheres of Justice: A Defense of Pluralism and Equality* (New York: Basic, 1983). [describes how to achieve "complex" equality by ending domination without at the same time repressing differences]

Watts, Alan W. *Nature, Man, and Woman* (New York: Vintage, 1970). [contrasts Western hostility to nature with Eastern traditions that honor it]

Webb, Walter Prescott. *The Great Frontier* (Boston: Houghton Mifflin, 1952).

Weber, Max. *The Protestant Ethic and the Spirit of Capitalism*, trans. Talcott Parsons (New York: Charles Scribner's Sons, 1958).

_____. *From Max Weber: Essays in Sociology*, trans. and ed. H. H. Gerth and C. Wright Mills (New York: Galaxy, 1958).

Weiner, Tim. *Blank Check: The Pentagon's Black Budget* (Waltham: Little, Brown, 1991).

Weizenbaum, Joseph. *Computer Power and Human Reason: From Judgment to Calculation* (San Francisco: W. H. Freeman, 1976). [on the limits and dangers of computational rationality]

Whitehead, Alfred North. *Science and the Modern World* (New York: Macmillan, 1925).

_____. *Modes of Thought* (New York: Free Press, 1968).

Whitehead, Barbara Dafoe. "Dan Quayle Was Right," *Atlantic Monthly*, April 1993, pp. 47–84. [broken families produce broken children]

Whitmont, Edward C. *Return of the Goddess: Femininity, Aggression, and the Modern Grail Quest* (London: Routledge & Kegan Paul, 1983). [an exploration of deep feminism from a Jungian perspective]

Wiener, Norbert. *The Human Use of Human Beings: Cybernetics and Society* (Boston: Houghton Mifflin, 1954). [the seminal work]

Wilkinson, Richard G. *Poverty and Progress: An Ecological Perspective on Economic Development* (New York: Praeger, 1973).

Will, George F. *Statecraft as Soulcraft: What Government Does* (New York: Touchstone, 1983).

Williams, Rosalind. *Notes on the Underground: An Essay on Technology, Society, and the Imagination* (Cambridge: MIT Press, 1990).

Williams, William Appleton. *Empire as a Way of Life: An Essay on the Causes and Character of America's Present Predicament Along With a Few Thoughts About an Alternative* (New York: Oxford University Press, 1980). [the classic "revisionist" history of the Cold War and the rise of the national-security state]

Wills, Garry. *Inventing America: Jefferson's Declaration of Independence* (New York: Vintage, 1979).

Wilson, Edward O. *The Diversity of Life* (Cambridge: Harvard University Press, 1982). [a magisterial overview of the life process and humanity's baneful effects on it]

Wilson, James Q. *The Moral Sense* (New York: Free Press, 1993). [argues that innate moral sentiments not only exist, they are the sine qua non of any social order]

Winner, Langdon. *Autonomous Technology: Technics-Out-of-Control as a Theme in Political Thought* (Cambridge: MIT Press, 1977).

Wolin, Sheldon S. *Politics and Vision: Continuity and Innovation in Western Political Thought* (Boston: Little, Brown, 1960).

_____. *The Presence of the Past: Essays on the State and the Constitution* (Baltimore: Johns Hopkins University Press, 1989).

Woolf, Virginia. *A Room of One's Own* (New York: Harvest, 1957). [one of the first, and still one of the best, feminist critiques; beautifully written; remarkable (and laudable) for its lack of cant, rancor, or self-pity]

World Commission on Environment and Development. *Our Common Future* (New York: Oxford University Press, 1987). [the so-called Brundtland Commission report]

Worster, Donald. *The Wealth of Nature: Environmental History and the Ecological Imagination* (New York: Oxford University Press, 1993).

Wright, Robert. *The Moral Animal: Evolutionary Psychology and Everyday Life* (New York: Pantheon, 1994). [describes how we are slowly coming to understand what is "natural" for human beings, knowledge that has revolutionary social implications]

Young, Michael D. *The Rise of the Meritocracy, 1870–2033: An Essay in Education and Equality* (Baltimore: Penguin, 1967).

About the Book
and Author

This long-promised sequel to Ophuls's influential and controversial classic *Ecology and the Politics of Scarcity* is an equally provocative critique of the liberal philosophy of government. Ophuls contends that the modern political paradigm—that is, the body of political concepts and beliefs bequeathed to us by the Enlightenment—is no longer intellectually tenable or practically viable. Our attempt to live individualistically, hedonistically, and rationally has failed utterly, causing a comprehensive crisis that is at once political, military, economic, ecological, ethical, psychological, and spiritual. Liberal politics has abandoned virtue, rejected community, and flouted nature, thereby becoming the author of its own demise.

By exposing the intrinsically contradictory and self-destructive character of Hobbesian political systems, Ophuls subverts our conventional wisdom at every turn. Indeed, his impassioned text reads more like a Greek tragedy than a conventional political argument. He critiques feminism, multiculturalism, the welfare state, and a host of other "liberal" shibboleths—but Ophuls is not yet another neoconservative. The aim of his thesis is far more radical and progressive, offering a political vision that entirely transcends the categories of liberal thought. His is a Thoreauvian vision of a "politics of consciousness" rooted in ecology as the moral and intellectual basis for governance in the twenty-first century. Ophuls holds that a polity based on a renewed erotic connection with nature offers a genuine solution to this crisis of contemporary civilization and that only within such a polity will it be possible to fulfill the worthy liberal goal of individual self-development.

Ophuls's work will interest and challenge a wide spectrum of readers, though it will not necessarily be well liked or easily accepted. No one will put down this book with his or her settled convictions about American culture intact, nor will readers ever again take modern civilization and its survival for granted.

William Ophuls is a former member of the U.S. Foreign Service and has taught political science at Northwestern University. He is the author of *Ecology and the Politics of Scarcity*, which won the International Studies Association's Sprout Prize and the American Political Science Association's Kammerer Award.

INDEX

Abortion, 69
Abstraction. *See* Rationalism
Abundance
    as goal of modern political economy, 41–44, 120, 135
    as illusory, dishonest, or paradoxical, 43, 149, 150, 151–152, 157–158, 166–168, 174
    of New World, 35, 57
    true nature of, 160, 176
    See also Affluence; Poverty; Primal society; Scarcity; Thermodynamic accounting
Accounting. *See* Thermodynamic accounting
Acton, John Emerich Edward Dalberg, 1st baron, 215, 249
Adams, John, 58, 63
Adatto, Kiku, 84
Addiction
    to drugs, 50, 151, 165, 246, 251, 267
    and escape into anesthesia, 224–226
    as intrinsic to modern political economy, 115, 131–133, 135, 171, 174, 213, 222, 267
Administrative state. *See* Despotism
Affluence
    in conflict with autonomy, 105
    as creator of public squalor, 127
    as fallacious and frustrating, 10, 115, 120, 121–131, 135, 148–149, 152, 173
    as support for despotism, 260
    See also Abundance; Addiction; Consumption
African-Americans. *See* Slavery
Agriculture
    in America, 59–60, 64, 113–116, 241
    and decline of family farming, 62, 64, 113–116, 137
    invention of, 17–19
    parasitic versus symbiotic, 99–101
    political consequences of, 18–22, 95, 115
    and thermodynamics, 8, 10, 99–101
    and war, 20–22
Alienation, 22, 191–194, 199, 204–206, 207–209, 211, 222, 250, 267. *See also* Moral Entropy; Rationalism; Religion
Amazon, 5, 7, 278
American Council of Education, 130
Ancient civilizations, 21–23, 25, 96, 124
Anesthesia. *See* Addiction
Anima mundi, 183, 189
Animism. *See* Participation (primary)
Arendt, Hannah, 50, 109, 213, 221, 282
Aristotle, xii, 30, 125, 160(n), 185, 228, 229
    on equality, 146, 149
    on household economy, 104–105, 109
    on rule of life, 23, 268
    on slavery, 96, 99
    on wisdom and virtue, 269, 280
Athens. *See* Greece

Authoritarianism. *See* Despotism
Authority. *See* Governance
Automobile, 62, 64, 126, 127, 155, 217

Bacon, Francis, 179, 185–190, 198, 214
Bali, 10, 99–101
Barbarism, 57, 74, 91–93, 203–204, 213
Barfield, Owen, 206, 284
Barnet, Richard J., 94, 95, 101–102
Bateson, Gregory, 177, 178, 197, 211, 284
Bayley, David H., 234–235
Bell, Daniel, 136, 283
Berlin, Isaiah, 271
Bernays, Edward, 87
Berry, Wendell, 262–263, 272, 273
Biotechnology, 9(n), 215, 217
Blake, William, 192
Bloomsbury group, 48, 49
Boorstin, Daniel J., 86, 282
Bourgeoisie, 29, 40–41, 47, 106, 109, 112, 136, 145, 189
Brave New World. *See* Huxley
Brundtland Commission, 157
Buddha, 22, 125
Burke, Edmund, 49, 137, 191, 223, 229, 231–232, 233, 236, 244, 268
Burnham, David, 253

Campbell, Joseph, 193, 282
Capitalism, 29, 38, 52, 107, 111, 123–125, 129–130, 149, 170, 189, 241. *See also* Economic development; Market economy; Marx
Carroll, Lewis, 152
Cherokee. *See* Native Americans
Chesterton, G. K., 205
Children, 66–67, 251–252
Christian church
    moral legacy of, 45, 47
    in struggle with Science, 179–182
    virtues and vices of, 23–25
    See also Morality; Religion
Citizenship. *See* Democracy.
Civilization
    based on stolen goods, 95–97
    destructiveness of, 94–95, 267, 274–275
    dynamic of, 15
    four great ills of, 95–97, 121
    fragility of, 46(n)
    as megalomaniac, 177–178, 217–218, 267
    necessity to reinvent, 273–274, 277–278
    as politically oppressive, 18–19, 21–22, 96–97
    prehistoric basis of, 17
    as problematic, x, 2, 15, 20, 270, 274, 277–278
    as synonymous with economic development, 95